The Religious Geography of Mzuzu City in Northern Malawi

Copyright 2018 Zeenah Sibande

All rights reserved. No part of this publication may be reproduced, stored in a retrieval system, or transmitted in any from or by any means, electronic, mechanical, photocopying, recording or otherwise without prior permission from the publishers.

Published by
Luviri Press
P/Bag 201 Luwinga
Mzuzu 2
Malawi

ISBN   978-99960-98-16-1
eISBN 978-99960-98-17-8

Luviri Books no. 15

Luviri Press is represented outside Africa by:
African Books Collective Oxford (order@africanbookscollective.com)

www.mzunipress.blogspot.com

www.africanbookscollective.com

Editorial assistance and cover: Daniel Neumann

The Religious Geography of Mzuzu City in Northern Malawi

Zeenah Sibande

Luviri Books no. 15

Mzuzu

2018

Dedication

This work is dedicated to my father, Jastone Sibande, for shouldering the huge responsibility of educating me. Further, to my late mother, Flourah Ngulube, for her caring, spiritual and moral support rendered to me; may her Soul rest in peace.

Acknowledgements

I thank God the Almighty for the guidance, understanding, wisdom and protection He provided to me during my time of study.

I give thanks to my Supervisor Professor Klaus Fiedler for his tireless guidance and direction throughout the research project. Thank you for taking me to the next stage of academic life.

Furthermore, I thank Mr. Rodney Mshali, my Geography lecturer and supervisor. Thank you very much for imparting to me geographical concepts which has helped to come up with this paper. I thank Mr. Tchuwa in the GIS lab who introduced me to cartography.

I would also like to thank Mzondwase Moyo for the secretarial help she rendered to me. I thank Charles Chabinga for his tireless help in producing maps. I also thank Mrs Tiwonge Chirwa and Abner Simfukwe for arranging and ordering this paper into a better format.

In addition, I thank my wife, Kettie Harawa, and our three children; Yewo, Tawonga and Mwabi for their patience, love and encouragement during the study period. I also thank Rev Dr T.P.K. Nyasulu and Rev. J.P.U. Mwale (Deputy General Secretary) for their tireless support and encouragement from the Synod Office. I thank you, Sirs.

Contents

Editors' Foreword	17
Chapter One: Introduction	21
Chapter Two: Origin and Diffusion of Religions in Mzuzu	30
2.1 Geographical Information	30
2.2 Historical Background	34
2.2.1 First Settlement in Mzuzu	34
2.2.2 The Settlement from 1900 to Date	37
2.3 Origin and Diffusion of Religions in Mzuzu	38
2.3.1 African Traditional Religion	39
2.3.2 Christian Religion	42
2.3.3 Islam	52
2.3.4 Hindu Religion	55
Chapter Three: Location and Places of Religious Worship Centres in Mzuzu	56
3.1 Religious Places in Lupaso Ward	56
3.1.1 Dunduzu Baptist Convention of Malawi	56
3.1.2 Nkhorongo Seventh-day Adventist Church	57
3.1.3 Dunduzu Seventh Day Baptist Church	59
3.1.4 Dunduzu Seventh - day Baptist Original Church	60
3.1.5 Dunduzu New Apostolic Church	61
3.1.6 Dunduzu Living Waters Church	62
3.1.7 Msiru Chipangano Church	63
3.1.8 St Teleza Dunduzu Roman Catholic Church	64
3.1.9 Muwela Traditional Healing Centre	65
3.1.10 Dunduzu Chekina Temple of Assemblies of God Church	66
3.1.11 Lupaso Good News Revival Church	67
3.1.12 Lupaso Kalibu Kwa Yesu Church	69
3.1.13 Lupaso Full Gospel Church of God	70
3.1.14 Lupaso Assemblies of God Church	71

3.1.15 Lupaso Seventh-day Adventist Church 72
3.1.16 Luwinga Grace Community Pentecostal Church 73
3.1.17 Area 1B Inspired Gospel Church 74
3.1.18 Area 1B International Pentecostal Church 75
3.1.19 Dunduzu Jesus Missionary Church 76
3.1.20 Nkholongo New Apostolic Church 77
3.1.21 Area 1B Charismatic Redeemed Ministries and International Church 77
3.1.22 Luwinga Baptist Convention of Malawi Church 78
3.1.23 Area 1B Church of Christ 79
3.1.24 Nkholongo Church of Christ 80
3.1.25 St Fostina Roman Catholic Church 81
3.1.26 Luwinga Evangelical Baptist Church of Malawi 82
3.1.27 Area 1B Cornerstone Presbyterian Church 83
3.1.28 Kang'ona Presbyterian Church of Malawi 84
3.1.29 Kang'ona Church of the Nazarene 84
3.1.30 Kang'ona African International Church 85
3.1.31 Area 1B Way of Life Church 86
3.1.32 Luwinga Africa National Church 87
3.1.33 Luwinga Assemblies of God Church 88
3.1.34 Nkholongo Mboni za Yehova Kingdom Hall 89
3.1.35 Kang'ona Living Waters Church 90
3.1.36 Kanyika Seventh-day Adventist Church 90
3.1.37 Chumbi Seventh-day Adventist 91
3.1.38 Nkholongo Good Samaritan Ministry 92
3.1.39 Luwinga Holy Trinity Anglican Church 93
3.1.40 St Mary's Convent 94
3.1.41 Luwinga African Evangelical Church 95
3.1.42 Luwinga Apostolic Church of Great Britain 95
3.1.43 Viyele Assemblies of God Church 96

3.1.44 Luwinga Holy Spirit Filled Ministry 97

3.1.45 Mzuzu Bible College Church of Christ............................... 98

3.1.46 St Augustine Roman Catholic Church 99

3.1.47 Area 1B Mosque 100

3.1.48 Lunyangwa Church of the Nazarene............................. 101

3.1.49 Lupaso CCAP Church.. 102

3.1.50 Viyele CCAP Church 103

3.1.51 Kachere CCAP Church 104

3.1.52 Luwinga United Methodist Church............................... 105

3.1.53 Kubwezeretsa Sabata la Yehova Church....................... 106

3.1.54 Luwinga Church of Africa Presbyterian 107

3.2 Religious Places in Chiputula Ward 108

3.2.1 Chiputula CCAP Church... 108

3.2.2 Chiputula St Michael's Lutheran Church of Central Africa 109

3.2.3 Chiputula Church of Christ.. 110

3.2.4 Chiputula New Apostolic Church................................... 111

3.2.5 Chiputula Charismatic Redeemed Ministry International 111

3.2.6 Chiputula Pentecostal Holiness Association.................. 112

3.2.7 Chiputula Assemblies of God Church 113

3.2.8 Chiputula Ambassadors for Christ Ministries 114

3.2.9 Chiputula St Pius Catholic Church.................................. 115

3.2.10 Chiputula African National Church 116

3.2.11 Chiputula Mtambo Ministry 117

3.2.12 Chiputula Seventh-day Adventist Church.................... 118

3.2.13 Chiputula Calvary Family Church 119

3.2.14 Chiputula Mosque 120

3.2.15 Chiputula Lutheran Church... 120

3.2.16 Chiputula Zambezi Evangelical Church........................ 121

3.3 Religious Places in Kataba Ward 122

3.3.1 Kataba CCAP Church... 122

- 3.3.2 Chasefu Seventh-day Adventist Church 124
- 3.3.3 Kataba Assemblies of God 125
- 3.3.4 The Redeemed Christian Church of God 126
- 3.3.5 Mzuzu Pentecostal Church 126
- 3.3.6 St Peters Convent of the Sisters of the Holy Rosary 127
- 3.3.7 Mzilawayingwe CCAP Church 128
- 3.3.8 Chiputula Jehovah's Witnesses Kingdom Hall 129
- 3.3.9 Pentecost Christ Church International 130
- 3.3.10 One More Time Christian Movement 131
- 3.3.11 Mzilawayingwe Last Reformed Church 131
- 3.3.12 St Peter's Parish 132
- 3.3.13 Chasefu Church of African Presbyterian 134

3.4 Religious Places in Zolozolo Ward — 135

- 3.4.1 Holy Family Catholic Church 135
- 3.4.2 Zolozolo Brethren Christian Assembly 136
- 3.4.3 Zolozolo Seventh-day Baptist Church 137
- 3.4.4 Zolozolo CCAP Church 137
- 3.4.5 Mganthira CCAP Church 138
- 3.4.6 Upper Zolozolo New Apostolic Church 139
- 3.4.7 Zolozolo West New Apostolic Church 140
- 3.4.8 African National Church 141
- 3.4.9 Chiputula Chipangano Church 141
- 3.4.10 Zolozolo Power Ministry of the Living God Church 142
- 3.4.11 Ching'ambo Word of Faith Temple International 142
- 3.4.12 Zolozolo West Seventh-day Adventist Church 143
- 3.4.13 Zolozolo East Seventh-day Adventist Church 144
- 3.4.14 Matope CCAP Church 145
- 3.4.15 Zolozolo Bethsaida Fellowship 145
- 3.4.16 Heart Healing Ministries 146
- 3.4.17 Zolozolo West Full Gospel of God Church 147

3.4.18 Zolozolo West Baptist Convention of Malawi Church 147
3.4.19 Zolozolo West Assemblies of God Church 148
3.4.20 Zolozolo West Chipangano Church 148
3.4.21 Zolozolo West Roman Catholic Church 149
3.4.22 Zolozolo West Church of Christ 149
3.4.23 Botanic Church of Christ 150
3.4.24 Chiputula Church of Christ 151
3.4.25 Ching'ambo Churches of Christ 151
3.4.26 Ching'ambo Free Methodist Church 152
3.4.27 Ching'ambo Zion Christian Church 153
3.4.28 Ching'ambo Mosque 154
3.5 Religious Places in Chibavi Ward   154
   3.5.1 Chibavi CCAP Church 154
   3.5.2 Chibavi Emmanuel Pentecostal Ministries 155
   3.5.3 Chibavi Community of Christ Church 156
   3.5.4 Chibavi Cornerstone Presbyterian Church 156
   3.5.5 Chibavi Salvation Army Church 157
   3.5.6 Chibavi Christian Hope Assembly Church 158
   3.5.7 Chibavi Last Church of God 159
   3.5.8 Chibavi St Benadeta Catholic Church 159
   3.5.9 Chibavi Agape Life Church International 160
   3.5.10 Chibavi Assemblies of God Church 161
   3.5.11 Chibavi African International Church 161
   3.5.12 Chibavi Chewasene Mosque 162
   3.5.13 Chibavi Enlightened Christian Gathering Ministry 163
   3.5.14 Chibavi Ephata Ministry 163
   3.5.15 Chibavi Last Church of God 164
   3.5.16 Chibavi Providence Industrial Mission 165
   3.5.17 Chibavi Come to Jesus Ministry 166
   3.5.18 Chibavi Christ Alive Family Church 166

- 3.5.19 Chibavi Seventh-day Adventist Church 167
- 3.5.20 Chibavi Living Waters Church 167
- 3.5.21 Chibavi Baptist Convention Church 168
- 3.5.22 Chibavi Bible Believers Church 169
- 3.5.23 Chibavi Bible Believers Church 2 169
- 3.5.24 Chibavi Central Mosque 170
- 3.5.25 Chibavi African International Church 171
- 3.5.26 Chibavi Apostolic Faith Mission 171
- 3.5.27 Chibavi New Apostolic Church.............................172
- 3.5.28 Chibavi Chipangano Church................................173

3.6 Religious Places in Mchengautuwa Ward — 174

- 3.6.1 Kaviwale Gospel Pentecostal Church 174
- 3.6.2 Kaboko Gospel Pentecostal Church.......................174
- 3.6.3 Kaviwale Victory Assemblies of God Pentecostal Church 175
- 3.6.4 Katoto Baptist Convention Church 176
- 3.6.5 Kaviwale Grace Fellowship 176
- 3.6.6 Kaviwale Seventh-day Adventist 177
- 3.6.7 Kaviwale Church of Christ..................................178
- 3.6.8 Soweto African International Church 178
- 3.6.9 Mchengautuwa Chipangano Church 179
- 3.6.10 Mchengautuwa Seventh-day Adventist Reform Movement Church..180
- 3.6.11 Mchengautuwa Church of Africa Presbyterian 180
- 3.6.12 Mchengautuwa New Apostolic Church 181
- 3.6.13 Sonda Assemblies of God Church........................182
- 3.6.14 Sonda Christ Rock Church..................................182
- 3.6.15 Sonda Bethel Tabernacle Church 183
- 3.6.16 Maria Temple..183
- 3.6.17 St Paul's Anglican Church 184
- 3.6.18 Mchengautuwa Kingdom Gospel Church 185

3.6.19 St Joseph Roman Catholic Church 186
3.6.20 Mchengautuwa Baptist Convention Church 186
3.6.21 Mchengautuwa Gospel of God Church 187
3.6.22 Mchengautuwa St Albert Catholic Church 188
3.6.23 Mchengautuwa Seventh-day Adventist Church 189
3.6.24 Mchengautuwa Christian Love Church 189
3.6.25 Mchengautuwa CCAP Church 190
3.6.26 Kaviwale CCAP Church 191
3.6.27 God's Will Church 192

3.7 Religious Places in Katoto Ward   192
   3.7.1 Chibanja Jehovah's Witnesses Kingdom Hall 192
   3.7.2 Chibanja Moravian Church 193
   3.7.3 Katoto Assemblies of God Church 194
   3.7.4 International Christian Assemblies Church 195
   3.7.5 Katoto New Apostolic Church 195
   3.7.6 Katoto Calvary Family Church 196
   3.7.7 Chithira Peace Ministries 197
   3.7.8 Christ Citadel International Church 198
   3.7.9 Katoto Medicine Ministry Church 198
   3.7.10 SOS Living Waters Church 199
   3.7.11 Mzuzu Winners Chapel Church 200
   3.7.12 Chisomo Baptist Church 200
   3.7.13 Hilltop Kandaha Mosque 201
   3.7.14 Kawuwa Seventh–day Adventist Church 202
   3.7.15 Katoto Bible Believers Church 202
   3.7.16 Victory Christian Temple 203
   3.7.17 Glorious Light Church 204
   3.7.18 Mzuzu Baptist Convention Church 205
   3.7.19 Mzuzu International Pentecostal Holiness Church 206
   3.7.20 St Mark's Anglican Church 206

3.7.21 Jomo Kenyatta Road Church of Christ 207
3.7.22 Mzuzu Central New Apostolic Church 208
3.7.23 Police CCAP Church 209
3.7.24 City Chipangano Church 209
3.7.25 Mzuzu Central Mosque.. 210
3.7.26 Hindu Servants Semaj 211
3.7.27 Masjd Anwarullmadina Mosque 212
3.7.28 Mzuzu Seventh–day Adventist Central Church 212
3.7.29 Mzuzu CCAP Church 213

3.8 Religious Places in Masasa/Msongwe Ward   215
   3.8.1 Moyale Anglican Church 215
   3.8.2 St Joseph Roman Catholic Church 215
   3.8.3 Moyale CCAP Church 216
   3.8.4 Mzuzu Government Secondary School CCAP Church........... 216
   3.8.5 Msongwe Trinity CCAP Church 217
   3.8.6 Msongwe New Apostolic Church.. 218
   3.8.7 Masasa Assemblies of God Church....................................... 218
   3.8.8 Masasa Unity Pentecostal Church 219

Chapter Four: Religion in Mzuzu by Numbers   221
   4.1 Places of Worship   221
      4.1.1 Location 221
      4.1.2 Worship Structures.. 223
   4.2 Worship Centres and Membership   224
      4.2.1 Membership Accession.. 225
      4.2.2 Relationship between Membership and Attendance 226
      4.2.3 Women Proportion in Worship Centres............................. 228
      4.2.4 Language in Services of Worship.. 229

Chapter Five: The Geographical Distribution of Religions and Denomination   232
   5.1 Locational Settlement of Religions and Denominations   232

- 5.1.1 African Traditional Religion 233
- 5.1.2 Hindu Religion 234
- 5.1.3 Islam 235
- 5.1.4 Christian Religion 236
- 5.2 Religious Infrastructure and Physical Development — 242
  - 5.2.1 Christian Sacred Structures 243
  - 5.2.2 Islamic Places of Worship 249
  - 5.2.3 Hindu Places of Worship 252
  - 5.2.4 African Traditional Religious Shrines 253
- 5.3 Geographical Origin of Members — 254
- 5.4 Religious Membership — 255
  - 5.4.1 Factors Influencing Membership in Worship Centres 256
- 5.5 Membership and Attendance at a Worship centre — 259
  - 5.5.1 Lack of Commitment 259
  - 5.5.2 Social Commitment 260

Chapter Six: Religious Worship Places as Social Centres — 266

- 6.1 Social Groups — 266
  - 6.1.1 Brotherhood 266
  - 6.1.2 Social Interaction 267
  - 6.1.3 Protection 267
  - 6.1.4 Social Guidance 268
  - 6.1.5 Information and Assistance 268
- 6.2 Worship Participation by Age — 269
  - 6.2.1 Youth Participation 269
  - 6.2.2 Tender Love and Care 271
  - 6.2.3 Worship Services are more Attended by Women 271
  - 6.2.4 Adult Participation 272
- 6.3 The Role of Women in Worship Centres — 273
  - 6.3.1 Women Participation at Worship Centres 273
  - 6.3.2 Females are more than Males 276

- 6.3.3 Social Groupings 277
- 6.3.4 Adaptability to Healing and Deliverance 278
- 6.3.5 Protection and Social Guidance 279
- 6.3.6 Position of Women in Leadership 279
- 6.4. Religions and Denominations whose Women are not Participating in Leadership ... 280
  - 6.4.1 Islamic Religion 280
  - 6.4.2 Hindu Religion 281
  - 6.4.3 Christian Religion 281
  - 6.4.4 Those who Allow Women in Leadership 282
- 6.5 Language ... 286
  - 6.5.1 Dominant Languages in Worship Centres 287
  - 6.5.3 Chitumbuka 289
  - 6.5.4 Chichewa 289
  - 6.5.5 English 291
  - 6.5.6 Language Influences Worship 292
- 6.6 Culture of Healing and Deliverance in Worship Centres ... 292
  - 6.6.1 Prophecy 294
  - 6.6.2 Healing and Deliverance 295
- 6.7 Geography of Conflicts and Splits in Worship Centres ... 296
  - 6.7.1 Conflicts and Disagreements 296
  - 6.7.2 Splits 298
- 6.8 Interreligious Relations ... 299
  - 6.8.1 Respect and Value 301

Chapter Seven: Religious Social Ministries in Mzuzu ... 302
- 7.1 The Significance of Religions in the Development of Education ... 302
  - 7.1.1 The Genesis of the System of Formal Education 303
  - 7.1.2 Primary Education from the 1930s to Date 305
  - 7.1.3 Secondary Education 313
  - 7.1.4 Higher Learning Institutions 319

7.1.5 Theology and Religious Studies 324
7.2 Contribution of Religions to Medical Care #wrong map below   327
   7.2.1 Spatial Distribution of Religious Medical Care 327
   7.2.2 St John's Hospital 328
   7.2.3 Nkhorongo Seventh-day Adventist Hospital 329
   7.2.4 St John of God Mental Hospital 329
   7.2.5 Private Seventh-day Adventist Clinics 330
7.3 Religious Human Rights   331
   7.3.1 Church and Society 333
   7.3.2 Catholic Commission for Justice and Peace 334
7.4 The Influence of Religions on Mass Communication   337
   7.4.1 Voice of Livingstonia Radio 337
   7.4.2 Radio Tigabane 339
   7.4.3 Radio ABC (Mzuzu Sub-Station) 340

Chapter Eight: Conclusion and Recommendations   **343**
8.1 Important Observation: Rural Expansion   344
8.2 Developments during the Study Period (2013 to 2015)   346
   8.2.1 Church Growth 346
   8.2.2 Birth of New Churches 347
   8.2.3 Churches that are Diminishing in Size 348
   8.2.4 Church Buildings 350
8.3 Future Expectations   352
   8.3.1 Expansion of Religions and Denominations 352
   8.3.2 Position of Women 353
   8.3.3 Language 354
8.4 Recommendations   354
Bibliography   **356**
Appendices   **365**

Abbreviations

ABC	African Bible College
ADMARC	Agricultural Development and Marketing Cooperation
ATR	African Traditional Religion
CAP	Central Africa Conference
CCAP	Church of Central Africa Presbyterian
CCJP	Catholic Commission for Justice and Peace
CDC	Commonwealth Development Cooperation
CLAIM	Christian Literature Association in Malawi
CHAM	Christian Health Association of Malawi
Dr	Doctor
ESCOM	Electricity Supply Commission of Malawi
GPS	Geographical Positioning System
HIV/AIDS	Human Immunodeficiency Virus/Acquired Immune Deficiency Syndrome
ICT	Information Communication Technology
MA	Master of Arts
Mzuni	Mzuzu University
NBS Bank	New Building Society Bank
OPD	Out Patient Department
PhD	Doctor of Philosophy
Rev	Reverend
SADC	Southern Africa Development Cooperation
SDA	Seventh-day Adventist
SEDOM	Small Enterprise Development of Malawi
TEEM	Theological Education by Extension in Malawi

Editors' Foreword

Religious geography is a new field of inquiry in Malawi. But it is a deserving field, and much could have been done, as religion influenced greatly the political development of Malawi. For a thousand years or so the territory of what is now Malawi looked largely east and west for outside communication. The Yawo were long distance traders, connecting the Copperbelt (Shaba) with the Coast, and along this route Islam entered Malawi. The Yawo collected it from the Coast, and Swahili traders brought it overland from the Coast to the Lake.

The Christian missionaries changed the direction of communication from East - West to South - North, coming in via the rivers Zambezi and Shire and using the Lake as the "road" to the North, even trying to extend that road further northwards to Lake Tanganyika.

The fight of missions and government against the slave trade-oriented Malawi South to North, and though the Yawo chiefs were defeated, the Pax Britannica speeded up the spread of Islam up to about 1910, when the expansion stopped because the Christian missions seemed to offer a more progressive school system than Islam did at that time. When the Western powers decided to divide up Africa amongst themselves, the missionaries, who had come earlier and had no colonial interests, did not agree with the Berlin settlement, which declared Southern Malawi to be part of the Portuguese zone of interest. The British government made in 1890 a treaty with Portugal that the Shire should be the boundary of their mutual spheres, confirming the Berlin settlement. The Blantyre missionaries organized a big public relations campaign and "forced" the British government to break the Lisbon 1890 treaty and declare a Protectorate over, initially, Southern Malawi. That Southern Malawi is surrounded on three sides by Mozambique is due to the agitation of the Scottish missionaries for British rule in order to keep the Portuguese out. Without their efforts, would there have been a country called Malawi? Maybe, but definitely not in today's shape.

Religion equally produced the strange geography that Likoma and Chizumulu islands, so close to the shore of Mozambique, belong to Malawi, though each is surrounded by Mozambiquan territorial waters, and the Livingstonia missionaries also arranged that the Ngoni Kingdom of Chief Mbelwa got annexed to the British Empire on its own accord in 1904.

Once the borders of Malawi had been settled, the Overtoun Institution attracted students from even neighbouring countries and its graduates were much sought after in Tanzania, Zambia, Zimbabwe and South Africa. The labour migration routes became also routes for religious interaction, Malawian churches following their members and the returning *machona* bringing new varieties of the Christian faith, foremost the Zionist churches.

In the first decades the missionaries tried to organize the Christian faith geographically by comity agreements, trying to give each (Protestant) mission its own territory. Success was limited, not the least because the people did not like the idea.

Over the decades more and more missions came in, and the *machona* brought several churches and missions, and over the period of more than 150 years Malawi developed a strong religious diversity, especially on the Christian side, much of which has found expression in geographical terms, and which may be understood through the study of religious geography.

In most books on religious history there are sketch maps that only involve some geographical locations, but we have not found a study devoted exclusively to religious geography in Malawi, so there is much that could be done. Where to start? Anywhere is right, so why not in Mzuzu. We are therefore happy to present this first study by Zeenah Sibande, based on the work he did for his MA in Theology and Religious Studies at Mzuzu University (supervised by Rodney Mshali for Geography and Klaus Fiedler for Religion). We wish that this book be a starting point for further inquiry into the religious geography in Malawi, which is so varied that it is worth to be explored from many different angles.

Rodney Mshali and Klaus Fiedler

April 2018

Chapter One: Introduction

Religious Geography is a growing field developed from geography and religion which deals with the impact of geography, i.e. place and space, on religious beliefs and vice versa. Religion lies at the foundation of culture in the fabric of society, gives identity in many societies less dominated by modern technology, is a binding force and a dominant rule of daily life.[1] The main reason to study religious geography is that some of the many interesting questions about how religions develop, spread and impact on people's lives are rooted in geographical factors, and they can be studied from a geographical perspective.[2] The real value of most geographical studies of religion is in describing spatial patterns, partly because these are often interesting in their own right but also because patterns suggest causes and processes. This study deals with space and place, and of movements between places.

Religious geography is a discipline of which the German geographer, A. Heihner, once remarked that it is *"der schwerste und heikelste Teil geographischer Betrachtung"* (the most difficult and delicate part of geographical thought), has not developed into a branch of human geography on its own comparable to economic, settlement, population or political geography, although there were efforts in this direction.[3] Whilst religion is not a central theme in contemporary geography, it has not been overlooked completely and has been developed into a sub discipline within geography in the name of Geography and Religion.

Religious geography and geography of religion are the two approaches adopted in recent work in dealing with the impact of geography on religious beliefs. The former looks at the role of religion in shaping people's perception of the world and where and how people fit into it. It explores the role of theology and cosmology in constructing and understanding the universe. The latter is concerned not so much with religion per se, but with the many different ways in which religion is expressed. It sees religion as a human institution and explores its social, cultural and environmental impacts. Most geographical research has

---

[1] H.J. de Blij and Peter O. Muller, *Human Geography: Culture, Society and Space,* New York: John Wily and Sons, 1995, p. 297.

[2] Chris Park and J. Hinnells (eds), *Religion and Geography, Companion to the Study of Religion*, London: Routledge, 2004, p. 1.

[3] Reinhard Henkel, *Christian Missions in Africa. A Social Geographical Study of the Impact of their Activities in Zambia*, Berlin: Reimer, 1989, p. 17.

tended to be of the second type, and that approach underpins the rest of the research under study.

Religious geography looks at the relationship between religion and geography where geographical ideas influence religion and religion influences geography. Traditionally, religious geography can be seen by the influences of religion in shaping cosmological understandings of the world. From the sixteenth and seventeenth century, the study of religious geography mainly focuses on mapping the spread of Christianity and other religions.[4]

Other traditional approaches to the study involved the theological explorations of the working of nature—a highly environmentally deterministic approach which identified the role of geographical environments in determining the nature and evolution of different religious traditions.

At first scholars seemed to think that religion and geography had little in common, most people interested in the study of religion had little interest in geography and vice versa. However, scholars today have started developing interest in the subject. Thus, geographers are less concerned about religion per se, but are sensitive to how religions as a cultural feature affects social, cultural, political and environmental systems.[5] The point of focus is not the specifics of religious beliefs and practices, but how these religious beliefs and practices are internalized by adherents, and how these processes of internalization influence, and is influenced by social systems.[6] Religious experiences and the beliefs in religious meanings transform physical spaces into sacred space. These perceptions and meanings influence the way such spaces are used, and the personal, spiritual meanings developed in using such scared spaces. The religious experiences and beliefs transform the cultural landscape.

The religious beliefs in Mzuzu are an indication of religious geography spread out in space and time. The religious beliefs and practices are internalized by adherents and are influenced by their social systems. The

---

[4] Lily Kong, *Geography and Religion: "Trends and Prospects"* http://phg.Sage.pub.com/cg1/pdf (extract /14/3/355) Progress in Human Geography 14(3): 355 - 371, 15.10.2012.

[5] Religion and Geography, http://en.Wikipedia.org/wiki/Religion and Geography, 15.10.2012.

[6] Lily Kong, *"Religious Schools for Spirit (f) or Nation,"* Environment and Planning, Society and Space 23.4.2005: http://dx.doi.org/10.1068 % 2&d3 94.

inhabitants of Mzuzu are religious with different religions. The American cultural geographer Yifu Tuan said that the religious person is the one who seeks coherence and meaning in his world and religious culture is one that has a clearly structured world view.[7] The religious impulse is to tie things together; therefore, all human beings in Mzuzu are religious, if religion is broadly defined as the impulse for coherence and meaning. The strength of the impulse varies from person to person. Religions and denominations of Mzuzu have become seemingly linked with particular tribal groups, cultures, racial groups, in certain quarters, political systems and life styles.

Geographers in Mzuzu study the process by which religions, like other cultural characteristics, are diffused from one location to another, resulting in a distinctive spatial distribution. The distribution of religion is generated by a process of spatial interactions diffused from a point of origin to the other places in accordance with distinctive pattern of communication.[8] Geographers identify the differences in spatial distributions and diffusion of the major universalized and ethnic religions. Universalized religions attempt to appeal to all people, not just to residents of one cultural background or location. In contrast, the religious principles of an ethnic religion are more likely to be based on physical characteristics of particular locations on the earth's surface. Consequently, an ethnic religion carries meaning primarily for people either living in or as attracted to a particular environment. An ethnic religion has typically a more clustered geographic distribution, while universalized religions have been adopted across cultural barriers and language boundaries.[9] Religious persuasion does not lead people to change the language they speak but it induces adherence to profess a new faith, while conversion is a means of spreading beliefs in receptive communities.[10]

The original religion of Mzuzu is African Tradition Religion (ATR) practiced by Tonga and Ngoni respectively, when they first settled in Mzuzu before

---

[7] Chris Park, *Religion and Geography*, Chapter 17 in J. Hinnells, *Routledge Companion to the Study of Religion*, London: Routledge, 2004, p. 1.

[8] James M. Rubenstein, *The Cultural Landscape. An Introduction to Human Geography*, Miami: Miami University, 1999, p. 162.

[9] H.J. de Blij and Peter O. Muller, *Human Geography: Culture, Society and Space*, New York: John Wily and Sons, 1995, p. 297.

[10] Ibid.

they moved out of Kaning'ina. The traditional religions were special forms of ethnic religions distinguished by their small size, their unique identity with localized cultural groups not yet absorbed into modern society, and their close ties to nature. Although the religion cannot be seen in an organized form today, the practices and beliefs are still among the people.[11] The religious rituals are passed on from one generation to the other by word of mouth. The other religions of the area are the universalized religions, especially Christianity and Islam. These have become more important over the years. Many Christian groups and Muslims have sent missionaries to Mzuzu and the number of adherents has increased. The adherents of different religions have diffused far and wide.

The demarcation of religious centres and the distribution of religious adherents are based on population growth, distance and some physical geographical barriers.[12] The religious adherents have their own belief when deciding to which faith and religious centre they should belong. They are bound to worship at a religious centre of their religion, no matter how far the centre might be.

Many join a religious centre of worship of their historical or cultural background. Worship centres have more nominal roll than the actual number of worship attendance. The majority of religious adherents are women. Worship centres are dominated by the productive age group. New members join worship centres by migration, birth and conversion. Some religions and denominations have permanent worship structures while some have temporary structures or no worship structure of their own.

The location of religious worship centres in Mzuzu has different characteristics from each other. Some religions and denominations have located their worship centres strategically within the jurisdiction of their religious adherents, located on demand delivery. However, the quality of a worship centre depends upon the area of location. Muslim mosques are located at the centre of attraction or busy areas i.e. trading centres. African Traditional Religious centres are located in the remote areas or out of the city, where people are living village or mixed life. Some religions and denominations are located in high density areas; many of

---

[11] For a study of this issue among the Ngonde, see Joyce Mlenga, *Dual Religiosity in Northern Malawi. Ngonde Christians and African Traditional Religion*, Mzuzu: Mzuni Press, 2016.

[12] CCAP Mzuzu Presbytery Minutes, 31.9.2012.

them have no church structures of their own and for those who have it, they have temporary church structures.

The movement of religious adherents in Mzuzu is something worrisome. Worship centres are located almost everywhere; however, the movement of religious adherents, passing worship centres closer to their houses to worship centres far from their residential areas is currently common. The unity of worship centres depends upon the historical and cultural background of such centres. Religious adherents join worship centres which has historical and geographical connection to their traditional religions or denominations. The connection is based on religion or denomination of their home of origin, parents, or a close ally and not on the need of worshippers. Worship centres have been distributed in such a way that it divides people of the same residential area who virtually share all things together, and who sometimes speak the same language, having the same ethnic background and make their living in similar way.

Many religious adherents go to worship centres to attend services on foot and very few of them travel by car or bicycle. Due to long distances they are travelling to worship centres, many adherents of respective worship centres do not attend services of worship regularly. Contrary to their religious beliefs and traditions, religious adherents restrict themselves to a worship centre of their traditional background when they have no problems which may need prayers, however, when they have problems which need prayers, they see no choice but to go to any worship centre, one or several, where they have been told that they can be helped.

I carried out this research as an insider. I am a church minister of the Church of Central Africa Presbyterian, Synod of Livingstonia, working in Mzuzu Presbytery; former moderator of Mzuzu Presbytery, and now Mzuzu Presbytery Clerk, former parish minister at Lupaso CCAP Church, and now parish minister at Mchengautuwa CCAP Church. I have the advantage of having an inner knowledge of religions and denominations in Mzuzu. My position helped me to access research information comfortably during the research process. However, I have tried as much as possible not to be biased so that the research exercise was carried out objectively.

The main objective of the study was to establish the religious geography of Mzuzu, through the study of all places of worship and religious social ministries. In order to achieve this aim these were the specific objectives in this study:

a) To locate all religious worship centres.
b) To gather relevant statistical information on all religious worship centres and to map out religious worship places and religious social institutions.
c) To analyze the data by denominational families.
d) To investigate the relationship between church attendance and the nominal role of church membership.
e) To find out the role and position of women in worship places.
f) To find out the role of language in worship places.
g) To find out the activities of religious social institutions.
h) To investigate the dynamics of origin and diffusion of religions in Mzuzu.

Since my research covers two disciplines, Religion and Geography, methods for both fields were used. A Geographical Positioning System (GPS) Receiver was used to collect geographically referenced data on religious facilities (i.e. worship Centres and Religious Social Institutions).

GIS software (Arc View 3.2) was used to visualize the data on a computer in form of a map, a spatial relationship and pattern was then developed. Worship centres and Religious Social Institutions were identified by snowball sampling technique. Localities of worship centres and Religious Social Institution were recorded using Eastings and Northings (UTM System).

This study is descriptive and analytical with the aim of showing, through dealing with selected issues, major aspects of religious reality in Mzuzu. Quantitative method was used in order to create a full picture of the distribution of religious centres as in 2013. This was based on a full coverage of religious centres. For analyzing the data, I have used the qualitative approach in an attempt to understand the data and their meaning.

Data was collected through questionnaires and oral interviews; existing literature relevant to the research topic was also reviewed. Questionnaires were used as data collection tools relative to worship centres. This procedure of administering these tools was adopted considering the perceived level of knowledge of respondents. In some cases, intended responses were obtained through probing questions. Both open and close ended questions were used depending on the information required. In depth discussions in focus groups at some centres were also used to allow more flexibility in data collection.

The basis is a comprehensive study with limited sampling and full accuracy in terms of places of worships as of 2013 December. The church building data collected is equally comprehensive. Data on church and mosque attendance were corrected from informants. The reliability is not 100% but as a researcher it presents me with a fair picture of reality. The information on the history of individual worship centres was collected from informants and was of necessity selective but quite appropriate to establish trends and approximations. Data on women and leadership in worship centres was obtained through informants and was checked by my personal observations and experience in worship centres.

The area under study is Mzuzu, the largest urban centre (latitude 11°27'S and 34°01'E longitude) in the Northern Region of Malawi, and the third largest city in Malawi. Mzuzu is the regional capital city of the Northern Region of Malawi. The city consists of 17 wards, with a total population of 133,968 according to the 2008 population and housing census. Mzuzu has a population growth rate of 4% per annum.

For the survey, a distinction was made between membership and attendance. Since few churches have properly maintained membership rolls, here again the picture is estimated but the data obtained still give a fair overall picture of the relative strength of the various demonstrations and also on the relationship between membership and church attendance. There were cases where the attendance was more than the membership; for example, in worship centres where they are well known for programmes of healing and deliverance, like at God's Will Church. However, normally membership is higher than attendance in most worship centres.

A third part of the survey, again aiming at full coverage, addressed some selected specific research questions such as:

    a) How is the numerical relationship between women and men?
    b) How far do women participate in leadership?
    c) What efforts are being made to increase membership?
    d) What is the dominant language of worship?

The data found and reproduced in this book cannot be used for precise comparison. In the following chapter, each of the described elements will be analyzed, and where appropriate it will be done in form of a survey of the whole city. In other instances, I have analyzed trends and supported them by anecdotal evidence.[13] The information obtained from the survey has been triangulated with existing information published or unpublished where relevant.

The field of this thesis is Religious Geography and therefore I do not take sides on religious adherents nor on the many differences between the Christian denominations. In classifying the Christians, I follow the historical typology developed by Klaus Fiedler which traces the denominations to their revival roots and classifies them in that way.[14] His typology starts with the Reformation, but for the church history of Malawi, it is sufficient to take the Reformation as the starting point. This typology distinguishes the following groups of the churches:

1. The churches of the Reformation.
2. The churches with a Pietist or Puritan background.
3. The churches of the Great Awakening.
4. The Evangelical churches.
5. The Restorationist Churches.
6. The Pentecostal Churches.
7. The Charismatic Churches.

This classification leaves out the Great Orthodox Church which has congregations in and near Blantyre, but not in Mzuzu. The Jehovah's Witness do not understand themselves as a Christian Church, but due to their origin, the Restorationist Revival, they are included among the Restorationist Churches. There is no category in this classification called African Independent (or Founded or Initiated) Churches as "African Independent Churches" is not a theological, but a sociological definition,[15] but I have used this category for sociological analysis together with other categories like migrant churches or language use.

The Non-Christian are less diverse than Christianity. In African Traditional Religion, I distinguish between the traditional type which has no regular worship and congregation and the modern type which may have those.

---

[13] Some such anecdotal evidence is included in the survey in chapter two but I have added further details through interviews and observations.

[14] Klaus Fiedler, *Missions as the Theology of the Church. An Argument from Malawi*, Mzuzu: Mzuni Press, 2015, p. 9.

[15] African Independent Churches are sociologically qualified by the absence of the White Man or the European connection, though theologically they may be poles apart from each other as are the Zionists and the Presbyterian Church of Africa (Blackman's Church).

Islam is categorized by the distinctions that Muslims use: Qudiriyya, Sunni, and Sukuti.[16] Hinduism is worldwide highly divers but only one form is represented in Mzuzu. Other religions that are represented in Malawi like Rastafarianism or Bahai have no organized presence in Mzuzu.

---

[16] There are real differences in spite of the common emphasis on Muslim unity.

Chapter Two: Origin and Diffusion of Religions in Mzuzu

This section provides the origin and diffusion of religions in 'Mzuzu'.[17] The section provides information in three parts; geographical, historical and religious diffusion in the study area. The first part deals with the geography of Mzuzu while the second part addresses the historical background and the third part is about the diffusion of religions in the study area.

2.1 Geographical Information

The area under study is the religious worship centres in Mzuzu, part of the northern region of Malawi *(Figure 2-1)*. Malawi is located south of the equator in sub–Saharan Africa. It covers a total area of 118,484 km^2 of which 94,276 km^2 is land area and the remaining part is covered by lakes. The country is divided into three regions; northern, central and southern; and the area under study is located in the northern region. Malawi as a nation is a God-fearing country,[18] it has many religions'[19] and

---

[17] 'Mzuzu' is a name given later to the area under study. At first the area was called Kajililwe or Kavuzi by the Tonga people, who were the first occupants of the land, when the Ngoni people occupied the land they called the place Kaning'igca translated Kaning'ina, meaning hanging. The word referred to small rain clouds which used to hang over the top mountain range of the area. The rain clouds could give rains soon after their appearance; hence the place was called Kaning'ina by the Ngoni. The name Mzuzu was given with the coming of Tung Oil Estate. The place had so many *Vizuzu* trees; it happened that Boardman, the estate manager, was failing to call the name Vizuzu, hence, he pronounced it Mzuzu. Later people started emulating his pronunciation and eventually the name changed from Kaning'ina to Mzuzu.

[18] The Right Honourable Khumbo H. Kachale, Former Vice President of the Republic of Malawi, Speech at Katawa CCAP Church at Silver Jubilee Celebrations, 23.12.2012.

[19] 'Religion' is a system of belief in and worship of one or more gods.

'denominations,[20] and the Christian religion is the largest religion in the northern region and Mzuzu in particular.[21]

Mzuzu is the largest urban centre in the northern region and the third largest city of the country after Lilongwe and Blantyre. Therefore, it plays an important role as a regional centre in the settlement hierarchy of Malawi.[22]

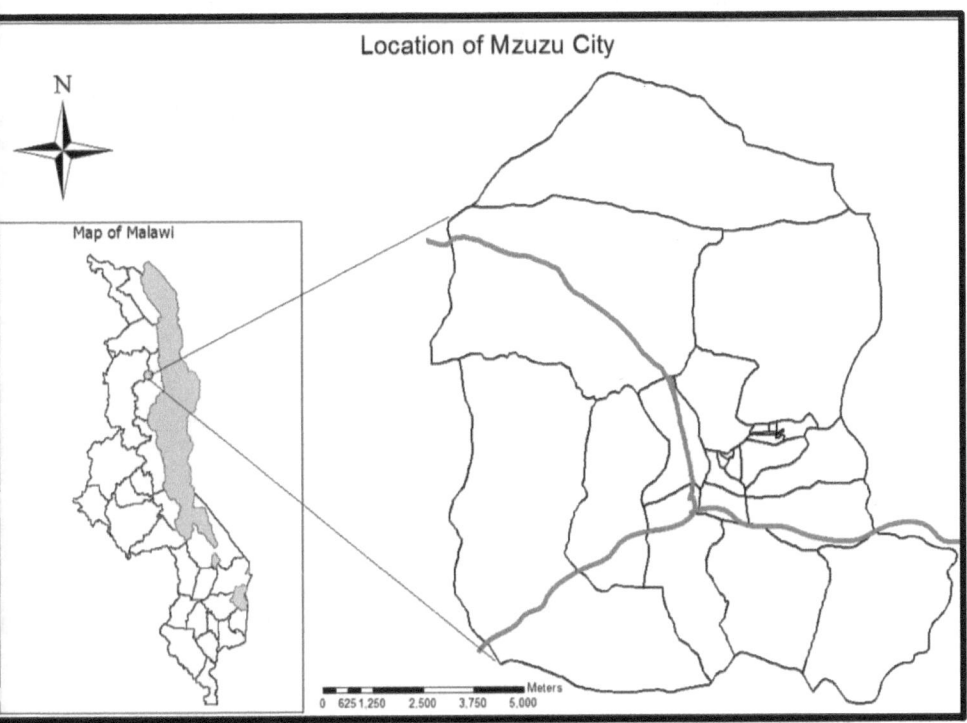

Figure 2.1: Location of Mzuzu City

The area under study is located at the northern end of the South Viphya Plateau on the edge of the Rift Valley escarpment at the altitude between 1,200 m and 1,370 m above sea level. It is bordered by the Viphya Mountains to the north and south and by the Kaning'ina

---

[20] 'Denomination' is a group of people having the same religious beliefs as a subdivision of a religion.
[21] According to the 2008 census figures 95.1% of the population belongs to one of the many Christian churches. Mzuzu Urban Profile Final Review 2008-2009, Mzuzu City, 2009, p. 24.
[22] Mzuzu Urban Profile Final Review 2008- 2009, Mzuzu City, 2009, p. 10.

mountains to the east. Mzuzu city area has been developed on a saddle of Kaning'ina, Choma and Nkhalapya or Viphya mountains. Most of the area lies in the Lunyangwa River basin with flatter, gently sloping land with ridges and gullies to the east and south.

The boundary of the area is Lusangazi to the south, Nkhorongo to the north, Mganthira to the east and Sonda to the west. The area consists of 17 wards, covering a total land area of 142.85 km² *(Figure 2.2)*. According to the 2008 population and housing census, Mzuzu had a population of 133,968 with a growth rate of 4.4% per annum.[23]

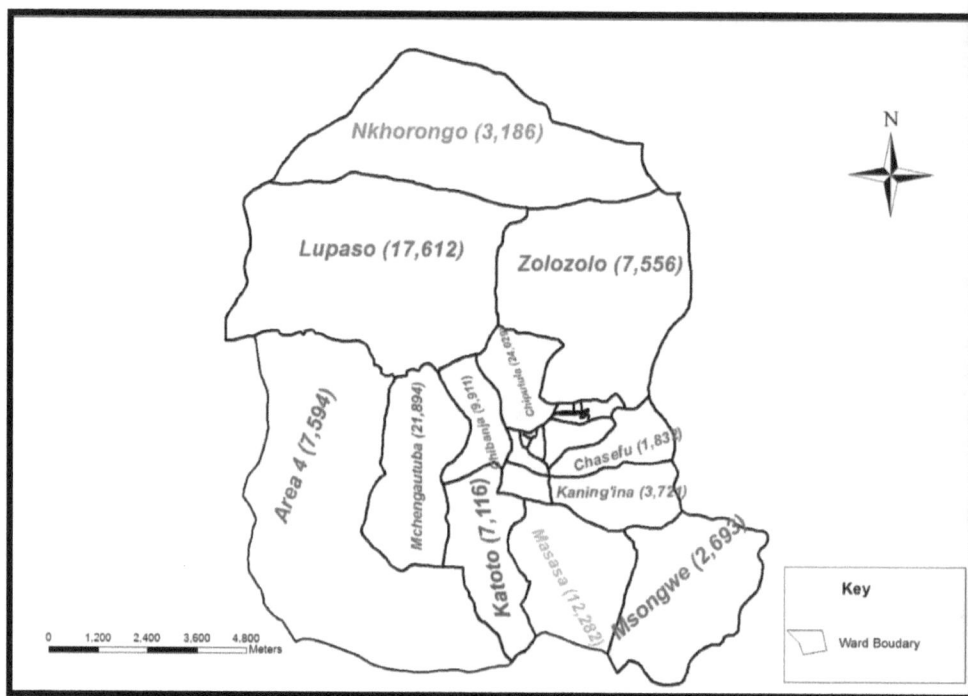

Figure 2.2: Map showing Wards and Population in Mzuzu (NSO, 2008)

---

[23] Mzuzu Urban Profile Final Review 2008- 2009, Mzuzu City, p. 18.

The census reveals that Mzuzu has a high number of socio-economically active people and a lower child dependency rate *(Figure 2.3)*.

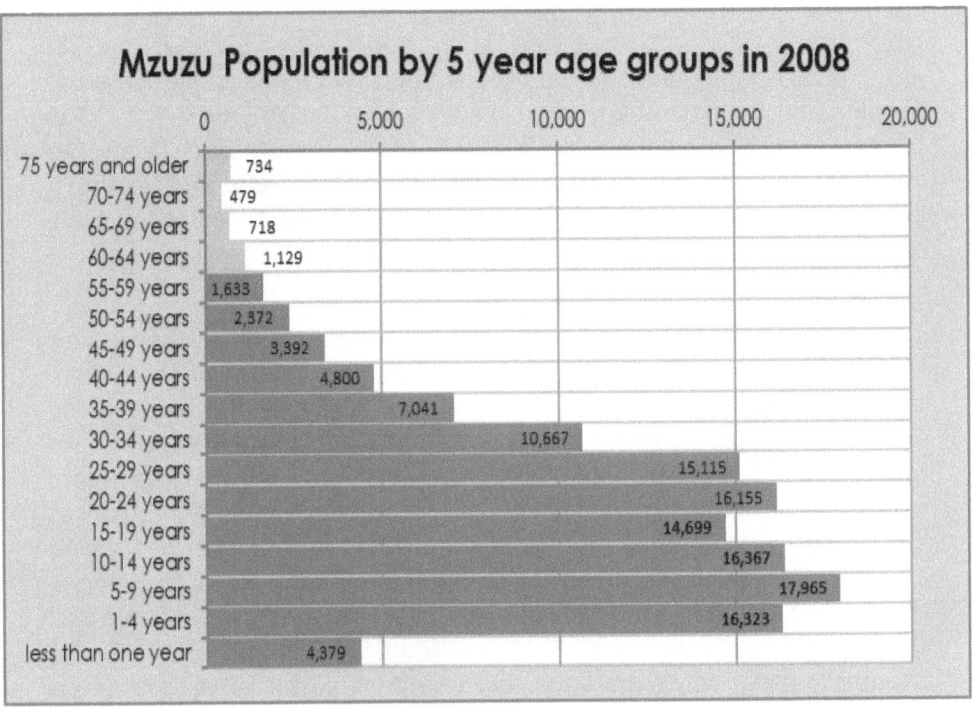

Figure 2.3: Mzuzu Polulation by age groups (Mzuzu City, 2009)

The area under study has been experiencing rural and urban migration from surrounding and far areas due to being a regional administrative centre and business attraction. The Mzuzu economy is undergoing a rapid change at this time, shifting from a mainly administrative Centre for northern Malawi to a commercial regional centre.[24] Due to its strategic position along the northern corridor, it already has become an important trading centre especially for imported products from China and other countries.[25]

---

[24] Mzuzu Urban Profile Final Review 2008- 2009, Mzuzu City, p. 18.
[25] Ibid.

2.2 Historical Background

2.2.1 First Settlement in Mzuzu

There was a time when the area under study had no people; the first group of people to settle in the area when it was mere jungle were the Tonga under Mankhambira, who called the area Kajililwe or Kavuzi.[26] The Tonga people settled at the eastern side of the present-day state lodge and later became subjects of the Ngoni under Mabulabo and *'Induna'*[27] Mayayi Chiputula Nhlane. The Tonga came to the hills of Kaning'ina while running away from Ngoni raids. This caused the Tonga to grow cassava at Kaning'ina, a food which the Ngoni did not like.[28]

The second group of people who occupied Mzuzu was the Ngoni under Mabulabo with the most notable Ngoni regiment leader of the Tonga, *Induna* Chiputula Nhlane. Chiputula Nhlane settled at the present day Chiputula location while other people resided in an area between Mganthira and where police and Mzuzu Hotel are today.[29] The Ngoni people called the place Kaning'igca, translated into Tumbuka as Kaning'ina. At that time, the whole of the Ngoni village was called Elangeni. The Ngoni settlement at Kaning'ina was for easy raiding among the Tonga who were at Chintheche, Mdyaka, Nkhata Bay, Bandawe and Kuwirwi. One great enticement to the Ngoni settlement was the Tonga gardens, so that when the Ngoni became hungry, they met their needs from Tonga gardens.[30]

The third group of people was the Scottish missionaries who came to Kaning'ina in 1878. Kaning'ina station was established as one of the two pioneer settlements in search of a permanent mission station, a better site than Cape Maclear. The station was established to the west of the

---

[26] Int. Rev L.N. Nyondo, General Secretary of CCAP Synod of Livingstonia, 12.4.2013.

[27] 'Induna', is a person who acts in between the chief and his subjects. Nobody can go directly to the chief without going through his Induna.

[28] C.Z. Mphande, Some Aspects of the History of the Tonga up to 1934, Dissertation, University of Malawi, 1968/69, p. 4.

[29] D.I. Nkhoma, The Northern Ngoni, A Political System, Dissertation, University of Malawi, 1968/69, p. 8.

[30] John McCracken, *Politics and Christianity in Malawi 1875-1940. The Impact of the Livingstonia Mission in the Northern Province*, Blantyre: CLAIM-Kachere, 2008, p. 92.

new state lodge, at a ridge in between where Msongwe CCAP church and the new Kaning'ina church are established respectively.[31] The Kaning'ina station rapidly developed as a focus for both the discontented Tonga who normally resided in Ngoni country and Tonga who having fled from the Ngoni country and settled under Mankhambira, who complained that they were being treated as slaves by him and asked permission to settle with the Scottish missionaries.[32] On January 1879, little more than six weeks after the foundation of the station, 314 villagers attended the Sunday service. By September it was reported in Scotland that upwards of 2000 people had come under mission influence at Kaning'ina, though many of these appear to have been temporary visitors, who used the presence of the mission as a protective shield against the Ngoni while they gathered their upland crops. Once the cassava had been collected

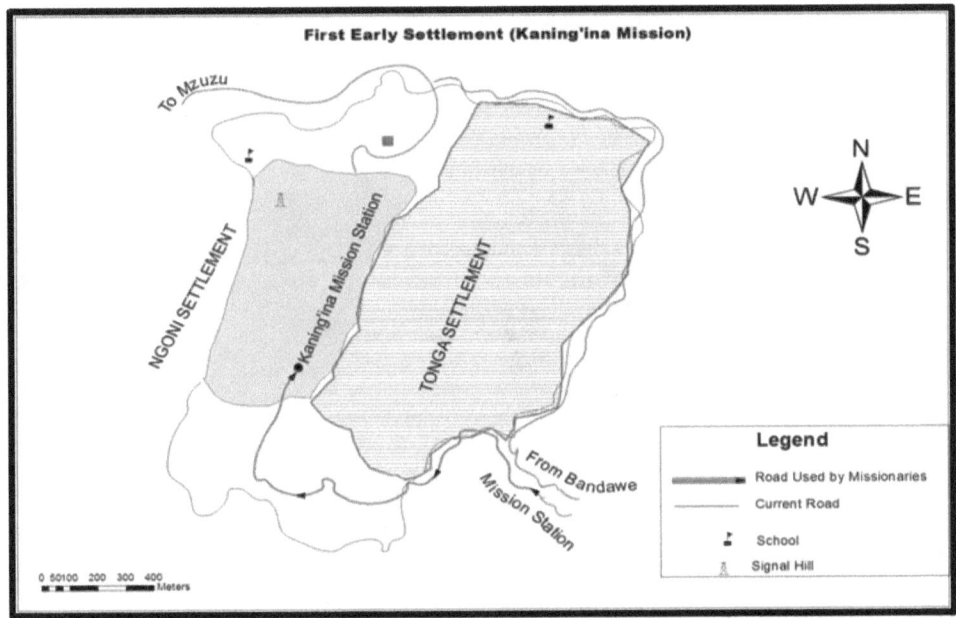

Figure 2.4 Map of first set of settlement (Kaning'ina Mission)

---

[31] Int. Opson Thole, Mzuzu Museum Office, Department of Culture and Heritage, 4.4.2013.

[32] John McCracken, *Politics and Christianity in Malawi 1875-1940. The Impact of the Livingstonia Mission in the Northern Province,* Blantyre: CLAIM-Kachere, 2008, p. 94.

and eaten, attendance at church fell and most people returned to their villages.³³ However, the Kaning'ina mission post survived until October 1879 and was closed, apparently because Dr Robert Laws was afraid of the difficulties which might arise on account of its exposed position in the no-man's land between the Ngoni in the hills and the Tonga.³⁴ The mission post was re-opened in Ngoni land at Njuyu in 1882, which later came back to Mzuzu via Ekwendeni. Figure 2.4 shows the first settlement.

The first three groups of people who settled in Mzuzu migrated elsewhere due to the Tonga rebellion. The immediate cause of the rebellion was the sudden death of Mayayi Chiputula Nhlane, Induna of Mabulabo. After his death, the Tonga found a chance to rebel and join

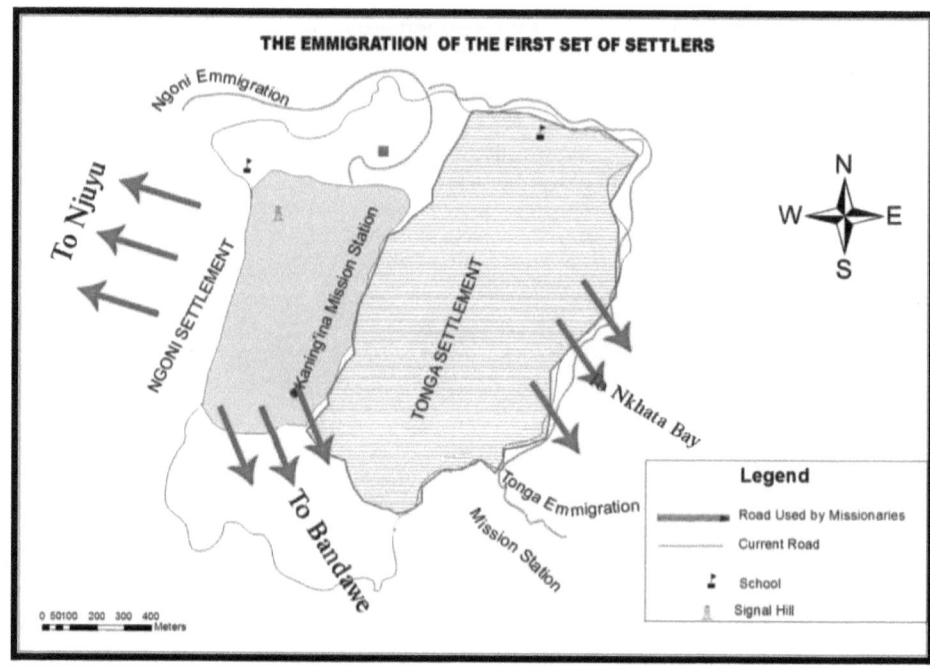

Figure 2.5: Map showing the emmigration of the first settlers.

---

³³ Ibid.

³⁴ T. Jack Thompson, *Christianity in Northern Malawi: Donald Fraser's Missionary Methods and Ngoni Culture*. Leiden, New York, 1995, p. 41, John McCracken, *Politics and Christianity in Malawi 1875 – 1940. The Impact of the Livingstonia Mission in the Northern Province,* Blantyre: CLAIM-Kachere, 2008, p. 89.

their friends at the lake.[35] The Ngoni people moved to Njuyu area following chief Mabulabo who settled at Elangeni while the family of Induna Chiputula Nhlane settled at Hoho near Njuyu Mountain. The Scottish missionaries went back to Bandawe Station. The map *(Figure 2.5)* shows the emigration of the first set of settlers.

2.2.2 The Settlement from 1900 to Date

The present state of Mzuzu originated from the permanent settlement of Mafuta Kaunda, Luwinga Singini and the Common Wealth Development Cooperation (CDC). The first group to settle in Mzuzu was Mafuta Kaunda, a Tonga by tribe, who came from Bula and settled at Mganthira. There are two theories of settlement around these people: The first theory is that the Kaunda people could have remained in the area as they were subjects of Ngoni Chiefs and did not leave the area together with their friends who rebelled against the Ngoni. It is suggested that when their fellow Tonga rebelled against the Ngoni, the Kaunda people remained loyal until when the Ngoni had to leave the place for Njuyu settlement, so that some of the Kaundas even went with the Ngoni people. This is the reason why we find the Kaunda people at Mzalangwe area in Mzimba district.[36] The other theory is that at first the Kaunda people left the place following the Tonga rebellion and came back later.

The first theory has some shortfalls. The reaction against the theory is that the Kaunda people would not remain with the Ngoni while their friends had rebelled against them and went down to the lake. The other issue is that at that time people used to be known by tribes, as a cultural identity. It would have been difficult to lose such identity and be on their own as a family group. Therefore, it is believed by many people that the Kaunda people came back later and settled at Mganthira.[37]

The second group of people who settled in Mzuzu were the Luwinga Singini. The group migrated from Ekwendeni. Originally, the Singini people came from Usisya in Usingini area; they were taken captives by

---

[35] C.Z. Mphande, *Some Aspects of the History of the Tonga up to 1934*, Chancellor College, University of Malawi 1968/69, p. 4.
[36] Int. Florah Ngulube, Church Elder and Ngoni Women Christian Counsellor, Mzalangwe CCAP, 21.3.2013.
[37] Int. Opson Thole, Mzuzu Museum Office, Department of Culture and Heritage, 4.4.2013.

the Ngoni and settled at Ekwendeni.[38] Luwinga Singini migrated from Ekwendeni to Mzuzu due to polygamy; he married 36 wives, and he wanted to find enough space for his family.[39] Luwinga Singini first settled at Mganthira, a place where 'Mzuzu Technical College'[40] is today situated. In 1930 they moved out of the place to the present day Luwinga area, because Mganthira became a reserved area for Tung Oil Estate.

The third group was the Commonwealth Development Corporation who came to establish Tung Oil Estate in 1947. The Commonwealth Development Corporation was the engine of growth of the study area; it influenced the regional administrative and service centre to be transferred from Mzimba Boma to Mzuzu. The movement of administrative offices and service centre from Mzimba to Mzuzu made Mzuzu settlement to develop rapidly in all sectors of life.[41]

2.3 Origin and Diffusion of Religions in Mzuzu

Religions in Mzuzu are as old as the first habitation of people in the area. Religion being a system of belief in and worship of one or more gods becomes inextricable linked with a particular tribe, racial group, ethnic group, culture, political and environmental system, and people's lifestyle, so that it becomes difficult to imagine one without the other. The point of focus is not on the specifics of religious beliefs and practices, but on how the religious beliefs and practices are internalized by adherents, and how these processes of internalization influence social systems and are influenced by it.[42] Thus, religious geographers study the process by which religions, as a cultural feature, diffuse from one location of origin to the other. The diffusion process results in a distinctive spatial distribution, generated by a process of spatial interaction that is diffused from a point of origin in accordance with a distinctive pattern of a communication network.[43] The process of religious diffusion is important because religion is a major force in the spreading of cultural values. Religious geographers

---

[38] Int. Wayinga Singini Group Village Headman, Lupaso, 6.4.2013.

[39] Ibid.

[40] Mzuzu Technical College area is where the first Luwinga Singini was buried in 1924. Luwinga area has taken the name of Luwinga Village while at first the area was called Lupaso.

[41] Mzuzu Urban Profile Final Review 2008-2009, Mzuzu City, 2009, p. 10.

[42] Religion and Geography, en.wikipedia org/wiki, 15.10.2012.

[43] Religion and Geography, en.wikipedia org/wiki, 15.10.2012.

have noted the characteristics of religious distribution and diffusion of the universal and ethnic religions in a way that universal religions attempt to appeal to all people of different cultural background, races and location, while an ethnic religion bases its appeal on the physical characteristics of a particular location, tribe or ethnic group.[44]

This being the case religions in Mzuzu have originated from different cultural groups and migrated into the area starting from when the first inhabitants came. Some religions and denominations are older than others, basing on when they were introduced in the area; however, diffusion of these religions and denominations differs, depending upon the type and characteristics of a particular religion and denomination. Religions and denominations started from a remarkably small area, through the growth of the study area in terms of population and urbanization, religious faiths have diffused far and wide.

The largest religion in Mzuzu is Christianity and to a minor degree Islam and Hindu. The 2008 census figure shows that 95.1% of the population belongs to one of the many Christian churches, 4.2% are Muslims and 0.6% has another religious orientation.[45] There is religious tolerance within the city and this fact unites people of Mzuzu.[46]

2.3.1 African Traditional Religion

Following the migration of people to the study area, African Traditional Religion[47] was the first religion to be practiced by the first inhabitants of

---

[44] An ethnic religion carries meaning primarily for people either living in or attracted to the particular environment, having a clustered geographical distribution, while the universalized religions of the world have been adopted across cultural barriers and language boundaries. H.J. de Blij and Peter O. Muller, *Human Geography: Culture, Society and Space,* New York: John Wily and Sons, 1995, p. 297. – For Mzuzu see: Zeenah Sibande, "Religious Geography: Investigation of Christian Distribution around CCAP Church Centres in Mzuzu City," MA Module, Department of Theology and Religious Studies, Mzuzu University, 2013, p. 18.

[45] Malawi Population and Housing Census Report, 2008.

[46] Mzuzu Urban Profile Final Review 2008- 2009, Mzuzu City, 2009, p. 18.

[47] In traditional African culture there was no separate compartment known as African Traditional Religion, for Traditional Religion permeated the whole of life. One could not point to anything and classify it as secular, for all of life was sacred with spiritual dimensions. Strictly speaking, African Traditional Religion is not a religion as understood in the West, a set of dogmas, but is life experiential.

the area, Tonga and Ngoni respectively, from the day of their arrival. The religion originated from their respective tribal cultural backgrounds. Worship places were established at Kaning'ina Mountain by the Ngoni and at Kavuzi by the Tonga.[48] The religion was composed of three basic components: belief in the Supreme Being, the spirit world (spirits are subordinate to the Supreme Being), and 'mystical powers'.[49] This has been emphasized throughout the history of this religion in Mzuzu.

Tonga people did not have shrines, oftentimes worship was taking place where a medicine man was discharging his/her duties, where medicine or mystical powers were given to the victims of circumstances, such as bad luck, sickness, and misfortunes, or for protection.

Village Headman Kabunduli Mtete, being the head of the Tonga tribe in this area, was also the religious leader; he was regarded as super human with strange mystical powers, from him religion diffused to all family heads.[50] Vimaso Mwale was a notable Tonga medicine man, head of the family of Mankhambila, a warrior trained by Ngoni when Tonga people were taken captive by the Ngoni of Mzimba. He came back from Mzimba and joined his friends at Kajilirwe during the Tonga rebellion as a famous warrior and medicine man. The name Vimaso was given to him because when he had gone to war and killed enemies, he used to cut off their heads and stuck them to a stick with eyes wide open.

Similarly, Ngoni Traditional Religion of Mabilabo originated from Emdla-kude village of Chief Mabilabo at Elangeni and diffused to all family heads. In Mzuzu the religion was headed by Induna Chiputula Nhlane and Prophets. The religion did not have a shrine for worship; they used to

---

The religion centres on man, the whole emphasis is upon man gaining the power needed to live a good life. Life revolves around man and his interests and needs (Richard J. Gehman, *African Traditional Religion in Biblical Perspective*, Nairobi, 1993, p. 19).

[48] Int. Rev. Kapombe Mwale, Director, Theological Education by Extension in Malawi, Mzuzu, 12.8.2014.

[49] The whole psychic atmosphere of African village life is filled with belief in mystical powers. People know that the universe has a power, or force in addition to the ancestral spirits, spirits and the Supreme Being, which affects everyone for better or for worse (John Mbiti, *African Religion and Philosophy*, London SPCK, 1969, p. 92).

[50] Int. Rev Kapombe Mwale, Director, Theology Education by Extension in Malawi, Mzuzu, 12.8.2014.

have annual religious festivals and occasional worship when they were faced with calamity.[51] Family headmen, village headmen, and chiefs were taken to be the religious leaders depending upon different levels of community gathering and diviners and prophets were the ones asking the will of the Supreme Being through the ancestral spirits. The common spirit diviners were *Dhlozi* and *Isangoma*. Kalengo Tembo, father of Mawelera and Makhala Tembo, was a notable diviner or prophet in Mzuzu who used to gather people at Kaning'ina Mountain for religious affairs. One of a notable annual religious festival was *Incwala*,[52] a traditional first fruits festival. The *Incwala* ceremony had two religions meanings; first was giving thanks to a Supreme Being through the ancestral spirits for giving them the year's harvest and at the same time asking permission to start eating the harvest.[53] The second meaning was a kind of medicine taken by a king from the spirits to strengthen both him and the whole tribe and that is why the ceremony welded together the nation and often preceded with war raids.

---

[51] Ngoni people used to face different calamities, such as famine, draught, pests and diseases, or death. When the calamity was on a national level, they were going to Emdlakude village with a black ox used as part of worship. Prayers were said to the Supreme Being through ancestral spirits in front of an oxen and when the oxen urinated while praying then it was an indication that the spirits accepted their prayers and presented their request to the Supreme Being who had accepted too.

[52] *Incwala* was the traditional annual feast of the first fruits among the Ngoni. This was first commented on by A.T. Bryant in his book, The Zulu People. The ceremony involved every man and woman, every young bride, every carrier-boy, and every girl, wended their way together to the regimental headquarters of their male folk, the boys carrying the sleeping mats and karosses of their fathers and elder brothers, the girls a food supply for at least a week. It was a national gathering expressing the unity of the Ngoni tribe. Later such meetings could no longer be held when the tribe stopped raiding. Therefore, the unity of the tribe was expressed in the National Christian conventions (T. Jack Thompson, *Ngoni, Xhosa and Scot, Religious and Cultural Interaction in Malawi*, Zomba: Kachere, 2007, p. 78). See also T. Jack Thompson, *Christianity in Northern Malawi: Donald Fraser's Missionary Methods and Ngoni Culture*, Leiden, New York, 1995, p. 89, Donald Fraser, *The Autobiography of an African*, London, 1925, p. 142-43, A.T. Bryant, *The Zulu People*, Pietermaritzburg, 1949, p. 515; W.A. Elmslie, *Among the Wild Ngoni*, Edinburgh, 1899, p. 309.

[53] Int. Opson Thole, Mzuzu Museum, Department of Culture and Heritage, 4.4.2013.

The African Traditional Religion in Mzuzu has originated from Tonga and Ngoni traditional religious background. The religion, however, has gone through to citizens of Mzuzu far and wide. The diffusion of the religion is without physical structure; rather it is through people's' life style. Members of Traditional Religions are nowadays at the same time members of other religions.

The type of diffusion of African Traditional Religious is contagious. The religion remains essentially cultural, being transmitted by word of mouth from one generation to the other. Although the religious worship centres cannot be clearly seen in an organized form today, the practices and beliefs are among the people with the basic component of belief in mystical power and ancestral spirits.[54] Religious worship centres are commonly where medicine men/women are discharging their duties. Religious centres have no nominal rolls; they are like clinics, where people are free to visit any time as long as they feel that they will receive their 'wants'.[55]

2.3.2 Christian Religion

The second religion in Mzuzu was the Christian religion established at Kaning'ina in 1878. The Christian religion at Kaning'ina was under what later became the CCAP Synod of Livingstonia established by Livingstonia missionaries from Scotland and South Africa. The Kaning'ina Christian worship centre was for both Ngoni and Tonga who at that time were around the area.

The missionaries came to Kaning'ina from Bandawe Mission Station through a path similar to the present-day road Chintheche - Mzuzu via Lwana Atonga,[56] and settled at Kaning'ina ridge, east of the present-day

---

[54] Witchcraft, sorcery and crises are great temptations; Reliance upon the ancestors is a felt need during times of emergency, even for many Christians. The traditional help derived from the medicine man/woman is often felt strongly during times of great need (Richard J. Gehman, *African Traditional Religion in Biblical Perspective*, Nairobi, 1993, p. 19).

[55] African Traditional Religions centre on man. The whole emphasis is upon man gaining the power to live a good life. Life revolves around man and his interest and needs. God is the explanation of man's origin and sustenance; it is as if God exists for the sake of man (John S. Mbiti, *African Religions and Philosophy*, London: SPCK, 1969, p. 92).

[56] Int. Rev. H.M. Nkhoma, Former General Secretary, CCAP Synod of Livingstonia, 14.7.2013.

State Lodge. The Kaning'ina centre was established by William Koyi and Alexander Riddel, however, it operated for eleven months and was closed. Later, a permanent worship centre was opened at Njuyu,[57] through which it later came back to Mzuzu at Lupaso via Ekwendeni Mission Station. The Christian religion came first to Mganthila in Mzuzu in 1900 and moved to Lupaso in 1930. In 1950 Mzuzu CCAP worship centre developed from Lupaso where Mzuzu CCAP Church is situated. The two CCAP worship centres have diffused far and wide in Mzuzu. Some of these worship centres are; Katawa, Zolozolo, Viyele, Chiputula, Kachere, Chibavi, Mchengautuwa, Msongwe. Figure 2.6 below indicate how the CCAP Churches have been diffused over time. Following the introduction of the Christian religion by Livingstonia Mission, many Christian denominations and groups were introduced into the area. In 1942 signs of Seventh-day worship started in Mzuzu at Nkholongo. Ephraim Chibambo, a member of Ekwendeni CCAP and a teacher

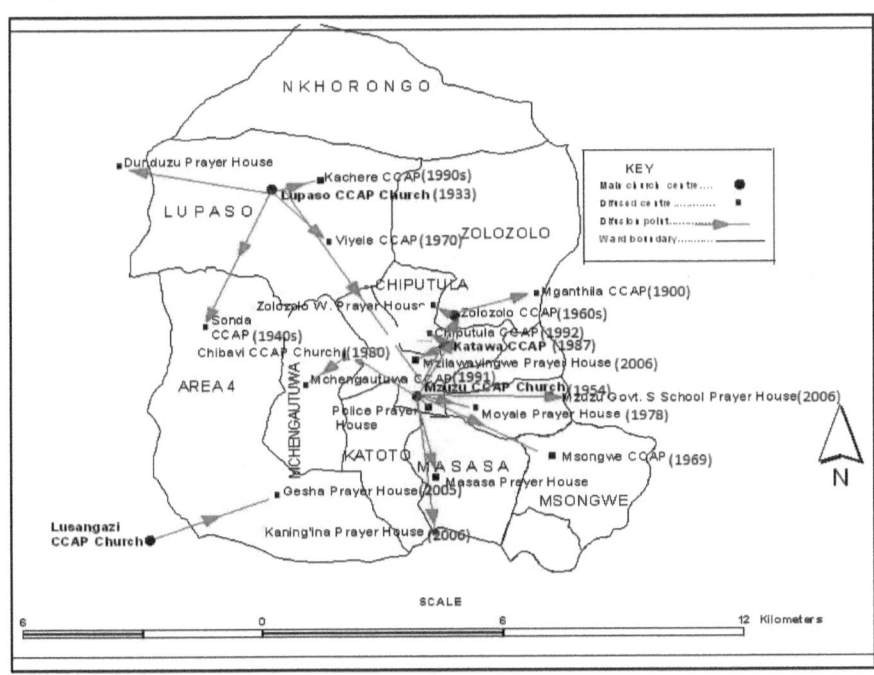

Figure 2.6 Diffusion of CCAP Churches

---

[57] T. Jack Thomson, *Christianity in Northern Malawi: Donald Fraser's Missionary Methods and Ngoni Culture*, Leiden, New York: Brill, 1995.

withdrew his membership together with his family from CCAP and started a church which was to address his spiritual quest for truthful worship which was not found in CCAP. He started a church at Nkholongo with his own family by the name of Truth Seekers. Many people joined the church; rules of worship were similar to Seventh-day Adventist.[58] When the news of this church was heard at Luwazi Seventh-day Mission, Pastor Davie William Ludlow from Luwazi visited the church in 1945 and on the same day the church became part of Seventh-day Adventist under Luwazi Mission. There are 12 Seventh-day Adventist churches that have originated from Nkholongo Seventh-day Adventist background. The concept of seventh-day worship in Mzuzu originated from this background and today we have Seventh-day Baptists, original, Central Africa Conference and Adventist. Figure 2.7 below indicate how the Seventh-day Churches have been diffused over time.

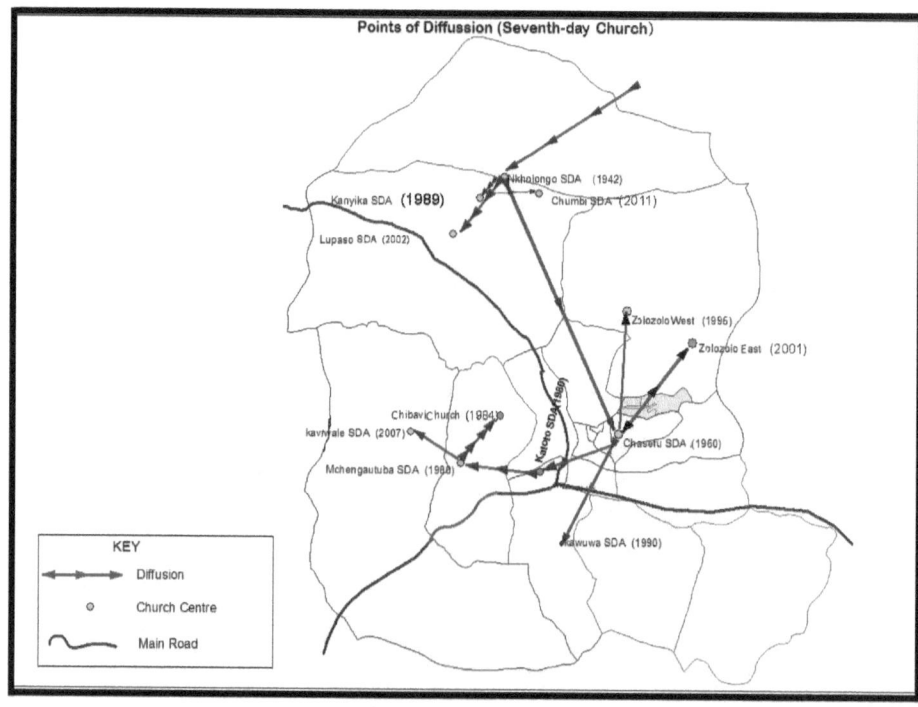

Figure 2.7: Diffusion of Seventh-day Churches

---

[58] Int. Doctor Mnthali, one of the first members of Nkhorongo Seventh–day Adventist Church, Nkhorongo, 28.8.2013.

The first Anglican Church was started in Mzuzu in 1950 by Anglicans working in Mzuzu. The church started as fellowship by Europeans who were fellowshipping in their houses as members of the Anglican Church working with the Tung Oil Estate and the regional administrative centre. Later Africans too started house fellowships separated from Europeans. The two groups joined each other sometime later when the Europeans had constructed a church at St. Mark's.[59] All Anglican congregations in Mzuzu have originated from St Mark's Church. Figure 2.8 below indicate how the Anglican Churches have been diffused over time.

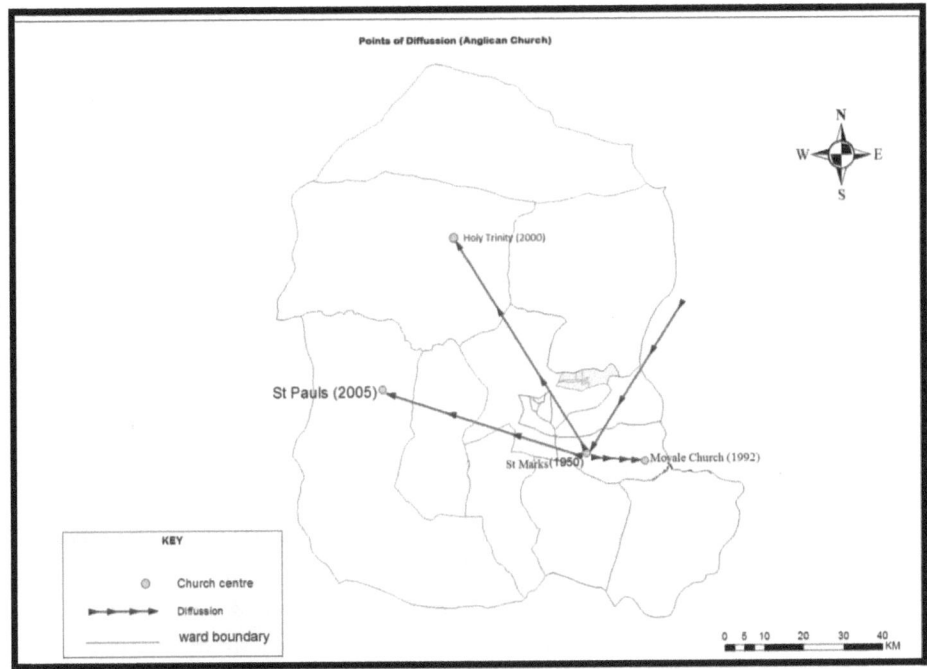

Figure 2.8: Diffussion of Anglican Churches.

In 1950 the first African Instituted Church started in Mzuzu. This was Chipangano which came from Nkhata Bay and was situated at Chiputula. The church came following her adherents who were working with Tung Oil Estate. The first Chipangano church was built at Chiputula which later was moved to Kaning'ina. Many African Instituted Churches came to

---

[59] Int. Arch Deacon James Kennan Chifisi, Vicar General, Anglican Diocese of Northern Malawi, Mzuzu, 3.10.2013.

Mzuzu following the background of Chipangano Church such as; Last Church of God, African National Church, and Church of African Presbyterian. Figure 2.9 below indicate how the Chipangano Churches have been diffused over time.

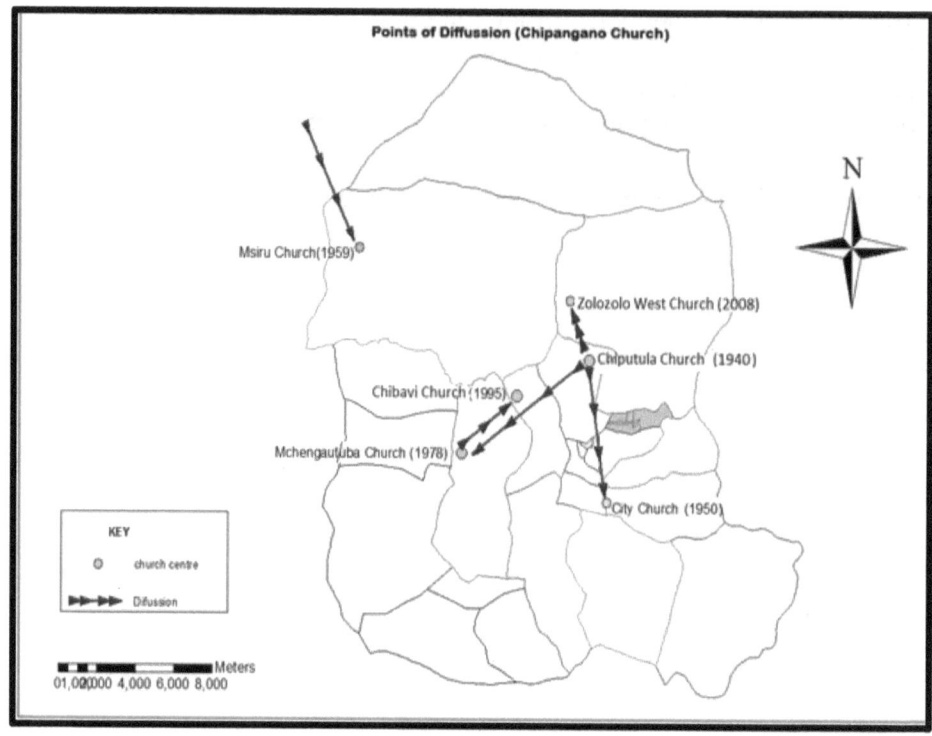

Figure 2.9: Diffusion of Chipangano

In 1954 the Roman Catholic Church came to Mzuzu from Katete in a search of a central place for the establishment of an administrative centre for the Roman Catholic Church in the north.[60] The idea to establish a Diocesan centre in Mzuzu coincided with the development of the study area, which resulted from the introduction of the Tung oil estate and the transfer of government administrative offices from Mzimba Boma. At that time the area had already members of the Roman Catholic Church, who were working with the Tung oil estate and government administrative offices. In 1954 Monsignor Marvel St. Denis started a worship centre at Lunyangwa which was called St. Peter's. Monsignor Denis came from Katete Mission. St. Peter's worship centre became the

---

[60] J. Coolen, *The History of Mzuzu Diocese*, Mzuzu, 1989, p. 69.

administrative centre of Mzuzu Diocese and Monsignor Marvel St. Denis became the first Bishop of the Diocese. St. Peter's worship centre developed into many worship centres in Mzuzu such as; St. Albert, Holy Family, St. Augustine, St. Theresa, St. Fostina and St. Bernadette.

In 1954 Monsignor Marvel St. Denis started a worship centre at Lunyangwa which was called St. Peter's. Monsignor Denis came from Katete Mission. St. Peter's worship centre became the administrative centre of Mzuzu Diocese and Monsignor Marvel St. Denis became the first Bishop of the Diocese. St. Peter's worship centre developed into many worship centres in Mzuzu such as; St. Albert, Holy Family, St. Augustine, St. Theresa, St. Fostina and St. Bernadette. Figure 2.10 below indicate how the Roman Churches have been diffused over time.

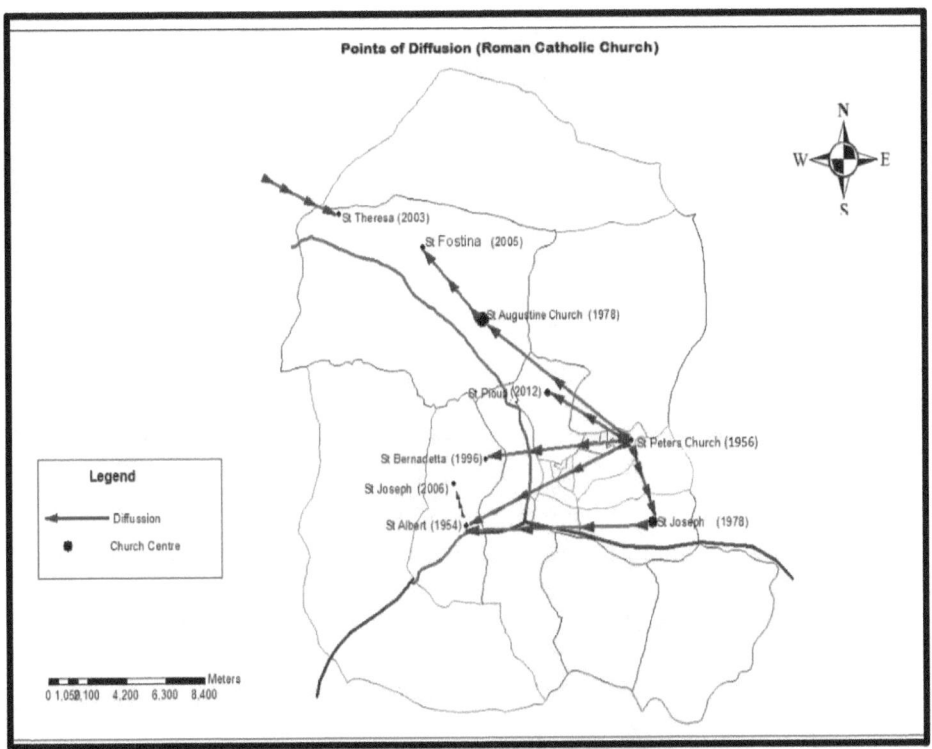

Figure 2.10: Diffiusion of Roman Catholic Churches

In 1965 came after the Roman Catholic another church that had its origin in the Restorationist Revival, the Church of Christ. It came to Mzuzu as a fellowship organized by members of the church who had joined it well before coming to Mzuzu. The first appearance of Church of Christ in

Mzuzu was through a fellowship started at Zolozolo east. When the fellowship had grown into a church, Pastor Chilambo from Chinyolo in Rumphi was sent to Mzuzu to nurture the church at Zolozolo. In 1968 the church was moved to Jomo Kenyatta at Kaning'ina. All other Church of Christ Congregations originated from Jomo Kenyatta at Kaning'ina. Figure 2.11 below indicates how Churches of Church of Christ have diffused over time.

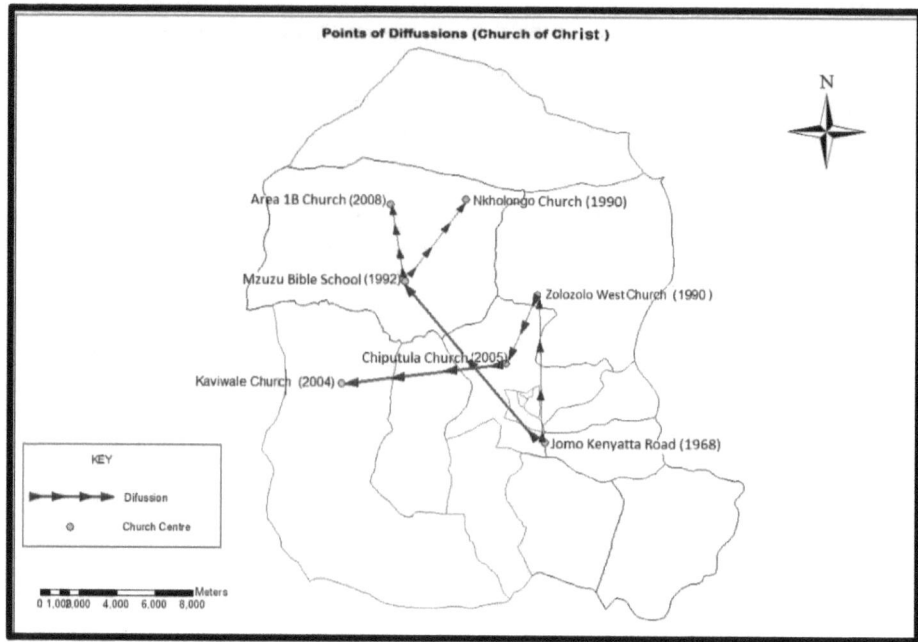

Figure 2.11 Diffusion of Church of Christ

In 1970 New Apostolic worship started in Mzuzu. The church started as a fellowship by members of the church working in Mzuzu who came from Bwengu area in Rumphi. These people were members of Bwengu Church and when they came to Mzuzu they started a fellowship which resulted into a church. The first church was built at Zolozolo east in 1974 with the help of Germany missionaries. From Zolozolo the church diffused to other areas (Figure 2.12).

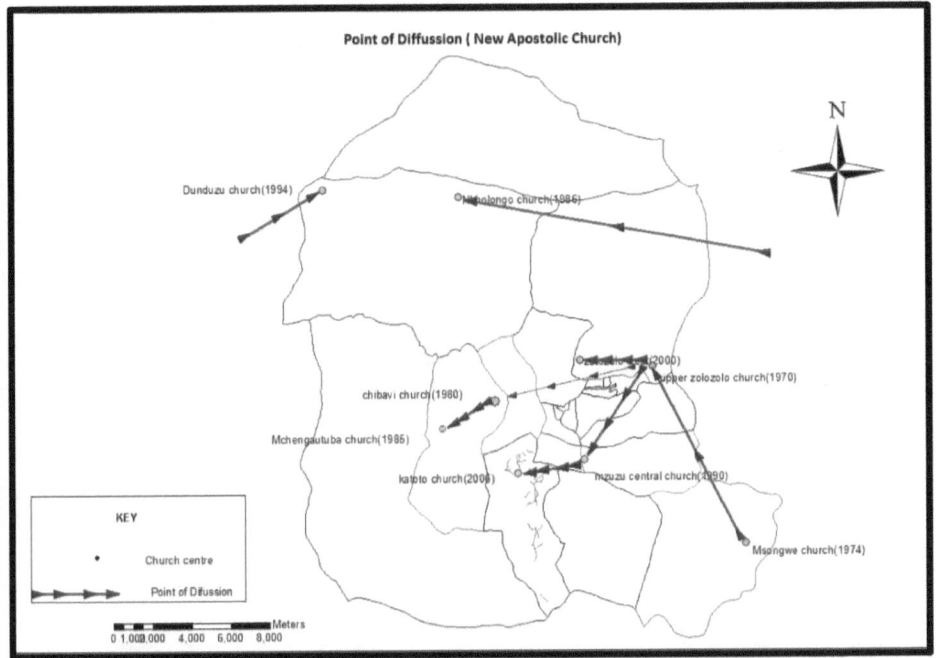

Figure 2.12: Diffusion of News Apostolic Churches

In 1972 the Baptist Convention of Malawi started in Mzuzu. The church was started by Njolomole Phiri and Missionary Swafford, who were on a church planting tour in northern Malawi. Njolomole and Swafford had a series of evangelism campaigns in Mzuzu which resulted in the establishment of bible study and fellowship groups at a rented shop of Chimpozo at the old market.[61] When the fellowship had matured, it became a church. The church was built at Kaning'ina and from there all Baptist Convention Churches in Mzuzu have come (Figure 2.13).

---

[61] Hany Longwe, *Christians by Grace – Baptists by Choice, A History of the Baptist Convention of Malawi*, Zomba: Kachere, 2011, p. 79.

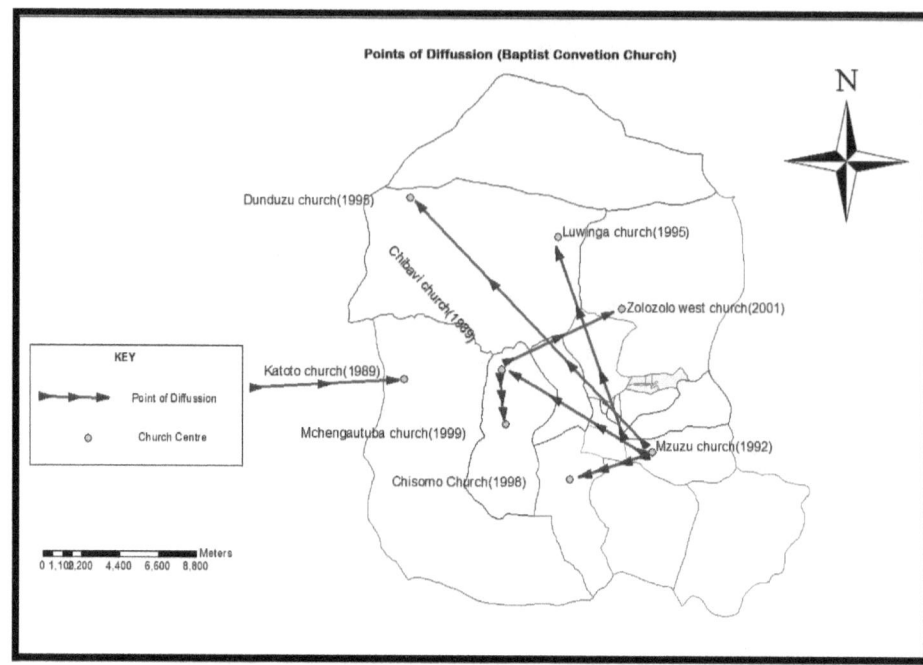

Figure 2.13: Diffussion of Baptist Convention Churches.

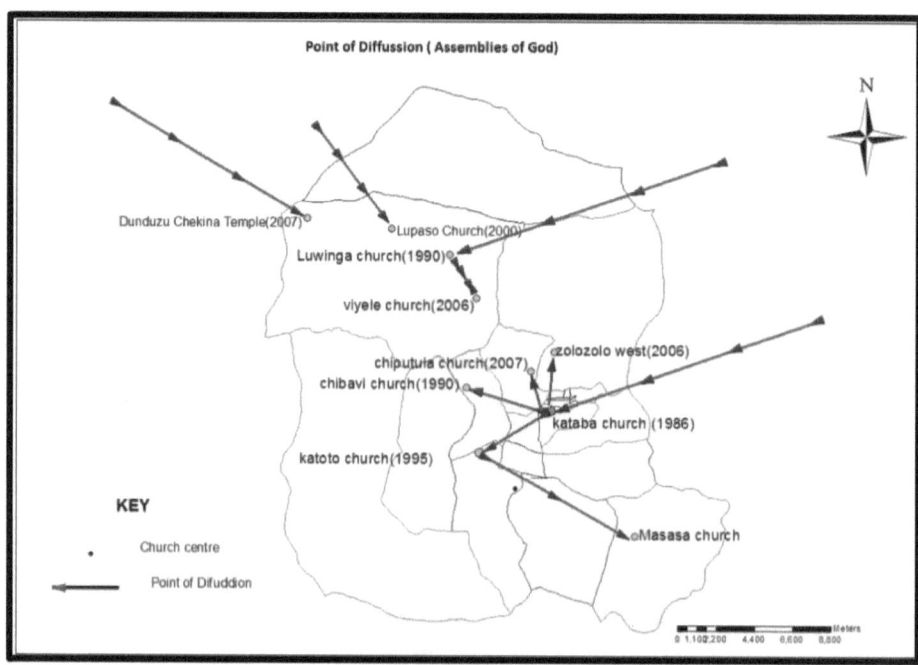

Figure 2.14: Diffussion of Assemblies of God

In 1982 the first Pentecostal Church was established in Mzuzu at Chibavi, the Apostolic Faith Mission. The church started through a project of church planting initiated by Lilongwe Apostolic Faith College. After the coming of Apostolic Faith Mission to Mzuzu, many other Pentecostal denominations have come to Mzuzu of which the Assemblies of God (1986) is the biggest of all Pentecostal denominations in Mzuzu. Figure 2.14 is a map showing how the assemblies of God has spread over the years.

Lupaso Good News Revival Church is the first Charismatic church to be established in Mzuzu in 1987 followed by others, like Chiputula Calvary Family Church in 1990. In 2002 another Charismatic church was established in Chiputula. The church did not come from somewhere else but was established by Bishop Mark Kambalazaza, who organized an open-air rally at Chiputula Primary School ground for one week.

Christian religion in Mzuzu originated from relocation diffusion. Christian denominations have come from outside Mzuzu and located themselves at respective places in Mzuzu. These places are points of origin on which denominations have spread to other areas within Mzuzu through the type of expansion diffusion in a way of contagious diffusion. The contagious diffusion has been achieved by means of evangelism activities, births and transfers.

Evangelistic Activities

Christian denominations have been diffused from their point of origin to others through evangelistic activities. The activities are deliberate means of converting people to their denominations. The commonest activities are; "Open-air rallies",[62] door to door visitations and provision of social services, i.e. in marriages, funerals, helping the needy, cheering the sick.

---

[62] 'Open-air rallies' originated from Donald Fraser's Sacramental Conventions introduced in Ungoni, first at Ekwendeni in 1898. Fraser based his idea for the convention on the old Scottish highland tradition of the communion season. Here in Malawi at Ungoni, the Scottish highland tradition was with the most important traditional festivals – the Ngoni feast of the first fruits, *Incwala*. The sacramental convention was mobilizing people from long distances constructing temporary grass huts for a week; the climax of it all was communion and baptism. The practice is a backbone in the evangelistic campaign in the CCAP church centres, though with some renovations. See Jack Thompson, *Ngoni, Xhosa and Scot, Religion and Culture in Malawi*, Zomba: Kachere, 2007, pp. 76-80.

When these activities have been carefully done, it mobilizes many people to join Christian denominations; hence worship centres diffuse from one centre to the other.

By Birth

Many Christians are members by birth.[63] The majority of Christians are born from parents where either one or both are Christian members. When a child is born in a Christian family, he or she is introduced to the Christian faith of the particular denomination to which the parents belong. Denominations are connected to parenthood whereby they are popularly known as genealogical denominations. Christian parents give birth to a Christian child and that child to another Christian child. Through this, the statistics of a particular worship centre grows hence that centre diffuses to another centre.

By Transfer

People migrate to Mzuzu to attain various social opportunities; employment, business, education and residence. When they come to Mzuzu, some of them are followers of the Christian religion. They do come with transfer letters or without and when they are contacted by members of their particular denominations they join a worship centre of their respective denomination. Such admission is known as Christians by transfer.[64] Through this, Church membership grows as a result worship centres' diffusion to different places.

2.3.3 Islam

The Christian religion has been followed by other religions such as Islam. In 1960 the Islamic religion came to Mzuzu while following her adherents working in Mzuzu. The Islamic religion came from Ekwendeni pioneered by Indians, Wali Karim and Hasan Gero, who were worshiping at Ekwendeni while residing in Mzuzu. The first mosque was established at Old Town near the hardware market. It is this mosque where all mosques in Mzuzu have come from.

---

[63] The growth rate is at 4.4% as per 2008 census report, Mzuzu Urban Profile Final Review 2008- 2009, Mzuzu City, 2009, p. 20.

[64] Annual Life and Work Forms and Statistics of CCAP Synod of Livingstonia, Congregational Christian Admission Roll Book, 2014, p. 1.

The type of diffusion of the Islamic religion has been relocation diffusion. This involves the initial group of people moving from one worship centre to a new location. The type of diffusion has been achieved by means of ziyala/Dawah, Building of Mosques, Madrassas and Alms Giving.

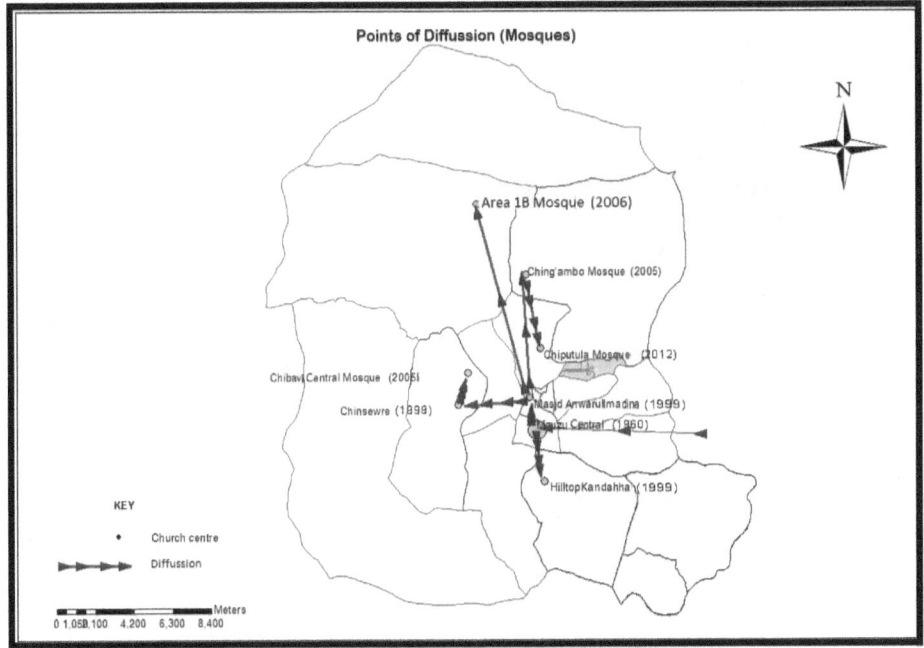

Figure 2.15: Diffussion of Mosques

Ziyala and Dawah

These are open-air rallies done at an open-air ground. These are non-denominational; rather they are open to anybody who wishes to attend. Ziyala and Dawahs are often done when they are opening a new location.

Building of Mosques

It is believed that the idea for opening more mosques was initiated during the reign of President Bakili Muluzi towards the end of 1990.[65] Individual members of the Islamic faith sometimes have a pleasure on their own to build a mosque at any place they want, when the mosque has been built, they appoint the in charge of the mosque and later

---

[65] Willemijn van Kohl, "Ummah in Zomba: Transnational Influences in Reformist Muslims in Malawi", *Religion in Malawi*, Nov. 2010 – Nov. 2011, p. 28.

Muslim worshippers start worshiping at the new worship centre. The new mosque attracts worshippers and it is relatively visible within their contact areas. With this, the presence of the Islamic religion in Mzuzu could no longer be ignored after being marginalized for a long time.

Madrassa

Some Islamic worship centres have started because of Islamic schools. Due to long distances some madrassas were opened closer to where Muslim children are residing. This eventually has made these madrassas to be Islamic worship centres as well. The Islamic schools provide basic learning of Quran, Hadith, and related Islamic subjects with the inclusion of basic Arabic writing and reading. However, of late, they do provide Malawi government education of primary and secondary education. Students are attracted to join Muslim schools because of various gifts they receive from Madrassas. Some have been interested because of the provision of scholarships for students who want to go further with education.[66]

Growth of Islamic Faithful

Islamic worship centres has been diffused from the point of origin to another because of the growth of her faithful. The numbers of Muslim believers are increasing because of migration and the increased birthrate of Muslim members. The other reason is alms giving; a true Muslim believer is supposed to give something to his/her neighbour once a year. In most cases this is done 9 days after Ramadan. However, there is a general practice that during Fridays Indian Muslims are sharing gifts to beggars who walk into their shops. The practice seems to be alms giving but not a traditional one. Through the tradition of giving, it is believed that some people become attracted and join the Islamic faith. The increased numbers of Muslim members increase the number of worship centres.

---

[66] In access to further education, young Malawian Muslims find the opportunity to create their own moral and ideological identity that gives them the courage to break free from the social and cultural structures of community and family. Through the development of a better educated and internationally oriented Islamic elite in Malawi and their proclamation of Islamic identity, they cleared the way for the quest of recognition and equal representation within their national environment.

2.3.4 Hindu Religion

In 1994 came another religion originated from India which had no territorial base in Mzuzu; it was started by Rasck Patel and his family. The religion does not have a communal worship centre, however each family has her own worship centre in the family house, unless during annual festivals.

The type of diffusion of the Hindu religions is relocation diffusion. The religion is diffused by migrants from east India who were born and brought up as Hindus. Migrants from India who were born and brought up Hindu come to Mzuzu with Hindu religion, and worship centres are per family houses. Each family house is a worship centre. The religion has remained essentially a cultural religion of South East Asia.[67] The religion is more than a faith; it is a way of life.

Conclusion

Religions and denominations in Mzuzu have developed numerous worship centres with many adherents. Citizens of Mzuzu belong to one religion or the other, the only difference is on individual commitment. Some members are more committed to their religion or denomination while others are just nominal. Mzuzu has developed from a raiding area of the Ngoni against the Tonga, a Tung Oil estate and regional administrative centre into a strategic area for religious activities. The study area is a radiating light of the concept of God, and its importance is doubtless unsurpassed throughout the Ngoni region, the northern part of Malawi.[68]

---

[67] Int. Rasck Patel, Founding Member of Hindu Religion in Mzuzu, Mzuzu, 5.10.2013.
[68] Int. Inkosana Luwinga Singini, Senior Group Village Headman Luwinga, 6.4.2013.

Chapter Three: Location and Places of Religious Worship Centres in Mzuzu

This section provides the location and places of religious worship centres found in Mzuzu, the worship centres include: Christian churches, fellowships and ministries, Muslim mosques and madrassa, and places of Traditional healers. Places of religious instructions are also mentioned, unless they are part of a church or a mosque. These places are divided in wards. This detailed presentation in Chapter 3 will be the base for further analysis in the following chapter.

3.1 Religious Places in Lupaso Ward

3.1.1 Dunduzu Baptist Convention of Malawi

The church is at Dunduzu area located off Mzuzu - Ekwendeni Road from Dunduzu Road Block to Nkhorongo area. The church is next to Dunduzu Roman Catholic Church and Muwela Traditional Clinic.

The church started as a result of a rally held at Lupaso Full Primary School, the rally was conducted by a team from Mzuzu Baptist Convention Church under the leadership of George Mwase in 1995.[1] The rally yielded many people who needed someone to nurture them in a church community. Mzuzu Baptist Convention Church requested Burton Kaminja Nyirenda and his wife, Maria, to lead the church.[2] Kaminja assisted by Leonard Shaba first met the new church on 28th January 1995. There were 41 members at that meeting and 26 of them were baptized.[3] The Church members were congregating in one of the classrooms of Lupaso Primary School in the early days. The situation did not please the School Management Committee of Lupaso Full Primary School,[4] who had a ruling from the proprietor, CCAP Synod of Livingstonia, saying that no church, should be worshiping in their classrooms. The School

---

[1] Int. Leya Phiri, Dunduzu Baptist Convention Church Sunday school Teacher, Dunduzu, 27.8.2013.

[2] Int. Thandi Mbeya, Member of Dunduzu Baptist Convention Church, Dunduzu, 27.8.2013.

[3] Int. Thomas Gondwe, Treasurer of Lupaso Primary School Management Committee, Lupaso, 27.8.2013.

[4] Int. Burton Kaminja Nyirenda, Pastor at Dunduzu Baptist Convention Church and Former Appointed Leader of the Church, Area 1B, 28.8.2013.

Management Committee asked the Baptist leadership to stop congregating at Lupaso School. The Baptist leadership took the matter to Inkosana Luwinga, who ruled that the church had to leave the school and find a place for the church elsewhere.[5] In fear of continued fight, the Baptists stopped meeting at the School and began meeting at Mbeya's house. They moved out of Mbeya's house to another house within Mbeya village, because the first Mbeya's house was rented elsewhere. The movements started reducing church membership, upon realizing that, the Church started constructing her own church in 1997 and it was completed in 2000. The church building accommodates 60 people. The first leaders of the church were Burton Kaminja Nyirenda, Charles Winstone Ngoma and Nelson Mfune, while Maria Nyirenda and Mrs. Mkandawire were deacons. Church leadership is dominated by men.

The average church attendance is 25 people, of whom women are in the majority. The church is dominated by the age group from 25 to 50 years. New members join the church by conversion; however, there is no new convert to the church apart from her old members.[6] The Mbeya family is dominating the church because at one time worship was taking place in the houses of the Mbeya family. During the service of worship, Tumbuka is the dominant language.

3.1.2 Nkhorongo Seventh-day Adventist Church

Nkhorongo Seventh-day Adventist Church is at the centre of Nkhorongo area. The church is located at the four ways road junction of Dunduzu Road Block off to Nkhorongo Luwinga road and Area 1B Market to Choma Road. The church is surrounded by Nkhorongo Clinic, Nkhorongo Primary School and Nkhorongo Community Day Secondary School.

Nkhorongo Seventh-day Adventist Church is the first Seventh-day Adventist Church in Mzuzu,[7] started by Ephraim Chibambo in February

---

[5] Int. Thomas Gondwe, Treasurer of Lupaso School Management Committee, Lupaso, 27.8.2013.

[6] Int. Leya Phiri, Dunduzu Baptist Convention Church Member and Sunday School Teacher, Dunduzu, 27.8.2013.

[7] Int. S.B. Nyirongo, Mzuzu Seventh-day Adventist Central Church Leader, Katoto, 24.9.2013.

1942.[8] Chibambo came from Chibambo village at Ekwendeni Mission; he stopped teaching at Ekwendeni CCAP Mission School and gave up his church membership of CCAP, together with his family, with the idea of starting a church and school of his own.[9] He left the CCAP Church in search of the truthful worship which he did not find in CCAP.[10] He came to Nkhorongo at a place called Kafwiri where he started his church and school; he called the church Truth Seekers or the Company of Truth Mission. He started the church with his family members, school students and students' parents'.

Ephraim Chibambo was visited by Pastor Devie William Ludlow, a Seventh-day Adventist missionary and a teacher at Luwazi Seventh-day Mission, in 1945. The two discussed and agreed on the possibilities of how Luwazi Mission could take over Nkholongo Church and School to be part of Seventh-day Adventist Church. The school and the church were finally taken over by the Seventh-day Adventist under Luwazi Mission the same year. At the same time, Ephraim Chibambo, the founder of Nkholongo Church and School was taken to Luwazi and later to Malamulo for clinical medical training.[11] When he had finished training, he came back to Nkhorongo, where finally, he became dissatisfied with the Seventh-day Adventist teachings and decided to go back to Ekwendeni and re-join CCAP Church. Ephraim Chibambo died a CCAP member at Ekwendeni Mission Station Church.

Nkhorongo Seventh-day Adventist Church started with 15 people and later more members joined the church because of the school. New members join the church through "efforts",[12] by transfers,[13] by birth[14]

---

[8] Int. Doctor Munthali, Nkhorongo Seventh-day Adventist Church Member and One of the First Students and Member of Chibambo's Church/School, Nkhorongo, 28.8.2013.

[9] Int. Doctor Munthali, Nkhorongo Seventh-day Adventist Church and One of the First Students and Member of Chibambo's Church/School, Nkhorongo, 28.8.2013.

[10] Int. Kafwiri Nyirongo, Village Headman, Nkhorongo, 28.8.2013.

[11] Ibid.

[12] "Efforts" are open-air rallies done once a year for 21 days during evenings. Baptism of those converted during efforts is done on the last day of the effort.

[13] Church members move from one area where they had been already members of the church to another church of the same denomination elsewhere.

and personal witnessing.[15] The average church attendance as of now is 300,[16] of whom the majority are women. The church has more youth of 10–35 years of age than adults. The church is dominated by the Nyirongo, Mnthali and Nyirenda families who are found around Nkhorongo area.[17]

The common language of the church is Chichewa while English and Chitumbuka are used on special occasions. The church leadership is dominated by men.

3.1.3 Dunduzu Seventh Day Baptist Church

Dunduzu Seventh-day Baptist Central African Conference Church is at Dunduzu area, under Group Village Headman Kadambo. The church is 250 m south of Dunduzu Road Block.

The church came from Zambia in 1910 by Mkandawire, a migrant labourer in Zambia, father of Gandakata Mkandawire. Mkandawire went to Zambia for work, while there he came into contact with members of the Seventh–day Baptist CAC Church who converted him and join the church. After baptism, he was filled with unwavering passion to bring the church home to Ekwaiweni. When he came home, he worked tirelessly in converting people for his church; the church was established before he went back to Zambia where he died.[18]

In 1955 the church was moved from Ekwaiweni to Dunduzu by Gandakata Mkandawire. The movement was in response to the movement of Ekwaiweni village from Ekwaiweni to Dunduzu area in search for enough land due to population increase.[19] Ekwaiweni area is situated west of Dunduzu area, 3 km from where Dunduzu church is

---

[14] Children are born and brought up in the church where their parents are members.
[15] Personal witnessing is another means of joining the church where members of the church shares the doctrine and policy of their church to non-members who eventually some of them become part of the church community.
[16] Church attendance record, 2013.
[17] Int. S.B. Nyirongo, Mzuzu Seventh Day Adventist Central Church Leader, Katoto, 24.9.2013.
[18] Int. Plate Phiri, Dunduzu Seventh-day Baptist CAC School Sabbath Teacher, Dunduzu, 27.8.2013.
[19] Int. Ronald Jere, Village Headman, Dunduzu, 29.7.2012.

situated. While at Dunduzu, the church started with two people, Gandakata and his wife, eventually, many people joined them and the number went up to 95. The first families to join the church were Bingo Jere, Shaddreck Jere and William Mkandawire.

The church has experienced a split, initiated by the teachings of New Zealand missionary, Ronald Barr, who wanted to restore the original Seventh–day Baptist of the 1887. Many members of the church accepted the teachings and became follows of Ronald Barr (Balala). With this development, Mr Lwanda, who was considered to be the most senior member of the church at that time, and 12 other members decided to leave the church building and continued worshiping as Seventh–day Baptist CAC at Chipangano Church building. When Dunduzu Seventh - day Baptist CAC Church got organized at Chipangano Church building, they built their own church in 2009.

The church building of Dunduzu Seventh - day Baptist CAC has the capacity of 100 people. The average church attendance is 65 people,[20] majority of whom are women. The dominant age group of the church is 20 to 50 years. The majority of church members are coming from the surrounding villages of Dunduzu area while a few are coming from far distances. New members join the church by birth and conversion. Nobody can become a member of the church without going through baptism by immersion after going through three months of intensive baptism classes.

Church leadership is dominated by men. The dominant language of the church is Chitumbuka.

3.1.4 Dunduzu Seventh - day Baptist Original Church

Dunduzu Seventh- day Baptist Original Church is at Dunduzu area at Njalanthowa II Village, 0.5 km South of Dunduzu Road Block.

Dunduzu Seventh-day Baptist Original Church is a breakaway of Dunduzu Seventh-day CAC Church. The breaking away happened in 2006, initiated by the teaching of New Zealand missionary, Ronald Barr, who wanted to restore the original Seventh–day Baptist Church principles.[21] The Central office in Lilongwe was not happy with the teachings of Balala (Barr) and

---

[20] Church attendance book, 2013.
[21] Int. Luckson Kanyinji, Dunduzu Seventh–day Baptist Original Church Member, Dunduzu, 27.8.2013.

he was asked to leave the country for his home, New Zealand. Instead of him going to New Zealand, he went around the country enticing church members to take up the reforms he was introducing. The reforms of Ronald Balala at Dunduzu Church were introduced by Bingo Jere, who was a senior church elder at that time.[22] When those who were against the teachings of Ronald Balala went out of the church building, those who remained there changed the name of the church from Seventh–day Baptist CAC to Seventh–day Baptist Original.

The church remained with 36 people, three quarters of the original church. The dominant church members were: Bingo Jere, Shadreck Mkandawire and William Mkandawire. The present number of Christians is 71, while the average church attendance is 37.[23] Church membership is dominated by women. Most of church members are local villagers. New members join the church by birth and through door to door visitation. The newly converted members join baptism classes for three months before baptism.

Leadership of the church is restricted to men only; women leadership is only to their fellow women.[24] The church has women elders but they are not supposed to stand before men. The dominant language of the church is Chichewa, although almost all members are Tumbuka speakers.

3.1.5 Dunduzu New Apostolic Church

Dunduzu New Apostolic Church is located around Dunduzu Market, 100 metres north of Dunduzu Road Block, near Dunduzu Under Five Clinic.

The New Apostolic Church at Dunduzu started in 1994 as an outstation of Msiki New Apostolic Church.[25] The Church was started by Munjeheli Tembo who at first was a member of Msiki New Apostolic Church. The Msiki New Apostolic Church started by Kenwood Mkandawire of Ekwaiweni Village, a migrant labourer in Zambia. The church started when Mkandawire came home on holiday in 1950. When some people

---

[22] Int. Gift Kanyinji, Dunduzu Seventh–day Baptist Original Church Former Member, Dunduzu, 27.8.2013.
[23] Church attendance record book, 22.8.2013.
[24] Int. Agnes Chabibga, Dunduzu New Apostolic Church Member, Dunduzu, 20.7.2013.
[25] Int. Ronard Mkandawire, Dunduzu New Apostolic Church Elder, Dunduzu, 27.8.2013.

from Dunduzu area heard about the new faith at Msiki, they mobilized themselves and joined the Msiki New Apostolic Church. While people from Dunduzu area were worshiping at Msiki Church, they started complaining about long distance they were travelling to Msiki. Later Munjeheli Tembo asked permission from Msiki Church to open another church at Dunduzu area due to distance people were complaining about. When the permission was granted, the church at Dunduzu started. The church started with four families worshiping in the house of Ronald Mkandawire. The first convert of Dunduzu Church was Amosi Nkosi who later became Shepherd of the church.[26]

Dunduzu New Apostolic Church has a church building with the capacity of 70 people. The church has 80 people with the average church attendance of 43. The majority of church members are women. Most members of the church are coming from within Dunduzu catchment area. The dominant families of the church are Kenwood Nkosi and Mbeya.[27] The church is dominated by people from the age of 25 to 50 years. New members join the church by birth and face to face evangelism.[28] When new members have been converted, they undergo baptism classes before water baptism.

Church leadership is for men. Women are not supposed to preach in the presence of men, however, they are allowed to lead their fellow women at women groups or sisters groups.[29] Male youth have no opportunity to lead the church apart from youth groups. The church uses Chitumbuka as the main language.

3.1.6 Dunduzu Living Waters Church

Dunduzu Living Waters Church is at Dunduzu area, 250 m south of Dunduzu Road Block, near Dunduzu Seventh-day Baptist Central Africa Conference Church. Dunduzu Living Waters Church started as a result of a rally organized by Mzuzu Pentecostal Assemblies of Jesus Christ

---

[26] Int. John Phiri, Dunduzu New Apostolic Church Member, Dunduzu, 27.8.2013.
[27] Int. Chikosela Phiri, Dunduzu New Apostolic Church Member, Discipline Chairperson, Dunduzu, 27.8.2013.
[28] Where church members are sent out to evangelize face to face with non-believers and invite them to join the church.
[29] Int. Thandi Mbeya, Dunduzu New Apostolic Church Member, Dunduzu, 27.8.2013.

Mission in 2003.[30] The Pentecostal Assemblies of Jesus Christ Mission rally at Dunduzu area was quite successful, whereby many people surrendered their lives to Jesus Christ. The result of the rally was the beginning of Dunduzu Living Waters Church. The church started with 10 people, but without a leader. The Assemblies of Jesus Christ Mission requested Bishop Thunga and his wife to nurture the church. In 1999, while the church was steadily growing, Bishop Thunga stopped leading the church and joined politics. He lost the 1999 General Election and later, he died.[31] For four years, the church was without leadership and affiliation. Despite the problems the church was facing, they managed to survive locally. Within the four years period of struggle, the church managed to build a permanent church which was completed in 2003. When they had finished building a permanent church, they asked the Living Waters Northern Head Office for the possibilities of incorporating them.[32] The Living Waters Head Office accepted the offer; Bishop Chaula from Mzuzu Living Waters Main Church became the leader of the church while Pastor Simbeye was appointed Pastor of the church in 2003.

At the beginning the church had 53 members, while as of now; the number has been reduced to 40. The average church attendance is 32 people, of whom the majority are women. The dominant age group of the church membership is 12 to 30 years. New members join the church through open-air rallies and door to door visitation. The church has no baptism classes for the newly converted members. Members of the church come from within Dunduzu area.

Church leadership is given to men. The language of the church is Chichewa.

3.1.7 *Msiru Chipangano Church*

Msiru Chipangano Church is located at Dunduzu area, 0.5 km south of Dunduzu Road Block. The church is near to Living Waters Church.

The Msiru Chipangano Church started in 1959 by Kapale Soko. The church started as an outstation of Ekwaiweni Chipangano Main Church in a way of responding to the complaints people from Dunduzu area were

---

[30] Int. Musa Chimaliro, Community Development Officer, Dunduzu, 28.8.2013.
[31] Int. Kondwani Luhanga, Dunduzu Living Waters Church Executive Member, 28.8.2013.
[32] Int. Fiskani Kanyinji Former Church Member, Dunduzu, 29.8.2013.

complaining about long distance they were travelling and population growth of membership.[33] At that time many people were joining Chipangano Church because the church was adhering to traditional practices i.e., beer drinking, polygamy.[34] Kapale Soko who came from Soko village requested the Ekwaiweni Chipangano Main Church to start a church at Dunduzu.[35] When the permission was granted he started the church in the house of Goodwin Hara, an evangelist, who later became a Pastor of the church.

The church started with 16 congregants who later, grew to 72 people. The current average church attendance is 15 people of whom women are in the majority.[36] The majority of church members are married people, aged 35 to 50 years. New members join the church by marriage and personal evangelism.[37] The church baptizes new members without going through baptism class.

Leadership of the church is dominated by men. Women are taking smaller responsibilities; no woman can be a pastor. The dominant language of the church is Chitumbuka.

3.1.8 St Teleza Dunduzu Roman Catholic Church

St Teleza is a Roman Catholic Church, located at Dunduzu area along Nkhorongo - Dunduzu Road Block Road. The church is next to Dunduzu Baptist Convention Church, north of Dunduzu Road Block.

Jacob Chipeta, from Dunduzu area, started St Teleza Catholic Church in 2003. The church came from Msiki Catholic Church due to long distance which people from Dunduzu area were travelling.[38] When the permission to start the church was given from Msiki Church, all members who were

---

[33] Int. Kondwani Luhanga, Church Executive Member, Dunduzu, 28.8.2013.
[34] Int. Pastor Misheck Ngulube, Msiru Chipangano Church Pastor, Dunduzu, 28.8.2013.
[35] Int. Green Luhanga, Msiru Chipangano Church Convener, Dunduzu, 27.8.2013.
[36] Int. Pastor Misheck Ngulube, Msiru Chipangano Church Pastor, Dunduzu, 28.8.2013.
[37] Int. Pastor Misheck Ngulube, Msiru Chipangano Church Pastor, Dunduzu, 28.8.2013.
[38] Int. Agnes Ngulube, Msiru Chipangano Church Member, Dunduzu, 28.8.2013.

coming from Dunduzu area started congregating under a tree near Jacob Chipeta's house. The total number of Christians who started the church at that time was 20 people.[39]

St Teleza Catholic Church has a permanent church building with a capacity of 60 people. The average church attendance is 40 people of whom the majority are women.[40] New members join the church by birth and through marriage.[41] New members undergo baptism classes before baptism. The church is dominated by the families of Chipeta and Mbeya who are found at the centre of where the church is built.

The church is led by both sexes: men and women, however, men are dominating.[42] The common language used in the church is Chitumbuka.

3.1.9 Muwela Traditional Healing Centre

The Muwela Traditional Healing Centre is at Dunduzu area, located off Mzuzu - Ekwendeni Road from Dunduzu Road Block to Nkhorongo. The Healing Centre is next to St Teleza Dunduzu Roman Catholic Church.

Ngwaza Muwela Mbeya started Muwela Traditional Healing Centre in 1988, with the idea of helping people from physical and spiritual oppression.[43] Muwela was initiated to traditional healing by the spirits of his departed grandparents' who came to him through *vimbuza*.[44] When Muwela started suffering from *vimbuza*, he visited Mulauli and Chikanga, where it was revealed to him that the problem he was suffering from was the desire of his departed grandparents' spirits wanting him to be healing

---

[39] Int. Cecilia Nkosi, Chairlady of St Teleza Roman Catholic Church, Dunduzu, 26.8.2013.

[40] Attendance Record Book, St Teleza Roman Catholic Church, Dunduzu, 11.7.2013.

[41] Marriage, where a church member, a man or woman, marries outside the Catholic Church, the married person from outside the Catholic Church is requested to leave his or her church and join Roman Catholic Church for the marriage to be recognized and officiate by the church. Int. Jacob Chipeta, St Teleza Roman Catholic Church, Elder, Dunduzu, 27.8.2013.

[42] Int. Cecilia Nkosi, Chairlady of the St Teleza Roman Catholic Church, Dunduzu, 26.8.2013.

[43] Int. Ngwaza Muwela Mbeya, Muwela Traditional Healer, Dunduzu 30.8.2013.

[44] Int. Cecilia Nkosi, wife of Ngwaza Muwela Mbeya a Traditional Healer, Dunduzu, 30.8.2013.

people with traditional medicine. The responsibility of healing people given to Muwela is a gift from the departed spirits. Whenever he performs his duties; he waits for instruction from the spirits on what to do.[45]

Muwela has two days of official duties a week, Tuesday and Saturday, both in the evening. When all people are gathered in a temple where he does his duties, Muwela begins his duties by a service of worship for one hour before he starts helping people physically. The service of worship begins with prayer, then singing of hymns and choruses from various churches and ends with Bible preaching. Participants in the service of worship are patients, guardians and nearby people who comes as spectators. When the service of worship is over, he starts helping people physically. Muwela, through the revelation from his ancestral spirits, believes that certain diseases do not need medicine, to such diseases, prayer is the only solution.[46]

There is no specific average number of attendances; it all depends upon the availability of patients. Patients come from different areas, dominant areas are Mzuzu City and nearby areas of Nkhatabay, Mzimba and Rumphi Districts.[47] The language used during service of worship is Chitumbuka. Leadership is dominated by Muwela himself.

3.1.10 Dunduzu Chekina Temple of Assemblies of God Church

Dunduzu Chekina Temple of Assemblies of God is around Dunduzu Market area, located along Mzuzu – Ekwendeni Road, east of Dunduzu Road Block.

The church started in 2007, as a breakaway of Dunduzu Living Waters Church. The reason for the split was that Dunduzu Living Waters Church had no local leadership; leadership and support of the church was coming from Mzuzu Living Waters Main Church. Due to this, local people who view themselves that they could lead the church started scrambling for leadership, eventually the church split into two, Dunduzu Living Waters Church, and the other group led by Elias Soko, which later

---

[45] Int. Ngwaza Muwela Mbeya, Traditional Healer, Dunduzu, 30.8.2013.

[46] Int. Ngwaza Muwela Mbeya, Muwela Traditional Healer, Dunduzu, 30.8.2013.

[47] Int. Akim Banda, Patient at Muwela Traditional Healer Centre, Dunduzu, 30.8.2013.

became Dunduzu Chekina Assemblies of God Church. Eliase Soko started the church with a group of 20 people worshiping in his house. While there, the group decided to join Kalibu Kwa Yesu Church where later Elias Soko became Pastor of the church.[48]

In 2007 disagreements arose in the Kalibu Kwa Yesu Church over the mismanagement of funds from American missionaries. The funds were given to build a church, instead it was discovered that Pastor Eliase Soko used the money for building his own house at Katoto.[49] The earlier group which came with Elias Soko left the church and started assembling under a tree at Dunduzu. Later, the group asked the Luwinga Assemblies of God Church to take over the group which happened in the same year. The church became Dunduzu Chekina Temple of Assemblies of God Church.

The church has a temporal church structure with the capacity of 70 people. The average church attendance is 30 people. The majority of who are women. The church is dominated by age group of 12 - 25 years. Church membership is from within Dunduzu area. New members join the church through overnight fellowships and open-air crusades. New converts undergo baptism classes before baptism.

The dominant language of the church is Chichewa, and sometimes English. Church leadership is for men, women and youth. Currently the church is led by women, the church Pastor and other executive members are women.

3.1.11 Lupaso Good News Revival Church

Lupaso Good News Revival Church is at Lupaso area, located at Kamzimu Gondwe Village, 1 km west of Lupaso Primary School. The church is off Mzuzu – Ekwendeni Road from Keju Garage.

In 1984, Pastor Medson W. Milazi, from Thyolo, came to Mzuzu with a revival crusade at Katoto Secondary School ground. The results of the crusade were that many people surrendered their lives to Jesus Christ and the beginning of Good News Ministry where Lupaso Good News Revival Church came from.[50] Pastor Milazi opened three fellowship

---

[48] Int. Pastor MIlliam Nyirenda, Pastor at Dunduzu Assemblies of God Church, Dunduzu, 26.8.2013.
[49] Ibid.
[50] Int. Thomas Gondwe, Northern Coordinator of Good News Revival Church, Lupaso, 29.7.2013.

centres; Katoto Secondary School, Kamzimu Gondwe Village at Lupaso and Yohane Jere Village at Ekwendeni. In 1987, the Kamzimu Gondwe and Katoto Secondary School fellowship centres formed a church known as Lupaso Good News Revival Church.[51] The church started at Lupaso with 30 members, Pastor Medson Milazi was a visiting Pastor, while Justine Jungwana was a full-time pastor. While the church was growing, all members from Katoto Secondary School fellowship centre left and joined Mzuzu Living Waters Church.[52]

As the church was trying to reorganize itself from the loss of her members, another setback followed as the leadership broke and scramble.[53] The situation led to the splitting of the church into two groups. The first group was for those who wanted Pastor Justine Jungwana to remain their leader, while the other group wanted Pastor Sharpe-Sharpe Banda to be the leader. Those who wanted Pastor Sharpe-Sharpe Banda left the church and started another church at Dunduzu by the name of African Assemblies. Later the Sharpe-Sharpe church at Dunduzu failed and rejoined Lupaso Good News Church. While there, disputes arose again where the Sharpe-Sharpe group wanted to take control of the church leadership. This did not please the other group who eventually started their own church by the name Lupaso Good News Revival. The Sharpe-Sharpe group started another church called Kalibu Kwa Yesu, led by Pastor Eliase Soko.

The Lupaso Good News Revival Church reorganized itself, built a church structure with the capacity of 60 people. The church has 60 people with the average church attendance of 20 people, of whom children are in the majority. The church is dominated by Kamzimu Gondwe Village where the church is situated. New members join the church through overnight fellowships taking place every fortnight.

Chichewa is the common language used during church services and sometimes English when they have official church visitors. The church is led by men, women and youth.

---

[51] Int. James Longwe, Lupaso Good News Revival Church Member, Lupaso, 29.7.2013.

[52] Int. Yohane Gondwe, Lupaso Good News Revival Church Coordinator, Lupaso, 29.7.2013.

[53] Int. Justine Jungwana, Former Pastor at Lupaso Good News Revival Church, Sonda, 27.7.2013.

3.1.12 Lupaso Kalibu Kwa Yesu Church

Lupaso Kalibu Kwa Yesu Church is at Lupaso area. The church is at Kamzimu Gondwe village at Kasolota, near Keju garage. The church is located along the Mzuzu – Ekwendeni road, three hundred metres south of Keju garage.

The Church started in 1998 as a break-away from Lupaso Good News Church due to a leadership struggle.[54] Two groups emerged from Lupaso Good News Church, supporters of Pastor Sharpe-Sharpe Banda and those who supported Pastor Justine Jungwana. The Sharpe-Sharpe group left Lupaso Good News Church and started African Assemblies Church at Dunduzu.[55] The Sharpe-Sharpe church failed at Dunduzu and the group rejoined Lupaso Good News Church again. When the Sharpe-Sharpe group rejoined Lupaso Good News Church, conflicts arose again, when the Sharpe-Sharpe group wanted to take the whole leadership of the church.[56] However, it happened that things were not on the side of the Sharp-Sharp group; the group left Lupaso Good News Church for the final time and formed Kalibu Kwa Yesu Church under the leadership of Pastor Elias Soko in 2000.[57]

The Kalibu Kwa Yesu Church started with 20 people, worshiping in the house of Pastor Gondwe. While the church was still congregating at Pastor Gondwe's house, an American missionary who visited the church was impressed with the group and he asked them to find a place where he could build them a church.[58] The place for a church building was found 100 meters from the house of Pastor Gondwe. The American Missionary funded the church project where eventually it was alleged that Pastor Elias Soko diverted the funds for his own house at Katoto.[59]

---

[54] Int. Pastor Gondwe, Pastor at Lupaso Kalibu Kwa Yesu Church, Lupaso, 27.7.2013.
[55] Int. Thomas Gondwe, Former Church Member at Lupaso Kalibu Kwa Yesu Church, Lupaso, 27.7.2013.
[56] Int. Thomas Gondwe, Former Church Member at Lupaso Kalibu Kwa Yesu Church, Lupaso, 27.7.2013.
[57] Int. Pastor Milliam Nyirenda, Pastor at Dunduzu Assemblies of God Church, Dunduzu, 27.7.2013.
[58] Int. Pastor Gondwe, Pastor at Lupaso Kalibu Kwa Yesu Church, Lupaso, 27.7.2013.
[59] Int. Elise Chiumia, Member of Kamuzimu Gondwe Village, Lupaso, 30.7.2013.

Disagreement rose again in the church, Pastor Soko left the church and the American Missionary stopped funding the project while it was at roofing stage. Due to the failure to finish the church building, the church asked Assemblies of God, Mzuzu Main Church, to take over Kalibu Kwa Yesu Church. Mzuzu Assemblies of God Church took over the Kalibu Kwa Yesu Church and roofed the church building. After roofing the church, disputes arose again between old Kalibu Kwa Yesu Church members and the Assemblies of God leadership. The Assemblies of God Church leadership left the church, pulled out their iron sheets and started their own Assemblies of God Church at Golden Gift Private School at Lupaso.[60] The remnant reroofed the church and the church remained Kalibu Kwa Yesu.

The Kalibu Kwa Yesu Church has 50 members with an average church attendance of 20 people. The majority of church members are youth, from the age of 9 to 20 years. The church is dominated by the Gondwe families. New members join the church through fellowships and overnights done every week. The church has baptism classes for the newly converted members before baptism.

The church uses Chichewa as a church language. Leadership is for both men and women.

3.1.13 Lupaso Full Gospel Church of God

Lupaso Full Gospel Church of God is at Lupaso area, located at the road junction of Mzuzu-Ekwendeni Road off Lupaso Primary School Road. The church is 100 metres south of Lupaso Primary School.

Lupaso Full Gospel Church of God started with Mr. Kambichi in 2000. Kambichi came to Lupaso with the church from Lilongwe, where he had been working before coming to Mzuzu. While in Mzuzu, Kambichi was working with Lupaso Rural Housing. He started the church with his own family worshiping in his house; slowly people started joining him through house to house visitation and open-air rallies he used to organize every month.[61] When the church was still growing, Hardson Singini, a church

---

[60] Int. Ludalingwa Khonje, Former Church Member at Lupaso Assemblies of God Church, Lupaso, 27.7.2013.

[61] Int. Pastor Ziba, Church Pastor at Lupaso Full Gospel Church of God, Lupaso, 27.7.2013.

member, offered for free his own piece of land for church building.[62] As soon as they received the land, Kambichi started building the church. As they were about to finish the project, Kambichi got transferred and Pastor Ziba took over the leadership of the church. Pastor Ziba was one of the pioneers of the church who, at the time of its formation, was working at Lupaso.[63]

The Lupaso Full Gospel Church of God has a permanent church building with the capacity of 90 people. The church has 80 people with the average church attendance of 30 people of whom the majority are the youth. The dominant age group of church members is 9 to 25 years. The majority of church members are coming from Singini families. New members join the church through open-air rallies and door to door visitation. Those who have surrendered their lives to Jesus Christ go for baptism class before water baptism.

The language of the church is Chichewa. Leadership is free for both, men and women, although men are dominating.

3.1.14 Lupaso Assemblies of God Church

The Lupaso Assemblies of God Church is at Lupaso area, next to Lupaso Primary School, close to Golden Gift Private Technical School. The church is surrounded by Lupaso Primary School, Seventy-day Adventist Church and Golden Gift Private Technical School.

Lupaso Assemblies of God Church started in 2000 from Lupaso Kalibu Kwa Yesu Church. In 2000, people from Kalibu Kwa Yesu Church asked the Mzuzu Assemblies of God Main Church to take over the church due to leadership problems and infrastructural development.[64] The Mzuzu Assemblies of God Main Church sent Pastor Henry Moyo to nurture the church which had 40 members. In 2002, Pastor Henry Moyo got transferred and Pastor Chilambo took over the church.

Although the Kalibu Kwa Yesu Church handed over the church to Assemblies of God, old members of the church were not happy with

---

[62] Int. Hardson Singini, Church Member at Lupaso Full Gospel Church of God, Lupaso, 2.1.2011.

[63] Int. Pastor Ziba, Church Pastor at Lupaso Full Gospel Church of God, Lupaso, 27.7.2013.

[64] Int. Mrs Patrick Longwe, Member of Kamuzi Gondwe Village, Lupaso, 2.1.2011.

pastors from Assemblies of God. What they wanted was that the Assemblies of God Church should be giving material support while Pastors and church leadership should be for the old Kalibu Kwa Yesu Church group.[65] This confusion made the church to split into two: old Kalibu Kwa Yesu, with about three quarters of the church membership, and Lupaso Assemblies of God. The Assemblies of God group left the church building and started worshiping where Pastor Chilambo was renting a house until when they fund a rentable room at Golden Gift Private Technical School.[66] When Pastor Chilambo left Lupaso for Likoma, Pastor George Ndau took over the church. In 2005, Pastor George Ndau found a place for a church building, which is next to Lupaso Primary School ground.

Lupaso Assemblies of God Church is renting at Golden Gift Private Technical School while they are building their own church. The church has 71 people with an average church attendance of 45 people. The majority of church members are women and the dominant age group is 10 to 20 years.[67] New members join the church through transfers. New converts join the church through open-air rallies and door to door visitation. Newly converted members go for baptism class before water baptism.

Church leadership is for both sexes; however, men dominate. The church uses Chichewa as a common language.

3.1.15 Lupaso Seventh-day Adventist Church

Lupaso Seventh-day Adventist Church is at Lupaso area, next to Golden Gift Private Technical School. The church is 150 metres north east of Lupaso Primary School.

The church started in 2002 as an outstation of Luwinga Seventh-day Adventist Church. It started because of increased numbers of membership from Lupaso and the long distances people from Lupaso were travelling to Luwinga for church services, near Tobacco Auction

---

[65] Int. Pastor Gondwe, Pastor at Lupaso Kalimba Kwa Yesu Church, Lupaso, 27.7.2013.
[66] Int. Pastor George Ndau, Pastor at Lupaso Assemblies of God, Lupaso, 28.8.2013.
[67] Int. Pastor George Ndau, Pastor at Lupaso Assemblies of God, Lupaso, 28.8.2013.

Holdings. The church started as a result of the effort, which took place at Lupaso Primary School ground where 12 people gave their life to Jesus Christ.[68] The church started with 16 people, one male while the rest were women and children. Church members were worshiping in the diesel maize mill house until when they bought a piece of land from Banga and Frank Singini, where they built a poled grass thatched church.

The present church is a pitched poled iron sheet thatched church with the capacity of 80 people. The church has 60 members with an average church attendance of 45 people. The church is dominated by women. Church membership is from within Lupaso area, dominated by the Mugomphola Singini families. New members join the church by birth. New converts join the church through efforts and personal witnessing.

The church is led by both men and women; however, men are dominating in leadership. The common language of the church is Chichewa.

3.1.16 Luwinga Grace Community Pentecostal Church

The Luwinga Grace Community Pentecostal Church is at Luwinga area, located off Mzuzu - Ekwendeni road towards Southern Bottlers from Great Britain Church.

The church started in 2004, when the pastor of Luwinga Assemblies of God Church wanted to create a church out of his church for his son in-law. The Luwinga Assemblies of God Church started as an outstation of Ekwendeni Assemblies of God Church. Pastor Gondwe, a resident Pastor at Ekwendeni and over-seer of Luwinga Assemblies of God Church, refused to give permission to Luwinga Church to stand on its own.[69] In 2003 permission was granted, Luwinga Church became independent and Pastor Shakespeare Mvalo was appointed resident Pastor.

In 2004, Pastor Shakespeare Mvalo's daughter married Pastor Lukhele a situation which allegedly made Pastor Mvalo create two outstations out of Luwinga Church.[70] The created outstations were Homebound and

---

[68] Int. Yotam Banda, Second Company leader of Lupaso Seventh-day Adventist Church, Lupaso, 28.8.2013.

[69] Int. Moffat Nyirenda, Church Member at Luwinga Assemblies of God Church, Luwinga, 3.8.2013.

[70] Int. Ludalingwa Khonje, Chairperson at Luwinga Grace Community Pentecostal Church, Luwinga, 27.7.2013.

Viyele, Pastor Lukhele, son in-law of Pastor Mvalo, was given Home-bound outstation. The situation created divisions within the church; many people resisted to go to Home-bound, instead, they flocked to Viyele outstation. When the Viyele Church was progressing well with the help of Pastor Winfred Banda, it happened that Pastor Shakespeare Mvalo and Pastor Gondwe ordered the closure of the outstation in order to support Home-bound outstation.[71]

When the Viyele outstation was closed, the congregants declared not to be going anywhere; they asked permission from Dr Lazarus Chakwera, president of the Assemblies of God Church, to start their own church. The president allowed them to do so as long as they maintained the doctrine of the Assemblies of God Church. The church started with 26 people and Oswald Banda was the church Pastor. The constitution of the church was drawn from Church of Central Africa Presbyterian Synods of Livingstonia and Nkhoma, Baptist Convention of Malawi and Seventh-day Adventist.[72]

The congregation has a temporal church structure. The church membership is 60, while average church attendance is 35 people, of whom the majority is women. The church covers the whole of Mzuzu area. New members join the church through door to door visitation. The newly converted members undergo baptism classes before water baptism.

The church uses Chichewa as a common language. Leadership is open to women, men and youth, although men are dominating.

3.1.17 Area 1B Inspired Gospel Church

The Area 1B Inspired Gospel Church is located along Luwinga – Nkhorongo market road, three hundred metres North West of Area 1B market.

In 2012, Area 1B Inspired Gospel Church started by Pastor Chimwemwe Mbewe. The church started with family members of Pastor Chimwemwe Mbewe and Sister Towera Botha, who was living next to the Pastor's

---

[71] Int. Moffat Nyirenda, Church Member at Luwinga Assemblies of God, Luwinga Church, Luwinga, 3.8.2013.

[72] Int. Ludalingwa Khonje, Chairperson at Luwinga Grace Community Pentecostal Church, Luwinga, 27.7.2013.

house.[73] The church started while worshiping in the house of Pastor Chimwemwe Mbewe. Slowly, people joined the church through overnights done every two weeks and afternoon fellowships done every week on Wednesdays, Saturdays and Sundays.

The church has a temporal structure of Vigwagwa with the capacity of 40 people. The church has 30 people with the average attendance of 17. The majority of church membership are men. The dominant age group of the church is 15 to 35 years.[74] New members join the church through open-air rallies and fellowships. Newly converted members undergo baptism classes for two days before water baptism.

The common language of the church is English and Chichewa. Church leadership is for both men and women.

3.1.18 Area 1B International Pentecostal Church

Area 1B International Pentecostal Church is located along Luwinga – Nkhorongo market road, three hundred metres north – west of Area 1B Market.

Bishop Gertrude Mhlanga, former Chang'ombe Full Gospel Church member, started Area 1B International Pentecostal Church in 2003.[75] The church started when Bishop Gertrude was dismissed from Chang'ombe Full Gospel Church by the church Pastor, who was not happy with the gifts of the Holy Spirit manifested through her.[76] As soon as she was dismissed, she started a church with three people worshiping in her house at Kubwanga. Later, she moved from Kubwanga to Area 1B where she continued with her church in a house where she was renting.

Area 1B International Pentecostal Church has no church structure; service of worship is done inside the Pastor's house. The church has 30 people with average church attendance of 20 people. The church is dominated by women membership who happens to come for physical

---

[73] Int. Sister Towela Botha, Area 1B Inspired Gospel Church Member, Area 1B, 4.8.2013.
[74] Int. Mrs Chimwemwe Mbewe, Pastor's wife, Area 1B Inspired Gospel Church, Area 1B, 4.8.2013.
[75] Int. Pastor Gertrude Mhlanga, Church Pastor at International Pentecostal Church, Area 1B, 20.8.2013.
[76] Int. Bishop Gertrude Mhlanga, Church Pastor at International Pentecostal Church, Area 1B, 20.8.2013.

help from their day to day problems.[77] The dominant age group of the church is 20 to 45 years. New members join the church through sharing experiences which other people have gained from Bishop Gertrude Mhlanga.[78]

Church leadership is dominated by women; Pastor Petros Ziyendani is the only man in the church. The common language in the church is Chichewa.

3.1.19 Dunduzu Jesus Missionary Church

Dunduzu Jesus Missionary Church is at Dunduzu area. The church is located off Mzuzu – Ekwendeni road. The church is next to Dunduzu Baptist Convention Church.

The church of Dunduzu Jesus Missionary was started by Apostle Brown Mnthali in 2005. The church started with six people worshiping in the house of Apostle Mnthali at area 1B.[79] Slowly, the number of church members increased to 20 people. The development forced Apostle Mnthali to find a piece of land where he could build the church. The place was found at Dunduzu where they have built a church with funding from Jesus Missionaries in America. The church building has a capacity of 70 people. The average age group of church members is 12 to 30 years.

The average church attendance is 15 people, of whom the majority are women. The members are coming from Area 1B to the point that the nearest church member's house to the church centre is 2 km. New members join the church through door to door visitation and afternoon fellowships.[80] New converts join a baptism class for a month before water baptism.

The language of the church is English with Chichewa translation. Church leadership is for both sexes; but male dominated.

---

[77] Int. Pastor Petros Ziyendani, Assistant Church Pastor at International Pentecostal Church, Area 1B, 20.8.2013.
[78] Int. Agnes Nyirenda, International Pentecostal Church Member, Area 1B, 20.8.2013.
[79] Int. Apostle Brown Munthali, Dunduzu Jesus Missionary Church Founder, Area 1B, 22.8.2013.
[80] Int. Pastor Green Gondwe, Assistant Pastor at Dunduzu Jesus Missionary Church, Area 1B, 22.8.2013.

3.1.20 Nkholongo New Apostolic Church

Nkholongo New Apostolic Church is at Area 1B. The church is located along Luwinga-Nkholongo road.

In 1986, Priest Manda supported by Tafwakose Khata suggested to Doloba New Apostolic Church to start Nkholongo New Apostolic Church at Area 1B.[81] The suggestion made to Doloba Church was supported by all members who were coming from Luwinga to Doloba for worship. The suggestion came at a time when people from Luwinga area were complaining about long distances they were travelling to Doloba and there were an increased number of church members from Luwinga area. The suggestion was accepted and Nkholongo New Apostolic Church started as an outstation of Doloba Church in the house of Priest Manda who later asked village headman Vilume to give the church a piece of land where they could build a church.[82] When a piece of land was given, they built a temporary church in 1990, and in 2009, they built a permanent one with a capacity of 120 people.

The church started with 15 people, all of them were already members when they were at Doloba Church.[83] Today, the church has 120 members, of whom the majority are women. The average church attendance is 70 people. The majority of church members are from the age of 25 to 50 years. New members join the church through house to house visitation and by birth. Newly converted members attend baptism classes before water baptisms.

The language of the church is Chitumbuka. The leadership of the church is for men.

3.1.21 Area 1B Charismatic Redeemed Ministries and International Church

The Area 1B Charismatic Redeemed Ministries and International Church is located along Luwinga – Nkholongo via Area 1B Market road, hundred metres west of Area 1B Market.

---

[81] Int. Pasipano Honde, Church Treasure at Nkholongo New Apostolic Church, Area 1B, 10.8.2013.

[82] Int. Akim Banda, Nkholongo New Apostolic Church Member, Area 1B, 10.8.2013.

[83] Int. Pasipano Honde, Church Treasure at Nkholongo New Apostolic Church, Area 1B, 10.8.2013.

At first, people from Luwinga and Area 1B were worshiping at Chiputula Church. Due to long distances people were travelling, Chiputula Church decided to open a sub-branch at Area 1B in 2009.[84] The church started with 10 people worshiping in Good Samaritan Hall.[85] The church worship centre was moved from Good Samaritan Hall to a Pastor's house near Area 1B Market because the majority of church members were coming from the area around Area 1B Market. The other reason was that the church wanted to have more days and time for church activities than what they were experiencing at Good Samaritan where they were given Sundays only.

The church has no permanent structure; they are using a Vigwagwa shelter built at the Pastors house. The church has 40 members of whom women are in the majority, the average church attendance is 30 people. The dominant age group of church members is 15-30 years.[86] New members join the church through door to door visitation. New converts join baptism class before water baptism. The majority of church membership comes from Roman Catholic and Pentecostal background.

The language of the church is English with Chichewa translation. Leadership of the church is dominated by men.

3.1.22 Luwinga Baptist Convention of Malawi Church

The Luwinga Baptist Convention of Malawi Church is at Area 1B, located at Thawi; near Luwinga transmitter.

Mzuzu Baptist Church in partnership with Jimmy Hodges Ministries International held a rally at Thawi in 1995.[87] The leader of the rally was George Mwase. At the rally, many people surrendered their lives to Jesus Christ and those who gave their life to Jesus Christ were asked to meet the following Sunday at the same place. On the following Sunday, 16

---

[84] Int. Pastor Isaac Kabwetsa, Church Pastor at Area 1B Charismatic Redeemed Ministries and International Church, Area 1B, 10.8.2013.
[85] Int. Gertrude Mwakiyoka, Church Secretary at Area 1B Charismatic Redeemed Ministries and International Church, Area 1B, 10.6.2013.
[86] Int. Clifford Nyangulu, Area 1B Charismatic Redeemed Ministries and International Church Secretary, Area 1B, 10.8.2013.
[87] Int. Pastor Burton Kawinja Nyirenda, Church Pastor, Luwinga Baptist Convention of Malawi, Area 1B, 12.8.2013.

people reported back, who later became members of the church.[88] The church started very well; however, it needed someone to nurture the new church. Mzuzu Baptist Church requested Thomas Chirwa, deacon leader, to Pastor the church.

Luwinga Baptist Church has 120 members with average church attendance of 85 people, of whom the majority are women. The majority age group is from 25 to 45 years.[89] Members of the church come from a wider area. New members join the church through transfers and open-air rallies. Newly converted members join baptism class before water baptism.

Church leadership is dominated by men. The language of the church is Chichewa.

3.1.23 Area 1B Church of Christ

Area 1B Church of Christ is located in Willison Moyo Village. The church was started by Kenson Mtambo and Kumwenda, who were working as cooks at Mzuzu Church of Christ College at Luwinga. In 2008, Kenson Mtambo and Kumwenda asked permission from Mzuzu College Church of Christ to start a church at Area 1B.[90] When permission was granted all members of Church of Christ from Area 1B were requested to start a church at Area 1B. The church started with eight people, congregating at Area 1B Primary School. Area 1B Church of Christ started on a good note; however, it was lacking leadership. The situation forced the Nkholongo Church of Christ to appoint Roy Simon Banda to lead the church.[91] At that time the church had 19 members. When the situation stabilized they built their own church.

The dominant age group of the church is 10 to 20 years. The church has more women than men.[92] The average church attendance is 45 people. New members join the church through transfers and by birth. Newly

---

[88] Int. Seyani Nainja, Church Elder, Luwinga Baptist Convention of Malawi, Area 1B, 12.8.2013.

[89] Int. Pastor Burton Kaminja Nyirenda, Church Pastor, Luwinga Baptist Convention of Malawi, Area 1B, 12.8.2013.

[90] Int. Kenson Mtambo, Area 1B Church of Christ Member, Area 1B, 20.8.2013.

[91] Roy Symon Banda, Area 1B Church of Christ Member, Area 1B, 20.8.2013.

[92] Int. Margret Kasambala, Area 1B Church of Christ Member, Area 1B, 20.8.2013.

converted members join the church through open-air rallies and face to face witnessing. New converts join baptism class after water Baptism.

The Church leadership is for men only. The dominant language of the church is Chitumbuka.

3.1.24 Nkholongo Church of Christ

Nkholongo Church of Christ is at Area 1B, located along Nkholongo – Luwinga via Habitat road. The church is near Area 1B Habitat area and next to newly built Luwinga sports complex.

Nkholongo Church of Christ started in 1990 as a substation of Mzuzu College Church of Christ. The idea to start the church was initiated by Mr. Manda who was an old man at that time who could not manage to go for worship at Chamalaza Church of Christ at Kapirimtende, where people from that area were worshiping.[93] When the Manda Village saw the need of having a church in their village, they took up the matter with Chamalaza Church where the request was accepted. Although the request was accepted, the church did not start at that time due to lack of skills on how to start a church.[94]

The idea to start the church was fulfilled by pastor Chilambo who at that time was a Pastor at Mzuzu College Church of Christ. Pastor Chilambo started the church through a rally he organized at Manda Village ground. At the rally, many people surrendered their lives to Jesus Christ and these people were requested to meet again the following Sunday. The following Sunday, 11 people reported for worship and that was the beginning of Nkholongo Church of Christ. The church started while worshiping in the house of J.J. Manda who also was given a responsibility of nurturing the church. J.J. Manda later became Pastor of Church of Christ and he was appointed deputy director to Jade at Mzuzu Church of Christ College. The church remained in J.J. Manda's house for a long time until when they had finished building their own church.[95]

---

[93] Int. Roy Symon Mtambo, Former Church Member at Nkholongo Church of Christ, Area 1B, 20.8.2013.

[94] Int. M. Manda, Church Member at Nkholongo Church of Christ Member, Area 1B, 20.8.2013.

[95] Int. Roy Symon Mtambo, Former Church Member at Nkholongo Church of Christ, Area 1B, 20.8.2013.

The church has an average attendance of 30 people, of whom women are in the majority. New members join the church by birth and transfers, while newly converted members join the church through face to face witnessing and open-air rallies. New converts go for water baptism before joining baptism class.

Leadership of the church is for men. The language of the church is Chitumbuka.

3.1.25 St Fostina Roman Catholic Church

St Fostina Roman Catholic Church is at Area 1B in Vilume Village next to St Fostina Primary School.

The St Fostina Church started as an outstation of St Augustine Church at Viyele. Jane Francis Jere and Stellah Nyirenda initiated the idea to ask the St Augustine Church to open an outstation at Area 1B.[96] The reason for wanting to have a church at Area 1B was the increased number of members at Area 1B and long distances worshippers were travelling for church services to St Augustine. The request was first presented when Father Phiri was Priest In-Charge at St Augustine; however, he turned down the request. The request was remembered when Father Phiri got transferred, and it was Father Chinula who allowed Christians from Area 1B, Nkholongo and Lupaso to start an out station at Area 1B in 2005. The church started with five families worshiping at St Fostina Primary School, which had been built with a help of MK 1.4 million from Prof John Ryan.[97]

St Fostina Church is building a permanent church with a capacity of 200 people. The church has 120 members, with average church attendance of 70 people. The majority of church members are women. New members join the church through transfers and by birth. Newly converted members join the church through marriages; such members join baptism classes before water baptism.[98]

---

[96] Int. Vwalakata Msiska, Church member, St Fostina Roman Catholic Church, Area 1B, 14.8.2013

[97] Int. Bakita Nyirongo, Church member, St Fostina Roman Catholic Church, Area 1B, 14.8.2013

[98] Int. Jane Francis Jere, Church Member, St Fostina Roman Catholic Church, Area 1B, 14.8.2013.

The church uses Chitumbuka as a common language. Leadership of the church is free for both male and female; however, men are taking the leading role.

3.1.26 Luwinga Evangelical Baptist Church of Malawi

Luwinga Evangelical Baptist Church of Malawi is at Area 1B. The church is located in between Home bound and Area 1B, near new Habitant for Humanities home at Village headman Vilume.

Luwinga Evangelical Baptist Church started by Pastor Lancaster Mfungwe who at the time of beginning the church was working with Forestry Department in Mzuzu.[99] The department of Forestry in Mzuzu sent Pastor Mfungwe to Liwonde on duty. While there he met a Canadian missionary, who asked him to establish a church in Mzuzu. Pastor Mfungwe was excited with the news and when he came back to Mzuzu, he convinced Masoni Zimba and Godwin Lwinga to start a church.[100] They started a church at Mchengautuwa with three people. The church was moved from Mchengautuwa to Lupaso and finally to Area 1B at Vilume Village in 2002.

When the church was finally established at Vilume Village, Pastor Mfungwe asked Pastor Jere and Mrs Belness Nyafulirwa to help him in running the church. Pastor Jere and Belness Nyafulirwa moved door to door asking people to join the church and promised them to be awarded with scholarship fund for whoever joins the church or for their children.[101] Many people of the school age group joined the church, and the total number at that time was 150.[102] The church at the early stage was congregating under a Muwula tree.

Luwinga Evangelical Baptist Church has a church building with the capacity of 100 people. The average church attendance is 10 people, of

---

[99] Int. Osvey Kumwenda, Church Elder at Luwinga Evangelical Baptist Church of Malawi, Area 1B, 13.8.2013.

[100] Int. Emily Banda, Church Member, Evangelical Baptist Church, Area 1B, 13.8.2013.

[101] Int. Osvey Kumwenda, Church Elder at Luwinga Evangelical Baptist Church of Malawi, Area 1B, 13.8.2013.

[102] Int. Osvey Kumwenda, Church Elder at Luwinga Evangelical Baptist Church of Malawi, Area 1B, 13.8.2013.

whom the majority are youth of school going age.[103] New members joined the church through promises made door to door that they were to be given scholarship fund for those who join the church. New members join a question class for one year before water baptism.

The language of the church is Chitumbuka and a little Chichewa. Church leadership is free for both men and women though dominated by men.

3.1.27 Area 1B Cornerstone Presbyterian Church

Area 1B Cornerstone Presbyterian Church is at Kang'ona area. The church is located at the four ways road junction of Viyele – Lupaso and Area 1B market.

Area 1B Cornerstone Presbyterian Church is a sub-station of Chibavi Cornerstone Church. The church started due to long distances church members from Area 1B were travelling to Chibavi church. The church started in 2011 with three adults and eight children aged five to ten.[104] The beginning of the church was as a fellowship conducted in the house of Sellah Msiska. Many people were joining the fellowship because of healing and deliverance services, which were taking place every Saturdays.[105] When the number of participants was growing, church leaders decided to look for a bigger room, which they happened to find in a newly constructed private secondary school belonging to Mr Nyirongo within the area.[106]

The church is still renting a class room from Mr Nyirongo. The total number of church members is 25, while the average church attendance is 18 people. Women are more in the church than men. Membership comes from the whole of Luwinga, Lupaso and Nkholongo areas. New members join the church through door to door evangelism, fellowships and open-air rallies. Newly converted members join baptism class before water baptism.

---

[103] Int. Allen Lwimba, Church Elder, Luwinga Evangelical Baptist Church of Malawi, Area 1B, 13.8.2013.
[104] Int. Towela Munthali, Church Elder, Area 1B Cornerstone Presbyterian Church, Area 1B, 12.8.2013.
[105] Int. Sellah Msiska, Church Elder, Area 1B Cornerstone Presbyterian Church, Kang'ona, 12.3.2013.
[106] Int. Eliah Nkhunika, Church Elder, Kang'ona Presbyterian church of Malawi, Kang'ona, 12.8.2013.

The basic language of the church is Chitumbuka. Leadership of the church is dominated by men.

3.1.28 Kang'ona Presbyterian Church of Malawi

Kang'ona Presbyterian Church of Malawi is at Kang'ona area, located along Area 1B to Kaka road.

Chiweza Banda, who came from Blantyre to work with Mzuzu University, was the one who established a Presbyterian Church of Malawi in Mzuzu.[107] The church started in 2003 at Mzuzu University with the family of Chiweza Banda. The first people to join the church of the family of Chiweza Banda were Clement Ngulube, Efridah Phiri and Peter Matola. While they were worshiping at Mzuzu University, they found a piece of land at Kang'ona where they built a church.[108] After they had finished building a church in 2008, they decided to move out of Mzuzu University and started worshiping at their own church at Kang'ona. On the same day, when the church was moving to Kang'ona Church, members of the church got divided into two groups, the first group went to Kang'ona, while the other group went to Katoto Secondary School.[109] The church at Kang'ona had 30 people under the leadership of Pastor Chipeta.

The church has 70 members; with average church attendance of 35 people. The church has more women than men. The dominant age group is 15 to 40 years. New members join the church through open-air rallies and door to door evangelism. New converts go straight for baptism without going through baptism class.

The language of the church is Chichewa. Church leadership is for both sexes; male and female.

3.1.29 Kang'ona Church of the Nazarene

Kang'ona Church of the Nazarene is at Robert Singini village in Kang'ona area. The church is located along Area 1B - Kaka road.

---

[107] Int. Pachalo Honde, Church Member, Kang'ona Presbyterian church of Malawi, Area 1B, 12.3.2013.

[108] Grace Zimba, Church Deacon, Kang'ona Presbyterian church of Malawi, Area 1B, 14.8.2013.

[109] Clement Ngulube, Church Elder, Kang'ona Presbyterian church of Malawi, Area 1B, 12.8.2013.

In 2007, Rev. Samson Singini from Lunyangwa Nazarene Church organized Jesus film show evangelism campaign for three days at Kang'ona Orphan Care ground.[110] After three days of a film show, many people surrendered their lives to Jesus Christ. Those who gave their lives to Jesus Christ were asked to meet the following Sunday at the same place.[111] The first Sunday service of worship gathered in Kang'ona Orphan Care Hall with 18 people. Some of the first members who joined the church were Kondwani Mzumara, Mrs. Mhango and Maliseni Mughogho. Before the church came to Kang'ona, there were five people who were worshiping at Lunyangwa Church. The coming of the church at Kang'ona lessened the distance the five people used to travel when going for worship at Lunyangwa.

When the church was still worshiping at Kang'ona Orphan Care, they managed to find a piece of land where they built the temporary church shelter. The church moved to a temporary shelter where later they built a permanent one with the capacity of 70 people. The church has 60 members with an average church attendance of 21. The church has more women than men. New members join the church through Jesus film shows and open-air rallies. Newly converted members join the church baptism class before water baptism.

The common language of the church is Chichewa. Leadership of the church is for both sexes; male and female, however males are dominating.

3.1.30 Kang'ona African International Church

Kang'ona African International Church is located in Robert Singini Village near Kang'ona Orphan Care.

The church started as a sub-station of Chibavi African International Church. The church started at Kang'ona because church members from Kang'ona were complaining of the long distances they were travelling to Chibavi for services of worship. The other reason was that members from Kang'ona were increasing such that they were able to become a church. In 1998, John Nyirenda and Abel Mhango supported by pastor Kanyinji

---

[110] Int. Temwache Mzumala, Church Member at Kang'ona Church of the Nazarene, Kang'ona, 14.8.2013.

[111] Int. Winter Chima, Church Elder at Kang'ona Church of the Nazarene, Kang'ona, 14.8.2013.

asked the Chibavi Church to allow people from Luwinga to start their own church.[112] The request was accepted in the same year. The Chibavi church organized a big rally in the same year, which resulted into the beginning of Kang'ona church. The church started with 15 people worshiping under a tree near Kang'ona Orphan Care ground.

The Kang'ona Church has a permanent church with the capacity of 60 people. The church has 70 members with average church attendance of 45. The majority of church members are women. The church has more married group of 35–50 Years of age than the youth.[113] The dominant members of the church are people from Karonga and Chitipa. New members join the church through transfers. New converts join the church through person to person witnessing, where they are told of doctrine and policies of the church.[114] New converts join a baptism class for one day before water baptisms.

Church readership is for men. The language of the church is Chitumbuka.

3.1.31 Area 1B Way of Life Church

Area 1B Way of Life Church is located south of Area 1B Market along Area 1B - Kang'ona Road.

The church was started in 2011 by Pastor Paul David Malani who was a church elder of Area 1B Assemblies of God Church. In 2011, the pastor of Area 1B Assemblies of God Church was alleged to have misused church money and he was taken to police where it was said that he was charged with theft.[115] The situation disappointed church members and many of them stopped worshiping. It was at this time when Paul David Malani reorganized the scattered group and convinced them to start a new church.[116] The church started with 10 people worshiping at Good

---

[112] Int. Ester Mhoni, Church Elder at Kang'ona African International Church, Kang'ona, 17.8.2013.

[113] Int. Martine Chima, Church Elder at Kang'ona African International Church, Kang'ona, 17.8.2013.

[114] Int. Ester Mhone, Church Elder at Kang'ona African International Church, Kang'ona, 17.8.2013.

[115] Int. Memory Maroni, Church Member, Area 1B Way of Life Church Area 1B, 17.8.2013.

[116] Int. Idah Nkhonjera, Church Member, Area 1B Way of Life Church Area 1B, 17.8.2013.

Samaritan Hall. Some of the prominent members of the church at that time were Mpira, Paul, Longwe and David. When the church was growing in numbers, they decided to withdraw from worshiping at Good Samaritan Hall and occupied the abandoned church of Area 1B Assemblies of God in 2012.[117]

The church has 20 members with church attendance of 12 people. The majority of church members are children of below 15 years. New members join the church through door to door visitation.

The language of the church is English with Chichewa interpretation. Leadership is for men.

3.1.32 *Luwinga Africa National Church*

The Luwinga Africa National Church is in Area 1B, South of Area 1B market.

Symon Kamukhati Mkandawire from Chilumba initiated the beginning of Luwinga African National Church. In 1964, Kamukhati was arrested by Mzuzu Police at Chilumba and detained at Mzuzu Police for three days.[118] When he was released, he went to Village Headman Wayinga Singini and asked him for the possibilities of starting a church in Mzuzu. Wayinga Singini introduced him to Inkosana Luwinga Singini, and after that, he was given a piece of land at Area 1B to start a church.[119] Symon Kamukhati did not start a church in Mzuzu by himself, instead, when he went back home, he sent Robert Mzumara to start the church. Robert Mzumara started the church through a rally he organized at Area 1B in 1964. After the rally, the church was established and Robert Mzumara went back home. Matrone Makhwawa became the first Pastor of the church while S. Mbewa became the first Session Clerk. The church started with 32 people, some of the first members who started the church were Matrone Makhwawa, H. Kondowe and Kanjauke Gondwe.

Luwinga Africa National Church has a permanent church with the capacity of 200. The church has 200 members with average church

---

[117] Int. Memory Maroni, Church Member, Area 1B Way of Life Church Area 1B, 17.8.2013.
[118] Int. Yohane Beka Mkandawire, Church Member at Luwinga Africa National Church, Luwinga, 20.8.2013.
[119] Int. Nkhwima Mkandawire, Church Member, Luwinga Africa National Church, Luwinga, 20.8.2013.

attendance of 150 people. The church has more women than men. Many members of the church are coming from Karonga, Chilumba and Mpherembe.[120] New members join the church through transfers and by birth. New converts join the church through person to person witnessing. Newly converted people join baptism class for two days before baptism.

The church uses Chitumbuka as the common language. Leadership of the church is for men.

3.1.33 Luwinga Assemblies of God Church

Luwinga Assemblies of God Church is in Area 1B, south of Area 1B market.

The Luwinga Assemblies of God Church started as an outstation of Ekwendeni Church. The church started in 1990 because church members were complaining about long distances they were travelling from Luwinga to Ekwendeni for church services and there was an increased number of church membership from Luwinga area who could stand as a church.[121] The church started with 25 people worshiping at Humbu Business College. The first people to start the church were Mr and Mrs B. Banda, Mr and Mrs R. Khonje and Shakespeare Mvalo, the first Pastor of the church.[122] The church moved from Humbu Business College to where it is now in 2001. It was in 2003 when the Luwinga Church became a full church independent from Ekwendeni Church.

The church has a permanent church building with the capacity of 500 people. The church has 330 members with average church attendance of 260 people. The majority of church members are women. The church dominant age group is below 35 years of age.[123] New members join the church through transfers. Newly converted members join the church

---

[120] The African National Church started at Chilumba, Karonga by Symon Kamkhati Mkandawire. He then went to Mpherembe to his brother, where he introduced the church. These areas are very much familiar with the church hence they take lead in membership. Int. Yohane Beka Mkandawire, Church Member at Luwinga Africa National Church, Luwinga, 20.8.2013.

[121] Int. R. Khonje, Former Church Elder, Luwinga Assemblies of God Church, Lupaso, 19.8.2013.

[122] Int. Moffat Nyirenda, Church Elder, Luwinga Assemblies of God Church, Area 1B, 18.8.2013.

[123] Int. Offat Nyirenda, Church Member, Luwinga Assemblies of God Church, Area 1B, 18.8.2013.

through open-air rallies. New converted members join baptism class before water baptism.

The common Language of the church is Chichewa or English with Chichewa interpretation. Church leadership is for both sexes; male and female.

3.1.34 Nkholongo Mboni za Yehova Kingdom Hall

Nkholongo Mboni za Yehova Church is located north east of Area 1B market. The church is located along Area 1B market to Area 1B Habitat for Humanity road.

Nkholongo Church started in 1996 as a branch of Chibavi Church. People like W.J. Lungu, J.K. Mendele and Msiska asked the Chibavi Church to consider distance which church members from Area 1B and Nkholongo were travelling to Chibavi Church.[124] In their request, they also asked the church to consider the mobility of children and the growth of membership from Area 1B and Nkholongo areas. The Chibavi Church responded to the request by granting permission to start a branch of Mboni za Yehova Church at Area 1B. The church started with 20 people, 12 elders and 6 children, worshiping under a tree.[125]

The Nkholongo church has a permanent church building with the capacity of 60 people. The average church attendance is 45 people. The church has more men than women. The dominant age group is 20 to 45 years.[126] New members join the church through transfers, the majority of whom come from Mzimba and Nkhata-bay. New converts join the church through door to door visitation and magazine. Converted members join baptism class for one year before water baptism.

The common language of the church is Chichewa. Church leadership is for men only.

---

[124] Int. Lilian Mendela, Church Member, Nkholongo Mboni Za Yehova Church, Area 1B, 19.8.2013.
[125] Int. Christina Mhango, Church Member, Nkholongo Mboni Za Yehova Church, Area 1B, 19.8.2013.
[126] Int. Lilian Mendela, Church Member, Nkholongo Mboni Za Yehova Church, Area 1B, 19.8.2013.

3.1.35 Kang'ona Living Waters Church

Kang'ona Living Waters Church is at Kang'ona area, west of Kang'ona Orphan Care. The church is located in Robert Singini village.

Kang'ona Living Waters Church started in 2000 as a branch of Mzuzu Living Water Main Church, Mount Zion Living Waters Church. At first all people from Luwinga, Nkholongo and Lupaso were worshiping at Mount Zion Living Waters Church.[127] In the year 2000, Mount Zion Living Waters Church management discovered that church members from Luwinga were travelling long distances for church services to Mzuzu. It was also discovered that membership from these areas was increasing who could make a church of their own. This made the church management to decide that all people from Luwinga, Lupaso and Nkholongo should have their own church at Kang'ona. The church started with 43 people worshiping at Nkholongo Primary School. Later, the church moved from Nkholongo to Kang'ona area because more church members were coming from Area 1B, Luwinga and Lupaso.

The church at Kang'ona has no permanent church building; instead they are using a temporary Vigwagwa church. The church has 60 members with average church attendance of 45 people. The majority of church members are women. The dominant age group of church members is 15-35 years. New members join the church through transfers. New converts join the church through door to door visitation and open-air rallies. The newly converted members join baptism class for four months before water baptism.

The church uses Chichewa as a common language. Church leadership is for both sexes.

3.1.36 Kanyika Seventh-day Adventist Church

Kanyika Seventh-day Adventist Church is at Area 1B, north east of Area 1B market. The church is along Area 1B Market to Area 1B Habitat for Humanity road.

The church started in 1987 as an outstation of Luwinga Seventh-day Adventist Church. The church started because members from Area 1B were complaining about long distances they were travelling for church

---

[127] Int. Agatha Phiri, Church Member at Kang'ona Living Waters Church, Area 1B, 20.8.2013.

services at Luwinga.[128] Luwinga church accepted the complaints considering distance and the growth of membership from Area 1B and they gave them mandate to start a church at Area 1B. Kanyika Church started with 50 people under the leadership of Gogo Gomezgani Nyasulu, Z.A.K. Chiwanda and T. Kamanga. The church started in the house of Gogo Gomezgani Nyasulu who at that time had just retired from Lunjika Seventh-day Adventist Mission as a Parish pastor and principal of the institution.[129] The church stopped from worshiping in the house of Nyasulu when they had finished building a temporary church, where the permanent one is built.

The church has 200 members with average church attendance of 150 people. Women are dominating church membership. The dominant age group is 15 to 45 years. The church is dominated by members who come from Lunjika and Luwazi. New members join the church through transfers and by birth. New converts join the church through efforts and Voice of Prophecy.[130] New converts go for water baptism after they had finished their training course.

The church uses Chichewa as the main language. Leadership is free for both sexes; however, men are dominating.

3.1.37 Chumbi Seventh-day Adventist

Chumbi Seventh-day Adventist Church is at Nkholongo Area in Chumbi Village east of Mzuzu Academy. The church is located off Nkholongo to Luwinga road from Nkholongo ESCOM storage to Luwinga area.

The church started in 2011 as an outstation of Kanyika Seventh-day Adventist Church. The Kanyika Church thought of starting Chumbi Church because of the growth of membership around the area.[131] The church started as a result of an effort organized by Kanyika Church at Chumbi.

---

[128] Int. Graswell Mgunda, Church Elder at Kanyika Seventh-day Adventist Church, Area 1B, 13.8.2013.

[129] Gogo Gomezgani Nyasulu was among the early pastors who witness the transition of powers from White missionaries to Malawian Pastors.

[130] Voice of Prophecy is where people learn by correspondences who eventually become members of the Church. Int. Graswell Mgunda, Church Elder, Kanyika Seventh-day Adventist Church, Area 1B, 13.8.2013.

[131] It is by law to Seventh – day Adventist that when members of a certain section are more than 30, the said section can be an outstation or branch from where the section belongs.

Chumbi Church started with 40 people, of whom some were members from Kanyika Church who were coming from Chumbi area, and some were those who surrendered their lives during the effort.[132] Kanyika Church asked L.G. Nyirongo, E.K. Kayira and W.E Nkhata to nurture the newly started church. Chumbi Church is under construction, so they are using a temporary church structure.

The church has 50 members with average church attendance of 35 people. The church is dominated by women. The dominant age group is from 15-45 years.[133] Members of the church are coming from nearby villages. New converts join the church through efforts and Voice of Prophecy pamphlets. Baptism for new converts is done when they have finished a training course of Voice of Prophets or after 21 days of effort.

The church uses Chichewa language. Leadership is for both sexes; although men are dominating.

3.1.38 Nkholongo Good Samaritan Ministry

Nkholongo Good Samaritan Ministry is at Nkholongo area. The ministry is located at the four ways road junction of Luwinga - Nkholongo road and Area 1B market to Area 1B Habitat for Humanity road.

Nkholongo Good Samaritan Ministry was started in 2000 by Rev J.D. Kavalo who was working with SEDOM.[134] The ministry started as a fellowship with 6 people worshiping in the house of Rev. J.D. Kavalo. As the fellowship was growing, they stopped congregating at the house of Rev J.D. Kavalo and started fellowshipping at African Evangelical Church. Later, they went on renting the house of Bitwel Kawonga at Area 1B. Finally, when they completed building their own house, they stopped renting and moved to their own house.

Nkholongo Good Samaritan Ministry is an interdenominational fellowship aimed at helping orphans, and widows with funding from

---

[132] Int. Graswell Mgunda, Church Elder, Kanyika Seventh-day Adventist Church, Area 1B, 13.8.2013.

[133] Int. Ettah Kayira, Church Member, Chumbi Seventh-day Adventist Church, Area 1B, 13.8.2013.

[134] Int. Rabson Mzumala, Youth Leader at Nkholongo Good Samaritan Ministry, Luwinga, 20.8.2013.

United States of American.[135] The ministry is divided into three groups; widows, microloan, and youth. The ministry has 100 members of whom all meet on Saturdays afternoon for prayers. Membership is only for those who are registered in the three programs.

The common language is Chichewa. The ministry has leadership crisis whereby at present there is no permanent leadership.[136] However, both male and female are free to lead

3.1.39 Luwinga Holy Trinity Anglican Church

Holy Trinity Anglican Church is at Luwinga area, located along Luwinga to Nkholongo road. The Church is between Radio ABC and Luwinga African Evangelical Church of Malawi.

The church of Holy Trinity started in 2000 as an outstation of St Mark's Anglican Church in Mzuzu. Mr Chola requested St Mark's Anglican Church to allow members from Luwinga area to start a church at Luwinga due to the long distances members from Luwinga were travelling to St Mark's Anglican Church and that membership of Luwinga area was big enough to run the church.[137] Many people at St Mark's Church supported the idea so that in 2000, St Mark's Church, in consultation with the Diocese, started Luwinga Holy Trinity Church. On the day they were launching Luwinga church, the Diocese distributed free maize to people who came to participate in the function.[138] The church started with 20 people, of whom the prominent families were: Edward Nkhata, Christina Banda, Edward Phiri, Huka Mponda and Filimon Banda. The church started worshiping at Humbu Business College, then, it went to Mzuzu Teachers College and finally to where they have constructed a church building.

Luwinga Holy Trinity Church has a permanent church structure with the capacity of 300 people. The church has 270 members with an average church attendance of 200 people. The church has more women than

---

[135] Int. Justina Msofi, Member, Office Worker at Nkholongo Good Samaritan Ministry, Area 1B, 20.8.2013.
[136] The first leader was Rev J.D. Kavalo, upon his death, Rev Samson Maleka took over the leadership who unfortunately also died. At present Justina Msofi is the interim leader.
[137] Int. Jessie Phiri, Church Elder at Holy Trinity Anglican Church, Area 1B, 21.8.2013.
[138] Int. Maxwell Phiri, Church Elder at Holy Trinity Anglican Church, Area 1B, 21.8.2013.

men. People from Likoma and Nkhotakota are dominating the church.[139] New members join the church through transfers and by birth. Newly converted people go through baptism class before water baptism.

The language of the church is Chichewa. Church Leadership is free for both sexes; however, only married members under church procedures are allowed to lead the church.

3.1.40 St Mary's Convent

'St Mary's Convent'[140] is at Luwinga area, located along Luwinga to Nkholongo road, 200 metres east of Radio ABC.

St Mary's Convert belongs to the Anglican Diocese of Northern Malawi. The convent is the house of Anglican nuns of the northern Diocese of Malawi founded in 2002. The idea of having nuns in the northern Diocese of Malawi was to have a special group of people who could dedicate themselves to praying for the Diocese.[141] The convert started in 2002 with three nuns. Later, one nun dropped, however, three more joined, making a total number of five.[142] Nuns use the chapel for prayers, eight times a day. The chapel is also used for worship and celebration of mass. Nuns are the only users of the chapel, unless on special occasions, when other people can be allowed to use it i.e. on mass.

New members join the convent by recruitment.[143] There is no specific location where nuns could come from.

Nuns use English for the divine office,[144] while, when celebrating mass, Chichewa is used. Leadership is only for nuns.

---

[139] Anglican Church has its origin from Likoma, there was no any other church at Likoma apart from Anglican as opposed to the case today.

[140] Oswald Jimmy Banda, The Role of Women in the Anglican Diocese of the Northern Malawi, MA, Mzuzu University, 2013.

[141] Int. Sister Mather Theu, one of the nuns, St Mary's Convert, Luwinga, 21.8.2013.

[142] Int. Father A. Chitowe, former Chaplain at St Mary's Convert is at Luwinga, 6.4.2012.

[143] Int. Sister Mather Theu, one of the nuns, St Mary's Convert, Luwinga, 21.8.2013.

[144] The Divine office is the nuns' prayers eight times a day.

3.1.41 Luwinga African Evangelical Church

The Luwinga African Evangelical Church of Malawi is located along Luwinga to Nkholongo road, next to Luwinga Holy Trinity Anglican Church.

The church started in 1991 by Rev Gregory, a missionary from United Kingdom, and Pastor Mpezeni. The two were sent by African Evangelical Church headquarters in Lilongwe to plant churches in Malawi. They started a church by organizing people through revival meetings, fellowships, open-air rallies and door to door evangelism. They also provided relief maize to people who were badly affected by hunger of 1991.[145] The relief maize made more people to come for fellowships and revival meetings where the church was congregating. Within three weeks of church plantation, church members had risen to 250 people. As more people were flocking to join the church, it was discovered that the house from where services of worship was taking place became small, as a result Rev Gregory and Pastor Mpezeni built a church with funding from African Evangelical Mission. The first people to join the church were the families of Msongolo Kondowe, J. Ngonga and Chimutu Nyirenda.

The church had a good beginning with 2,500 people, later, membership dropped to 50 people because they stopped giving relief maize.[146] The average church attendance is 25 people, of whom children of 10 years below are in the majority. New members join the church through transfers and by birth.

The language of the church is Chichewa. Leadership of the church is for both sexes; however, males are dominating.

3.1.42 Luwinga Apostolic Church of Great Britain

The Luwinga Apostolic Church of Great Britain is at Luwinga area. The church is located along Mzuzu - Ekwendeni road, near Injena Filling Station, 100 m north – east of Mzuzu University.

The church was started by Rev. Christopher Mzomela Ngwira, a Zionist, who was converted into Apostolic Church of Great Britain while at

---

[145] Int. Pastor Christopher Mzomela Ngwila, Church Pastor at Luwinga African Evangelical Church of Malawi, Luwinga, 21.8.2013.
[146] Ibid.

Rumphi Secondary School.[147] When Rev Ngwira finished his secondary education at Rumphi, he came to Zolozolo in 1990 to start a church while looking for employment. He started a church through door to door visitation and house to house fellowships. As the fellowship was growing, he started a church in his house at Zolozolo.[148] The church started with 10 families; four from Zolozolo and six from Luwinga, giving him a total of 20 members. The church management decided to open another branch at Luwinga because many members of the church were coming from Luwinga. The other reason was that people from Luwinga complained about the difficulties they were facing when crossing rivers on their way to Zolozolo Church. Before the opening of Luwinga branch, Rev Ngwira moved from Zolozolo to Luwinga, so that the church at Luwinga started in his house.

The Luwinga church grew into a Parish whereby Zolozolo church was reduced to a substation under Luwinga. The church has 120 members with average church attendance of 80 people. The church has more women than men. New members join the church by conversion through door to door visitation and women's' fellowships. Newly converted members join baptism classes before water baptism.

The church uses Chichewa as a common language. Leadership is free for both sexes; however, men are dominating.

3.1.43 *Viyele Assemblies of God Church*

Viyele Assemblies of God Church is at Luwinga, located off Mzuzu - Ekwendeni road

The church started in 2006 as a result of the marriage of Pastor Lukhele, who was an associate Pastor at Rumphi.[149] Pastor Lukhele married a daughter of Pastor Shakespeare Mvalo, who was the pastor at Luwinga Assemblies of God. The father-in-Law of Pastor Lukhele asked Pastor Gondwe, Zonal superintendent, to open branches to Homebound and Viyele so that his son-in-law secures a place in Mzuzu.[150] Two branches

---

[147] Int. Mary Mnthali, Wife of the Church Pastor at Luwinga Apostolic Church of Great Britain, Luwinga, 21.8.2013.
[148] Ibid.
[149] Int. Vincent Kumwenda, Church Member, Viyele Assemblies of God Church, Viyele, 23.8.2013.
[150] Int. L. Khonje, Former Church Member, Viyele Assemblies of God Church, Lupaso, 21.8.2013.

were created; Pastor Lukhele was posted at Homebound. Many members were not happy with his posting, so they left the branch for Viyele branch where there was no Pastor. The situation did not please Pastor Gondwe and Mvalo as a result they closed Viyele church.[151] Later, Pastor Lukhele was asked to leave homebound branch and reopen Viyele branch.

Pastor Lukhele with the support from his father-in-law restarted the church at Viyele in his house. He started the church as a fellowship with nearby neighbours; later, he visited those who knew him while at Homebound. When the number of church membership was growing, they went on renting the abandoned beer hall building. After staying there for some time, they left the building because the owner, Vidame Mkandawire, wanted the building for the original use of beer drinking. They left the building for another of Vidame's houses, and finally, they constructed their own temporary church building with the capacity of 100 people.

The church has 90 members of whom the majority are women. The dominant age group of church membership is 15-35 years. Church members join the church through conversion. New converts join the church through open-air and door to door evangelism.

Church leadership is for everyone as long as he/she has leadership skills. The language of the church is Chichewa.

3.1.44 Luwinga Holy Spirit Filled Ministry

The Luwinga Holy Spirit Filled Ministry is located two hundred metres North West of Luwinga market, West of Luwinga Post Office.

The Ministry was started in 2011 by Prophet Obadiah Mwale at his house in Area 1B. The Ministry started as a family fellowship of Prophet Obadiah and his wife, when neighbours and other people started seeing signs and miracles done through prophet Obadiah Mwale, they started joining him so that the house became small.[152] In order to solve the problem of space, Prophet Obadiah wanted to construct a temporary shelter at his house; however, before he did that he was contacted by a

---

[151] Int. Vincent Kumwenda, Church Member, Viyele Assemblies of God Church, Viyele, 23.8.2013.
[152] Int. Dickson Nkhoma, Evangelist, Luwinga Holy Spirit Filled Ministry, Luwinga, 22.8.2013.

member from Enlightened Christian Gathering Ministry who offered him a temporary church hall belonging to Enlightened Christian Gathering Ministry at Luwinga.[153] The result was that the two ministries joined together, they retained the name of Holy Spirit Filled Ministry while using the hall belonging to Enlightened Christian Gathering.

The ministry meets every Monday and Friday afternoon from 2 pm to 5 pm. The average church attendance is 30 people, of whom the majority are women. The ministry is for all people around Luwinga area.

The common language of the ministry is Chichewa. Prophet Obadiah Mwale speaks in English while someone interprets into Chichewa.[154] Leadership is for both sexes; while preaching is for the prophet and Pastors only.

3.1.45 Mzuzu Bible College Church of Christ

Mzuzu Bible College Church of Christ is at Luwinga area, west of Mzuzu University, behind Social Community Offices.

The church started as a result of opening a Bible College. The Bible College was opened by James D. Rujat who came as a missionary from United States of America to Chinyolo in Rumphi.[155] Rujat started training Pastors and teachers at Chinyolo while looking for a central place for the college. In 1989, he left the mission in the hands of John Thensen and came to Mzuzu where he established a college along Jomo Kenyatta road, behind Northern Region Police Station. The Malawi Government refused to give him permission to start a college there; instead, he was instructed to open up a college at Luwinga.[156] He started a College at Luwinga in 1992 while the church remained behind at Jomo Kenyatta. Few months later, the church started at Luwinga College with 30 people.[157] Membership of the church was from two groups, the first

---

[153] The Enlightened Christina Gathering is a Ministry/Church belonging to Prophet Shepherd Bushiri.

[154] Int. Pastor Thyelani Sibande, Luwinga Holy Spirit Filled Ministry, Luwinga, 20.8.2013.

[155] Int. Elengtone Harawa, College Lecture at, Mzuzu Bible College Church of Christ, Luwinga, 20.8.2013.

[156] Int. World Nyoni, College Lecturer at Mzuzu Bible College Church of Christ, Luwinga, 20.8.2013.

[157] Int. Sakhani Nyirenda, College Lecturer at Mzuzu Bible College Church of Christ, Luwinga, 20.8.2013.

group was students who came from different places, and the second one was those who came from Jomo Kenyatta Church. The church started while worshiping at a Dining Hall until when a permanent church was built.

The average church attendance, when the college is in full session, is 110 people while off session it becomes 30. The majority of church members are men. New members join the church by transfers.[158]

The common language of the church is Chitumbuka. Leadership of the church is for men.

3.1.46 St Augustine Roman Catholic Church

St Augustine Roman Catholic Church is at Luwinga area, located at St Augustine market. The church is 150 metres north of Mzuzu University. It is surrounded by St Augustine market and St Augustine Primary school.

St Augustine church started with 20 people in 1978 as an outstation of St Peter's Parish. The idea of starting a church was to provide spiritual help to Roman Catholic students who were studying at Mzuzu Teachers Training College.[159] Roman Catholic students were complaining about time spent and long distances they were travelling to St Peter's Church for worship. When the request was accepted at St Peter's Church, the church started as a small Christian Community gathering in Mzuzu Teachers Training College classroom. Fr Jeremia Oarealy, a teacher at Mzuzu Teachers Training College and Vicar General of Bishop Jean Louise Jobidon living in the Bishop's house, started the church.[160]

When the church was established at Mzuzu Teachers Training College campus, all members of Roman Catholic members around Luwinga area were ordered to start worshiping at Mzuzu Teachers Training College. The order was accepted; many members joined the church so that a classroom became small. Looking at the situation of limited space at the college, people like, M.G. Zulu, Mathews Ngwira, Patrick Nyirenda, Dr D.M. Ndengu and Elias Zulu asked the Vicar General for the possibilities

---

[158] Int. Elengtone Harawa, College Lecturer at Mzuzu Bible College Church of Christ, Luwinga, 20.8.2013.
[159] Int. Bulukutu Chirwa, Church Elder, St Augustine Roman Catholic Church, Luwinga, 8.8.2013.
[160] Int. Edwine Mhoni, Church Elder, St Augustine Roman Catholic Church, Luwinga 8.8.2013.

of opening a Parish.[161] In 1984, Bishop Jobidon of Mzuzu Diocese and the Vicar General accepted the request. Church members managed to find a piece of land where they constructed a church building in 1986. The white fathers were the In- Charge of the Parish and the first Parish priest was father Ditchen.

The church has 400 members with average church attendance of 300 people. The church capacity is 400 people. The majority of church members are woman. The dominant age group of church members is 10 – 45 years.[162] New members join the church through transfers, marriages and by birth. Newly converted members join baptism class before water baptism.

The language of the church is Chitumbuka and English. Church leadership is for both men and women, however, men are dominating.

3.1.47 Area 1B Mosque

The Area 1B Mosque is located near Area 1B market, east of the market.

The Mosque was started in 2009 by Gogo Chause. The idea of starting a Mosque at Area 1B was to ease the distance Muslims living at Area 1B were travelling to Mzuzu town mosques for worship.[163] Before Area 1B mosque, Muslims from Area 1B and Luwinga were worshiping at Hilltop, Hardware and Matabwa Mosques. The idea of starting a mosque at Area 1B was discussed at Area 1B market by different Muslims.[164] The Mosque at Area 1B started with 40 people, 30 men and 10 women, children were not involved because there were no activities for them.

The area 1B mosque has a temporal Mosque. The average worship attendance is 30 people, of whom the majority are women. The mosque is dominated by people from Mangochi and Nkhota-kota. Mosque members are both Sunni and Quadiriyah. New members join the Mosque by birth and through transfers.

---

[161] Int. Edmon Mkandawire, Church Elder, St Augustine Roman Catholic Church, Luwinga, 8.8.2013.
[162] Int. Bulukutu Chirwa, Church Elder, St Augustine Roman Catholic Church, Luwinga, 8.8.2013.
[163] Int. Sheik Zambali Juma, Sheik of Area 1B Mosque, Area 1B, 8.8.2013.
[164] Int. A Gama, Mosque Member, Area 1B Mosque, Area 1B, 8.8.2013.

The language at the Mosque is Chichewa. The central leadership is for men while women are responsible for the women's group only.

3.1.48 *Lunyangwa Church of the Nazarene*

Lunyangwa Church of the Nazarene is at Luwinga area, located along Mzuzu - Luwinga road close to TEVET.

Lunyangwa Church of the Nazarene was started by Rev M.C. Gondwe in 1978. In his early days, Rev Gondwe was supported by American missionaries, Walter Meya and Dundo, who were teachers at Bangwe College of the Nazarene Church.[165] Rev M.C Gondwe was sent to Mzuzu when he had finished his ministerial studies at Bangwe Nazarene College. When he came to Mzuzu, he was told to meet Mpachika and Zuwa, who were already members the church. When the three met, they discussed about the possibilities of starting a church. The church started as a fellowship in the house of Rev M.C. Gondwe where he was renting. Rev M.C. Gondwe reached out to people by giving them second hand clothes and organizing football teams for children and youth.[166] This made many people join the church more especially youth. Very soon his house became small and they moved to Mpachika's house. Later, with the help of Walter Meya and Dundo, they built a church where Rev. Gondwe was renting a house.

The average church attendance for today is 80 people of whom the majority are children from 10 – 15 years.[167] New members join the church through transfers and by birth. The majority of church members come from Blantyre and Lilongwe. New converts join the church through open-air evangelism and Jesus film. New converts join baptism class before water baptism.

The church is led by both sexes; male and female. The church uses Chichewa as a common language.

---

[165] Int. Rev Voster T.K. Mhango, Parish Minister at Lunyangwa Church of Nazarene, Luwinga, 8.8.2013.
[166] Int. Mercy Longwe, Church Elder at Lunyangwa Church of Nazarene, Luwinga, 8.8.2013.
[167] Int. Rev. Voster T.K. Mhango, Parish Minister at Lunyangwa Church of Nazarene, Luwinga, 8.8.2013.

3.1.49 Lupaso CCAP Church

Lupaso CCAP Church is located off Mzuzu - Ekwendeni road from Lupaso Bus stage towards Nkholongo. The church is hundred metres north of Lupaso Primary School.

Lupaso CCAP Church is the first permanent church in Mzuzu where all CCAP churches in Mzuzu have originated from. The church started in 1933 as a branch of Ekwendeni Mission Station. The idea for starting a church at Lupaso was to provide spiritual help and formal education to people living in Luwinga village.[168] The first church as well as school was at Luwinga, were Petroda Filling Station is situated. Church leaders at that time were Saulos Mkandawire and Wadilika Singini. In 1946, when Luwinga village started expanding to other nearby places, the church and school moved from Luwinga to Lupaso. Lupaso area was considered to be a central place to surrounding villages of Chimaliro, Khalani Msiska and Kafwiri Nyirongo from Nkholongo, Kamuwimbi Mhoni, Kamzimu Gondwe, Bob Mkandawire, Katumbi, Nyirenda and Msowoya and Lupaso. People like Samson Mbuto Katumbi, Samuel Filenyanga Ngwira, and Thundu Mkandawire initiated the movement of the church from Luwinga to Lupaso. At Lupaso, the church started under a Muwula tree, later, they moved into a classroom.[169] They built a temporal church structure and later, they built a permanent one. In 1989, the church moved hundred metres north of where it was. The church became a congregation from Mzuzu congregation in 1984.[170]

The church started with students and their parents. Students were not allowed to come for primary education alone without attending church Sunday services together with their parents.[171] The church has 500 members with an average church attendance of 350 people. The church capacity is 600 people. The church has more women than men. New members join the church through transfers and by birth. New converts

---

[168] Int. Village Headman Bob Mkandawire, Lupaso, 5.5.2012.

[169] There was a big Muwula tree with spread out branches, which was providing good shade to people. Int. Village Headman Bob Mkandawire, Lupaso, 5.5.2012.

[170] The first Church in Mzuzu is Lupaso which was under Ekwendeni congregation; the first congregation was Mzuzu which was comprised of Lupaso, Mzuzu and Lusangazi. Int. Rev G.J. Msowoya, Retired Minister of the CCAP Synod of Livingstonia, Lupaso, 5.5.2012.

[171] Int. Samuel Thundu Mkandawire, Church Elder at Lupaso CCAP Church, Lupaso, 14.11.2013.

join the church through door to door and open-air evangelism. New converts join baptism class before water baptism.

The church is led by both sexes; male and female, however men are dominating. The common languages of the church are Chitumbuka and English.

3.1.50 Viyele CCAP Church

Viyele CCAP Church is at Luwinga area, located off Mzuzu - Ekwendeni road from Mzuzu University Bus Stage towards airport transmitter. The church is 150 metres north east of Mzuzu University and 50 metres west of St Augustine Market.

Viyele CCAP Church started in 1978 as a result of the opening of Mzuzu Teachers Training College.[172] Before 1978, students from Mzuzu Teacher Training College were worshiping at Lupaso church. Johnstone Langa, K.J. Mhango and Zondiwe Mbano, all tutors, asked Lupaso church to allow students from Mzuzu TTC to be worshiping at the campus. When the permission was granted, they started worshiping in the Dining Hall. The church started with 35 people, all of them were students, tutors and tutors' families.[173]

The church stopped worshiping at Mzuzu Teachers Training College because of the desire to start Sunday school. The College Management Committee did not allow the CCAP Church to use other places within the campus for Sunday school; instead, they were advised to look for a possible place outside the campus.[174] When the matter was reported to Lupaso Church, the Lupaso Church sent Fiskani Mwandira and Frank Banda to find a place where they could start Sunday school. The place was found free of charge from Bingu Singini who was Village Headman Luwinga. They started Sunday school under a Muwula tree in early 1980. In 1984, Lupaso Church declared that all those worshiping at Mzuzu Teachers Training College campus should leave the campus and start congregating where the Sunday school was operating.[175] Soon after the

---

[172] Int. Anitah Shaba, Session Clerk, Viyele CCAP Church Viyele, 4.12.2012.
[173] Int. Samuel Thundu Mkandawire, Church Elder at Lupaso CCAP Church, Lupaso, 14.11.2013.
[174] Int. Samuel Thundu Mkandawire, Church Elder at Lupaso CCAP Church, Lupaso, 14.11.2013
[175] Int. A. Makwakwa, Session Clerk at Viyele CCAP Church, Viyele, 14.11.2013.

church had moved out of the campus, many people from Luwinga area joined the church. In 1999 the church became a congregation under the name of Viyele.[176]

Viyele Church has three services each Sunday, the average church attendance with respective church services of English and Chitumbuka is 700 people, of whom the majority are women.[177] The church has 2000 members. The capacity of the church is 800 people. New members join the church through transfers and by birth. New converts join the church through open-air rallies. Newly converted members join baptism class before water baptism.

The church uses Chitumbuka and English. The church is led by both sexes.

3.1.51 Kachere CCAP Church

Kachere CCAP Church is at Area 1B, located along Nkholongo - Luwinga road via Area 1B market. The church is 150 metres Eat of Area 1B market.

Kachere CCAP Church came from Lupaso CCAP Church in 2003. The church started by identifying a place for future development before initial plans for a church.[178] The place was found in 1984 by Vincent Moyo, Edward Kamanga and Dolinas Nyama, who were members of Lupaso Church while living at Area 1B. In 1990, church members from Area 1B asked Lupaso Church to give them permission to start Sunday school at the identified place in order to ease long distances children were travelling.[179] When permission was granted, they started Sunday school classes under pine trees planted in 1984. As the number of children was increasing, they built a small church structure for Sunday school.

In 2003, Lupaso vestry under the leadership of Samuel Thundu Mkandawire asked church members from Area 1B to start a church where the Sunday school was operating. The idea for starting a church at Area 1B was supported by many members who considered the growing membership of Area 1B and also long distances people were travelling to

---

[176] Kang'ona Session Minutes, 28.3.1999
[177] Viyele Church Attendance Book, 11.7.2013
[178] Int. K. Mwenechanya, Church Elder at Kachere CCAP Church, Area 1B, 12.11.2013.
[179] Int. Unious Jenda Moyo, Session Clerk, Kachere CCAP Church, Area 1B, 12.11.2013.

Lupaso. When Members from Area 1B accepted the idea, they renovated the Sunday school structure into a suitable church building. The church started with 120 people, of whom 20 were church elders. In 2007, the church became a congregation by the name Kachere in memorial to a small planted Kachere tree which was removed when renovating the church building.[180]

The church has 900 people with an average church attendance of 650 people for Chitumbuka and English services. The church capacity is 450 people. The church has more women than men.[181] New members join the church through transfers and by birth. New converts join the church through open-air and door to door evangelism.

The dominant languages of the church are Chitumbuka and English. Leadership is for both sexes; male and female.

3.1.52 Luwinga United Methodist Church

Luwinga United Methodist Church is located off Mzuzu - Ekwendeni road from Mzuzu University Bus Stage towards airport transmitter. The church is 155 metres north- east of Mzuzu University, next to Viyele CCAP Church.

In 2004, Rev Copeland Nkhata was sent to Mzuzu from Blantyre to start United Methodist Church. The church started with five people fellowshipping in the house of Rev Nkhata at Katoto where he was renting.[182] When people like Hastings Mkandawire, Francis Mzumara and many others who were already members who joined the church while in Blantyre, Lilongwe and Zimbabwe heard about the coming of United Methodist Church to Mzuzu, they joined the church where Rev. Nkhata was renting. As many people were joining the church, the house of Rev Nkhata became small, as a result the church moved to Mzuzu University. Later, people like; Lister Mhoni, Rose Mhoni and Pastor Mwale were sent to Mzuzu as missionaries from Tanzania. Pastor Mwale was renting a house at Viyele which later was sold to the church together with the surrounding piece of land. It is on that piece of land where the church

---

[180] Int. Samuel Thundu Mkandawire, Church Elder at Lupaso CCAP Church, Lupaso, 14.11.2013.
[181] Strategic Planning Committee Report, 22.10.2013
[182] Int. Hannah Kamoto, Church Elder, Luwinga United Methodist Church, Viyele, 1.10.2013.

has been built. The church moved out of Mzuzu University to a new place after completing building a temporary church shelter. As of now, they have completed building a permanent church where they are worshiping.

The church capacity is 200 people. The church has 100 people with average church attendance of 70 people. The majority of church membership are women. The dominant church age group is 14 to 35 years. The majority of church members come from Kasungu north and Jenda.[183] New members join the church through transfers. New converts join the church through fellowships. New converted members join baptism class before water baptism.

The language of the church is Chichewa. Leadership of the church is for both sexes.

3.1.53 Kubwezeretsa Sabata la Yehova Church

Kubwezeretsa Sabata la Yehova Church is in Nkholongo area, located along Dunduzu Road Block - Nkholongo road close to the road junction of Lupaso.

In 1992, Thole who came from Lilongwe to Mzuzu, working with the Tobacco Control Commission of Malawi, came with Kubwezeretsa Sabata la Yehova Church in Mzuzu. He started a church with seven people from his own family in his house at St Augustine where he was renting.[184] Slowly Thole was joined by other people through face to face evangelism and by others who were already members of the church who joined from elsewhere before coming to Mzuzu.[185] The first people to join the church were; Set Longwe, Chisale Bechani Banda, Lameck Mnthali and Mandabwisa Kalua. As many people were joining the church, the house of Thole became small, Mandabwisa Kalua, member of the church, gave his own piece of land for free to the church where the church building

---

[183] The Pastor of the church come from the areas of Kasungu north and Jenda, therefore people from these areas are following their home colleague.

[184] Int. Chimbwemtuba Chipeta, Former Member at Kubwezeretsa Sabata la Yehova Church, Lupaso, 30.9.2013.

[185] Int. A. Nyirenda, close friend of Mandabwisa Kalua, Lupaso, 30.9.2013.

was built.[186] When they completed building a church, they left the house of Thole and went where the church was built.

The church of Kubwezeretsa Sabata la Yehova worships on Saturdays. When they go for worship, they put off shoes and put on sack cloths, like what John the Baptist was wearing. The average church attendance is 35 people, of whom the majority are men. The church is dominated by Chewa people from Lilongwe. New members join the church through transfers. New converts join the church through face to face evangelism and feasts done at night.[187]

The language of the church is Chichewa. Church leadership is only by men.

3.1.54 Luwinga Church of Africa Presbyterian

Luwinga Church of Africa Presbyterian is at Luwinga area. The church is located along Luwinga - Nkholongo road, where they have built Luwinga sports complex next to Area 1B Habitat for Humanity.

The Luwinga Church came from Masasa in 1993. At first all people in Mzuzu who belonged to Church of Africa Presbyterian were worshiping at Masasa. Due to long distances people were travelling and due to the growth of membership, they decided to divide the church into three branches: Luwinga, Zolozolo and Mchengautuwa.[188] The division of branches from Masasa was spearheaded by B.K. Manda, former Pastor of Last Church of God while in Blantyre and supported by Kamanga and Mhoni.[189] The Luwinga Church started with seven people worshiping in the house of B.K. Manda. When more people started joining the church, the house became small as a result they moved to a *Muwula* tree, where they bought a piece of land for church building. When they had finished building a permanent church, they started worshiping in the church. Any day from now, the church is about to move from the present place to in

---

[186] Mandabwisa was the first convert with the church because he was the first person to be contacted with Thole; both of them were working with the same company where Mandabwisa was working as a watchman for Thole.
[187] Int. Chimbwemtuba Chipeta, Former Member at Kubwezeretsa Sabata la Yehova Church, Lupaso, 30.9.2013.
[188] Int. Rev Benneck Mwase, Parish Minister at Luwinga Church of Africa Presbyterian, Luwinga, 10.10.2013.
[189] B.K. Manda was experienced Church leader with vision and dedication. People were easily convinced to his idea.

between Luwinga Seventh-day Church and Southern Bottlers because at the present place, the government is building a Sports Complex Centre.

The average church attendance is 25 people, of whom the majority are women. New members join the church through transfers. The majority of church members come from Nkhata Bay and Chilumba in Karonga.[190] New converts join the church through individual contacts. Newly converted members join baptism class before water baptism.

Church leadership is for both sexes; male and female, although men are dominating. The language of the church is Tumbuka.

3.2 Religious Places in Chiputula Ward

3.2.1 Chiputula CCAP Church

Chiputula CCAP Church is at Chiputula, located at the centre of Chiputula Ward, along Mzuzu Airport - Kataba Market road.

In 1992, Hezekiah Mhlanga and M.Z.L. Kamanga proposed to Kataba Session to allow people from Chiputula area to start a substation of Kataba Church at Chiputula area.[191] The reason to start a church at Chiputula was due to the growth of membership at Chiputula area. The other reason was that church leaders from the two areas used to be in conflicts due to social differences where people from Chiputula were considered to be of low class.[192] Kataba Church under the leadership of Rev. M.M.D. Sibande accepted the proposal. The church started with afternoon prayers while Sunday morning services were still at Kataba Church. The Church started with 50 people worshiping at the house of Hezekiah Mhlanga. They stopped going to Kataba Church for Sunday morning services when they had built a temporary church shelter in 1998. Chiputula Church became a congregation in 2009 under the influence of Hezekiah Mhlanga, Frezar Chunga and M.Z.L. Kamanga, although, Daniel Chirwa and Gehazi Janda from Kataba Church resisted from allowing Chiputula branch to become a congregation.[193]

---

[190] The church started from Nkhatabay by Rev. Yesaya Zerenje Mwase and moved to Chilumba. These places have become strongholds of the church.
[191] Int. Steven Moyo, Session Clerk, Chiputula CCAP Church Chiputula, 5.9.2013.
[192] Int. Frezar Chunga, Deputy Session Clerk at Chiputula CCAP Church, Chiputula, 5.9.2013.
[193] Ibid.

The first church building they built at Chiputula was grass thatched with a capacity of 90 people, later they built a permanent church with the capacity of 800 people. The church has 1500 people of whom the majority are women. The church has two services; the average church attendance is 500 people. The dominant age group of the church is below 45 years. New members join the church through transfers and by birth. Newly converted members join the church through open-air evangelism. When converted; they join baptism class before water baptism.

The basic languages of the church are Chitumbuka and English. Male, female and youth are free to lead the church; however, men are dominating.

3.2.2 Chiputula St Michael's Lutheran Church of Central Africa

St Michael's Lutheran Church of Central Africa is situated in Chiputula area, located at the central area of Chiputula, along Mzuzu Airport - Kataba Market road.

The Church started in 1986 with the initiative of Rev. R.G. Cooks who came to Mzuzu from a visit to Mpherembe. While at Mpherembe, Rev. Cooks was told of Harawa, a church member who was in Mzuzu, who joined the church while at Mpherembe but he did not open a church in Mzuzu. When Rev. Cooks came to Mzuzu, he went to the house of Harawa at Mzilawayingwe where they discussed about the possibilities to start a church.[194] Harawa accepted to start the church; he started the church as a fellowship with his family and family friends. When the church was established, Rev. R.G. Cooks left Mzuzu and went to Lilongwe.

The church became more established when Chilambo, a student minister, came to Mzuzu on practical work. When Chilambo came to Mzuzu, he came to the house of Harawa where he was living. Chilambo worked hard to develop the church, he did door to door evangelism and open-air rallies.[195] Through these activities, he discovered some people who were already members of the church but they did not know about the existence of their church in Mzuzu. At the same time many people

---

[194] Int. S. Phiri, Church Elder, St Michael's Lutheran Church of Central Africa, Chiputula, 21.8.2013.
[195] Ibid.

were being converted and joined the Church. The church grew and they built a temporary church shelter at where the present one is built.

The church building has a capacity of 200 people. The church membership is 100; the average church attendance is 60 people. The church has more women than men. The dominant age group of the church is 20 to 40 years. The majority of church members are coming from Enukweni.[196] New members join the church through conversion and, through door to door visitation. Converted members join baptism class before water baptism.

The dominant language of the church is Chitumbuka. Church leadership is for men only.

3.2.3 Chiputula Church of Christ

Chiputula Church of Christ is in Chiputula area, located along Ching'ambo to Chiputula Centre road.

The Church started in 1989 as a branch of the Kenyatta Road Church. Pastor Magona started the church while worshiping in his house, until when a church was build.[197] The Church started because of the growth of membership at Chiputula and at the same time Chiputula members were complaining about long distances they were travelling for church services to the Kenyatta Road Church of Christ. The church started with three families.

The church has 50 members and an average church attendance of 36 people. The majority of church membership are women. The dominant age group of the church is 20 to 35 years.[198] New members join the Church through transfers. Newly converted members join the Church through door to door visitation. When they are converted, they join baptism class for three months before water baptism.

The leadership of the church is for men only. Chichewa is the common language in the church.

---

[196] Enukweni was the first place to be evangelized in the north; the church came from the centre to the north. The Church came to Malawi in 1963 and was first established in Chiradzulu.

[197] Int. Zione Mawaya, Church Member at Chiputula Church of Christ, Chiputula, 21.8.2013.

[198] Int. Baulen Chitsulo, Church Member at Chiputula Church of Christ, Chiputula, 21.8.2013.

3.2.4 Chiputula New Apostolic Church

Chiputula New Apostolic Church is in Chiputula area, located at the road junction of Ching'ambo from Chiputula road The Church is surrounded by Chiputula Church of Christ and Charismatic Redeemed Ministry International.

The church started in 2000 as a branch of Zolozolo New Apostolic Church. The idea to start Chiputula Church was initiated by Stocker Gondwe, Kapinda and Kamanga who were tired of long distances to Zolozolo for church services.[199] The three mentioned people agreed to present their complaint to Zolozolo Church. When the request was presented, Zolozolo Church agreed to open a branch at Chiputula; however, they were cautioned to build a church first before starting a congregation. The Chiputula people did not take the caution seriously; they started a church with 15 people worshiping in the house of Stocker Gondwe.[200] Later, they bought a piece of land where they built a temporal church structure, the development which made them to move from the house of Stocker Gondwe to the temporal Church building.

Chiputula New Apostolic Church has a permanent Church building with the capacity of 100 people. The average church attendance is 90 people. The majority of church members are women. The dominant age group of church membership is from 25 to 45 years. New members join the Church through transfers and conversion. New converts join the Church through social works.[201] Converted members join baptism class for two years before water baptism.

The basic language of the Church is Chitumbuka. Church leadership is for men only.

3.2.5 Chiputula Charismatic Redeemed Ministry International

Chiputula Charismatic Redeemed Ministry International is located along Chiputula to Ching'ambo road at the road junction of Chiputula market

---

[199] Int. Grades Soko, Church Member, Chiputula New Apostolic Church, Chiputula, 22.8.2013.
[200] Int. Stocker Gondwe, Church Elder at Chiputula New Apostolic Church, Chiputula, 22.8.2013.
[201] Int. Grades Soko, Church Member at Chiputula New Apostolic Church Chiputula, 22.8.2013.

Centre road. The Church is next to Chiputula Pentecostal Holiness Association Church.

The Church was started in 2002 by Bishop Mark Kambalazaza who organized an open-air rally at Chiputula Primary School ground for one week.[202] The result of the rally was that many people surrendered their lives to Jesus Christ. When Bishop Kambalazaza saw the fruits of the rally, he requested all those who surrendered their lives to Jesus Christ to come the following week at the same place for worship. He entrusted the responsibility of nurturing them in the hands of Gogo Phiri and Bambo Chilindilira.[203] When those people reported what Bishop Kambalazaza asked them to do, Bambo Chilindilira and Gogo Phiri led the worship service and later they were told how they will go about with worshiping. The church went on as a fellowship done in different people's houses together with open-air rallies conducted in different places of Chiputula. When they were tired of moving from house to house they started worshiping at Chiputula Primary School.[204] Later, they bought a piece of land where they have built a church.

The church started with 40 people of whom the majority were from the age of 12 to 25 years.[205] The church has 110 members with average church attendance of 80 people; the majority of them are women. The church capacity is 150 people. New members join the church through conversion; due to door to door visitation. Newly converted members join baptism class for one week before being baptized by water.

Leadership of the church is dominated by men. The language of the church is Chichewa.

3.2.6 Chiputula Pentecostal Holiness Association

Chiputula Pentecostal Holiness Association is located along Chiputula centre - Ching'ambo road. The church is next to Chiputula Charismatic Redeemed Ministry International.

---

[202] Int. Juness Kita, Church Member at Chiputula Charismatic redeemed Ministry International, Chiputula, 21.8.2013.
[203] Ibid.
[204] Int. Sucios Kazifere, Church Member, Chiputula Charismatic Redeemed Ministry International, Chiputula, 21.8.2013.
[205] Ibid.

Chiputula Pentecostal Holiness Church started at Zolozolo in 2005. The Church came from Zambia to Chitipa in 1932 and further to Mzuzu at Zolozolo in 1994. Pastor Jones Nyirenda started the Church at Zolozolo through fellowships and open-air rallies.[206] When many people had joined the fellowship, they stopped worshiping in the house of pastor Nyirenda and started worshiping at Zolozolo Primary School while renting one of the class rooms. Due to the raising of rental costs and remoteness of the place, they decided to move the church from Zolozolo Primary School to Royal Private Secondary School near Mzuzu Stadium.[207] While at Royal Private Secondary School, the church managed to buy a piece of land at Chiputula where they built a Church. When the people had finished building a church, they all left Royal Private Secondary School class and moved into their own church at Chiputula. The Chiputula Pentecostal Holiness Association Church started with 82 people of whom the majority were youth of below 20 years. The Church had four elderly people who were above 30 years at that time.

The average church attendance is 150 people, of whom the majority are women. New members join the church through transfers and conversion. The majority of Church members come from Chitipa, Mpherembe and Jenda.[208] Newly converted members join the Church through good neighbourhood which Church members show to their neighbours.[209] When people are converted, they go straight for water baptism.

The Church uses English and Chichewa languages. Leadership is male dominated.

3.2.7 Chiputula Assemblies of God Church

Chiputula Assemblies of God Church is located in Chiputula area, along Chiputula Centre - Ching'ambo road. The Church is near Chiputula Pentecostal Holiness Association Church.

---

[206] Int. Pastor Wilbert Msukwa, Church Pastor, Chiputula Pentecostal Holiness Association, Chiputula, 19.8.2013.
[207] Int. Abel Msiska, Church Clerk, Chiputula Pentecostal Holiness Association, Chiputula, 19.8.2013.
[208] Jenda, Chitipa and Mpherembe are old Centres of the Church, in these Centres; there are big Churches which act as Missionary stations.
[209] Int. Akim Saka, non Church member, neighbour to Chiputula Pentecostal Holiness Association Church, Chiputula, 19.8.2013.

The Church started in 2007 as a branch of Kataba Assemblies of God Church. People from Chiputula area were going to Kataba for church services; however, due to long distances people from Chiputula were travelling for church services at Kataba, Pastor Mrs. Chatayika decided to ask Kataba Church to give her permission to start a branch at Chiputula.[210] The idea was accepted and the church was started with 14 people. Pastor Mrs Chatayika had been trained as a pastor in Zomba where her husband was working as a policeman. When her husband had retired from work, they went to Chiputula where they built their house. As she was starting Chiputula Church, Kataba Church gave her Mr. Mphenisi and Mr. and Mrs. Mhango to help her in running the church.[211] The church started in the house of Mr. and Mrs. Mhango before building their own church. Pastor Mrs. Chatayika made a series of door to door visits and held open-air rallies, which made it possible to mobilize more people to join the church.

Chiputula Assemblies of God Church has a permanent Church building with the capacity of 100 people. The church has 125 members with average church attendance of 90 people. The majority of church members are women. The dominant age group of the church is below 30 years.[212] New members join the Church through transfers, by birth and conversion. Newly converted members join the church through door to door visits and open-air rallies. Converted members join baptism class for three months before water baptism.

The language of the church is Chichewa, while leadership is dominated by men.

3.2.8 Chiputula Ambassadors for Christ Ministries

Chiputula Ambassadors for Christ Ministries is located along Mzuzu Airport - Chiputula Market road. The Church is 150 metres west of Chiputula market.

---

[210] Int. Jemsom D. Mtawali, Church elder, Chiputula Assembles of God Church, Chiputula, 19.8.2013.

[211] Int. Chiyala Manse, Church elder, Chiputula Assembles of God Church, Chiputula, 19.8.2013.

[212] Int. Chiyala Manse, Church elder, Chiputula Assemblies of God Church, Chiputula, 19.8.2013

The ministry started in 2008 with 14 members from Scripture Union and Student Christian Organization of Malawi, of whom the majority were CCAP members.[213] Jastus Hacred Godwings Mwalughali, a prominent member of the Church of Central Africa Presbyterian, initiated the idea of starting Chiputula Ambassadors for Christ Ministries because many youth of CCAP were not attending Sunday afternoon prayers with the reason that prayers were dull and fit for adults.[214] The ministry wanted to keep the youth busy on Sundays with prayers instead of doing things which might ruin their lives.[215] The ministry started congregating in a rentable house of Mr. Makwakwa. Many people joined the ministry through Jesus film shows which were borrowed from Life Ministry.

The average worship attendance is 30 people, of who the majority are youth of 16 to 30 years of age. Female are in the majority than male. The ministry has more members from south and central region of Malawi. New members join the ministry through overnight fellowships.

Leadership of the ministry is dominated by men. The dominant language is English with Chichewa translation.

3.2.9 Chiputula St Pius Catholic Church

Chiputula St Pius Catholic Church is in Chiputula area, located along Chiputula - Ching'ambo road.

St Pius Catholic Church started in 1982 as Mphakati of St Peters and in 2012 the Mphakati became an outstation of St Peters church.[216] The idea for a church at Chiputula was initiated by Handrigde Chilambo and Samuel Banda, the two asked St Peters church to consider long distances which old people and Sunday school children were travelling from Chiputula to St Peters Church and the growth of Chiputula Mphakati which grew into seven Mphakati.[217] St Peters Church accepted the

---

[213] Int. Dalitso Makwakwa, Ministry Member, Chiputula Ambassadors for Christ Ministries, Chiputula 19.8.2013.

[214] Int. Rodah Hara, Ministry Members, Chiputula Ambassadors for Christ Ministries, Chiputula, 19.8.2013.

[215] Ibid.

[216] Int. Juliana Msukwa, Church leader, Chiputula St Pious Catholic Church, Chiputula, 19.8.2013.

[217] Mphakati is a small Section where Christian families are grouped together for prayers in their residential area. A number of mphakati make a branch and branches make a Church centre.

request; Chiputula area was granted the status of an outstation. The church started with 300 church members, the majority of whom were members aged 25 years and above while youth of 12 to 20 years of age used to go to St Peters because of multiple church activities done at St Peters Church.[218]

When St Pius Church was still Mphakati, they built a church with the capacity of 500 people. The average church attendance is 400 people, of whom the majority are women. New members join the Church through transfers and by birth. Newly converted members join the Church through marriage. New converts join baptism class for a year before water baptism.

The language of the Church is Chitumbuka. Church leadership is dominated by men.

3.2.10 Chiputula African National Church

Chiputula African Church is in Chiputula area, located off Chiputula - Ching'ambo 500 metres South of Chiputula Primary School.

Chiputula African National Church started by Pastor Mfuni who came from Chilumba to Chiputula in 1980. Mfuni and others were worshiping at Area 1B Church. Due to long distances people from Chiputula and Zolozolo were travelling to Area 1B for church services and due to the growth of church members in these areas, they decided to start another branch at Mzuzu stadium.[219] The Mzuzu Stadium Church experienced raising rental costs which made them to move out of the stadium. When the church was moving out of the stadium, it got divided into two branches, Chiputula and Zolozolo; Pastor Mfuni led the Chiputula Church.[220] The Chiputula church started with seven people worshiping in the house of Pastor Mfuni, of whom the majority of them were people from Chilumba who came to Mzuzu for employment. Slowly, Pastor

---

[218] Roman Catholic Churches have many activities in worship which attract people to join the Church. Many young people or children are used to perform these activities in worship. Many youth/ Children from Chiputula Church are worshiping at St Peters because at St Peters children are used to the maximum in worship activities than at Chiputula.

[219] Int. Suzen Mwasinga, Church Member at Chiputula African Church, Chiputula, 19.8.2013.

[220] Int. Wezzie Mhango, Pastor's Wife at Chiputula African Church, Chiputula, 19.8.2013.

Mfuni and other church members bought a piece of land where they built a church with a capacity of 120 people.

The church has 130 members with average Church attendance of 100 people, of whom the majority are women. The Church is dominated by the married age group. The majority of church members come from Karonga and Chitipa. New members join the Church through transfers. New converts join the church through marriage; when converted, they go straight for baptism.[221]

The central leadership of the church is done by men. The dominant language of the church is Chitumbuka.

3.2.11 Chiputula Mtambo Ministry

Chiputula Mtambo Ministry is in Chiputula area, located along Chiputula sub-market to Airtel transmitter road. The ministry is found south of Chiputula Primary School.

Chiputula Mtambo Ministry started in 2012 by Gideon Mtambo through the calling from God in a form of a vision.[222] When Mtambo received the call, he started door to door visitation, open-air rallies and evening fellowships.[223] Slowly, the number of members grew up; they stopped moving from house to house and started worshiping at a central place in the house of Gideon Mtambo. Later, his house became small; one of his members surrendered a place, outside her house where they built a temporary church shelter for worship. They moved to a new place where worship is done on a daily basis. The ministry started with 20 people.

The average worship attendance is 33 people, of whom the majority are women.[224] The ministry has more married people from the age of 25 to

---

[221] Simon Kamkhate started African Church because of marriage. He was suspended from CCAP because he married a second wife; he moved from CCAP and started a Church which accommodates all those who have two or more wives or are second wives.

[222] He saw God calling him in form of vision to start a ministry. He was given a responsibility to deliver people, especially women, from spiritual and physical oppressions.

[223] Int. Gedion Mtambo, Founder of Chiputula Mtambo Ministry, Chiputula, 19.8.2013.

[224] The ministry is full of women. There are about 50 members of whom five are men.

40 years. Mtambo Ministry is not a church; all members of the ministry belong to different churches. The majority of ministry members come from Chitipa and Nkhatabay. The ministry focuses much on deliverance. New members join the ministry through seeking deliverance.

The language of the ministry is Chitumbuka. Leadership is by women.

3.2.12 Chiputula Seventh-day Adventist Church

Chiputula Seventh-day Adventist is found in Chiputula area, located along Kataba market - Mzuzu airport. The church is 50 metres north of Chiputula Mosque.

The church started in 2013 as an outstation of Chasefu Seventh-day Adventist Church. The first attempt to start a church was done in 2010, however, the church failed and was withdrawn to Chasefu Church because the majority of church members from Chiputula area were not ready to stand on their own and they had no church building.[225] The church restarted in 2013 through an effort organized by Maranatha group from America. The Church started with 200 people of whom the majority were those who were found at the effort and the remaining few were those who were worshiping at Chasefu while coming from Chiputula area.[226] The Maranatha group was so impressed with the results of the effort, as a result they erected an iron poled church within a week at the same place where the effort took place.

The church has 115 members with the average church attendance of 90 people, of whom the majority are women. The dominant age group of church membership is 10 to 35 years.[227] The church is dominated by members from Lunjika and Luwazi areas. New members join the church through transfers and by birth. Newly converted members join the church through efforts.

The language of the church is Chichewa. Church leadership is predominantly by men.

---

[225] Int. Wedson Luhanga, Church Elder, Chiputula Seventh - day Adventist Church, Chiputula, 28.8.2013.

[226] Int. Milliam Kumwenda, Former Member of Chasefu Seventh-day Adventist Church, Katawa, 28.8.2013.

[227] Int. Wedson Luhanga, Church Elder, Chiputula Seventh - day Adventist Church, Chiputula, 19.8.2013.

3.2.13 Chiputula Calvary Family Church

Chiputula Calvary Family Church is at Chiputula area, located along Mzuzu stadium to Zolozolo road. The Church is 50 metres west of Kataba Plane Crashed area.

The Church was started in 1990 by Pastor L.H.K. Banda who formerly was a pastor of Mzuzu Assemblies of God Church.[228] Pastor Banda resigned from Mzuzu Assemblies of God Church because the Church was failing to take care of him and the family. Before he resigned, he reported the matter of his welfare at Mzuzu to the National Head Office of Assemblies of God Church where he was given a chance to choose, either to resign and go to his own home or to start or join any other church.[229] The decision from the Head Office did not please him and it made him to remain in the church for a while. While he was still thinking the matter over, Apostle Madalitso Mbewe asked him to start Calvary Family Church in Mzuzu. He further asked the National Head Office's opinion over the matter where he was accepted to take up the offer. He started the Church with his own family members worshiping in his house. Slowly, he started visiting members of Assemblies of God, door to door, and other members of difference churches, eventually, many people abandoned their churches and joined Calvary Family Church.[230] When the number of Church members became bigger, they started worshiping at Mzuzu Stadium Hall until they had finished building their own church.

The church building has a capacity of 200 people. The church membership is 130, with average church attendance of 100 people. Women are more than men. The dominant age group of the church is from 15 to 30 years. New members join the church through transfers. Newly converted members join the church through open-air rallies. When converted, they join baptism class before water baptism.

---

[228] Int. Gogo Ester Jere, wife to Pastor L.H.K Banda, Chiputula Calvary Family Church, Chiputula, 20.8.2013.

[229] Ibid.

[230] Pastor L.H.K. Banda was good at pastoral work and many people loved him. Members of Mzuzu Assemblies of God Church were not happy with the way the Head Office in Lilongwe was treating him. When they heard that he had joined Calvary Family Church, they did not regret; hence many of them followed him. Int. Gogo Ester Jere, wife to Pastor L.H.K Banda, Chiputula Calvary Family Church, Chiputula, 20.8.2013.

Church leadership is dominated by men. Chichewa is the main language of the church.

3.2.14 Chiputula Mosque

Chiputula Mosque is located along Kataba - Chiputula market Centre road. It is 50 metres south of Chiputula Seventh-day Adventist.

The Mosque started in 2012 as a break away from Lower Chasefu Mosque.[231] The reason for breaking away was that Muslims from Chiputula area wanted to be together with a madrassa which was started by Sheik Yusufu at Chiputula in 2000. Members from Lower Chasefu Mosque refused the request from Chiputula and this made members from Chiputula area to break away and join their madrassa. Chiputula Mosque was started by sheik Yusufu, a teacher at Chiputula Madrassa, and Samuel Banda, an early Islamic leader in Mzuzu since 1970.[232] Chiputula Mosque started with 30 people in a Mosque built by an Asian in 2012.

The Mosque has 60 members, with average Mosque attendance of 45 people; the majority of them are children.[233] The Mosque is dominated by people from Mangochi and Nkhotakota. New members join the Mosque by transfers and by birth. Newly converted members join the Mosque through open-air rallies and deliberate discussions and debate. When converted, they become members of the Mosque.

Leadership of the Mosque is done by men. Preaching is done by men, although men and women are worshiping in separate rooms. The common language is Chichewa.

3.2.15 Chiputula Lutheran Church

Chiputula Lutheran Church is at Chiputula area, located along Kataba market to Mzuzu airport via Chiputula Market centre road. The church is at the eastern side of Chiputula CCAP church.

---

[231] Int. Samuel Banda, Chiputula Mosque Member, Chiputula, 20.8.2013.
[232] Int. Fatuma Banda, Chiputula Mosque Member, Chiputula, 20.8.2013.
[233] Chiputula Mosque followed the Madrassa, therefore the majority of membership are children and women. In most cases men are found in town working, and they do worship at Hardware or Vigwagwa Mosques.

In 1992 a group of crusaders from Mpherembe, led by Shaba, held a rally at Chiputula ground.[234] Shaba and his team were church planters from Mpherembe. The team at Chiputula followed Nyirenda, who was a member of the Lutheran Church at Mpherembe before coming to Mzuzu to look for employment. Although Nyirenda was a Lutheran Church member, he did not introduce the church is Mzuzu. The results of a rally at Chiputula ground were fruitful whereby many people surrendered their lives to Jesus Christ and that was the beginning of the Lutheran Church in Mzuzu. The church started with eight people worshiping in the house of Jailos Zimba. Slowly, through door to door visitation and open-air rallies, many people joined the church. They found a piece of land where they built a temporary church shelter for worship, later; they built a permanent church at the same place.

The average church attendance is 70 people, of whom the majority are women. The dominant age group of the church is from 10 to 25 years.[235] New members join the church through transfers. Newly converted members join the church through open-air rallies and door to door visitation. When converted, they join baptism class before being baptized by water.

The leadership of the church is for men only. The common language of the church is Chichewa.

3.2.16 Chiputula Zambezi Evangelical Church

Chiputula Zambezi Evangelical Church is at Chiputula area, located along Kataba market to Mzuzu Airport via Chiputula Main Market road. The church is 40 metres south of Chiputula CCAP Church.

Chiputula Zambezi Evangelical Church was the first Zambezi Evangelical church to come to Mzuzu. The church was started in 1990 by two student pastors, Mwayi Kamuyambeni and Wilford Banda, from Zambezi Evangelical Theological College in Blantyre.[236] The student Pastors were sent to Mzuzu to open a branch of Zambezi Evangelical Church in Mzuzu.

---

[234] Int. Milliam Soko, Church Member at Chiputula Lutheran Church, Chiputula, 20.8.2013.
[235] Int. J. Nyirenda, Church Elder at Chiputula Lutheran Church, Chiputula, 20.8.2013.
[236] Int. Pastor Wells Mwajumu, Church Pastor at Chiputula Lutheran Church, Chiputula, 20.8.2013.

The two pastors started a church by visiting some individuals who were already members of Zambezi Evangelical Church before coming to Mzuzu.[237] The purpose of a visit was of introducing a church to them. The individual members received the church and together they worked hard to establish a church at Chiputula.[238] They organized door to door visitations, open-air rallies and fellowships. Worship started in the house of Pastor Mwai Kamyambeni, later; they found a piece of land where they built a temporary church structure and eventually a permanent one with the capacity of 200 people.

The church has 130 members with the average church attendance of 115 people, of whom the majority are women. The dominant age group of the church is 15 to 35 years. New members join the church through transfers. The majority of church members come from the southern region, especially Ntcheu[239] and Blantyre.[240] New converts join the church through open-air rallies and door to door visitations. Converted members join baptism class before water baptism.

The dominant language of the church is Chichewa. Church leadership is dominated by men.

3.3 Religious Places in Kataba Ward

3.3.1 Kataba CCAP Church

Kataba CCAP Church is located off Mzuzu - Zolozolo road at Lower Chasefu. The church is 50 m north east of Ukani Private Schools.

Before 1987 Kataba was a section under Mzuzu CCAP Church where Sunday afternoon and midweek prayers were being conducted. In 1987, Rev M.Z. Chavula, senior Presbytery Clerk residing at Ekwendeni CCAP Mission Station, directed the Mzuzu Session to grant Kataba section the

---

[237] Int. John Chiphwanya, Church Member at Chiputula Lutheran Church, Chiputula, 20.8.2013.

[238] Int. Pastor Wells Mwajumu, Church Pastor at Chiputula Lutheran Church, Chiputula, 20.8.2013.

[239] Ntcheu was one of the early centres of Zambezi Industrial Mission.

[240] Ntcheu and Blantyre are old historical places of Zambezi Evangelical church; hence more people from these areas became members of the church than other areas Int. Pastor Wells Mwajumu, Church Pastor at Chiputula Lutheran Church, Chiputula, 20.8.2013.

full status of a prayer house as well as a congregation.[241] Rev Mbezuma Mfuni, Parish Minister of Mzuzu Congregation at that time, and Mzuzu session accepted the directive from Rev. M.Z. Chavula.

In May 1987, Kataba Section became a congregation; however, many people from Kataba and Mzuzu as well were not happy with the decision because Kataba was not ready to be a congregation at that time since the section was without a church building and had few church members.[242] Daniel Chirwa, J.M. Mhoni, Victoria Thole and Pauline Nkhwazi visited Kataba members door to door encouraging them to accept the decision of being a congregation. The first service of worship was Holy Communion which was conducted under a Muwula tree with 150 members in 1987.[243] After the Holy Communion service, Kataba Church forced herself to join Zolozolo Church where there was a church building until when they had finished building a church.[244] They finished building the church in early 1990 and they left Zolozolo Church to Kataba Church building with 400 church members. The capacity of the church building is 900 people.

Kataba Church has 900 members. The average church attendance is 600 people, of whom the majority are women. The dominant age group of the church is from 25 to 50 years.[245] New members join the church through transfers, by birth and marriage. New converted members join the church through door to door visitation, open-air rallies and social services. Newly converted members join baptism class before water baptism.

English and Tumbuka are the two languages used in the church. Leadership is for both male and female, although men are dominating.

---

[241] Int. Rev. M.Z. Chavula, Retired Reverend of CCAP Synod of Livingstonia, Mzuzu, 14.12.2012
[242] Int. Steven Nkhoma, Church Elder at Katawa CCAP Church, Katawa, 21.8.2013.
[243] Int. Selfridge Ng'ambi, Session Clerk at Katawa CCAP Church, Katawa, 21.8.2013.
[244] Int. Rev. M.M.D. Sibande, Formal Parish Minister of Katawa CCAP Church, Viyele, 14.12.2012.
[245] Int. Selfridge Ng'ambi, Session Clerk at Katawa CCAP Church, Katawa, 21.8.2013.

3.3.2 Chasefu Seventh-day Adventist Church

Chasefu Seventh-day Adventist Church is at Kataba area, located off Mzuzu - Zolozolo road at Lower Chasefu. The church is 50 metres east of Kataba CCAP church.

The church started in 1970 as a branch of Nkholongo Seventh-day Adventist Church, initiated by Pastor Yakonia Beza who was a Pastor at Nkholongo Church.[246] Pastor Yakonia Beza was forced to come up with the idea of starting a branch at Chasefu, because people from Kataba and surrounding areas were travelling long distances to Nkholongo for church services. Chasefu Church started with five notable families; Chiumia, Gunde, Mafuta, Mwale, Malikembu, worshiping under a Mpapa tree. The official opening of the church was done through an effort which took place for 21 days. Slowly, new members were joining the church as a result they built a temporary church building where later they built a permanent one. When the church became independent, Yakonia Beza became the first pastor.

The church building has a capacity of 600 people. The church membership is 600 with average church attendance of 400 people, of whom the majority are women. The dominant age group of the church is from 16 to 40 years. The majority of church members come from the original mission stations of 'Luwazi',[247] Nkholongo and Lunjika.[248] Newly converted members join the church through efforts.

The language of the church is Chichewa. Leadership is for both sexes; although men are dominating.

---

[246] Int. Arther Chirwa, Former Church Member of Chasefu Seventh-day Adventist Church, Chibavi, 10.12.2010.

[247] For the history of Luwazi Mission, see Amos Bula, *The Development of Seventh-day Adventist Luwazi Mission since its Establishment in 1928 up until 2003*, Mzuni Document, Department of Theology and Religious Studies, Mzuzu University.

[248] Int. Arther Chirwa, Former Church Member of Chasefu Seventh-day Adventist Church, Chibavi, 10.12.2010. For the history of Lunjika SDA Mission, see Macleard Banda, *The Remnant and its Mission. An Investigation into the Interaction of the Seventh-day Adventist Church with Society in Malawi*, PhD, Department of Theology and Religious Studies, Mzuzu University, 2014.

3.3.3 Kataba Assemblies of God

The church is in Kataba area, located off Mzuzu - Zolozolo road at Lower Chasefu. The church is near Kataba CCAP Church and south west of Chasefu Seventh-day Adventist.

Kataba Assemblies of God Church started in 1986 as a house fellowship.[249] Individual members of Assemblies of God who came from Lilongwe and Blantyre where the church was first established were meeting as a fellowship in the house of R.K. Mhoni who was working with Mzuzu High Court. The official opening of the church was done in 1986 through a revival meeting conducted at Mzuzu Upper Stadium ground by a team from Lilongwe Assemblies of God.[250] The leader of the revival team was Evangelist Daniel Sheffer who came from the United States of America. The results of the revival meeting were that many people surrendered their lives to Jesus Christ and also the formation of Kataba Assemblies of God Church. The church started with 60 people worshiping at Mzuzu Stadium Hall until when they had built a church at Chasefu.[251] Pastor Ruben Jere was the first Pastor of the church, through him a temporary church was built at Chasefu.

The church has a church building with the capacity of 400 people. They are 300 members in the church with an average church attendance of 250 people. The majority of church members are women. The church is dominated by the age group of 15 to 30 years. New members join the church through transfers and by birth. New converts join the church through door to door visitation, home cells and open-air rallies. Newly converted members join baptism class before water baptism.

The dominant language of the church is English with Chichewa interpretation.[252] The church is led by both sexes.

---

[249] Int. Rev. Owen Mwale, Parish Minister, Katawa Assemblies of God Church, Katawa, 21.8.2013.

[250] Int. Rev. Edina Mwale, Assistant Pastor, Katawa Assemblies of God Church, Katawa, 21.8.2013.

[251] Int. Rev. Owen Mwale, Parish Minister, Katawa Assemblies of God Church, Katawa, 21.8.2013.

[252] The System of preaching in English with Chichewa interpretation was introduced by Evangelist Daniel Shaffer, when he was establishing Chasefu Church at Mzuzu Upper Stadium.

3.3.4 The Redeemed Christian Church of God

The Redeemed Christian Church of God is in Upper Chasefu area, located off Mzuzu - Zolozolo road. The church is 200 metres north-east of Mzuzu Stadium.

The church came to Mzuzu from Lilongwe in 2011 by Pastor Chauma.[253] Pastor Chauma started the Church as a house fellowship at Chiwanja where he was renting. He worked hard on door to door visitations and evening fellowships until the church was established. He started the church with eight people, while the Church was growing; Pastor Chauma resigned from redeemed Christian Church of God and joined Calvary Family Church.[254] Pastor Kamtukule from Lilongwe Head Office came and took over the leadership of the Church. The church was officially opened by Pastor Divide Emeke Emela from Nigeria in 2012 at Chiputula. From that time, the Church moved from different rental houses until eventually they found an abandoned church hall at upper Chasefu where they are operating.

The average church attendance is 25 people, of whom the majority are women. The church is dominated by the age group of 13 to 30 years. New members join the Church through conversion. New converts join the church through" call your friend" and door to door visitation. When converted, they join baptism class before water baptism.

The leadership of the church is free for both sexes. The basic language of the church is English with Chichewa translation.

3.3.5 Mzuzu Pentecostal Church

Mzuzu Pentecostal Church is in St John's area, located along Mzuzu - Marymount road. The Church is 100 metres north-east of St John's Hospital and 50 metres west of Ilala Lodge.

The Church was started in 1985 by Pastor Samuel Banda in his house.[255] However, some says that Pastor Samuel Banda did not start the church;

---

[253] Int. Peter Chawawa, Church Elder, Chasefu Redeemed Christian Church of God, Upper Chasefu, 21.8.2013.

[254] Pastor Chauma abandoned the Church because the Redeemed Christian Church Head Office in Lilongwe was not supporting him; hence, he joined Calvary Family Church.

[255] Int. Pastor Trevour Mwambila, Associate Pastor, Mzuzu Pentecostal Church, St. John's, 22.8.2013.

rather he just joined the missionary Pastor Nepard who served with him in establishing the church amicably. For those who says that he started the church says that he started the Church with five people; all of them were from his family. Pastor Banda established the Church through door to door visitations and open-air rallies. Many people joined his church as a result his house became small and they went on renting at Mzuzu Stadium. The first converts of Mzuzu Pentecostal Church were Joyce Trindade and Trevour Mwambila, who later became an Associate Pastor of the Church. Mzuzu Pentecostal Church was growing steadily; however, the Church Head Office in Lilongwe sent Nepard, a missionary, to facilitate the growth of the Church.

It is alleged that when Pastor Nepard came to Mzuzu, he took over leadership of the church; which was not accepted by church members. All church members, apart from Joyce Trindade, wanted Pastor Samuel Banda to continue leading the church. [256] As a result of this, the church got split into two groups, 40 people went behind Pastor Samuel Banda while Joyce Trindade and Trevour Mwandila followed pastor Nepard. The group of pastor Banda abandoned the church and joined Calvary Family Church while the group of Pastor Nepard remained Mzuzu Pentecostal Church who started worshiping at the house of Pastor Nepard. Pastor Nepard, Trevour Mwambila and Joyce Trindade intensified door to door visitations and open-air rallies, and slowly people joined them. They bought a piece of land at St John's where they built a temporary church and later a permanent one.

The average church attendance is 130 people, of whom the majority are women. The church is dominated by the age group of 18 to 35 years. New members join the church by conversion. Newly converted members join the church through open-air rallies. When converted they join baptism class before water baptism.

The church uses English and Chichewa languages. Leadership of the church is for both sexes.

3.3.6 St Peters Convent of the Sisters of the Holy Rosary

St Peter's Convent of the Sisters of the Holy Rosary is in St John's area, located along Mzuzu town to Marymount road. The convent is

---

[256] Ibid.

surrounded by St John's Hospital to the north, St Peters Catholic Church and St Peters Primary School to the west.

St Peters Convent of the Holy Rosary took over from the Convent of Mary Medical Missionaries.[257] The Convent of Mary Medical Missionaries at St John's Hospital started in 1962 when St John's Hospital was being built. The main duty of the convent was to help the sick spiritually and physically. The Mary Medical Missionaries handed over the St John's hospital to Mzuzu Diocese in 2000.[258] At the same time, the convent of Mary Medical Missionaries was taken over by sisters of Holy Rosary.

The convent of Sisters of the Holy Rosary is responsible for providing spiritual and physical help to the sick at St John's hospital; they also dedicate themselves to prayers in the chapel. The chapel is used by convents for personal prayers and occasionally mass upon request. At present there are five nuns. New members join the convent by transfers.

The convent uses English as the dominant language and Chichewa or Chitumbuka. Leadership is for women only.

3.3.7 Mzilawayingwe CCAP Church

Mzilawayingwe CCAP Church is in Mzilawayingwe area, located along Mzuzu Stadium - Chizaso Maize Mill road. The church is 300 metres west of Mzuzu Stadium.

The church started in 2006 when Charity Msukwa asked Kataba Session to recognize Mzilawayingwe section to be holding Sunday afternoon and midweek prayers. Kataba Session accepted the request and started looking for a place where they could build a church. The Session bought an abandoned Church building belonging to African Light Church.[259] They renovated the building and started using it as a CCAP Church. The Church started with 50 people. Mzilawayingwe Church as an outstation of Kataba CCAP Church holds Sunday morning services at Kataba Church

---

[257] Int. Jane Banda, Convent Member, St Peters Convent of the Sisters of Holy Rosary, St John's, 22.8.2013.

[258] Int. Alice Ngulube, Employee at St John's Hospital, St John's, 22.8.2013.

[259] Int. James Phiri, Church Member, Elder, Mzilawayingwe CCAP Church Mzilawayingwe, 22.8.8.2013

while Sunday afternoon and midweek prayers are being done at Mzilawayingwe church.[260]

The average Church attendance is 120 people, of whom the majority are women.[261] New members join the Church through transfers and by birth. New converts join the Church through marriages, door to door visitation and sectional prayers. New converts join baptism class before water baptism.

The language of the church is Chitumbuka. The leadership of the Church is for both sexes.

3.3.8 Chiputula Jehovah's Witnesses Kingdom Hall

The Church (Kingdom Hall) is in Mzalawayingwe area, located 100 metres south of Mzuzu Stadium.

Chiputula Jehovah's Witness is a breakaway of Zolozolo Jehovah's Witness. Zolozolo Jehovah's Witness had four services of worship; English, Chitumbuka, Chichewa and Signs. It was the Chichewa service of worship group who decided to break away from Zolozolo church and find a place of their own.[262] The breaking from Zolozolo Church was because they wanted enough time for worship since the Chichewa group was too big which needed a church of their own.[263] The idea of breaking away was presented to Zolozolo Church by Potani Mwale and Stanly Bwanali. When permission was granted, the whole Chichewa group of 120 people left Zolozolo Church and started a church west of Ukani Private School in 2010. Later, the church moved out of the place to the present one because they were in conflict with the Muslims who originally had started a mosque at the place.[264]

---

[260] Int. Charity Msukwa, Chairlady of Mzilawayingwe CCAP Church, Mzilawayingwe, 22.8.2013.

[261] Int. Kayange, Church Elder at Mzilawayingwe CCAP Church, Mzilawayingwe, 22.8.2013.

[262] Int. Mary Banda, Church Member at Chiputula Jehovah's Witness, Mzilawayingwe, 22.8.2013.

[263] Int. Stanly Bwanali, Church Member at Chiputula Jehovah's Witness, Upper Stadium, 22.8.2013.

[264] Int. Potani Mwale, Church Member at Chiputula Jehovah's Witness, Upper Stadium, 22.8.2013.

The average church attendance is 110 people, of whom the majority are women. The church is dominated by the age group of 15 to 35 years. New members join the church through transfers and by birth. The majority of church members are Chichewa speaking people. New converts join the church through door to door visitation. New converts join baptism class before water baptism.

The language of the church is Chichewa. Leadership is for men only.

3.3.9 Pentecost Christ Church International

Pentecost Christ Church International is in Mzilawayingwe area, located 100 metres east of Mzuzu Stadium.

The church was started by Bishop Alex Msikiti in 2003 as a breakaway from Mzuzu International Pentecostal Holiness Church. Bishop Alex Msikiti was a Pastor at Mzuzu International Pentecost Holiness Church. He was dismissed from the church by the National Head Office in Blantyre because of the disagreements between him and the National Office. The disagreements arose when Bishop Msikiti was enquiring from the Head Office on why churches from the north were not supported when all other churches from south and centre were being supported.[265] The disagreement was too big in the sense that the Head Office could not contain Bishop Msikiti as their Pastor anymore. He was ordered to prepare himself for two weeks and leave the church for his own home, Blantyre. However, he was not given transport for going home. Due to transport problems, he failed to go home; instead, he was encouraged by church members to start his own church.[266] Bishop Miskiti started Pentecost Christ Church International with 200 members from his former church. They bought a piece of land behind Pastor's house where they built a temporal church.

The average church attendance is 150 people, of whom the majority are women. The church is dominated by the age group of 14 to 40 years. New members join the church by conversion. New converts join the church through open-air rallies and deliverance sessions done at the

---

[265] Int. Pastor Tonny Mkamanga, Church Pastor at Mzuzu International Pentecost Holiness Church, Mzuzu, 2.9.2013.
[266] Int. Chricy Msikiti, Wife to Bishop Msikiti, Pentecost Christ Church International, Mzilawayingwe, 23.8.2013.

church on a weekly basis.[267] The language of the church is English with Chichewa interpretation. Church leadership is free for both sexes.

3.3.10 One More Time Christian Movement

One More Time Christian Movement is located along Mzuzu Stadium in Mzilawayingwe road. The church is 200 metres west of Mzuzu Stadium.

One More Time Christian Movement Church was started by Pastor Job Major Nyirenda in 2005. He started a church with a vision from God to deliver people from their sicknesses.[268] Pastor Nyirenda had no ideas on how to start a church until when he was called by his friend to escort him where he was going to cheer the sick. While there he prayed for the sick and they were healed. The incident gave him courage to start a church. He started a church with his family worshiping in his house. Later, he was joined by the family of John Mlowoka who together with him started visiting people door to door and delivering them from sicknesses. Many people joined him worshiping at his house where he erected a temporary church structure.

The church has two permanent members, the Pastor and the wife, while other members are coming on special reasons, i.e. healing and deliverance.[269] However, the average church attendance is four people, of whom the majority are women. The dominant language of the church is English translated into Chichewa by the wife. The leader of the church is the Pastor himself.

3.3.11 Mzilawayingwe Last Reformed Church

Mzilawayingwe Last Reformed Church is in Mzilawayingwe area, located along Mzilawayingwe - Chiputula road, behind Mzuzu Stadium. The church is 150 metres west of Mzuzu Stadium.

---

[267] The reason why Bishop Msikiti seemed to be loved by people of his former church is because of the gift of the Holy Spirit of deliverance. Many people have been helped from their physical and spiritual oppressions. Int. Chricy Msikiti, Wife to Bishop Msikiti, Pentecost Christ Church International, Mzilawayingwe, 23.8.2013.

[268] Int. John Mlowoka, Former Church Member of One More Time Christian Movement Church, Mzilawayingwe, 23.8.2013.

[269] Int. Pastor Job Major Nyirenda, Church Pastor, One More Time Christian Movement Church Mzilawayingwe, 23.8.2013.

The Church was started in 2003 by Rev Saka who came to Mzuzu from Nkhatabay to look for employment. Rev Saka, who was renting a house at Mzilawayingwe, was not happy to see members of Last Reformed Church, who were living at Mzilawayingwe, going to Zolozolo or Masasa for worship.[270] He talked to Mzilawayingwe Church members to have one Central place of worship. When Mzilawayingwe Church members accepted the idea, he went further asking Zolozolo and Masasa churches to allow Mzilawayingwe members to start a church in their area. The two churches accepted the request. The church started with eight people worshiping in the house of Gogo Nkhumbila Kanyaso while Rev Saka was a church minister.[271] Rev Saka did door to door evangelism whereby after a year the church become full and made them to change worship place from Gogo Nkhumbila Kanyaso's house to a rent at Royal Private Secondary school. Later, they bought a piece of land where they built a church building.

The church building has a capacity of 50 people. The average church attendance is 15 people, of whom the majority are women.[272] The church is dominated by the age group of 30 to 55 years. The majority of church members are people form Nkhatabay. New members join the church through transfers. New converts join the church through marriage. When converted, they join the church by water baptism without baptism classes.

The language of the church is Chitumbuka. Church leadership is for men only.

3.3.12 St Peter's Parish

St Peter's Parish is in St John's area, located near Marymount in Zolozolo. The church is surrounded by St John's Hospital, St Peters Primary School and Mzuzu Stadium.

---

[270] Int. Nkhumbila Kanyaso, Church Member, Mzilawayingwe Last Reformed Church, Mzilawayingwe, 23.8.2013.

[271] Int. Akim Banda, Church Member, Mzilawayingwe Last Reformed Church, Mzilawayingwe, 23.8.2013.

[272] The church has more women than men because of polygamy. Some men have married more than two wives, and all of them have joined the church. The church allows men too many as many wives as he can provide he can take care of them. Int. Nkhumbila Kanyaso, Church Member, Mzilawayingwe Last Reformed Church, Mzilawayingwe, 23.8.2013.

The Parish was started in 1955 by Bishop St Denis who came from Katete Mission. The idea to have a church in Mzuzu was to look for a central place which could help in coordinating worship centres in the northern region. Chiphaso Mission established a mission station in Lilongwe in 1935 to coordinate worship centres in the north. The Mission was transferred to Katete because Lilongwe proved to be an inaccessible place to reach from the northern region. Bishop St Denis from Northern Ireland was sent to Katete Mission[273] to help in running the missions and churches in the north. For easy coordination of churches in the north, Bishop St Denis thought to transfer headquarters of the Church from Katete to Mzuzu because Katete was not a central place for churches in the northern region, and the other reason was that Mzuzu became a provincial headquarters for the Northern Province.[274]

When he came to Mzuzu in 1954, he asked for a piece of land from the Provincial Commissioner, who happened to came from the same area, where he built the mission station. The Provincial Commissioner gave him two places, Katoto and Lunyangwa. He first built his house at Katoto before building a church at Lunyangwa. Bishop Denis converted people through material help i.e. sewing needles, money, sending children to school for free at Mzuzu CCAP Primary School and door to door visitations. His activities made him to become closer to people to the extent that he was sniffing tobacco with them.[275] The first gathering of a church at St Peters was done in 1955 with 30 people.

The church has a church building with the capacity of 700 people. The church has 900 members with average church attendance of 600 people, of whom the majority are women. The church is dominated by the age group of 14 to 45 years. The majority of the church members are coming from Chitipa, Karonga and Kasungu in areas of original Roman Catholic Mission Stations. New members join the church through transfers and by

---

[273] Sister Enestina Chirwa was the first person to be baptized at Katete Mission. Sister Chirwa became the first Roman Catholic nun in the northern region. The father of Sister Enestina Chirwa was a worker at Katete Mission, who became a Roman Catholic Christian while in Zimbabwe. Int. Bonavential Mvula, Church Member at St Peters Church, Chiputula, 23.8.2013.
[274] Int. Mbulukutu Chirwa, Church Member at St Augustine, Lupaso, 23.8.2013.
[275] Int. Bonavential Mvula, Church Member at St Peters Church, Chiputula, 23.8.2013.

birth. New converts join the church through marriages. Newly converted members join baptism class before water baptism.

The church has two languages; English and Chitumbuka. Leadership is by men only.

3.3.13 Chasefu Church of African Presbyterian

Chasefu Church of African Presbyterian is in Kataba area, located off Mzuzu - Zolozolo road and Chasefu Seventh-day Private Secondary School.

The Church started from Masasa Church of African Presbyterian in 1993. Church of African Presbyterian started at Masasa. The Masasa Church was divided into four branches; Masasa, Mchengautuwa, Luwinga and Chasefu because people from different places were complaining about long distances they were travelling to Masasa for worship services.[276] One of the people who requested the division of Masasa Church was Type Msumba who also happened to start Chasefu Church. The Chasefu Church was under the leadership of Type Msumba who offered his house at Zolozolo to be a worshiping centre. Slowly, the church started growing and the house became small. Type Msumba gave the church his own piece of land at Zolozolo to west for free to build a church. When the church was being built, Type Msumba took back his land because of the suspension he was given when he quarrelled with a friend.[277] The church left the place and went to Mzilawayingwe where they were renting a house. Later, they asked the City Assembly to give them a piece of land in Upper Chasefu where they have built a church.

The church building has a capacity of 300 people. There are 300 members in the church with an average church attendance of 250 people. The majority of church members are women. The church is dominated by the age group of 15 to 35 years. The majority of the church members are people from Chilumba and Nkhatabay.[278] New members

---

[276] Int. Rev. Mwase, Parish Minister at Chasefu Church of African Presbyterian, Viyele, 23.8.2013.

[277] Int. Benweck Mwase, Church Elder at Chasefu Church of African Presbyterian, Kataba, 23.8.2013.

[278] Church members follow churches of their home areas. The church of Africa Presbyterian was started from Ching'oma in Nkhata bay and was quickly accepted at Chilumba and Chitipa. Many members of Church of African

join the church through transfers and by birth. New converts join the church through individual contacts and door to door evangelism, when converted they join baptism classes before water baptism.

The language of the church is Chitumbuka. Leadership is dominated by men.

3.4 Religious Places in Zolozolo Ward

3.4.1 Holy Family Catholic Church

Holy Family Catholic Church is in Upper Zolozolo, located off Mzuzu to Matete road. The church is situated within the premises of Mzuzu Technical College.

The church started in Mzuzu from Banga Technical Collage in Nkhata bay in 1960. Father Andrew Barre started the church in Mzuzu when Banga Technical College was moved from Banga in Nkhata bay to Mzuzu. The college was moved to Mzuzu because Mzuzu had electricity supply which was needed to run college machines, and because the college wanted to be closer to the Diocese. Holy Family Church started with the idea of providing spiritual help to students at Banga Technical College and then at Mzuzu Technical College. While in Mzuzu, the college felt the need for a local Roman Catholic community to be part of the Holy Family Catholic Church, and this made them to ask the St Peters Catholic Church to allow all church members living closer to Mzuzu Technical College to be worshiping at Holy Family Catholic Church.[279] When permission was granted, all Catholic members from Zolozolo and other surrounding areas started worshiping at the college together with students.[280] Holy Family Catholic Church was an outstation of St Peter's Parish before it became a Parish in 2013. The parish is governed by White Fathers' Missionaries who are not Diocesan Fathers.

The church has a church building with the capacity of 500 people. There are 400 members in the church with average church attendance of 300

Presbyterian are coming from these areas Int. Rev. Mwase, Parish Minister at Chasefu Church of African Presbyterian, Viyele, 23.8.2013.

[279] Int. John Kondowe Principle Mzuzu Technical Collage, Church Elder, Holly Family Catholic, Zolozolo, 24.8.2013.

[280] Int. Mukhondwa, Church member, Holly Family Catholic Church, Zolozolo, 24.8.2013.

people, of whom the majority are women. The church is dominated by the age group of 20 to 50 years. The majority of church members are people from Karonga and Chitipa. New members join the church through transfers and by birth. New converts join the church through marriages. When converted they join baptism class before being baptized.

Chitumbuka is the dominant language of the church. Leadership is dominated by men.

3.4.2 Zolozolo Brethren Christian Assembly

Zolozolo Brethren Christian Assembly is in Zolozolo area, located along Mzuzu Stadium - Mzuzu Technical College road. The church is 150 metres east of Zolozolo CCAP Church.

Zolozolo Brethren Christian Assembly started as a fellowship by Harvey Mkandawire and Piouson Halawa in 1997. The church started from an advertisement which was on the internet asking interested people from all nations to start a church of Brethren Christian Assembly with the help of Pastor Paul Pasco in Canada.[281] Harvey Mkandawire and Piouson Halawa responded to the advertisement and were permitted to start a fellowship. Later Pastor Paul Pasco from Canada came to Malawi at Mzuzu with an evangelism team. They organized a big rally at Mzuzu Stadium where many people surrendered their lives to Jesus Christ. Further Pastor Pasco organized door to door visitations and open-air rallies. His evangelistic campaign made many people to follow him; as a result, he started a central worship with 10 people at Chenda Hotel Hall.[282] Later, they bought a piece of land at Zolozolo where they have built a permanent church building.

The average church attendance is 30 people, of whom the majority are women. The church is dominated by the age group of 15 to 25 years. New members join the church by conversion through receiving material help.[283] All church members are given transport to and from church service. New converts join baptism class before being baptized.

---

[281] Int. Hyce Msukwa, Church Member, Zolozolo Brethren Christian Assembly, Zolozolo, 23.8.2013.

[282] Int. Mushali, Former Church Member, Zolozolo Brethren Christian Assembly, Zolozolo, 27.8.2013.

[283] Int. Hyce Msukwa, Church Member, Zolozolo Brethren Christian Assembly, Zolozolo, 23.8.2013.

The language of the church is English with Chitumbuka translation. Leadership is for men only.

3.4.3 Zolozolo Seventh-day Baptist Church

Zolozolo Seventh-day Baptist Church is located off Mzuzu Stadium - Mzuzu Technical College road.

The church was started in 1972 by members of the church who were already members of the church before coming to Mzuzu. Mrs Milliam Theu, Mzumara and Mazunda initiated the starting of the church by sensitizing other members of the church about the importance of starting the church in Mzuzu. The church started with seven families worshiping in old Mzuzu Stadium Hall. When the church was being established, Pastor Absalom Harawa was sent to Mzuzu to nurture the congregation.[284] In 1974, the church left Mzuzu Stadium Hall to Zolozolo where they built a temporary church building. They left Mzuzu Stadium Hall because Mzuzu City Assembly increased the amount of rental payments.

The church has a church building with the capacity of 70 people with an average church attendance of 40 people. The majority of church members are women. The dominant age group is from 25 to 40 years. New members join the church through transfers and by birth. New converts join the church through efforts, and material help given to the elderly and people with disabilities. New converts join baptism class before water baptism.

The dominant language of the church is Chitumbuka. Leadership is dominated by men.

3.4.4 Zolozolo CCAP Church

Zolozolo CCAP Church is located at the road junction of Mzuzu Stadium - Mzuzu Technical College road and Zolozolo - Luwinga road.

Zolozolo Church started in 1960 as an outstation of Mzuzu CCAP Church. Petros Lweska Nyirongo and Kamanje asked Mzuzu Session to give permission to Zolozolo section to start a church at Zolozolo in order to ease the problem of movement from Zolozolo to Mzuzu CCAP Church

---

[284] Int. Pastor Isaac Chisi, Church Pastor at Zolozolo Seventh-day Baptist Church, Zolozolo, 3.9.2013.

due to poor road network.[285] At that time there was no possible road network to town apart from via Matete - St John's Hospital road. The Mzuzu Church accepted the request and the church started with 15 people worshiping under a Muwula tree until when they had built a glass thatched church at where they have constructed a Manse. The church became a congregation from Kataba session in 1989 under Rev Franklin Chunga.[286]

Zolozolo Church has two Sunday services, English and Chitumbuka, respectively. The church has 1600 members with an average church attendance of 700 people in both services. The majority of church members are women. The dominant age group is 18 to 50 years. New members join the church through transfers and by birth. New converts join the church through door to door visitation and open-air evangelism. New converts join baptism class before water baptism.

Languages of the church are Chichewa and English respectively. Leadership is for both sexes.

3.4.5 Mganthira CCAP Church

Mganthira CCAP Church is located off Marymount to Luwinga road at Lunyangwa Research Station towards Lunyangwa Research Offices.

Mganthira CCAP Church started 1900 as an outstation of Ekwendeni Mission Station. The idea to start a church was to give spiritual and formal education to people of Mafuta Kaunda and Luwinga Singini living at Mganthira area.[287] (Refer here to Chapter Two page 19). Further the church continued giving spiritual help to people who were working with the Tung Oil Estate at Mganthira and nearby villages after Mafuta Kaunda and Luwinga Singini had left the area.[288] When Tung Oil Estate had stopped from working in the area, Lunyangwa Research Station took over the area, and the church restarted again giving spiritual help to

---

[285] Int. Groscestar Sangano, Session Treasurer at Zolozolo CCAP Church, Zolozolo, 10.9.2013.

[286] Rev. Franklin Chunga started Zolozolo Congregation when he came back from living in Scotland. The money he used to start with building the church was given to him when he was leaving Scotland for Malawi.

[287] Int. Spinord Kaunda, born and brought up at Mganthila (1915 to 1930), Lupaso, 5.10.2012.

[288] Int. Agnes Nhlema, Mzuzu Presbytery women's Coordinator, whose father was teaching at Mganthila Primary School in 1954, Lupaso, 10.12.2011.

people working with Lunyangwa Research Station and to the surrounding villages. The church started by congregating under a *mpapa* tree and later for a long time they were worshiping in a class room which was burnt by Village Headman Mafuta Kaunda in a way of protesting against using the school for recruiting his people for World War 1. Since then worshippers went back to mpapa tree until when a certain general manager of Lunyangwa Research Station who was a member of CCAP Church gave them a piece of land where they build a church. The church had moved in three phases; it first started during Mafuta Kaunda and Luwinga Singini time and it stopped, then it restarted during Tung Oil Estate and it stopped, and finally it restarted during Lunyangwa Research Station to the present day. The church today is an outstation of Zolozolo CCAP Church.

The church building has a capacity of 80 people. The church has 100 members with average church attendance of people. The majority of church members are women. New members join the church through transfers and by birth. New converts join the church through door to door visitations. New converts join baptism class before being baptized by water.

The language of the church is Chitumbuka. Church leadership is for both sexes.

3.4.6 Upper Zolozolo New Apostolic Church

Upper Zolozolo New Apostolic Church is in Zolozolo area, located hundred metres south east of Zolozolo CCAP Church.

The Church started in 1970 as a fellowship among people who were already members of the church who came from Bwengu area in Rumphi to look for employment in Mzuzu. The church started with five people worshiping in the house of Henwood Mkandawire; however, the official opening of the church was done in 1974 by a group of German missionaries led by Apostle Felenades.[289] The German group came from Zambia to Mzuzu through Bwengu, where there was an existing church. While in Mzuzu, they organized a big open-air rally and door to door visitations. The results of the rally were that many people surrendered

---

[289] Int. Kondwani Chatata, Church Member at Upper Zolozolo New Apostolic Church, Zolozolo, 16.9.2013. – Felenades seems to refer to Apostle Hubert Howes Fernades (1910-1976), Bishop Rhodesia, Zambia and Malawi.

their lives to Jesus Christ and the beginning of a New Apostolic Church at Zolozolo. Apostle Felenades built a church at Zolozolo.[290]

The church building has a capacity of 100 people. There are 80 members in the church and the average church attendance is 60 people, of whom the majority are women. The dominant age group is 20 to 45 years. New members join the church through transfers and by birth. The church is dominated by people from Rumphi. New converts join the church through door to door visitations. The newly converted members join baptism class before being baptized by water.

The language of the church is Chitumbuka. Church leadership is for men only.

3.4.7 *Zolozolo West New Apostolic Church*

Zolozolo West New Apostolic Church is in Zolozolo area, located hundred metres west of Zolozolo centre.

The church was started in 2000 as a branch of Upper Zolozolo New Apostolic Church. Zolozolo West New Apostolic Church started by Apostle Msiska and Apostle Nzima. The church started because of increased number of church members at both areas, Upper Zolozolo and Zolozolo West.[291] The church started with 50 people of whom the majority were elderly.

The church building has a capacity of 100 people. There are 120 members in the church with an average church attendance of 60 people. The majority of church members are women. The dominant age group of the church is 40 to 60 years. The church is dominated by people from Rumphi district. New members join the church through transfers and by birth. New converts join the church through home cell prayers. The newly converted members join baptism class before water baptism.

Church leadership is for men only. The language of the church is Chitumbuka.

---

[290] Int. Clement C. Makwakwa, Church Member at Upper Zolozolo New Apostolic Church, Zolozolo West, 10.9.2013.

[291] Int. Clement C. Makwakwa, Church Member at Zolozolo West New Apostolic Church, Zolozolo West, 10.9.2013.

3.4.8 African National Church

Zolozolo African National Church is located at the centre of Zolozolo, hundred metres south of Zolozolo CCAP Church.

The Church was started in 1970 by members of Chilumba African National Church who came to Mzuzu to look for employment. Mchunga, Mbale and Kaluba started African National Church at Zolozolo because they could not afford to go and worship at Luwinga African Nation Church at Area 1B due to long distances. The church started with 15 people worshiping in Mzuzu Stadium Hall. They stopped from worshiping in Mzuzu Stadium Hall because they were failing to pay rents; as a result, they built a temporary church at Zolozolo.

The average church attendance is 100 people, of whom the majority are women. The church is dominated by people from Chilumba and Chitipa.[292] New members join the church through transfers. New converts join the church by marriage and evangelism.[293] New converts join baptism class for three weeks before being baptized by water.

The church is led by men. The language of the church is Chitumbuka.

3.4.9 Chiputula Chipangano Church

Chiputula Chipangano Church is at Lower Zolozolo area, located at the four ways road junction of Chiputula to Zolozolo Clinic road and Zolozolo to Luwinga road.

Chiputula Chipangano Church was started in 1940 by Chazuka Kaunda and G. Kayira who came from Chintheche to Mzuzu on church plantation tour.[294] The church started with four people worshiping in a glass thatched house where Chazuka Kaunda and G. Kayira were renting. The first converts were Chikundula, Sackson Phiri and Mvula who later

---

[292] Chilumba and Chitipa are the early areas of African National Church. Int. Yohane Beka Mkandawire, Church Member at Luwinga Africa National Church, Luwinga, 20.8.2013.

[293] The most attractive policy of African National Church is marriage. The policy gives freedom to anyone who wants to marry more than one wife, Int. Yohane Beka Mkandawire, Church Member at Luwinga Africa National Church, Luwinga, 20.8.2013.

[294] Int. Yilinase Chisi, Church Member at Chiputula Chipangano Church, Lower Zolozolo, 10.9.2013.

became Pastors of the church. The church left a rented house to where they built a church building.

The average church attendance is 80 people, of whom the majority are women. The dominant age group of the church is 25 to 50 years. New members join the church through transfers. New converts join the church through face to face evangelism. Converted members go straight for water baptism without going to baptism class.

The language of the church is Chitumbuka. The church is led by men.

3.4.10 Zolozolo Power Ministry of the Living God Church

Zolozolo Power Ministry of the Living God Church is in Lower Zolozolo area, located along Zolozolo CCAP Church - Matope road, hundred meters east of Zolozolo Clinic.

The church was started by Daniel Kamanga in 1994. It started as a fellowship worshiping in the house of Daniel Kamanga. Daniel Kamanga and his wife were later joined by Leanard Beza and Felimon Kaluba. The founder of the church was a former member of Zolozolo CCAP Church; he decided to leave Zolozolo CCAP Church while looking for freedom of worship where he could sing choruses and do deliverance.[295]

The church is still worshiping in the house of Daniel Kamanga. The average church attendance is 20 people, of whom the majority are women. The dominant age group of the church is 18 to 25 years. New members join the church by conversion.[296] New converts join baptism class before being baptized by water.

The language of the church is Chichewa. Leadership of the church is dominated by men.

3.4.11 Ching'ambo Word of Faith Temple International

Ching'ambo Word of Faith Temple International is in Chiputula area, located along Chiputula central - Ching'ambo road at Mandingo Private Secondary School.

---

[295] Int. Pastor Daniel Kamanga, Church Pastor at Zolozolo Power Ministry of the Living God Church, Lower Zolozolo, 10.9.2013.
[296] Ibid.

The church was started in 2005 by Bishop Mwalindima, who came from Blantyre to plant a church in Mzuzu.[297] Bishop Mwalindima started the church as a fellowship with his wife and his family worshiping in his house. The fellowship was later joined by a group of people who were involved in healing ministry. When the group of members became bigger, they changed the worshiping place to Chiputula Primary School where they focused their worship on healing people rather than on pastoral care. In 2013, the fellowship group was joined by another fellowship under the leadership of Wyson Alex Mbewe. The two groups became one church and they decided to move from worshiping at Chiputula Primary School to Mandingo Private Secondary School. The church discourages her believers from going to hospital for treatment rather it encourages them to depend upon prayers when someone is sick.

The church has 20 members with average church attendance of 12 people, of whom the majority are women. The dominant age group of the church is 20 to 35 years. The majority of church members come from Mulanje. New members join the church through conversion. New converts join the church through door to door visitation. New converts join baptism class before being baptized by water.

The language of the church is Chichewa. Church leadership is dominated by men.

3.4.12 Zolozolo West Seventh-day Adventist Church

Zolozolo West Seventh-day Adventist Church is located at the road junction of Zolozolo to Luwinga from Lower Zolozolo market towards Upper Zolozolo.

The church started in 1995 as an outstation of Chasefu Seventh–day Adventist Church. The idea to start a church at Zolozolo West came from Gogo Siwo, an old man, who was unable to walk to Chasefu church. The man asked elders from Zolozolo West to consider the long distances old people and children were travelling from Zolozolo West to Upper Chasefu for church services.[298] Lt. Nyondo took up the idea and asked Chasefu Church to give permission to start a church at Zolozolo west in

---

[297] Int. Pastor Wyson Alex Mbewe, Church Pastor, Ching'ambo Word of Faith Temple International Church, Lower Zolozolo, 10.9.2013.
[298] Int. Davie Soko, Church Elder, Ching'ambo Word of Faith Temple International Church, Lower Zolozolo, 11.9.2013.

order to lessen long distances people were travelling for church services at Chasefu. When permission was granted, the church started out of a 21 days effort done at the house of Gogo Siwo.[299] After a 21 days effort, the church continued with 20 people worshiping in the house of Gogo Siwo for one year. Later Mr. B.E.S. Msowoya a church member gave a piece of land to a church where they built a church.

The church building has a capacity of 200 members. Church membership is 220 with the average church attendance of 180 people, of whom the majority are women. The dominating age group of the church is 13 to 40 years. The majority of church members come from Mzimba and Nkhatabay. New members join the church through transfers and by birth. Converts join the church through efforts. New converts go for baptism after attending baptism class.

The language of the church is Chichewa. Church leadership is dominated by men.

3.4.13 Zolozolo East Seventh-day Adventist Church

Zolozolo East Seventh-day Adventist Church is in Upper Zolozolo area, located off Zolozolo - Matope road.

The Church started in 2001 as an outstation of Chasefu Seventh-day Adventist Church. The reason to start the church was in consideration of the growth of membership at Zolozolo East and long distances people were travelling to upper Chasefu for church services. The church started out of a 21 days effort organized by people from Chasefu Church under the leadership of F.C. Kamanga and P.C. Mhoni. The results of the effort were that many people surrendered their lives to Jesus Christ which led to the beginning of Seventh-day Adventist Church in the area. The church started with 15 people worshiping at Zolozolo Primary School for two years. Later, the church bought a piece of land where they built a church and started worshiping there.

The church building has a capacity of 200 people. Church membership is 160 with average church attendance of 120 people, of whom the majority are women. The dominant age group of the church is 20 to 40 years. The majority of church members come from Mzimba and Nkhata-

---

[299] Traditionally, Seventh-day Adventist Church starts out of 21 days, an open-air rally or crusade. Int. Arther Chirwa, Former Church Member of Chasefu Seventh-day Adventist Church, Chibavi, 10.12.2010.

bay. New members join the church through transfers and by birth. New converts join the church through efforts. New converts go for baptism class before being baptized by water.

The language of the church is Chichewa. Leadership of the church is dominated by men.

3.4.14 Matope CCAP Church

Matope CCAP Church is in Lower Zolozolo area, located off Zolozolo to Luwinga road 300 metres from lower Zolozolo market towards upper Zolozolo.

Matope CCAP church started in 1998 as a substation of Katawa CCAP Church. Medson Y. Mzumara and I.M. Phiri asked Katawa Session to give permission to Christians from Matope to start their church to ease long distances they were travelling to Katawa church for church services.[300] Katawa session which was led by Rev M.M.D. Sibande accepted the request upon looking at the growth of membership in the area. The church started with 40 people worshiping in a glass thatched church. At present the church is under Zolozolo Session, however, in January, 2014, it will be an independent congregation.[301]

The church has 1300 members with an average church attendance of 600 people, of whom the majority are women. The dominant age group of the church is from 15 to 45 years. New members join the church through transfers and by birth. New converts join the church through door to door visitation and open-air rallies. New converts join baptism class before being baptism by water.

The church has two services English and Chitumbuka respectively. Church leadership is for both sexes; male and female, however, men are dominating.

3.4.15 Zolozolo Bethsaida Fellowship

Zolozolo Bethsaida Fellowship is in Lower Zolozolo area, located off Zolozolo - Luwinga road, 50 metres north of Matope CCAP Church.

---

[300] Int. Selfridge Ng'ambi, Session Clerk at Katawa CCAP Church, Katawa, 20.11.2013.
[301] CCAP Mzuzu Presbytery Budget Minute, 23.11.2013.

The fellowship was started by Gogo Molly Mhango in 2000. Molly Mhanga was a former member of Katawa CCAP Church; she was initiated to start a fellowship by Pastor Luhanga who organized a seminar at Mtayisi Hall for people who wanted to start a church, ministry and fellowship.[302] After the seminar, participants were ordained to preach the word of God and to lay on hands on the sick. Gogo Molly Mhango started a fellowship with her own family, later she was joined by 15 people. The fellowship is worshiping in the house of gogo Molly Mhango.

The average fellowship attendance is 10 people, of whom the majority are women. Fellowship members are coming from different churches. New members join the fellowship due to healing and deliverance.

The language of the fellowship is Chitumbuka. The fellowship is led by women.

3.4.16 Heart Healing Ministries

Heart Healing Ministries is in Chiputula area, located along Zolozolo - Ching'ambo road, close to Chiputula Primary School.

The church was started as a fellowship by Pastor Charles Chiwele in 2008. Pastor Charles Chiwele started a church with his wife and his family worshiping in his house. Later, he was joined by Chizaso Munyimbiri who became an assistant Pastor of the church. Many people joined the church because of healing miracles the Pastor was doing. The first converts were Mather Phiri and Ruth Chimutanda, whose relatives were healed after being bewitched by their fathers respectively.[303]

The average church attendance is 18 people, of whom the majority are women. The church is dominated by married people. New members join the church by conversion. The majority of church members are converted through healing miracles. New converts join the church without going through baptism classes.

The language of the church is Chichewa. The church leadership is dominating by men.

---

[302] Int. Gogo Molly Mhango, Founder of Zolozolo Bethsaida Fellowship, Lower Zolozolo, 11.9.2013.
[303] Int, Name Withheld.

3.4.17 Zolozolo West Full Gospel of God Church

Zolozolo West Full Gospel of God Church is located along Zolozolo to Ching'ambo road, at a place commonly known as Tchongwe.

The church started in 1997 as a branch of Mchengautuwa Church. The church started to ease the problem of long distances church members from Zolozolo West were travelling to Mchengautuwa for church services. The request to start a church at Zolozolo West was presented to Mchengautuwa Church by Mama Kachere and Mbewe. The permission was granted to start a church at Zolozolo West and the church started with three families worshiping in the house of Mama Kachere. The church later moved to where they built a temporary church where they bought a piece of land.

The church building has a capacity of 50 people. The membership of the church is 50 with average church attendance of 30 people, of whom the majority are women. The dominant age group of the church is 10 to 16 years. New members join the church by conversion. New converts join the church through door to door visitation and open-air rallies. Converted members join the church without going through baptism class.

The language of the church is Chichewa. The church is led by both sexes.

3.4.18 Zolozolo West Baptist Convention of Malawi Church

Zolozolo West Baptist Convention Church is in Ching'ambo area, located along Zolozolo - Lunyangwa road, close to Ching'ambo Primary School.

Zolozolo West Baptist Convention Church started as a branch of Chibavi Church in 2001. The church started because church members at Zolozolo West were travelling long distances to Chibavi for church services. When permission to start a church at Zolozolo West was granted, Rincon Sichali, Tafazatha Mbewe and Manji Nkhata affiliated the branch to Mzuzu Baptist Convention Church. The church started with nine people worshiping in the house of Rincon Sichali, later, they were worshiping in a rented house and finally moved to where they have built a church.

The church has 90 members with average church attendance of 70 people, of whom the majority are women. The dominant age group of the church is 12 to 25 years. New members join the church through transfers and by birth. New converts join the church through door to door visitation and open-air rallies. New converts join baptism class before being baptized.

The language of the church is Chitumbuka. Church leadership is for both sexes.

3.4.19 Zolozolo West Assemblies of God Church

Zolozolo West Assemblies of God is in Ching'ambo area, located along Zolozolo - Luwinga via Botanic road, next to Ching'ambo Primary School.

The Church started in 2000 as a branch of Katawa Assemblies of God Church. The church started in response to Pilingu and B. Phiri asking Kataba Church to consider the growth of church members at Zolozolo West and long distances people were travelling to Katawa Assemblies of God Church for worship.[304] When Katawa church accepted the request, the church started with nine people worshiping in the house of Pilingu. The church bought a piece of land where they built a church.

The average church attendance is 30 people, of whom the majority are women. The dominant age group of the church is 10 to 25 years. New members join the church through transfers. New converts join the church through open-air rallies and fellowship. New members join baptism class before being baptized by water.

The language of the church is Chichewa. Church leadership is for both sexes.

3.4.20 Zolozolo West Chipangano Church

Zolozolo West Chipangano Church is in Ching'ambo area, located along Zolozolo - Luwinga via Botanic road, 150 metres south of Ching'ambo Primary School.

The church started in 2008 as an outstation of Chiputula Chipangano Church. Rev. Juwa and Nyamphalo asked Chiputula Chipangano Church to consider the growth of church members at Zolozolo West and long distances people from Zolozolo were travelling to Chiputula for church services.[305] The Church started with 20 people worshiping in an abandoned church hall.

---

[304] Int. Bernard Mkwala, Church Member, Zolozolo West Assemblies of God Lower Zolozolo, 12.9.2013.

[305] Int. Catherine Mhone, Church Member at Zolozolo West Chipangano Church, Lower Zolozolo, 12.9.2013.

The church has 40 members with average church attendance of 30 people. The majority of church members are women. The church is dominated by married people from the age group of 30 to 50 years. New members join the church through transfers. New converts join the church through face to face discussions on policy and church doctrines.[306] New converts join the church without going through baptism class.

The language of the church is Chitumbuka. The church is led by men.

3.4.21 *Zolozolo West Roman Catholic Church*

Zolozolo West Roman Catholic Church is in Lower Zolozolo area, located along Zolozolo - Luwinga - Botanic road, 200 metres west of Ching'ambo Primary School.

The Church started in 1998 as an outstation of Zolozolo Technical College Holy Family Catholic Church. The idea to have a church at Zolozolo West was presented to Zolozolo Technical College Holy Family Catholic Church by Samuel Ngulube, Mhlanga and Ngoma. These people asked the church to consider the growth of church members in the area and long distances people were travelling for church services at Zolozolo Technical College Church.[307] When the Holy Family Catholic Church accepted the request, the church started with 20 people worshiping in a temporary church built where they bought a piece of land.

The church has 200 members with average church attendance of 150 people. The majority of church members are women. New members join the church through transfers and by birth. New converts join the church through marriages. New converts join baptism class before being baptized by water.

The language of the church is Chitumbuka. Church leadership is dominated by men.

3.4.22 *Zolozolo West Church of Christ*

Zolozolo West Church of Christ is in Lower Zolozolo area, located along Botanic - Chiputula road.

---

[306] Int. Manase Kaunda, Church Member at Zolozolo West Chipangano Church, Lower Zolozolo, 12.9.2013.
[307] Int. Mercy Wakisa, Church Member at Zolozolo West Catholic Church, Lower Zolozolo, 12.9.2013.

The church was started in 2005 from Jomo Church of Christ behind Regional Police Station. Rev. Theu, Chanjo Msiska, G.V. Vikhumbo and Precious Jere requested Jomo Church to consider the growth of church members at Zolozolo West and long distances people from Zolozolo West were travelling to church service at Jomo Kenyatta Church.[308] When the request was accepted, they started a church with 30 people worshiping under a *muwula* tree. They built a glass thatched church where they bought a piece of land. The church gave birth to Chiputula and Botanic churches.

The average church attendance is 50 people, of whom the majority are women. The dominant age group of the church is 12 to 25 years. New members join the church by birth and transfers. New converts join the church through door to door visitations. New converts go for water baptism without going through baptism class.

The church is led by men. The language of the church is Chitumbuka.

3.4.23 Botanic Church of Christ

Botanic Church of Christ is in Botanic area, located along Zolozolo - Luwinga - Botanic road, at Zolozolo Community Day Secondary School.

The church started in 2005 due to quarrels among Zolozolo West Church of Christ members. The quarrels were between people belonging to Tonga and Tumbuka tribes. These people were quarreling with each other for a long time because of leadership scrambles.[309] When Goodfully Kaunda, senior leader of the Tonga group, became a leader of the church, the Tonga group decided to leave the church and start their own church at Botanic.[310] The church started with 10 people worshiping at Zolozolo Day Secondary School. The first leaders of the church were Goodfully Kaunda, Chipeta and Choma.

---

[308] Int. Joseph Muzigula Banda, Church Elder at Zolozolo West Church of Christ, Lower Zolozolo, 12.9.2013.

[309] Int. Mary Luhanga, Church Member, Botanic Church of Christ, at Botanic, Lower Zolozolo, 14.9.2013.

[310] Goodfully Kaunda Senior Tonga leader convinced his fellow Tonga church members to start Church of Christ for Tonga Members to avoid further serious conflict between Tonga and Tumbuka tribes where Zolozolo West Church of Christ was heading to. The Tonga people were being accused of pride and self-righteousness Int. Mary Luhanga, Church Member, Botanic Church of Christ is at Botanic, Lower Zolozolo, 14.9.2013.

The average church attendance is 15 people, of whom the majority are women. The dominant members of the church are Tonga people. New members join the church by birth and transfers. New converts join the church through door to door visitations. New converts go for baptism without going through baptism class.

The language of the church is Chitumbuka. The church is led by men.

3.4.24 *Chiputula Church of Christ*

Chiputula Church of Christ is at Chiputula Primary School located along Zolozolo - Luwinga road.

The church started in 2005 due to quarrels at Zolozolo West Church of Christ. The quarrels were between people belonging to Tonga and Tumbuka tribes who were scrambling for leadership.[311] The Tonga people wanted Goodfully Kaunda to be the leader at Zolozolo West Church of Christ. When they succeeded with the plan, the Tumbuka group under the leadership of Chirwa, decided to leave the church and start their own church at Chiputula Primary School. The Church started with 15 people worshiping at Chiputula Primary School.

The average church attendance is 25 people, of whom the majority are women. The dominant members of the church are Tumbuka people. New members join the church through transfers and by birth. New converts join the church through door to door visitations. New converts go for water baptism without going through baptism class.

The language of the church is Chitumbuka. Church leadership is done by men.

3.4.25 *Ching'ambo Churches of Christ*

Ching'ambo Churches of Christ is in Ching'ambo area, located along Zolozolo to Luwinga road, near Churches of Christ maize mill and Free Methodist Church.

The church was started in 1980 by church members from Gowa Mission in Ntcheu who came to Mzuzu for employment.[312] The prominent people

---

[311] Int. Goodfully Kaunda, Church Member at Chiputula Church of Christ, Zolozolo West, 14.9.2013.

[312] Int. Vincent Kamphukusi, Church Member at Ching'ambo Churches of Christ, Ching'ambo, 12.9.2013.

who started the church at Ching'ambo were S.D. Lipenga, Kachingwe and Kakolo. The church started with 10 families worshiping under a *katope* tree, later they bought a piece of land where they built a glass thatched church. After some time, the church received a help of iron sheets from the Church Headquarters in Lilongwe for roofing the glass thatched church.

The church building has a capacity of 50 members. The church has 25 members with average church attendance of 15 people. The majority of church members are women. The dominant age group of the church is 15 to 30 years. The majority of church members are coming from Ntcheu District. New members join the church through transfers and by birth. New converts join the church through open-air rallies. New converts join baptism class before being baptized by water.

The common language of the church is Chichewa. The church is led by both sexes; however, men dominates.

3.4.26 Ching'ambo Free Methodist Church

Ching'ambo Free Methodist Church is in Ching'ambo area, located along Zolozolo - Luwinga road, near Ching'ambo Churches of Christ.

The church was started in 1993 by Pastor Maliwa who came from Lilongwe Church headquarters to plant a church in Mzuzu. He started a church with his family worshiping in his home, later he was joined by Nickson Mpulula, former Free Methodist pastor who left the church while at Karonga and joined United Method Church. These two pastors worked had to establish the church and after a year they had 10 families.[313] Pastor Maliwa stayed in Mzuzu for a year and left the church for Lilongwe, and Pastor Mathew Kawaza Banda took over his place. The Free Methodist Church had two worshiping centres each headed by a Pastor, Chibavi and Chiputula. Due to failure to pay rents for worshiping centres, the two groups decided to have one worshiping centre. They bought a piece of land at Ching'ambo and built a church with help from the head office in Lilongwe.

The church has 40 members with average church attendance of 25 people. The majority of church members are women. The church is

---

[313] Int. Pastor Mwiza Msiska, Church Pastor at Ching'ambo Free Methodist Church, Ching'ambo, 12.9.2013.

dominated by people from the Central Region.[314] New members join the church through transfers and by birth. New converts join the church through door to door visitations. New converts go for baptism without going through baptism class.

The language of the church is Chichewa. Church leadership is dominated by men.

3.4.27 Ching'ambo Zion Christian Church

Ching'ambo Zion Christian Church is in Ching'ambo area located off Zolozolo - Luwinga road close to Ching'ambo Free Methodist Church.[315]

The church started in 1987 by Mphuza Nkhata and Silver Mtonga who came from Mzimba to start a church in Mzuzu. Ching'ambo Zion Christian Church started with three families worshiping in the house of Sangwani Mhoni where they were renting. The first convert Sangwani Mhoni was working with Mzuzu Airport that eventually gave the piece of land where they have built a church.[316] The church attracted many people because of healing and dancing miracles done in the church three times a week.

The average church attendance is 50 people, of whom the majority are women. The church is dominated by sick people and guardians. The majority of church members are people from Mzimba District. New members join the church by conversion through the experiences of healing. New converts go for water baptism without going through baptism class.

The language of the church is Chitumbuka. The church is led by men only.

---

[314] Free Methodist Church is the only Free Methodist Church in Mzuzu. The church is familiar with people from Central Region unlike people from Northern and Southern Region. Int. Pastor Mwiza Msiska, Church Pastor at Ching'ambo Free Methodist Church, Ching'ambo, 12.9.2013.

[315] For a full study of the Zionist Churches in Malawi, see Ulf Strohbehn, *The Zionist Churches in Malawi. History – Theology – Anthropology*, Mzuzu: Mzuni Press, 2016. See also Verentina Chilamba, Impact of Zionist Church Teachings and Practices on Human Welfare: A Case study of Kaole (Mayani) Zionist Church, Mzuni Document, Department of Theology and Religious Studies, Mzuzu University.

[316] Int. Ephraim Mkandawire, Church Secretary, Ching'ambo Zion Christian Church, Ching'ambo, 12.9.2013.

3.4.28 Ching'ambo Mosque

Ching'ambo Mosque is in Ching'ambo area, located along Zolozolo to Luwinga road, 50 metres south of Ching'ambo market.

Ching'ambo Mosque was started in 2005 by Bambo Gama, Juma and Kaubwe. The mosque started at Ching'ambo because people of Ching'ambo area were travelling long distances to Vigwagwa or Hardware mosque in town for weekly prayers. Worship started with six people worshiping in a temporary Mosque with the capacity of 30 people.[317]

The average worship attendance is 30 people, of whom the majority are women. The dominant members of the Mosque are people from Mangochi. New members join the Mosque through transfers and by birth. New converts join the Mosque through open-air rallies. New converts join the Mosque without going through baptism class.

Languages of the Mosque are Yao and Chichewa. The Mosque is led by men.

3.5 Religious Places in Chibavi Ward

3.5.1 Chibavi CCAP Church

Chibavi CCAP Church is located at the centre of Chibavi area, 300 metres South-east of Chibavi market and 200 metres east of Chibavi Primary School.

The Church started in 1980 as an outstation of Mzuzu CCAP Church. The church started in consideration of the growth of membership of Chibavi area and long distances people were travelling for church service at Mzuzu CCAP Church.[318] Mama Moyo, Ziba, E.B.Y. Sibande and Mbizi presented the request to Mzuzu Church to allow Chibavi Section to become a prayer House. When permission was granted, the church at Chibavi started with 20 people worshiping under a *Katope* tree, where later they built a temporary church.

Chibavi prayer House became a congregation in 1993 because of the decree made by Rev. Aaron Longwe, parish minister of Mzuzu

---

[317] Int. Sheik Issah Kaliati, Leader of the Mosque Ching'ambo Mosque, Ching'ambo, 12.9.2013.

[318] Int. John Nyirenda, Session Clerk, Chibavi CCAP Church, Chibavi, 15.9.2013.

congregation, due to poor relationship between the church elders of Chibavi outstation and Rev Aaron Longwe. The centre of controversy was that church elders from Chibavi were reported to have refused to accept a call, *ntchemo*, of Rev. Aaron Longwe.[319] The refusal made the parish minister to become angry the with Chibavi section and made them a congregation on their own; however, due to this he eventually resigned as a parish minister of CCAP Synod of Livingstonia and started his own organization in Lilongwe.[320]

The church building has a capacity of 700 people. Church members are 1300 with average church attendance of 600 people, of whom the majority are women. The church is dominated by age group of 15 to 45 years. The majority of church members are from Chitipa and Karonga.[321] New members join the church through transfers and by birth. New converts joint the baptism class before being baptized by water.

The church has two languages, English and Chitumbuka. Church Leadership is for both sexes; however, men are dominating.

3.5.2 Chibavi Emmanuel Pentecostal Ministries

Chibavi Emmanuel Pentecostal Ministries is in Chibavi area, located off Mboni za Yehova road at Salvation Army Church, 50 metres west of Salvation Army Church.

The Ministry was started as a fellowship in 2008 by Prophet Gift Mwafongo. The fellowship started with 10 people worshiping in the house of Mai Nyakanyasko at Chinese Garden.[322] The first people to join the ministry were Agatha Theu, Andrew Mwanyongo and Rabecca Sayini. The ministry was joined by many people who made them to leave the house of Mayi Nyakanyasko to where they bought a piece of land. The

---

[319] Ntchemo appears to have originated the CCAP Synod of Livingstonia in 1928, when Rev. Yesaya Zerenje Mwase was called by Bandawe Congregation. Int. John Nyirenda, Session Clerk, Chibavi CCAP Church, Chibavi, 15.9.2013.

[320] Int. Moses Phiri, Deputy Session Clerk, Chibavi CCAP Church, Chibavi, 15.9.2013.

[321] The area is dominated by business people; therefore, the majority of business people in Mzuzu come from Chitipa and Karonga. Int. Moses Phiri, Deputy Session Clerk, Chibavi CCAP Church, Chibavi, 15.9.2013.

[322] Int. Joseph Kaunda, Church Secretary, Chibavi Emmanuel Pentecostal Ministries, Chibavi, 15.9.2013.

ministry has no permanent church structure; however, they are worshiping in a *vigwagwa* church.

The average worship attendance is 60 people, of whom the majority are women. The ministry is dominated by the age group of 15 to 35. New members join the ministry by conversion. New converts join the church through overnight prayers and "call your friend" evangelism. New converts join the baptism class for three months before being baptized by water.

The language of the church is Chichewa. The church leadership is for both sexes; however, men are dominating.

3.5.3 Chibavi Community of Christ Church

Chibavi Community of Christ Church is in Chibavi area, located at Majiga in Madimba area, along Mboni za Yehova road.

The Church started out of an open-air rally organized by Pastors John Mnthali and Goldrick Phiri and 16 people in 2010. The Chibavi rally was part of the open-air rallies which Pastor John Mnthali and Pastor Goldrick Phiri started in 1997 at Chiputula.[323] Pastors John Mnthali and Goldrick Phiri organized a big rally at Chibavi Primary School ground which yielded 16 people to Jesus Christ who eventually started the church at Chibavi. The first convert of the church was Fumbani Gondwe, Minus Mnthali and Kadali Mkandawire. The church changed the worshiping centre from Chibavi Primary School to where they have built a temporary church.

The average church attendance is 40 people, of whom the majority are women. New members join the church through conversion. New converts join baptism class before being baptized by water.

The language of the church is Chitumbuka. Church leadership is for both sexes.

3.5.4 Chibavi Cornerstone Presbyterian Church

'Chibavi Cornerstone Presbyterian Church'[324] is in Chibavi area, located along Chibavi market - Mchengautuwa road.

---

[323] Int. Pastor John Munthali, Parish Minister, Chibavi Community of Christ Church, Chibavi, 15.9.2013.

[324] For the history of Chibavi Cornerstone Presbyterian Church, see Austine Nyangu, A History of Zakumwamba Ministry and its Impact on the CCAP in

The church was started in 2005 by Winstone Timchindike Banda who had been suspended from Chibavi CCAP Church together with 40 other members for being involved in the formation of Zakumwamba Ministries.[325] Zakumwamba Ministry was an independent Ministry within Chibavi CCAP Church. Members of the ministry were warned to stop from attending the Ministry for it was not a recognized ministry in the CCAP Synod of Livingstonia.[326] Some members stopped while others continued; hence those who continued were suspended from the church. When Winstone Timchindike Banda was suspended, he was encouraged by his close friends; Richard Jere, Lemuel Nkhoma, Martin Chipeta and Henderson Luhanga to start a church. He started a church together with those he was suspended with; they started worshiping at his house before building their own church at the same place. The church is intending to start branches at Area 1B and in Chiputula.

The church building has a capacity of 100 people. Church membership is 70 with average church attendance of 50 people, of whom the majority are women. The dominant age group of the church is 30 to 50 years. New members join the church through conversion. Conversion is done through mass evangelism and man to man evangelism. New converts join baptism class before being baptized by water.

The language of the church is Chitumbuka. Church leadership is for both sexes.

3.5.5 Chibavi Salvation Army Church

Chibavi Salvation Army Church is in Chibavi area, located along Majiga in Madimba area, along Mboni za Yehova road.

The Church started at Chibavi area as a result of a big rally which took place at Katoto Secondary School ground in 2004. Chibavi Salvation Army Church was started by 10 converts of Katoto Secondary School ground rally; however, the prominent converts of the rally were Irene Gondwe and Chipeta who happened to come from Chibavi. When the rally was

---

Malawi, Mzuni Document, BA, Department of Theology and Religion Studies, Mzuzu University.

[325] Int. Rechard Jere, Session Clerk, Chibavi Cornerstone Presbyterian Church, Chibavi, 17.9.2013.

[326] Int. Sella Msiska, Church Elder, Chibavi Cornerstone Presbyterian Church, Chibavi, 17-9-2013.

over, Irene Gondwe and Chipeta convinced their fellow converts to start a church at Chibavi.[327] The church started at Chibavi worshiping in the house of Irene Chipeta. Later, they moved to old Njerenjere Private School where they managed to find a piece of land where they built a *vigwagwa* church. Captain Msikitela was sent to Chibavi Salvation Church to nurture the church in 2011.

The church building has a capacity of 60 people. Church membership has 40 people with average church attendance of 25 people, of whom the majority are women. The dominant age group of the church is 15 to 35. New members join the church through transfers and by birth. New converts join the church through open-air rallies and village visitation. New converts join baptism class before being baptized.

The church is led by both sexes. The language of the church is Chichewa.

3.5.6 Chibavi Christian Hope Assembly Church

Chibavi Christian Hope Assembly Church is in Chibavi area, located off St John's Hospital to Chibavi market road at Njelenjele towards Mchengautuwa road, 300 metres South –west of old Njelenjele Private School.

The church started as a fellowship with six families while worshiping at Chibavi Assemblies of God church.[328] Patrick Valosi Chirwa broke away from worshiping at Chibavi Assemblies of God Church and started his own church, worshiping in his house. When people started joining him, they changed the worship place to old Njelenjele Private School while looking for a suitable place where they could build a church. They bought a piece of land and built a church where they are worshiping now.

The church building has a capacity of 100 people. Church membership is 80 with average church attendance of 60 people, of whom the majority are women. The dominant age group of the church is from 14 to 20 years. New members join the church by conversion. New converts join the church through open-air rallies and door to door visitations. New converts go for water baptism before baptism class.

The language of the church is Chichewa. The church is led by both sexes.

---

[327] Int. Agnes Nkhata, Church Member, Chibavi Salvation Army Church, Chibavi, 17.9.2013.

[328] Int. Idah Nyirongo Semo, Church Member, Chibavi Christian Hope Assembly Church, Chibavi, 17-9-2013.

3.5.7 Chibavi Last Church of God

Chibavi 'Last Church of God'[329] is in Chibavi area, located along St John's Hospital - Chibavi market road.

The church started in 1984 as an outstation of Masasa last church. Dickson Zowana, Mackson Msiska and Live Mwambughi asked Masasa Church to consider long distances people from Chibavi were travelling to Masasa for church services.[330] The church started with 20 people worshiping under a *katope* tree. Later they built a church at the same piece of land.

The average church attendance is 100 people, of whom the majority are women. The church is dominated by people from Karonga.[331] New members join the church through transfers and by birth. New converts join the church through door to door visitation. New converts go for baptism class for one day before being baptized by water.

The language of the church is Chichewa. The leadership of the church is for men.

3.5.8 Chibavi St Benadeta Catholic Church

Chibavi St Benadeta Catholic Church is located at the centre of Chibavi area, between Chibavi CCAP Church and Chibavi Primary School.

The Church started in 1996 as an outstation of St Peters Church. Chibavi St Benadeta Catholic Church started at Chibavi in consideration of the growth of membership at Chibavi and long distances people were travelling for church services at St Peters.[332] The request for starting a

---

[329] For the Last Church of God, see; Wezzie Gondwe, *The Last Church of God and His Christ: Histories of Four Congregations in Nkhata bay District*, Mzuni Document, Department of Theology and Religious Studies, Mzuzu University. See also, Wezzie Gondwe, *A History of the Last Church of God and His Christ in Malawi from 1914 to 2015*, MA, Mzuzu University, 2015.

[330] Int. Rev. Hanfully Mwakalinga, Parish Minister Chibavi Last Church of God, Chibavi, 18.9.2013.

[331] The Last Church of God Church came to Mzuzu from Karonga; it came with Karonga Church Members who were work in Mzuzu. As a result, the dominant members of the church are people from Karonga. Int. Rev. Hanfully Mwakalinga, Parish Minister Chibavi Last Church of God, Chibavi, 18.9.2013.

[332] Int. Nichorous Kanyinji, Local church Council Chairperson, Chibavi St Benadeta Catholic Church, Chibavi, 18.9.2013.

church was presented to St Peters Church by Elias Msowoya, Francisco Banda and Mlenga. When permission was granted, the church started with 100 people worshiping at Chibavi Primary School. [333] Mbano, Nundwe and Soko offered a piece of land to the Church where they have built a church.

The church building has a capacity of 500 people. Members of the church are 300 with average church attendance of 250 people, of whom the majority are women. The dominating age group of the church is from 17 to 40 years. The majority of church members come from Chitipa and Karonga. New members join the church through transfers and by birth. New converts join the church through marriages. New converts join baptism class before being baptized by water.

The language of the church is Chitumbuka. Leadership of the church is dominated by men.

3.5.9 Chibavi Agape Life Church International

Chibavi Agape Life Church International is located along St John of God Hospital - Chibavi market road.

The church started in 1990 as a result of a rally organized by Apostle A.D. Mgala who came from Lilongwe to plant the church. [334] The rally was successful whereby people surrendered their lives to Jesus Christ and were grouped together to start a church. When the church started it needed someone who could nurture the church. The church was left in the hands of Mkandawire, Nkosi and Soko, and these were experienced people in running fellowships. The church started with fellowship meetings at old Njelenjele Private School. When people from the church headquarters came to Mzuzu for a follow-up; they discovered that the church was not growing, it had only six people.[335] This made the church headquarters to requested Pastor Mkandawire to lead the church. Pastor Mkandawire reorganized the church and people started joining the church which made them to build a permanent church.

---

[333] Int. Elias Msowoya, Church Member at Chibavi St Benadeta Catholic Church, Chibavi, 18.9.2013.

[334] Int. Jessie Msukwa, Church Member, Chibavi Agape Life Church International, Chibavi, 18.9.2013.

[335] Int. Pastor Mkandawire, Church Pastor, Chibavi Agape Life Church International, Chibavi, 18.9.2013.

The average church attendance is 70 people, of whom the majority are women. The dominant age group of the church is 20 years and above. New members join the church through transfers. New converts join the church through open-air rallies and door to door visitations. New converts join baptism class before being baptized by water.

3.5.10 Chibavi Assemblies of God Church

Chibavi Assembles of God Church is in Chibavi area, located along Tupa road.

The Church started in 1990 as a branch of Katawa Assemblies of God Church. Alfred Chitalo, Peter Kavuli and K. Gondwe asked Katawa church to consider the growth of membership at Chibavi and the long distances people from Chibavi were travelling to Katawa for church services.[336] When the request was accepted, the church started with 20 people worshiping in a rented house before building their own. Pastor W.K. Gondwe was the first Pastor to be sent to Chibavi church.

The church building has a capacity of 300 people. Church membership is 300 with average church attendance of 250 people, of whom women are in the majority. The dominant age group of the church is 15 to 25 years. New members join the church through transfers and by birth. New converts join the church though open-air rallies and bring your friend evangelism. New converts join baptism class before being baptized by water.

Church leadership is for both sexes. The languages of the church are English and Chichewa.

3.5.11 Chibavi African International Church

Chibavi African International Church is in the Centre of Chibavi, located South of Chibavi market, and 300 metres south of Chibavi Primary School.

The church started in 1985 as a branch of Katoto African Church International. Steven Nyirenda, Rogan Kumwenda and Winestead Msiska asked Katoto African Church to give permission to Chibavi Section to start their own church due to the growth of membership at Chibavi and long

---

[336] Int. Mather Jia Nyirenda, Church Member, Chibavi Assemblies of God Church, Chibavi, 18.9.2013.

distances people were travelling to Katoto for church services.[337] When permission was granted, the church started with 10 families worshiping under a *muwula* tree. The church built a temporary church at the same piece of land where later they built a permanent one.

The church building has a capacity of 200 people. Church membership is 120 with average church attendance of 100 people, of whom the majority are women. The church is dominated by married people and more especially those who have married more than one wife. The majority of church members come from Karonga and Rumphi. New members join the church through transfers. New converts join the church through face to face discussion on church policy.[338] New converts go for baptism without going for baptism class.

The leadership of the church is for men. The language of the church is Chitumbuka.

3.5.12 Chibavi Chewasene Mosque

Chibavi Chewasene Mosque is located 200 metres south of Chibavi New Apostolic Church.

The mosque was started in 1999 by Musa Ali, Juma Chaimbo and Yusuf Wilson. Chewasene Mosques started at Chibavi because of long distances Muslims from Chibavi were travelling to Vigwagwa or Hardware Mosque in town for weekly prayers. When people were organized they started worshiping in a *vigwagwa* mosque which was burnt down in 1999 due to the political struggle that arose when the United Democratic Front won the 1999 General Elections.[339] Later Fizer Karim built a permanent mosque for the Chibavi people. The mosque started with 55 people of whom the majority were people from Mangochi.

The mosque capacity is 100 people. Mosque membership is 80 people with average mosque attendance of 65 people, of whom the majority are women and youth. The majority of mosque members come from Mangochi. New members join the mosque by birth. New converts join

---

[337] Int. Winstead Msiska, Church Member at Chibavi African International Church, Chibavi, 18.9.2013.
[338] Int. Ester Mbala, Church Member, Chibavi African International Church Chibavi, 18.9.2013.
[339] Int. Brother Yusufu Dane, Madrassa Instructor, Chibavi Chewasene Mosque, Chibavi, 18.9.2013.

the mosque through door to door visitation, *madrassah* and *jalasa*.[340] New converts join mosque by confirmation and later joins instruction class.

The languages of a mosque are Arabic and Chichewa. The mosque leadership is for men.

3.5.13 Chibavi Enlightened Christian Gathering Ministry

Chibavi Enlightened Christian Gathering Ministry is in Chibanja area, located north of Chabanja Primary School.

The ministry started as a fellowship with seven people worshiping in the house of Fasale, a teacher at Luwinga Secondary School, at Area 1B in 2007.[341] The owner of the Ministry, Shepherd Bushiri, decided to transfer the worshiping Centre of the Ministry to an appropriate Centre in order to ease mobility of people from long distances. The Ministry moved from Area 1B to Chibanja, worshiping in a Garage at a plot of Maggie. While there, many people joined the church. This made them to look for a more spacious place; they bought a piece of land, near the same area, where they have built a *vigwagwa* church.

The *vigwagwa* church building has a capacity of 500 people. The average worship attendance is 20 people, of whom the majority are women. The dominant age group of the ministry is from 15 to 30 years.[342] New members join the ministry through fellowships, healing miracles and open-air rallies. The converted members join the church through joining baptism class for a month before being baptized by water.

The ministry leadership is male. The language of the Ministry is English translated into Chichewa.

3.5.14 Chibavi Ephata Ministry

Chibavi Ephata Ministry is in Chibavi area, located 200 metres south of Chibavi Day Secondary School.

---

[340] Jalasa, these are open-air demonstrations which children from Madrassah demonstrate to the general Public. Int. Brother Yusufu Dane, Madrassa Instructor, Chibavi Chewasene Mosque, Chibavi, 18.9.2013.

[341] Int. Chimwemwe Mkandawire, Pastor, Chibavi Enlightened Christian Gathering Ministry, Chibanja, 19.9.2013.

[342] Int. Prophet King Solomon Jere, church prophet, Chibavi Enlightened Christian Gathering Ministry, Chibanja, 19.9.2013.

The Ministry was started in 2005 by Pastor Jackson who came from Dar es salaam for church planting in Malawi. The coming of the ministry to Chibavi was through Josephine who introduced Pastor Jackson to Emma Kamwela upon his arrival in Mzuzu. Josephine came to know Pastor Jackson while in Dar es salaam where she went for healing from her sufferings.[343] Emma Kamwela received Pastor Jackson in her house and introduced him to her fellow friends with whom she was doing Bible Study. The Bible Study group of Emma Kamwela found a house for Pastor Jackson from where he started the ministry with the whole group of Emma Kamwela Bible Study. The first prominent members of the ministry were: Monica Gondwe, Nowa Kamwela, Zeleza Chilambo and Emma Kamwela. When the ministry was fully established, they bought a piece of land where they have built a church.

The church average worship attendance is 20 people, of whom the majority are women. The dominant age group of the ministry is from 25 to 40 years. New members join the ministry through conversion. Converted members join the ministry through healing miracles.[344] The converted members join baptism class before being baptized by water.

The ministry is led by both sexes; however, female is dominating. The language of the church is English translated into Chichewa.

3.5.15 Chibavi Last Church of God

Chibavi Last Church of God is located at the road junction of Chibavi market - Chinese Garden and Chibavi CCAP - Chinese Garden road.

The church started in 1975 by Rev. Matanje, who was working with the ministry of works in Mzuzu. He started a church with five people worshiping under a Katope tree, 50 metres west of where the present church has been built.[345] The church was removed from where it first started because it is where the road from Chibavi market to Chinese

---

[343] Int. Monica Gondwe, Church Member at Chibavi Ephata Ministry, Chibavi, 17.9.2013.

[344] The first person to be healed was Zeliya Chilambo, who at that time had suffered for five years without receiving any help. When she met Pastor Jackson, she was healed and she became a living testimony to many people who later joined the ministry. Int. Monica Gondwe, Church Member at Chibavi Ephata Ministry, Chibavi, 17.9.2013.

[345] Int. Standwell Mphaka, Church Member at Chibavi Last Church of God, Chibavi, 19.9.2013.

garden is going through. The first convert and a prominent member of the church is Mama Nkhata known as computer.

The church has 60 people with average church attendance of 45 people, of whom the majority are women. The dominant age group of the church is 25 to 50 years. The majority of church members come from Mzimba.[346] New members join the church through transfers. New converts join the church through face to face discussion of church policy. New converts join the church through baptism without going through baptism class.

The church leadership is dominating by men. The language of the church is Chitumbuka.

3.5.16 Chibavi Providence Industrial Mission

Chibavi Providence Industrial Mission Church is located 100 metres south of Chinese garden, along Chibavi market to Chinese garden road.

The church started in 2000 by individual members of Providence Industrial Mission who happened to come from Blantyre to work in Mzuzu.[347] Matola and Mphanje were the people who organized together all members of Providence Industrial Mission in Mzuzu to start a church. The church started with six families worshiping in the house of Matola. Later, they bought a piece of land where they have built a church. When the church was fully organized, the National Head Office of the church sent Pastor Wongani to nurture the church.

The church has 60 members with average church attendance of 45 people, of whom the majority are women. The dominant age group is 20 to 50 years. The majority of church members come from Blantyre.[348] New members join the church through transfers and by birth.

The leadership of the church is for men only. The language of the church is Chichewa.

---

[346] People from Mzimba District are dominating in the church because the church came with members from Mzimba District. Int. Standwell Mphaka, Church Member at Chibavi Last Church of God, Chibavi, 19.9.2013.

[347] Int. Gladess Maganga, Church Member at Chibavi Providence Industrial Mission Church, Chibavi, 19.9.2013.

[348] Providence Industrial Mission Church is dominated by members from Blantyre. The church started with members from Blantyre and remains dominated by members from Blantyre. Int. Gladess Maganga, Church Member at Chibavi Providence Industrial Mission Church, Chibavi, 19.9.2013.

3.5.17 Chibavi Come to Jesus Ministry

Chibavi Come to Jesus Ministry is in Chibavi area, located near Chinese garden. The Ministry is 150 metres south of Chinese garden.

The ministry started in 2009 by Prophet Sylvester Msowoya who at that time was studying Business Administration. Prophet Msowoya is a former member of Assemblies of God. He started his Ministry as a fellowship with five people worshiping in his house at Chibavi. When the number of worshippers was increasing, the house became small; as a result, they bought a piece of land, 50 metres south of the Pastor's house, where they have built a *vigwagwa* church.[349]

The church has 30 people with the average worship attendance of 25 people, of whom the majority are women. The dominant age group of worshippers is 20 to 35 years. New members join the ministry through prophecy, healing and deliverance done by the prophet himself. The ministry has neither baptism classes nor water baptism.

The leadership of the ministry is dominated by men. The language of the church is English translated into Chichewa.

3.5.18 Chibavi Christ Alive Family Church

Chibavi Christ Alive Family Church is in Chibavi area, along Chinese garden - Chibavi market road.

The church started in 2009 by Pastor Timothy Banda who came from Lilongwe for Church plantation. Pastor Timothy Banda started the church as a fellowship; he started with six people worshiping in his house.[350] He started a church at Luwinga where he first rented a house and then moved to Chibavi where he was renting a house of Kumwenda Kafukule. When the number of church members was increasing, they started worshiping at Chibavi Day Secondary School. Later they bought a piece of land where they built a *vigwagwa* church. The first and prominent converts of the church were Alnod Banda, John Kamanga and Albart Tembo.

---

[349] Int. Prophet Silvester Msowoya, Founding Member of Chibavi Come to Jesus Ministry, Chibavi, 19.9.2013.

[350] Int. Angellah Nyirenda, Church Member at Chibavi Christ Alive Family Church, Chibavi, 19.9.2013.

The church has 20 members, with average church attendance of 15 people, of whom men are in the majority. The church is dominated by people from the central region. New members join the church through conversion. New converts join the church through open-air rallies, and door to door visitations. The church has neither baptism classes nor water baptism.

The church is led by men. The language of the church is English translated into Chichewa.

3.5.19 Chibavi Seventh-day Adventist Church

Chibavi Seventh-day Adventist Church is in Chibavi area, close to Chibavi market.

The church stated in 1984 by members of Seventh-day Adventist who were worshiping at Nkholongo and Chasefu. The Chibavi members of Seventh-day Adventist led by P.L. Nyirenda and Gogo Shonga, agreed to start their own church at Chibavi in consideration of the growth of membership and long distances people were travelling for church services. The church started as a result of 21 days effort held at Chibavi Primary School ground. After the effort, they started a church with 48 people worshiping in the house of Mbizi, who was not a member of the church.[351] Later, they built their own church.

The church building has a capacity of 300 people. Church membership is 320 with average church attendance of 280 people, of whom women are in the majority. The dominant age group of the church is 12 to 25 years. The majority of church members come from Mzimba and Nkhatabay where there are old stations of the church. New members join the church through transfers and by birth. New converts join the church through efforts and discovery paper lessons. New converts who have attended efforts and discovery paper lessons go straight for baptism.

The language of the church is Chichewa. The leadership of the church is dominated by men.

3.5.20 Chibavi Living Waters Church

Chibavi Living Waters Church is in Chibavi area, 300 metres north of Chibavi market.

---

[351] Int. Elias Masingi, Church Member at Chibavi Seventh-day Adventist Church, Chibavi, 20.9.2013.

The church started in 2011 as a branch of Mzuzu Living Waters, Mount Zion Church. Franklin Banda, Lenard Nkunika and Hastings Kamoto requested Mzuzu Living Waters Church to consider the growth of membership at Chibavi and long distances people from Chibavi were travelling for church services at Mzuzu Living Waters Church.[352] Mzuzu Living Waters Church granted permission to Chibavi members to start a church in the area. The church started with 50 people worshiping at Chibavi Primary School. Later, the worshiping Centre was moved to Chibavi Secondary School where finally they found a piece of land where they have built a church.

The average church attendance is 60 people, of whom the majority are women. The dominant age group of the church is 12 to 35 years. New members join the church through transfers and by birth. New converts join the church through open-air rallies. New converts join baptism class before water baptism. The leadership of the church is for both sexes. The language of the church is Chichewa.

3.5.21 Chibavi Baptist Convention Church

Chibavi Baptist Convention Church is 200 metres south of Chibavi market.

The church was started in 1986 by Deacon Tegha. The church at first was a preaching point of Mzuzu Baptist Church. Deacon Tegha, Gama, Elina Msika and Silungwe requested Mzuzu Baptist Church to consider the growth of church membership at Chibavi and long distances people from Chibavi were travelling for church services at Mzuzu Baptist Church.[353] When permission was granted by Mzuzu Baptist Church, the Chibavi Baptist Church started with five families worshiping in the house of Benjamin Phiri. While there, they bought a piece of land where they built a temporary church, and after some time they built a permanent church.

The church building has a capacity of 200 people. The church has 100 members with average church attendance of 80 people, of whom the majority are women. The dominant age group of the church is 14 to 30 years. The church is dominated by people from the central and Southern

---

[352] Int. Closby Kanenga, Church Member, Chibavi Living Waters Church, Chibavi, 20.9.2013.
[353] Int. Manes Jere, Church Member at Chibavi Baptist Convention Church, Chibavi, 20.9.2013.

regions.[354] New members join the church through transfers. New converts join the church through marriages, open-air and "bring your friend" evangelism. Converted members join baptism class before being baptized by water.

The language of the church is Chichewa. The church is led by both sexes; however, men dominates.

3.5.22 Chibavi Bible Believers Church

Chibavi Bible Believers Church is in Chibavi area, located along Chibavi Market - Chinese garden road.

The church was started in 1990 as a branch of Hilltop Bible Believers Church. The church started at Chibavi due to the growth of church membership and long distances people from Chibavi were travelling to Hilltop for church services.[355] The church started with five families worshiping in the house of Daniel Mkwate. They eventually built a church.

The average church attendance is 60 people, of whom the majority are men. The dominant age group of the church is 20 to 45 years. The majority of church members are people from the Central region. New members join the church through transfers. New members join the church through tape ministry[356] and distribution of preaching discs.[357] New converts join the church through water baptism without going through baptism class.

The language of the church is Chichewa. The church is led by men.

3.5.23 Chibavi Bible Believers Church 2

Chibavi Bible Believers Church 2 is in Chibavi area, located east of Chibavi Day Secondary School and 100 metres west of Chibavi Enlightened Christian Gathering Ministry.

---

[354] Int. Christina Standfore, Church Member at Chibavi Baptist Convention Church, Chibavi, 20.9.2013.

[355] Int. Jenifa Kaunda, Church Member at Chibavi Bible Believers Church, Chibavi, 22.9.2013.

[356] Tape ministry is a Youth Programme, where Youth visit villages preaching.

[357] For more on the importance of tape and CD ministry for the Bible Believers, see Richard Gadama, The Bible Believers in Malawi: History, Teachings and Practice (1977-2011), MA, Mzuzu University, 2012.

The church was started in 2007 by Isaiah Nyirenda who broke away from Chibavi Bible Believers Church. Isaiah Nyirenda and his group abandoned Chibavi Bible Believers Church and started Chibavi Bible Believers Church 2 because Isaiah Nyirenda was not happy with the report that he was not selected to the position of a Pastor.[358] Isaiah Nyirenda could not believe that he failed the interview; therefore, he was disappointed and decided to start the same church within Chibavi area. He started the church with six families worshiping in his house. The church moved from his house to Mchengautuwa for a while, later, it came back to Chibavi occupying an abandoned church building next to Chibavi Enlightened Christian Gathering Ministry.

The average church attendance is 40 people, of whom the majority are men. The dominant age group of the church is 18 to 35 years. The majority of church members are coming from the Central Region. New members join the church through transfers. New converts join the church through Tape ministries and distribution of preaching disc. New converts join the church through water baptism without going through baptism class.

The church is led by men. The language of the church is Chichewa.

3.5.24 Chibavi Central Mosque

Chibavi Central Mosque is in Chibavi area, located hundred metres west of Chibavi market.

The Central Mosque came from Chibavi Chewasene Mosque in 2000. Chewasene Mosque was a small mosque while Muslims around Chibavi wanted a bigger mosque where they could pray five times a day including Fridays.[359] The idea to have a bigger mosque was initiated by Kennedy Adams Mbewe, Kaseno Chewasene and Magawe. As the numbers of Muslims members at Chewasene Mosque was increasing, Sheik Ibrahim Fikila Banda requested a piece of land from chiefs around Chibavi area where they could build a mosque.[360] When the piece of land was given,

---

[358] Precious Kaunda, Church Member, Chibavi Bible Believers Church, Chibavi, 22.9.2013.

[359] Int. Kennedy, Adam Mbewe, Chairperson of Chibavi Central Mosque, Chibavi, 22.9.2013.

[360] Sheik Ibrahim Fikila Banda was the first Sheikh at Chibavi Mosque and is the one who changed the face of the Islamic faith at Chibavi. Int. Kennedy Adam Mbewe, Chairperson of Chibavi Central Mosque, Chibavi, 22.9.2013.

they built a small sized mosque with the capacity of 10 people. Later a bigger mosque was built with funding from those who were rehabilitating mosques which were burned down during political struggle of 1999 General Election.

The average mosque attendance is 70 people, of whom the majority are women. The majority of church members are people from Mangochi and Nkhotakota. New converts join the mosque through marriages and charity work and undergo instruction and confirmation.

The mosque is led by men. The language of the mosque is Arabic translated into Chichewa.

3.5.25 Chibavi African International Church

Chibavi African International Church is in Chibavi area, located 200 metres north of Chibavi market.

The church was started in 1988 by members of the church, from various areas, who came to work in Mzuzu. The prominent members who started the church were Ana Shaba, Nyasambo and Nyamusuku.[361] The church started with eight people worshiping in the house of Ana Shaba. They bought a piece of land where they started worshiping under a mango tree while building a church.

The church building has a capacity of 100 people. The church membership is 80 with average church attendance of 60 people, of whom the majority are women. The dominant age group of the church is 25 to 50 years. The majority of church members are people from Karonga and Chitipa. New members join the church through transfers. New converts join the church through person to person witnessing. New converts join the *pangano* class before being baptized by water.

Church leadership is dominating by men. The language of the church is Chitumbuka.

3.5.26 Chibavi Apostolic Faith Mission

Chibavi Apostolic Faith Mission is in Chibavi area, located along Chibavi market - St John of God Hospital road and 200 metres south of Chibavi market.

---

[361] Int. Nyamunyasulu, Church Member at Chibavi African International Church, Chibavi, 22.9.2013.

The church was started in 1982 by Pastor Kenstone Nkhata who was sent to Mzuzu to plant a church after finishing training for pastorship at Lilongwe Apostolic Faith Mission College. He started a church with his wife in his house, through door to door visitations and house to house fellowships, slowly people started joining him and the group grew to 10 people.[362] As the number of church members was growing, they started worshiping under a mango tree where later they bought a piece of land where they built a church. The church and manse were built with finding from Bishop Bongartz, the overseer of all pastors of Apostolic Faith Mission in Malawi.

The average church attendance is 70 people, of whom the majority are men. The dominant age group of the church is 15 to 40 years. The church is dominated by people from central and southern regions. New members join the church through transfers. New converts join the church through door to door visitations and open-air evangelism. New converts join baptism class before being baptized by water.

The church is led by both sexes; however, men dominate. The language of the church is Chichewa.

3.5.27 *Chibavi New Apostolic Church*

Chibavi New Apostolic Church is in Chibavi area, located 350 metres south-East of Chibavi market and 100 metres south of Chibavi CCAP Church.

The church started in 1980 as a result of the closure of Masasa Church when they wanted to have one central church at Zolozolo.[363] The idea was that all Christians around Mzuzu town should have one central worshiping place at Zolozolo; hence, they closed Masasa church for Zolozolo. New Apostolic Christians from Chibavi led by Ngulube, Nkosi, Chirwa and Mr and Mrs Phiri decided to have their own worshiping centre considering long distances people might travel to Zolozolo central church.[364] The leadership of the central church accepted the idea and the

---

[362] Int. Agnes Chipeta, Church Member, Chibavi Apostolic Faith Mission, Chibavi, 22.9.2013.

[363] Int. Evangelist Andrew Zembo, Evangelist, Mzuzu Central New Apostolic Church, Mzuzu, 27.9.2013.

[364] Int. Mrs Njelenjele Sibande, Church Member, Chibavi New Apostolic Church, Chibavi, 22.9.2013.

church started at Chibavi with seven families worshiping under a mango tree. They built a temporary church where later they have built a permanent one.

The church building has a capacity of 200 people. Church membership is 180 with average church attendance of 150 people, of whom the majority are women. The dominant age group of the church is 30 to 50 years. New members join the church through transfers and by birth. New converts join the church through personal witnessing and door to door visitation. New converts join baptism class for three months before being baptized by water.

The church is led by men. Chichewa and Chitumbuka are the languages commonly used by the church.

3.5.28 Chibavi Chipangano Church

Chibavi Chipangano Church is located hundred metres east of Chibavi Day Secondary School.

The church was started in 1995 by Pastor Kondwani Nyirenda who quarreled with Pastor Tambulani Njikho for Pastorship while at Mchengautuwa Chipangano Church. Kondwani Nyirenda wanted to be an assistant Pastor at Mchengautuwa Church, however, Pastor Tambulani Njikho, a resident Pastor, did not see him qualified for the post.[365] The two disagreed over the issue, eventually; Pastor Kondwani Nyirenda and his supporters left the church and started their own church at Chibavi. The church started with 20 people worshiping in the house of Kondwani Nyirenda who later became the Pastor. Later, Pastor Kondwani Nyirenda bought a piece of land where they have built a temporary church.

The average church attendance is 45 people, of whom the majority are women. The dominant age group is 25 to 50 years. The majority of church members are coming from Mzimba and Nkhatabay. New members join the church through transfers. New converts join the church through face to face discussion of church policy. New converts join the church through water baptism without going through baptism class.

The dominant language of the church is Chitumbuka. Church Leadership is for both sexes; however, men are dominating.

---

[365] Int. Pastor Kondwani Nyirenda, Church Pastor at Chibavi Chipangano Church, Mchengautuwa, 26.9.2013.

3.6 Religious Places in Mchengautuwa Ward

3.6.1 Kaviwale Gospel Pentecostal Church

Kaviwale Gospel Pentecostal Church is in Kaviwale area, located along Enyezini road.

The church was started in 2000 by Bishop Pulex Msuku. The church broke away from Mchengautuwa Full Gospel Church due to controversy over the legitimacy of the leadership of Bishop Pulex Msuku.[366] In 1999, Bishop Pulex Msuku abandoned the church and contested for the 1999 parliamentary elections which he lost. When the General Election was over, Bishop Msuku rejoined the church in 2000 and he took over leadership of the church himself. Many church elders were against the move and when he discovered that, he decided to start his own church. Bishop Msuku broke away with 78 people and started his own church, by the name of Revival Ministries, worshiping at Mlinda Private School.[367] The church was joined with Gospel Pentecostal Church which later became Kaviwale Gospel Pentecostal Church. Due to leadership conflicts, Bishop Pulex Msuku left the church and started another church.

The average church attendance is 52 people, of whom the majority are women. The dominant age group of the church is from 15 to 30 years. New members join the church by conversion. New converts join the church through healing miracles and material support. New converts join the church through confirmation.

The church is led by both sexes; however, men are dominating. The language of the church is Chitumbuka.

3.6.2 Kaboko Gospel Pentecostal Church

Kaboko Gospel Pentecostal Church is in Wed Adams area located near Chipambo Primary School.

The church started in 2000 as a branch of Kaviwale Gospel Pentecostal Church. Victoria Msofi started a branch of Gospel Pentecostal Church at Kaboko, when she was called to visit her relative, Mrs Katazuka Msofi. While there, she prayed for a boy who was suffering from epilepsy and

---

[366] Int. Pastor Belson Mtonga, Church Pastor at Kaviwale Gospel Pentecostal Church, Kaviwale, 25.9.2013.
[367] Int. Lexer Kumwenda, Church Member at Kaviwale Gospel Pentecostal Church, Kaviwale, 25.9.2013.

he was healed. The incident made many people around the area to join her church at Mlinda Private Secondary School. Due to long distances people were travelling to Mlinda Private School for church services, they asked the church leadership to allow them to start their own church.[368] The church started with two families worshiping in the house of Mrs Katazuka Msofi. Later, they found a piece of land where they built a church.

The average church attendance is 40 people, of whom the majority are women. The dominant age group of the church is 15 to 35 years. New members join the church through conversion. The majority of church members are coming from Assemblies of God Church. New members join the church through healing miracles and material support, and they join the church through confirmation.

The church is led by both sexes. The language of the church is Chitumbuka.

3.6.3 Kaviwale Victory Assemblies of God Pentecostal Church

Kaviwale Victory Assemblies of God Pentecostal Church is in Kaviwale area located off Enyezini road, near Kaviwale Primary School.

The church was started in 2012 by Pastor Gift Sibale who was a church elder at Gesha Living Waters. Pastor Gift Sibale had some misunderstandings with Geisha Living Waters Church. The centre of controversy was that he was denied the right to become a pastor of Living Waters Church; as a result, he started his own church where he became a pastor.[369] Kaviwale Victory Assemblies of God Pentecostal Church started as a fellowship with two families worshiping in the house of Pastor Gift Sibale. As the church membership was growing, the church started worshiping at Kaviwale Primary School.

The average church attendance is 11 people, of whom the majority are men. The dominant age group of the church is 18 to 25 years. New members join the church by conversion. New converts join baptism class before being baptized by water.

---

[368] Int. Victoria Katazuka, Church Member at Kaboko Gospel Pentecostal Church, Kaviwale, 25.9.2013.

[369] Int. Victoria Katazuka, Church Member, Kaviwale Victory Assemblies of God Pentecostal Church, Kaviwale, 25.9.2013.

The leadership of the church is for both sexes. Chichewa is the common language of the church.

3.6.4 Katoto Baptist Convention Church

Katoto Baptist Convention Church is in Kaviwale area, located along Mchengautuwa to Kaviwale Primary School road.

The church started in 1978 through tracks titled *Kasi Nichitechi kuti Niponoskeke* (what should I do to be saved), which were received by Juma Ngwira, Wisdom Bota and Emelia Nkhata.[370] When these people had finished responding to the tracts they received, they sent them to Lilongwe. In response, two white missionaries, Swafford and Kennedy, followed up the addresses of those three people, they came to Mzuzu in the village of Titus Ngwira at Kaviwale and found those three people, and they introduced themselves to the village and asked the village to allow them to show the Jesus film. When permission was granted, they started showing the Jesus film which attracted many people who eventually surrendered their lives to Jesus Christ.[371] The church started with 30 people worshiping under a *Muwula* tree and later they built a church at the same place.

The church has 50 members with average church attendance of 40 people, of whom the majority are women. New members join the church through door to door visitation and open-air rallies. New converts join baptism class before being baptized by water.

The language of the church is Chitumbuka. Church leadership is for both sexes; however, men are dominating.

3.6.5 Kaviwale Grace Fellowship

Kaviwale Grace Fellowship is located at Kaviwale Primary School.

The fellowship was started in 2012 by Prophet Joseph Mphaniso Phiri. Prophet Joseph Phiri started a fellowship with four families worshiping in his house. The fellowship attracted many neighbouring families when

---

[370] Int. Alice Mbowe, Church Member, Katoto Baptist Convention of Malawi, Kaviwale, 25.9.2013.

[371] Int. Emelia Nkhata, Church Member, Katoto Baptist Convention of Malawi, Kaviwale, 25.9.2013.

prophet Phiri healed a child suffering from unknown diseases.[372] The first prominent families to join the fellowship were; Phiri, Ngulube, Ngoma and Manda. When the number of fellowship members became bigger, they changed the worshiping place from the prophet's house to Kaviwale Primary School.

The average worship attendance is 45 people of whom women are in the majority. The dominant age group of the fellowship is 15 to 30 years. New members join the fellowship through healing miracles and deliverance. The fellowship receives members of different churches. The fellowship has no baptism.

The language of the fellowship is Chichewa. Leadership of the church is for both sexes; however, men are dominating.

3.6.6 Kaviwale Seventh-day Adventist

Kaviwale Seventh-day Adventist Church is in Kaviwale area, located along Enyesini road.

The church started in 2007 as a branch of Mchengautuwa Seventh-day Adventist Church. The idea to start a church at Kaviwale came from two retired Pastors; Chavula and Jere, who asked the church leadership to consider long distances old people were travelling from Kaviwale to Mchengautuwa for church services and the advancement of the city boundary towards Kaviwale where there was need to find a piece of land for a future church.[373] The idea for a church at Kaviwale was adopted by Nkosi Mtenje and Luhanga, who presented it to Mchengautuwa Church for consideration.[374] Mchengautuwa Church accepted the idea and the church started at Kaviwale with 30 people worshiping at Kaviwale Primary School. Later, they bought a piece of land where they have built a temporary church.

The average church attendance is 50 people, of whom the majority are women. The dominant age group of the church is 10 to 25 years. The majority of church members are from Mzimba and Nkhatabay. New

---

[372] Int. Prophet Joseph Mphaso Phiri, Fellowship Pastor, Kaviwale Grace Fellowship, Kaviwale, 25.9.2013.

[373] Int. Chrisy Ng'anjo, Church Member, Kaviwale Seventh-day Adventist, Kaviwale, 26.9.2013.

[374] Nkosi, Mtenje and Luhanga were among influential church leaders from Kaviwale section who worked hard to start a church at Kaviwale.

members join the church through transfers. New converts join the church through efforts. Those who have been converted through efforts go for water baptism without baptism classes.

The language of the church is Chichewa. Church leadership is for both sexes; however, men dominates.

3.6.7 Kaviwale Church of Christ

Kaviwale Church of Christ is in Sonda area located south east of Mzuzu Silos.

The church started in 2004 as a branch of Mchengautuwa Church. Kaviwale Church of Christ started in consideration of the growth of Kaviwale membership and long distances people from Sonda area were travelling for church services at Mchengautuwa. J.S.V. Gondwe, Wiseman Msowoya and Baxter Nyirenda were among church elders who presented the request to Mchengautuwa to start a church of Christ at Sonda area. When Mchengautuwa Church accepted the request, they asked Sonda Church members to provide a piece of land where they could build a temporary church.[375] The church started with 36 people worshiping in a temporary church.

The average church attendance is 50 people, of whom the majority are women. The dominant age group of the church is 12 to 30 years. The majority of church members are coming from Mzimba. New members join the church through transfers. New converts join the church through open-air rallies and door to door visitation. New converts join the church through water baptism without going through baptism class.

The language of the church is Chitumbuka. Church leadership is for men.

3.6.8 Soweto African International Church

Soweto Africa International Church is in Kaviwale in Zamadula village, located along Mzuzu Silos road.

The church started in 2006 as an outstation of Chibavi Church. Soweto Africa International Church started due to growth of church members from Kaviwale and long distances people from Kaviwale were travelling to Chibavi for church services. Moses Msukwa, Kanyika, Simwela and

---

[375] Int. Chawanangwa Nkhonjera, Church Member at Kaviwale Church of Christ, Kaviwale, 26.9.2013.

Sikwese were among church leaders who initiated the start of a church at Kaviwale. The church started with 15 people worshiping under a *Muwula* tree, where later they built a church.

The church has 100 members with average church attendance of 60 people, of whom the majority are women. The church is dominated by the married age group. The majority of church members are from Chitipa. New members join the church through transfers. New converts join the church through face to face discussion of church policy.[376] New converts join the church through water baptism without going through baptism class.

The church is led by men. The language of the church is Chitumbuka.

3.6.9 Mchengautuwa Chipangano Church

Mchengautuwa Chipangano Church is in Mchengautuwa area, located along Mchengautuwa market to Target Private Secondary School road.

The church started in 1978 as a branch of Sonda Church. The reason why the church started at Mchengautuwa was in consideration of the growth of membership and long distances people from Mchengautuwa were travelling to attend church services at Sonda. The other reason was the advancement of the city boundary towards Mchengautuwa where there was a need to find a piece of land for a future church.[377] The church started with 16 people worshiping at a temporary church built where the permanent one now is. The church started under the leadership of Tambulani Njikho, Harson Nyirongo, Chiona, and Esnath Mseteka.

The church has 120 members, with average church attendance of 90 people, of whom the majority are women. The dominant age group of the church is 25 to 50 years. The majority of church members are coming from Mzimba and Nkhatabay. New members join the church through transfers. New converts join the church through water baptism without going through baptism class.

The dominant language of the church is Chitumbuka. Church leadership is for both sexes; however, men are dominating.

---

[376] Int. Febie Msuku, Church Member at Kaviwale church of Christ, Kaviwale, 26.9.2013.
[377] Int. Pastor Tambulani Njikho, Church Pastor at Mchengautuwa Chipangano Church, Mchengautuwa, 26.9.2013.

3.6.10 Mchengautuwa Seventh-day Adventist Reform Movement Church

Mchengautuwa Seventh-day Adventist Reform Movement Church is in Mchengautuwa area, located at Ulemu Mwanga Village near Jerejere Private Secondary School.

The church was started in 1995 by R. J. Msiska and R. Banda. The church started as a first branch of Karonga Church from where the first church started in Malawi. Seventh-day Adventist Reform Movement Church came from Tanzania to Karonga and R.J. Msiska and R. Banda were sent from Karonga to plant the church in Mzuzu. The two members started the church through door to door visitation while targeting Seventh–day Adventist Church members. The church planters taught about the need of reforming the Seventh–day Adventist Church to its original state which has been marred by new teachings.[378] The church started with nine families worshiping in the house of H.W.Z. Moyo, the first convert. When more people joined the church, they bought a piece of land and built a church.

The church has 30 members with average church attendance of 25 people, of whom the majority are women. The dominant age group of the church is 20 to 35 years. The majority of church members come from Karonga. New converts join the church through efforts, camp meetings and door to door visitations. New converts join baptisms class before being baptized by water.

The language of the church is Chichewa. The church is led by men only.

3.6.11 Mchengautuwa Church of Africa Presbyterian

Mchengautuwa Church of Africa Presbyterian is located along Chibavi to Mchengautuwa road, in between Mwenga Maize Mill and Zinazone Grocery.

The church was started in 1993 as a branch of Masasa. It started from the declaration made by Rev. Wyson Banda, parish minister at Masasa, who declared that Mchengautuwa, Zolozolo and Luwinga should have their own worshiping centres in consideration of long distances people

---

[378] Int. Grace Banda, Church Member at Mchengautuwa Seventh-day Adventist Reformed Movement, Mchengautuwa, 26.9.2013.

from these areas were travelling for church services at Masasa.[379] Judith Mlenga, Roggins Mkandawire and W. Kaunda supported the idea and they started a church at Mchengautuwa with 22 members worshiping in a house of Roggins Mkandawire. Later they bought a piece of land where they built a church.

The church has 90 members with average church attendance of 65 people, of whom the majority are women. The church is dominated by people from Chitipa, Karonga and Nkhatabay. New converts join the church through door to door visitation and open-air rallies. New converts join baptism class before being baptized by water.

The language of the church is Chitumbuka. Church leadership is for both sexes; however, men dominates.

3.6.12 Mchengautuwa New Apostolic Church

Mchengautuwa New Apostolic Church is located along Target Private Secondary School to Chibavi road

The church started in 1985 as a branch of Chiputula Church. Pastor George Kayira who was a pastor at Chiputula Church asked church members from Mchengautuwa section to open a worshiping centre at Mchengautuwa in consideration of the growth of membership and long distances people were travelling for church services at Chiputula.[380] Sanderson Mwala and Gelbart Nkosi supported the idea and started Mchengautuwa Church with 30 people worshiping in the house of Chisi. Later, Gondwe offered land free of charge to the church where they have built a church.

The church building has a capacity of 250 people. The church membership is 200 people with average church attendance of 150 people, the majority of whom are women. The dominant age group of the church is from 25 to 40 years. New members join the church through transfers and by birth. New converts join the church through open-air rallies. New converts join baptism class before being baptized by water.

The language of the church is Chitumbuka. The church is led by men.

---

[379] Int. Foreness Manda, Church Member at Mchengautuwa Church of Africa Presbyterian, Mchengautuwa, 26.9.2013.

[380] Int. Lighton Chirwa, Church Member at Mchengautuwa New Apostolic Church Mchengautuwa, 26.9.2013.

3.6.13 Sonda Assemblies of God Church

Sonda Assemblies of God Church is in Sonda area, located along Target Private School - Sonda road, and 300 metres west of Catharge Private Secondary School.

The church was started in 2008 by Pastor Joshua Msiska, worshiping at Sonda Primary School. However, the church failed to grow due to insufficient church members; as a result, they moved the church to Mchengautuwa leaving behind one church ember, F. Nyirenda, who was worshiping in her house.[381] In 2009 Chibavi Evangelism team came to Sonda and organized a big rally where eight people gave their lives to Jesus Christ. The Chibavi Evangelism team left the group of people in the hands of F. Nyirenda until when Pastor Mc Evans Gondwe took over leadership of the church.

The church has 45 members with average church attendance of 35 people, of whom the majority are women. The dominant age group of the church is 12 to 25 years. New members join the church through transfers. New converts join the church through door to door visitation and open-air rallies. New converts join baptism class.

The language of the church is Chichewa. Church leadership is for both sexes.

3.6.14 Sonda Christ Rock Church

Sonda Christ Rock Church is in Sonda area, located 200 metres west of Catharge Private Secondary School.

The church started in 2002 as a branch of Ching'ambo Church. The church was started by Fanny Singini who asked Ching'ambo church to consider the long distance she used to travel from Sonda to Ching'ambo for church service.[382] Pastor Soko accepted her request and she was given a go ahead to start the church. She started the church with 20 people while worshiping in her house. At first the church was known as a fellowship, but when the fellowship became a church, the number of members dropped to three people. The church started all over again with the three remaining people while worshiping at Sonda Primary School.

---

[381] Int. Pastor McEvens Gondwa, Church Pastor, Sonda Assemblies of God Church, Sonda, 26.9.2013.
[382] Int. Funny Singini, Church Member at Sonda Christ Rock Church, Sonda, 26.9.2013.

Slowly, more people were joining the church which made them to find a piece of land where they have built a church.

The church has 15 people with average church attendance of 10 people, of whom the majority are women. New members join the church through open-air rallies and door to door visitations. New converts join the church through water baptism without going through baptism class.

The language of the church is Chichewa. The church is led by both sexes.

3.6.15 *Sonda Bethel Tabernacle Church*

Sonda Bethel Tabernacle Church is in Sonda area located south of Sonda Primary School.

The church was started in 2011 by Pastor Augustine Chinoko, who got support from Isaac Chembezi, based in South Africa. Pastor Augustine Chinoko was a Baptist Convention Pastor serving at Enukweni Church. While there he was dismissed from serving at Enukweni Church due to some misunderstandings with church elders.[383] He came to Mzuzu where he met Isaac Chembezi who asked him to start a church in Mzuzu. Pastor Chinoko accepted the request; he started the church at Sonda with 10 people worshiping in his house. Slowly the number increased which made him to build a temporary church.

The average church attendance is 25 people, of whom the majority are women. The dominant age group of the church is 10 to 20 years. New members join the church by conversion. New converts join the church through door to door visitation and open-air rallies. New converts join the church by confirmation without going through baptism class.

The leadership of the church is for both sexes. The language of the church is Chichewa.

3.6.16 *Maria Temple*

Maria Temple is in Sonda area, located along Sonda Primary School - Luwinga Secondary School road. The temple is 300 metres north of Sonda Bethel Tabernacle Church.

Justina Maria Sakala started Maria Temple in 1997 with the idea of healing people from Physical suffering through the help from her

---

[383] Int. Coriness Chizumila, Church Pastor's wife, Sonda Bethel Tabernacle Church, Sonda, 26.9.2013.

ancestral spirits.[384] Justina Maria Sakala, a former member of Mchengautuwa CCAP Church, was initiated into traditional healing by the spirits of her departed aunts,[385] Jenala Sakala and Grace Longwe. She was initiated through the illness she suffered from in 1991 to 1993 while at Rumphi. It was revealed in her illness that in all her healing activities she will be doing, will haves to be done in prayer and worship through her ancestral spirits. She started her healing ministry with seven people in Bwangandu Village at Sonda. She changed the place to where she is now, because she was renting and the space was becoming small as many people were coming to her for help.

The official day for worship is Friday of every week, while the other days she just offers prayer. Worship services takes place in a temple where she leads the service. The average worship attendance is 25 people, the majority of whom are women. Worship participants are patients, guardians and visitors.

The temple is led by women only.[386] Chitumbuka is the common language used at the temple.

3.6.17 St Paul's Anglican Church

St Paul's Anglican Church is in Sonda area, located along Target Private School - Sonda road.

The church started in 2005 as an outstation of St Mark's Anglican Church in Mzuzu. Mayi Bai and B.N. Chirwa asked St Mark's Church to consider long distances people from Sonda were travelling for church services at St Mark's Church.[387] When permission was granted, the church started with seven people worshiping in the house of Mayi Bai. After a year, the church changed worshiping place to Mchengautuwa Primary School. When they were tired of paying rent at Mchengautuwa Primary School,

---

[384] Int. Justine Maria Sakala, Founding Member of Maria Temple, Sonda, 28.9.2013.

[385] Justina Maria Sakala has two departed aunts who are influencing the activities in her Temple, both of them died before she was born; Jenala died in 1916 while Grace died in 1919.

[386] The leadership of the temple is for women, in the sense that the owner of the temple is a woman. She does not associate herself with men; hence she might anger the spirits who are women as well.

[387] Int. Edward Phiri, Church Member, St Paul Anglican Church, Sonda, 28.9.2013.

they bought a piece of land from village headman Chiumia where they have built a permanent church. The church became a Parish in 2012, consecrated by Bishop Fanuel Magangani.

The church building has a capacity of 200 people. The church has 80 members with average church attendance of 50 people, of whom the majority are women. The dominant age group of the church is 25 to 50 years. The majority of church members are coming from Likoma and Nkhotakota. New members join the church through transfers and by birth. New converts join the church through open-air rallies. New converts join baptism class before being baptized by water.

The language of the church is Chichewa. Church leadership is done by both sexes.

3.6.18 Mchengautuwa Kingdom Gospel Church

Mchengautuwa Kingdom Gospel Church is in Mchengautuwa area, located along Mchengautuwa Market to Mzuzu Central Hospital road.

The church was started in 2003 by Pastor Moses Sichinga, who was sent to Mzuzu as a missionary from Karonga. He first started a church as a fellowship worshiping in his house together with his family. Slowly people joined the fellowship and the number of membership had gone up to five when they were officially starting a church at Chibanja. The church moved from Chibanja to Katoto Primary School, and finally moved to Mchengautuwa where they have built a church. Pastor Moses Sichinga abandoned the church when he found a better paying job; however, Pastor Yonah Mwale took over the church.[388]

The church has 40 members with average church attendance of 25 people, of whom the majority are women. The dominant age group of the church is 20 to 30 years. New members join the church by conversion. People get converted through door to door visitation and open-air rallies. New converts join a baptism class for two weeks before being baptized by water.

The language of the church is Chitumbuka. Church leadership is for both sexes; however, men are dominating.

---

[388] Int. Duncan Kayira, Church Member, St Joseph Roman Catholic Church, Mchengautuwa, 28.9.2013.

3.6.19 St Joseph Roman Catholic Church

St Joseph Roman Catholic Church is in Mchengautuwa area, located along Target Private School - Mchengautuwa Market road.

The church was started in 2006 as a substation of Katoto St Albert Church. The idea to start a church at this place came from Simon Ghambi, Benard Kayange and Tembo who were considering long distances people from the area were travelling to St Albert Church for church services.[389] When the idea was presented to St Albert Church, it was accepted and the church started with 70 people worshiping at Target Private School. Later they bought a piece of land where they built a permanent church building.

The church building has a capacity of 400 people. The church has 300 members with average church attendance of 200 people of whom the majority are women. The dominant age group of the church is 15 to 40 years. The majority of church members come from Chitipa and Karonga. New members join the church through transfers, by birth and conversion. New converts join the church through marriages. New Converts join the church through baptism class before being baptized by water.

The language of the church is Chitumbuka. Church leadership is dominated by men.

3.6.20 Mchengautuwa Baptist Convention Church

Mchengautuwa Baptist Convention Church is in Mchengautuwa area, located along Mchengautuwa market to Target Private School road.

The church was started in 1999 by Pastor Chisomo Nyirenda a member of Chibavi Baptist Convention Church before being a Pastor. When he became a Pastor, he opened Luwinga, Doloba and Mchengautuwa Baptist Convention Churches. He started Mchengautuwa Church with nobody accept his own family, he reached out to people through door to door visitation, and open-air rallies.[390] The first people to join the church were seven; among them were Kawonga, Steven Silungwe and Kondwani Zimbili. He started the church while worshiping in his house for one and a

---

[389] Int. Emmelina Kaluba, Church Member, St Joseph Roman Catholic Church, Mchengautuwa, 28.9.2013.

[390] Int. Kondwani Zimbiri, Church Member at Mchengautuwa Baptist Convention Church, Mchengautuwa, 28.9.2013.

half years, and then they moved the church to Target Private School and finally to where they built a permanent church.

The church building has a capacity of 200 people. The church has 100 members with average church attendance of 85 people, of whom the majority are women. The dominant age group of the church is 20 to 40 years. New members join the church through transfers and conversion and through door to door visitation and film shows. New converts join baptism class before being baptized by water.

The language of the church is Chichewa. The church is led by both sexes; however, men are dominating.

3.6.21 Mchengautuwa Gospel of God Church

Mchengautuwa Gospel of God Church is in Mchengautuwa area located in village headman Johana Masowi along Chibavi - Mchengautuwa Apositoli road.

The church of Mchengautuwa Gospel of God is popularly known as *Apositoli,* it started from Sonda in 1973. The church came to Sonda in 1964 initiated by Apostle Johana Masowi who wanted people of the same faith to live together.[391] Apostle Johana Masowi came to Malawi in 1960 and established the church at Matuli before he went back to Zambia. While in Zambia, he asked Patrick Hara, Smart Chirwa, Kuwale Banda and Swanord Zgobvu to find a place for the village of Gospel of God Church. The village was founded at Sonda, but because people wanted to be closer to town for easy market of tin smiting items, they moved to Mchengautuwa area.[392] The church village started with seven families, and Patrick Hara was the leader of the village. The church does not allow her members to go to the hospital when they are sick.

The church village has 400 people. The average worship attendance is 100 people, of whom women are dominating in participation.[393] The

---

[391] Int. Pastor John Smart Chirwa, Church Pastor, Mchengautuwa Gospel of God Church, Mchengautuwa, 28.9.2013.

[392] Int. Kuwale Banda, Church Member, Mchengautuwa Gospel of God Church, Mchengautuwa, 28.9.2013.

[393] The average total number of women in the church is bigger than men because most men are polygamist. However, the average church attendance is almost the same because when women are expectant, they are not allowed to

dominant age group of the church is 20 to 45 years. The majority of church members came from Mzimba. New members join the church by birth and conversion. New converts join the church through marriages, tin smiting and open-air rallies. Converted members join the church through baptism without going through baptism class.

The language of the church is Chitumbuka. The church is led by men only.

3.6.22 Mchengautuwa St Albert Catholic Church

Mchengautuwa St Albert Catholic Church is located in Bishop's area, two hundred metres north of Katoto Filling Station.

The church was started in 1954 by Bishop St Denis as a Bishop's Chapel. At that time people around Bishop's area were going to St Peters Church but due to long distances they were travelling for church services, Bishop Denis ordered all the weak and old people around Mchengautuwa to be worshiping in the Bishop's chapel.[394] The chapel became a worshiping centre for Bishop, priest, workers at the bishop's residence and the weak and old people from outside the Bishop's residence. The church started with 10 families, among them the influential members were David Ngoma, Gabriel Mhoni and Joseph Soko. As the number of worshippers was growing, the Bishop ordered the worshippers to go out of Bishop's chapel to Bishop's hall, and later he gave them a piece of land outside the Bishop's residence to build a church.[395]

The church building has a capacity of 400 people. The church membership is 350, with average church attendance of 260 people, of whom the majority are women. The dominant age group of the church is 15 to 45 years. New members join the church through transfers, birth and conversion. New converts join the church through marriages. Converts join baptism class before being baptized by water.

The leadership of the church is dominated by men. The language of the church is Chitumbuka.

---

attend church services. Int. Pastor John Smart Chirwa, Church Pastor, Mchengautuwa Gospel of God Church, Mchengautuwa, 28.9.2013.

[394] Int. Elizabeth Nzima, Church Member, Mchengautuwa St Albert Catholic Church, Mchengautuwa, 28.9.2013.

[395] Int. Daniel Mhoni, Retired Worker at Bishop's Residence, Mchengautuwa, 28.9.2013.

3.6.23 Mchengautuwa Seventh-day Adventist Church

Mchengautuwa Seventh-day Adventist Church is in Mchengautuwa area located along Bishop to Mchengautuwa Market road.

The church started in 1980 as a branch of Chibavi Church. The immediate cause to start a church was a 21 days effort which took place at Mchengautuwa ground. However, the idea to start a church at Mchengautuwa was based on the growth of church membership at Mchengautuwa and the long distances people were travelling for church services at Chibavi.[396] When the request to start a church was accepted, the church started at Mchengautuwa with seven families worshiping in the house of Weston Chilambo. The first leaders of the church while worshiping at Weston Chilambo were; Westone Chilambo, Masingi, Edward Ride and Mbeya. The church bought a piece of land at where Mchengautuwa Primary School has been built; then, they had to move to where they have built a church.[397]

The church building has a capacity of 350 people. The church membership is 300 with average church attendance of 250 people, of whom the majority are women. The dominant age group of the church is 15 to 45 years. New members join the church through transfers by birth and conversion. Conversion is done through efforts and door to door visitation. New converts join baptism class before being baptized by water.

The church is led by men. The language of the church is Chichewa.

3.6.24 Mchengautuwa Christian Love Church

Mchengautuwa Christian Love Church is in Mchengautuwa areas, located along Mchengautuwa SDA Church to Kaviwale road, two hundred metres west of Mchengautuwa SDA Church.

---

[396] Int. Kuwale Banda, Church Member at Mchengautuwa Seventh-day Adventist Church, Mchengautuwa, 28.9.2013.

[397] The place where Mchengautuwa Primary School has been built was first given to Mchengautuwa Seventh-day Adventist by Mzuzu City Assembly. The church built a temporary church building which was demolished when the primary school was being constructed. The present place where the church has been built was compensation to the lost one. Int. Kuwale Banda, Church Member at Mchengautuwa Seventh-day Adventist Church, Mchengautuwa, 28.9.2013.

The church was started in 1990 by Symon Msowoya. Symon Msowoya was a member of Karonga Christian Love Church; he left Karonga for Mzuzu to look for employment under the blessings of his Pastor, Benedictal Mwankenja.[398] While looking for employment in Mzuzu, he started a fellowship with gogo Msowoya in his house. The fellowship became big enough become a church. Members of the church were worshiping in his house before they moved to where they have built a church building.

The church building has a capacity of 100 people. The church membership is 80 people, with average church attendance of 70, of whom the majority are women. The dominant age group of the church is 15 to 35 years, the majority of church members are from Karonga.[399] New members join the church by conversion. People get converted through door to door visitation and open-air rallies. Converted members join baptism classes before being baptized by water.

The language of the church is English translated into Chichewa. Church leadership is dominated by men.

3.6.25 Mchengautuwa CCAP Church

Mchengautuwa CCAP Church is in Mchengautuwa area, located at the centre of Mchengautuwa along Bishop - Mchengautuwa market road.

The church started in 1991 as a prayer house of Chibavi congregation. People from Mchengautuwa requested Chibavi congregation to consider long distances they were travelling to Chibavi for church services and the growth of Mchengautuwa in terms of membership.[400] The idea to start a church was initiated by Newton Mbizi, Godfrey Kalivwati, Ronely Honde and Lisewell Mhone. Chibavi Session accepted the request, the church started with 15 families worshiping under a Muwula tree at where they have built Mchengautuwa Primary School. They built a temporary church

---

[398] Int. Donald Msowoya, Church Member at Mchengautuwa Christian Love Church, Mchengautuwa, 29, 9.2013.

[399] Christian Love Church came from Karonga, the founders of the church, both Karonga and Mzuzu branches, are people from Karonga; as a result, membership of the church is dominated by Karonga people. Int. Donald Msowoya, Church Member at Mchengautuwa Christian Love Church, Mchengautuwa, 29, 9.2013.

[400] Int. Godfrey Kalivwati, Church Elder at Mchengautuwa CCAP Church, Mchengautuwa, 29.9.2013.

at the same place before they had to move to where they have built a church.

The church building has a capacity of 1500 people. The church has 1600 members with average church attendance of 800 people, of whom the majority are women. The church is dominated by the age group of 20 to 50 years. New members join the church through transfers, by birth and conversion. New converts join the church through door to door visitation and open-air rallies. Converted members attend baptism class before being baptized by water.

The language of the church is Chitumbuka and English at respective church services. Leadership of the church is for both sexes; however, men are dominating.

3.6.26 Kaviwale CCAP Church

Kaviwale CCAP Church is in Kaviwale area, located along Bishop - Enyezini road west of Kaviwale Primary School.

The church started in 2005 as a prayer house of Sonda CCAP Church. The idea to start a church was a result of the growth of membership at Kaviwale area.[401] Lyson Chikoza, Vone Kayange, Sambo and Nelson Ngoma were the people who initiated the idea to start a church at Kaviwale. The church started with 20 people worshiping at Kaviwale Primary School before constructing a temporary church building at where they are intending to build a permanent church.

The church has 300 members with average church attendance of 200 people, of whom the majority are women. The church is dominated by the age group of 15 to 50 years. New members join the church through transfers, by birth and conversion. New converts join the church through door to door visitation and social services. Converted members attend baptism class before being baptized by water.

The language of the church is Chitumbuka. The church leadership is dominated by men.

---

[401] Int. Lyson Chikoza, Church Elder at Kaviwale CCAP Church, Kaviwale, 29.9.2013.

3.6.27 God's Will Church

God's Will Church is in Mchengautuwa area, located along Chibavi to Mchengautuwa via Njelenjele Private Secondary road.

The church started in 2010 by Pastor Frank Zebrone with the vision from God to help people spiritually and physically. God's Will Church started as a fellowship, worshiping in the house of Frank Zebrone who at that time was a member of Chibavi CCAP Church.[402] He started a fellowship with his own family and slowly he was joined by five more families. Zimba, Tcheleko, Nyiwanga and Mrs. Nyamunyirenda were the first members who were helping pastor Zebrone on how to start a church.[403] The church started in the Pastors house, and later they built a temporary church building before building a permanent one.

The church building has a capacity of 700 people. The church has 50 members with average church attendance of 500 people, of whom the majority are women. The dominant age group of the church is 15 to 40 years. New members join the church through healing and deliverance and a fortune seeker. These members are just participants; very few of them became converted members who can join baptism class before being baptized by water.

The language of the church is Chichewa. Church leadership is by men.

3.7 Religious Places in Katoto Ward

3.7.1 Chibanja Jehovah's Witnesses Kingdom Hall

Chibanja Jehovah's Witnesses Church is in Chibanja area, located along Chibanja - Luwinga road and 50 metres south of Kubwanga stage.

The church came to Chibanja from Chibavi in 2008. Before 2008 church members around Chibanja area were worshiping at Chibavi at a borrowed piece of land where they built a church.[404] Slowly the church was growing and it made them to think of building a bigger church. Before building a bigger church, they wanted to lease the plot but the

---

[402] Int. Costas Kamanga, Church Secretary, God's Will Church, Mchengautuwa 29.9.2013.

[403] Int. Costs Kamanga, Church Secretary, Gods Will Church, Mchengautuwa, 29.9.2013.

[404] Int. Mrs Edith Kamanga, church member, Chibanja Jehovah's' Witnesses Church, Chibanja, 30.9.2013.

City Assembly refused to process the lease, instead the City Assembly gave them another piece of land at Chibanja where they have built the church. When they had finished building the church, they left the borrowed plot and moved to a new place. The Chabanja church started with 100 people.

The church has 150 members with average church attendance of 100 people, of whom the majority are men. The dominant age group of the church is 15 to 30 years. New members join the church through transfers and by birth. The majority of church members come from Mzimba and Nkhatabay. New converts join the church through door to door, reading of magazines and public rallies. Converted members join baptism class for one year before baptism.

The church has three services in English, Chichewa and Chitumbuka, Church leadership is for men.

3.7.2 Chibanja Moravian Church

Chibanja Moravian Church is also in Chibanja area, located along Mzuzu – Karonga road and 200 metres North West of Chibanja bus stage.

The church started in 2002 by suspended church members from Mzuzu Lutheran Church.[405] The Bishop of the Lutheran Church in Malawi suspended some members of Mzuzu Lutheran Church who protested the transfer of their pastor whose wife was in poor health. The Mzuzu Lutheran pastor was being posted away of Mzuzu at the time when his wife was critically ill. The church protested against the transfer appealing to authorities to materialize the transfer when the pastor's wife got better. This did not go well with the Lutheran authorities whose Bishop suspended all the protesters. The protesters resisted the pressure and eventually asked the Moravian church in Tanzania to consider their positions.[406] The Moravian church in Tanzania accepted their request and asked Karonga branch to start a church in Mzuzu. The church started with 10 families worshiping in the house of evangelist Nathan Nkhata for a few months before renting at Katoto Secondary School. Later, they started worshiping in the house of Pastor Jeffrey Ngwaipiyana Chiona

---

[405] Int. Rev. Mourine Chikhawa, Church Pastor at Chibanja Moravian Church, Chibanja 30.9.2013.
[406] Int. Emily Nyirenda, Church Member at Chibanja Moravian Church, Chibavi, 30.9.2013.

until when they bought their own piece of land where they have built a church.

The church building has a capacity of 300 people. The church has 120 members with average church attendance of 70 people, of whom the majority are women. The dominant age group of the church is 15 to 30 years. The majority of the church members are from Chitipa.[407] New members join the church through transfers and conversion. New converts join the church through door to door visitation and open-air rallies. Converted members join baptism class before being baptized by water.

The church uses Chitumbuka and Chichewa languages. The church leadership is dominated by men.

3.7.3 *Katoto Assemblies of God Church*

Katoto Assemblies of God Church is located along St John of God Hospital - Sozibelelaini road.

The church started in 1995 as a branch of Kataba assemblies of God church. Ziba and Kawelama as leaders of Katoto section asked permission from Kataba Assemblies of God Church to consider them to start their own branch basing own the distances people were travelling to Kataba for church services. The request was answered through the crusade held at Katoto Secondary School ground which was led by Pastor Michael Danstane.[408] The crusade was successful whereby it gave birth to the church, the church started with 10 people worshiping at Katoto Secondary School Hall. Pastor Michael Danstane bought a piece of land where they have built a church.

The church building has a capacity of 400 people. The church has 250 members with average church attendance of 200 people, of whom the majority are women. The dominant age group of the church is 15 to 35 years. New members join the church through transfers, by birth and conversion. New converts join the church through home cell and annual

---

[407] Int. Moravian church came from Tanzania via Chitipa/ Karonga to Mzuzu. Chitipa district has more churches than any other district in Malawi. Int. Emily Nyirenda, Church Member at Chibanja Moravian Church, Chibavi, 30.9.2013.

[408] Int. Pastor Danwell Masamba, Church Pastor, Katoto Assemblies of God Church, Katoto, 30.9.2013.

conferences. Converted members join baptism class before being baptized by water.

The church is led by both sexes; however, men are dominating. The language of the church is English translated into Chichewa.

3.7.4 International Christian Assemblies Church

International Christian Assemblies Church is in Katoto area, located at Katoto Secondary School.

The church started as a separate branch of Assemblies of God Church in Malawi with the idea of accommodating those who feels not fitting in the existing churches in terms of culture, dressing and language.[409] The church reaches out to those living in contemporary culture, a culture which cannot be accepted in most traditional worshiping centres.[410] The International Christian Assemblies Church was started in Mzuzu from Lilongwe in 2000 by Pastor Macson Chimphungu. The church started with five families worshiping in the house next to Continental Bakery before they moved to Katoto Secondary School Main Hall.

The church has 50 members with an average church attendance of 40 people, of whom the majority are women. The dominant age group of the church is from 25 to 40 years. New members join the church by conversion. New converts join the church through call your friend and annual conferences. Converted members join baptism class before being baptized by water.

The church is led by both sexes. The language of the church is English translated into Chichewa.

3.7.5 Katoto New Apostolic Church

Katoto New Apostolic Church is located along St John of God Hospital - Sozibelelaini road.

---

[409] The church was started by the former president of the Assemblies of God of Malawi, Rev. Dr Lazarus Chakwera with the idea of reaching out to every human being. Int. Pastor Danwell Masamba, Church pastor of Katoto Assemblies of God Church, Katoto, 30.9.2013.

[410] Int. Pastor Danwell Masamba, Church pastor of Katoto Assemblies of God Church, Katoto, 30.9.2013.

The church started in 2006 as an outstation of Mzuzu New Apostolic Central Church. They started a church due to long distances people were travelling to Mzuzu Central Church for church services. Katoto New Apostolic Church started with eight families worshiping at Katoto Primary School before building their own church with the help from Blantyre New Apostolic Central Church.[411] Shepherd Kayira and, Brother Sibale were the organizers when starting the church at Katoto.

The church building has a capacity of 400 people. The church has 300 members with average church attendance of 250 people, of whom the majority are men. The church is dominated by people from Rumphi. New members join the church through transfers, by birth and conversion. New converts join baptism class before being baptized by water.

The church is led by men. The language of the church is Chichewa.

3.7.6 Katoto Calvary Family Church

Katoto Calvary Family Church is in Katoto area, located at Chithira Village along St John of God Hospital - Sozibelelaini Road and 250 metres north – east of Toyota Malawi.

The church started in 1999 as a branch of Chiputula Calvary Family Church. The proposal to start a church at Katoto came from Mponda, Pastor of the church, and Annie Kumwenda. Annie Kumwenda asked Chiputula Calvary Family Church to consider the growth of membership at Katoto and the long distances people were travelling to Chiputula for church services.[412] When permission was granted, the church started with 10 people worshiping at Our Time Private Secondary School before they went to Katoto Primary School, Katoto Secondary School and finally to where they have built a church.

The church building has a capacity of 700 people. The church has 100 members with average church attendance of 80 people, of whom the majority are women. The dominant age group of the church is 15 to 30 years. New members join the church through transfers and conversion. New converts join the church through outreaches, "call your friend" and

---

[411] Int. Brother Chisimu, Church Member, Katoto New Apostolic Church, Katoto, 30.9.2013.

[412] Ranker Kumwenda, Church Member at Katoto Calvary Family Church, Katoto, 30.9.2013.

open-air rallies. The converted members join baptism class before being baptized by water.

The language of the church is Chichewa. The church is led by both sexes; however, men dominate.

3.7.7 Chithira Peace Ministries

Chithira Peace Ministries is in Katoto area, located at Chithira Village and 240 metres north–east of Toyota Malawi.

The ministry was started in 2000 by Pastor Alick Vweza Banda. Chithira Peace Ministries started as a branch of Nkhatabay Peace Ministries. Alick Vwaza Banda, founder of Nkhatabay Peace Ministries, wanted to start a branch of his Ministry in Mzuzu. He started his Ministry at Area 1B where he was renting a house. He started Peace Ministries with his family worshiping in his house. While at Area 1B, he decided to move the worshiping centre to Ching'ambo when it was discovered that the influential members of the ministry were coming from Zolozolo and Chiputula.[413] The founder of the Ministry was unhappy with Ching'ambo worshiping centre, as a result he opened two more centres, Ziwazako and Our Time Private Secondary School, where, eventually, the three places joined together and found one common place at Katoto where they have built a worshiping centre.[414] The Katoto centre started with 20 people.

The average worship attendance is 90 people, of whom the majority are women. The dominant age group of the ministry is 20 to 40 years. New members join the ministry through conversion. Converted members join the ministry through "call your friend" evangelism and door to door visitation. The converted members join baptism class before being baptized by water.

The church is led by both sexes. The language of the church is Chichewa.

---

[413] Int. Allen Njakwa, Wife of Pastor Alick Vweza Banda Founding Member of Peace Ministries, Chithira, 20.9.2013.

[414] Int. Zilawa Chavwanga, Former Church Member of Peace Ministries, Katoto, 20.9.2013.

3.7.8 Christ Citadel International Church

Christ Citadel International Church is in Katoto area, located along at Chithira Village, off St John of God Hospital - Sozibelelaini road at Calvary Family Church towards Toyota Malawi.

The church started in 1995 by Mwendo Phiri, who was working with World Vision International Mzuzu Division. Mwendo Phiri was the only member of Christ Citadel International Church when he came to Mzuzu.[415] As he was in Mzuzu, he did not want to join any denomination; instead he started Christ Citadel International Church with his family. The church started as a fellowship worshiping in the house of Mwendo Phiri. Slowly more people started joining the church and they changed the worshiping place from Mwendo Phiri's house to a recreation centre at Viphya and then to where they have built their church.

The church building has a capacity of 300 people. The church has 70 members with average church attendance of 50 people, of whom the majority are women. The dominant age group of the church is 20 to 40 years. New members join the church by conversion; conversion is done through one to one witnessing and mass evangelism. New converts join baptism class before being baptized by water.

The leadership of the church is for both sexes. The language of the church is English translated into Chichewa.

3.7.9 Katoto Medicine Ministry Church

Katoto Medicine Ministry Church is in Katoto area, located at Chithira Village, close to St John of God Hospital.

The church was started in 2009 by Tryson Mphande, under the leadership of Pastor Mphapo who was in Blantyre. Pastor Mphapo asked Tryson Mphande, former member of Zolozolo CCAP Church, to start a church in Mzuzu. Tryson Mphande started a church with his family and five people more people worshiping in his house. When the number of church members became bigger, Pastor Mphapo came from Blantyre and took over leadership of the church who eventually changed the

---

[415] Int. Gray Kapanga, Church Member of Christ Citadel International Church, Katoto, 30.9.2013.

worshiping place from Tryson Mphande's house to Zolozolo Primary School and finally to where they have built a church today.[416]

The church building has a capacity of 300 people. The church has 80 members with average church attendance of 70 people, of whom the majority are women. The dominant age group of the church is 20 to 35 years. New members join the church by conversion, conversion is done through door to door visitation and open-air rallies. New converts join baptism class before being baptized by water.

The church is led by both sexes. The language of the church is Chichewa.

3.7.10 SOS Living Waters Church

SOS Living Waters Church is in Hilltop area, located along National Bank - Kawuwa road and 200 metres west of Kawuwa Primary School.

The church was started in 1990 by Pastor Kawomba who was sent by Apostle Ndovi to start Living Waters Church in Mzuzu. Pastor Kawomba started the church in his house with his family as a fellowship. When the number of fellowship members was growing, Pastor Kawomba decided to change the worshiping centre from his house to Katoto Secondary School Hall. The change of worship place marked the launching of Living Waters Church in Mzuzu.[417] The church bought a piece of land at Hilltop where they have built a church and a Bible School, from where they changed their worshiping Centre to date. The Bible School started with five students taught by Pastor Nyangulu and Chaula.

The church building has a capacity of 400 people. The church has 100 people with average church attendance of 80 people, of whom the majority are women. The dominant age group of the church is 15 to 40 years. New members join the church through transfers and conversion. Conversion is done through open-air rallies and personal contact. New convents join baptism class before being baptized by water.

The church is led by both sexes. The language of the church is English translated into Chichewa.

---

[416] Int. Pastor Mphapo, Church Minister at Katoto Medicine Ministry, Katoto, 30.9.2013.
[417] Int. Mrs Olive P.S. Msiska, wife of a church Pastor, SOS Living Waters Church, Hilltop, 2.10.2013.

3.7.11 Mzuzu Winners Chapel Church

Mzuzu Winners Chapel Church is in Hilltop area, located along National Bank - Kawuwa road and hundred metres to the south of SOS Living Waters Church.

The church came to Mzuzu from Lilongwe by Sister Chenda Mkandawire in 2005. Sister Chenda was converted when she was in Lilongwe before she came to Mzuzu. While in Mzuzu, she was joined by a friend and started a church through lunch hour fellowships at Chenda Hall. When the number of worshippers was increasing, they started open-air rallies, face to face and "call your friend" evangelism. When the fellowship became more of a church, they received a Pastor who eventually changed the worship place to a Baptist Church Hall at Hilltop.[418]

The church has 120 members with average church attendance of 70 people, of whom the majority are women. The dominant age group of the church is 20 to 30 years. New members join the church by conversion. Conversion is done through the provision of material help, open-air rallies and media advertisement. New converts join baptism class before being baptized by water.

Church leadership is for both sexes. The language of the church is English translated into Chichewa.

3.7.12 Chisomo Baptist Church

Chisomo Baptist Church is in Hilltop area, located a long National Bank - Kawuwa road and hundred metres west of Kawuwa Primary School.

The church was started in 1998 by Pastor H. Chapulapula, former Mzuzu Baptist Church pastor. Chisomo Baptist Church started as a brake away of Mzuzu Baptist Convention Church due to disagreements between Mzuzu Baptist Convention Church and Pastor H. Chapulapula. The disagreements were big enough and made Pastor Chapulapula to resign his membership from the church and started his own church.[419] When the Pastor was resigning from the church, he resigned together with 26 other church members, such as V. Muthali, P. Steven, Mwambagi, T.N. Phiri and Nkhwinika, who together with him started Chisomo Baptist

---

[418] Int. Brother Progress Mbumba, Church Evangelist at Mzuzu Winners Chapel Church, Hilltop, 2.10.2013.

[419] Int. Pastor Chapulapula, Church Pastor at Chisomo Baptist Church, Hilltop, 2.10.2013.

Church. The church started at Bazala Private School before they bought a piece of land where they have built a church. Chisomo Baptist Church also met in the Baptist Training Centre and after at Hilltop School (owned by the Munthalis).

The church has 150 members with average church attendance of 130 people, of whom the majority are women. The dominant age group of the church is 15 to 45 years. New members join the church through transfers and conversion. Conversion is done through, open-air rallies and door to door evangelism. New converts join baptism class before being baptized by water.

Chisomo Baptist Church building has a capacity of 600 people. The church is led by both sexes. The language of the church is Chichewa.

3.7.13 Hilltop Kandaha Mosque

Hilltop Kandaha Mosque is in Hilltop area, located along National Bank - Kawuwa road and two hundred metres to the north of Kawuwa Primary School.

The mosque started in 1999 with funding from Malawi Government as compensation for burnt mosques of 1999 General Election results. The results of General Election of 1999 caused riots between Muslims and non-Muslims in Mzuzu; as a result, same mosques were burnt down and destroyed.[420] The Malawi Government took up the responsibility to rebuild the destroyed mosques; the compensation was overestimated to the extent of building a complete new Kandaha Mosque which was not part of the destruction.[421] The administrators of the construction of Kandaha mosque were Brothers Mambo, Mkwanda and Husein. After finishing building the mosque, worship started with 30 people who were from Hardware and Matabwa mosques.

The average mosque attendance is 60 people, of whom the majority are men. The dominant age group of the worshippers is 25 to 45 years. The majority of the mosque members come from Mangochi. New members

---

[420] Int. Abdullah Solomon, Mosque worker, Hilltop Kandaha Mosque, Hilltop, 2.10.2013. See Ibrahim Milazi, "The Burning of Mosques in the North: Is it the Beginning or Climax of Political Fanaticism or Christian Fundamentalism in Malawi?" *Religion in Malawi*, No. 9, November, 1999.

[421] Int. Abdullah Solomon, Mosque worker, Hilltop Kandaha Mosque, Hilltop, 2.10.2013.

join the mosque through transfers and by conversion. Conversion is done through dawah (open-air rallies). New converts join an instruction class before being baptized.

The leadership of the mosque is by men. Arabic and Chichewa are the languages used in the mosque.

3.7.14 Kawuwa Seventh-day Adventist Church

Kawuwa Seventh-day Adventist Church is in Hilltop area, located along National Bank - Kawuwa road and 20 metres east of Kawuwa market.

The church started in 1990 as a branch of Chasefu Seventh-day Adventist Church. Kawuwa Seventh-day Adventist Church started in consideration of long distances people from Kawuwa were travelling to Chasefu for church services; and there was also growth of membership around the area.[422] When the request was presented to Chasefu Church, permission was granted to Kawuwa church members to start a church. The church first started at Elamuleni, and then it moved to Gezamugomo and finally came to Kawuwa.

The church building has a capacity of 400 people. The church has 200 members with average church attendance of 150 people, of whom the majority are women. The dominant age group of the church is 12 to 35 years. The church is dominated by people from Nkhatabay. New members join the church through transfers, by birth and conversion. Conversion is done through efforts and home cells. Converted members join baptism class before being baptized by water.

The church leadership is dominated by men. The language of the church is Chichewa.

3.7.15 Katoto Bible Believers Church

Katoto' Bible Believers Church'[423] is in Hilltop area, located along National Bank - Kawuwa road and hundred metres south of SOS Living Waters Church.

---

[422] Int. Lyness Phiri, Church Member, Kawuwa Seventh-day Adventist Church, Kawuwa, 2.10.2013.

[423] For a detailed study of the Bible Believers, see Richard Gadama, The Bible Believers in Malawi: History, Teaching and Practices (1979-2011), MA, Mzuzu University, 2012.

The Church started in 2004 from the closure of Msongwe Bible Believers Church. Msongwe Bible Believers Church started in 1990 by Pastor Kaluwa who was converted from CCAP through the teachings of Bible Believers Church. He started a church as a fellowship with his family worshiping in his house. When the number of fellowship members became bigger, they constructed a church at Msongwe where they were worshiping. Some of the church members, Harrison Kaluwa, Gelezi and Mkumbwa proposed to sell the Msongwe Church and open up a church at Hilltop because influential members were coming from Hilltop.[424] The ideal was accepted by the church; they sold the Msongwe Church building and started a church at Hilltop in 2004.

The church building has a capacity of 200 people. The church has 100 members with an average church attendance of 80 people, of whom the majority are women. The dominant age group of the church is 20 to 45 years. The majority of church members come from Chitipa. New members join the church through transfers and conversion. Conversion is done through open-air rallies and door to door evangelism. The converted members join baptism class before being baptized by water.

The leadership of the church is for men only. The language of the church is English translated into Chichewa.

3.7.16 Victory Christian Temple

Victory Christian Temple is in Mapale, located along Katoto - Hilltop road.

The church was started by Pastor and Mrs Moffat Phiri in 2001. The idea and all required support to start a church came from the wife of Pastor Moffat Phiri. Mrs Pastor Moffat Phiri is a white lady, married to Pastor Moffat Phiri while she was teaching at Lilongwe Assembles of God Bible School where Pastor Moffat Phiri was a student.[425] When they got married, they started teaching at Kande Bible School where they dropped and started a church in Mzuzu. The church started as a fellowship worshiping in the house of Pastor and Mrs Phiri at Katoto Housing Estate. While doing fellowship, they started door to door visitation which made many people to join the church and eventually

---

[424] Int. Alex Chiluwa, Church Member, Katoto Bible Believers Church, Kamuwa, 2.10.2013.
[425] Int. Shene Honde, Church Worker, Victory Christian Temple, Mapale, 3.10.2013.

moved the worshiping place to Skyways Private School, and then to Katoto Secondary School Hall and finally to a place where they have built their own church.

The church building has a capacity of 600 people. The church membership is 100 with average church attendance of 80 people, of whom the majority are women. The dominant age group of the church is 20 to 35 years. New members join the church by conversion. Conversion is done through giving out material help. Those converted join the church without going through any class of baptism.

The leadership of the church is for both sexes. The dominant language of the church is English translated into Chichewa.

3.7.17 Glorious Light Church

Glorious Light Church is located at Kawuwa Primary School.

The church started in 2003 with five people who were already members of the church from Karonga. Mai Kamweko Kalua, Davison Chikumba and Nyirenda among others came from Karonga to work in Mzuzu on transfers.[426] While in Mzuzu, they did not join any denomination instead they organized themselves doing fellowship within their houses. They asked Bishop Simama to give them a Pastor who could nurture them. Bishop Simama sent Pastor Mfune to nurture the church, he changed the worshiping place from Christian houses to Chenda Hall and finally at Kawuwa Primary School.

The church has 15 people with average church attendance of 10 people, of whom the majority are men. The dominant age group of the church is 25 to 35 years. The majority of church members come from Karonga. New members join the church through conversion. Conversion is done through open-air rallies, door to door visitation and provision of material help.[427] New converts go for baptism without joining baptism class.

The church is led by men. The dominant language of the church is Chichewa.

---

[426] Int. Pastor Chimwemwe Mangani, Church Pastor at Glorious Light Church, Kawuwa, 3.10.2013.

[427] The Glorious Light Church gives money to church members who have participated Sunday Service with the idea that it is the duty of the church to give help to people. Int. Pastor Chimwemwe Mangani, Church Pastor at Glorious Light Church, Kawuwa, 3.10.2013.

3.7.18 Mzuzu Baptist Convention Church

The Mzuzu Baptist Convention Church is in Kaning'ina area, located along Mzuzu - Nkhata bay road, 50 metres west of Malawi Broadcasting Cooperation (MBC).

The Church was started by Njolomole Phiri and Garry Swafford in 1972. These two people were on a church plantation tour in the northern region of Malawi. The church started as a result of bible study groups and fellowships organized by Njolomole Phiri and Garry Swafford in Mzuzu. The Baptist Convention Bible Study and fellowship groups in Mzuzu were meeting at the rented shop of Chimpozo near Taifa market, at old main bus depot.[428] When the number of worship member had fully grown, the place became small as a result; they bought a Masonic Lodge where they renovated the building into a church.[429] Mzuzu Baptist Convention Church later became the primary centre of all Baptist Convention activities in the northern region. Some of the earliest members who joined Mzuzu Baptist Convention Church with Njolomole Phiri and Swafford were Simbeye and Chikula. The church moved from the Masonic Lodge building to where they have built the church today because many people were suspicious and afraid to join them because people were failing to differentiate it from the activities of the former occupant.[430]

The church has a capacity of 500 people. The average church attendance is 300 people, of whom the majority are women. The majority of church members come from Nkhata bay. New members join the church through transfers, by birth and conversion. New converts join the church through door to door evangelism and open-air rallies. Newly converted members join baptism class before being baptized by water.

Languages of the church are English and Chichewa (with some Chitumbuka) for respective church services. The church is led by both sexes; however, men are dominating.

---

[428] Int. Aless Nyirenda, Church Member, Mzuzu Baptist Convention of Malawi Church, Kaning'ina, 3.10.2013.

[429] Int. Martha Phiri, Church Member, Mzuzu Baptist Convention of Malawi Church, Kaning'ina, 3.10.2013.

[430] For detailed information on the origin of Mzuzu Baptist Convention Church and Masonic Lodge building, see; Hany Longwe, *Christian by Grace – Baptists by Choice, A History of the Baptist Convention of Malawi*, Mzuzu: Mzuni Press, 2011, p. 79.

3.7.19 Mzuzu International Pentecostal Holiness Church

Mzuzu International Pentecostal Holiness Church is in Kaning'ina area, located along Mzuzu - Nkhata bay road and to the north-west of Malawi Broadcasting Corporation Studio.

The church started at Chiputula with Pastor Msikiti who came from Lilongwe in 1993. When Pastor Msikiti came to Chiputula, he started a church through fellowship with his family where they were renting a house.[431] Pastor Msikiti, through house to house visitation found members of International Pentecostal Holiness Church who joined the church before coming to Mzuzu, such as Mwakiwinga and Shaba, and this was the first group that joined the church at Chiputula.[432] As the number of church members was growing, the house in which they were worshiping became small; as a result they bought a piece of land where they built a temporary church and later a permanent one.

The church building has a capacity of 400 people. The church membership is 200 people with average church attendance of 130 people,[433] of whom the majority are women. The dominant age group of the church is 15 to 35 years. New members join the church through conversion. Conversion is done through door to door visitation, Home cells and open-air rallies. The church emphasizes spirit baptism.

The leadership of the church is for both sexes. The language of the church is English translated into Chichewa.

3.7.20 St Mark's Anglican Church

St Mark's Anglican Church is in Kaning'ina area located opposite the High Court and along the Mzuzu to Nkhatabay road.

---

[431] Int. Pastor Tony Mkamanga, Church Pastor at Mzuzu International Pentecostal Holiness Church, Kaning'ina, 3.10.2013.

[432] Int. Pastor Msikiti, Former Church Pastor of Mzuzu International Pentecostal Holiness Church, Mzilawayingwe, 18.9.2013.

[433] At first the majority of church members were coming from the south, but when Pastor Msikiti had left the church, he went away with the whole membership from south. However, in the today's membership the majority of them are coming from Rumphi because Pastor Mkamanga comes from Rumphi while Pastor Msikiti came from South. Int. Pastor Tony Mkamanga, Church Pastor at Mzuzu International Pentecostal Holiness Church, Kaning'ina, 3.10.2013.

St Mark's Anglican Church started as a combination of European and Malawian Anglican Church members in 1957. The Anglican denominational worship in Mzuzu had started in 1950. At first Europeans and Malawians were worshiping in the name of fellowships in selected homes in respective of colour, Europeans were meeting at the house of Sir Martin and Lady Rosevaere, while Malawians were meeting at the house of C. Chisale.[434] When the number of church members was growing, the a decided to build a church which could accommodate Europeans and the few educated Malawians in 1957. The church was consecrated by Bishop Frank Thorne. The first people who became part of membership of the church were; Martin Roseveare, the Commissioner of Police, staff from Tung Oil Plantation, C. Chisala and Edwin Mwase; after some time, the church was open to all Anglican Church members.[435]

The church has 500 members with average church attendance of 400 people, of whom the majority are women. The church is dominated by members from Likoma, Mangochi and Nkhotakota along the lake shore. New members join the church through transfers, by birth and conversion. Conversion is done through open-air rallies and material help. Converted members join baptism class before being baptized by water.

The church leadership is dominated by men. English and Chichewa are the common languages in the respective church services.

3.7.21 Jomo Kenyatta Road Church of Christ

Jomo Road Church of Christ is in Kaning'ina area, located along Jomo Kenyatta road, east of Regional Police Station.

The church started as a fellowship in 1968 at Zolozolo east. People who started the church were eight; amongst them were Patrick Ngwira, Franklin Mhango and Wickson Kumwenda. Church members organized themselves as a fellowship until when Pastor Chilambo was posted to Mzuzu to nurture Zolozolo church.[436] He changed the worship from fellowship to a church. He moved the church to where he bought a piece

---

[434] Int. Arch Deacon James Kenane Chifisi, Parish Minister, St Marks Anglican Church, Kaning'ina 3.10.2013.
[435] Int. Fr. Arther Chitone, Chaplain of St Mary's Convent, Luwinga, 11.8.2011.
[436] Int. Pastor Lingstone Mlotha, Church Pastor at Jomo Road Church of Christ, Kaning'ina, 3.10.2013.

of land at Kaning'ina where he built a temporary church and later a permanent one. In 1989, the church was joined by Bible School led by Jones D. Rujato who came from Chinyolo in Rumphi; however, the Bible School stayed for a short while and then found its place at Luwinga area.[437] Jomo Kenyatta Road Church of Christ became the centre of all Church of Christ activities in the northern region.

The church building has a capacity of 500 people. The church membership is 300 with average church attendance of 250 people, of whom the majority are men. The dominant age group of the church is 20 to 40 years. New members join the church through transfers, by birth and conversion. New converts join the church through door to door evangelism and open-air rallies. The converted members join baptism class before being baptized by water.

Chitumbuka is the dominant language of the church. The church is led by men only.

3.7.22 *Mzuzu Central New Apostolic Church*

Mzuzu Central New Apostolic Church is in Kaning'ina area, located along Jomo Kenyatta Road, East of the Regional Police Camp.

The church started in 1990 from the idea of building a central church in Mzuzu City. The idea of a central church came from New Apostolic World Headquarters in Germany who asked Mzuzu New Apostolic Churches to give them a place where they could build a central church for the city.[438] The place was provided by closing some other branches, i.e. Zolozolo, Moyale and Chibavi.[439] At first the central church was thought to be built at Zolozolo, however, the idea was dropped because Zolozolo was considered to be far from town and was not a central place for churches around the city. Mzuzu Central New Apostolic Church was built with funding from Germany, when the construction of the church building was finished; the building was handed over to church members to start using it. The church started with 300 people.

---

[437] Int. Elengtone Harawa, Lecture at Mzuzu Church of Christ College, Luwinga, 20.8.2013.

[438] Int. Evangelist Andrew Tembo, Church Evangelist, Mzuzu Central New Apostolic Church, Kaning'ina, 3.10.2013.

[439] Int. Nicely Nyirenda, Church Member at Msongwe New Apostolic Church, Msongwe, 11.10.2013.

The church building has a capacity of 500 people. The membership of the church 400 with average church attendance of 300 people, of whom majority are women. The dominant age group of the church is 25 to 50 years. The majority of church members are coming from Rumphi district.[440] New members join the church through transfers and conversion. New converts join baptism class for three months before being baptized.

The church is led by men only. Chichewa and Chitumbuka are common languages in the church.

3.7.23 Police CCAP Church

Police CCAP Church is in Police Camp, located west of the administration block.

The church started in 1990 as a branch of Mzuzu CCAP. Police CCAP Church members asked Mzuzu Session to consider the growth of membership at Police and the time limitation for Police Officers as they are required to work even if they could be off duty.[441] The Mzuzu Session, moderated by Rev. H.K. Mvula, accepted the request. The church started with 30 people worshiping in a Police Hall. The church has members from Police Station and surrounding areas.

The church has a capacity of 400 with average church attendance of 250 people, of whom majority are women. The dominant age group of the church is 15 to 45 years. The majority of the church members are from Police station. New members join the church through transfers and by birth.

The church is led by both sexes; however, men are dominating. The language of the church is Chichewa.

3.7.24 City Chipangano Church

City Chipangano Church is in Kaning'ina area, located along Jomo Kenyatta Road, East of the Regional Police Camp.

---

[440] More church members seem to come from Rumphi because the church started from Rumphi when it first come from Zambia before coming to Mzuzu at Zolozolo. Int. Nicely Nyirenda, Church Member at Msongwe New Apostolic Church, Msongwe, 11.10.2013.

[441] Int. Evans Masiyano, Chairperson at Police CCAP Church, Police Station, 5.10.2013.

The church was started in 1950 by church members from Phiri in Nkhatabay who came to work with Tung Oil Plantation in Mzuzu. Chipangano Church was started by Isaac Chazuka Kaunda, a teacher who taught at Phiri CCAP Primary School in Nkhatabay. The church came to Mzuzu with its first converts who happened to be taught by him at Phiri Primary School and they were working in Mzuzu. The church in Mzuzu started at Chiputula, but later, when Isaac Chazuka Kaunda came to Mzuzu, he changed the worship place and established it at this present place.[442] The Chipangano Church went back to Chiputula under the leadership of Kapoli because of the Tung Oil Estate owner who claimed back their land. In 1978, when Tung Oil Estate was almost abandoned, Chipangano Church claimed back their land. Mzuzu City Assembly gave back their land and advised them to build a bigger church; the advice made them to close all other branches within the City and built one church at the present place.[443] The church attracted many members because it was giving freedom to worshippers to do what seemed restrictive from the mainline churches.

The church has 110 members with average church attendance of 60 people, of whom the women are in the majority. The church is dominated by the age group of 25 to 50 years. The majority of church members come from Nkhatabay. New members join the church through transfers and by birth.

The church is led by men. The language of the church is Chitumbuka.

3.7.25 *Mzuzu Central Mosque*

Mzuzu Central Mosque, commonly known as Hardware Mosque, is in Old Town, located next to Hardware Market.

The mosque came to Mzuzu as a substation of Ekwendeni Mosque in 1960. Mzuzu Central Mosque was started by Indians, Wali Karim (Kalimu) and Hassam Gero, together with Malawian Muslims from Mangochi and Nkhotakota who were working with Indians. Hasan Gero and Wali Kareem asked permission from Ekwendeni Mosque to allow Muslims from Mzuzu to start their own mosque in consideration of the growth of

---

[442] Int. Rev. Principal Wisman Kayira, Church Principal, City Chipangano Church, Kaning'ina, 5.10.2013.
[443] Int. Rev. J.P. Nyirenda, Church Coordinator at City Chipangano Church, Kaning'ina, 5.10.2013.

membership in Mzuzu and the long distances people from Mzuzu were travelling for worshiping at Ekwendeni.[444] When permission was granted, they started worshiping in a temporary Mosque built by Wali Karim and Hassam Gero at where the present mosque has been built. The Mosque is for both Indians and Malawians.

The mosque has a capacity of 600 people. The mosque membership is 500 with average worshiping attendance of 400 people, of whom the majority are women. The dominant age group of the mosque is 15 to 45 years. The majority of mosque members come from Mangochi and Nkhotakota. New members join the Mosque through transfers and conversion. Conversion is done through job opportunities working under Muslim Indians.

The languages of the mosque are Arabic and Chichewa. The mosque is led by men.

3.7.26 Hindu Servants Semaj

Hindu servants *Semaj*, servants of community, is located in every Hindu house.

The worship of Hindu Servants Semaj came from Eastern India by Rasck Patel, owner of Classic Centre, in 1994. Rasck Patel was joined by Swang in the worship making two families. Hindu Servants Semaj worship has no central church building. Church members worship in their family houses from 7 pm to 8:30 pm every Tuesdays except when they have a common worship of anniversaries.[445] The church has different gods, about 32 billion, however, the most common ones are Senknr (creator), Bratua (spirit) and Vishan (sustainer), and all gods were created through these three gods.[446]

The average worship attendance depends upon the size of the family. The total number of Hindu worshippers is 100 people of whom the majority are youth. The church is dominated by Indians. New members join the church through transfers and by birth

---

[444] Int. H.H. Munthali, working with H.H. Wholesalers, Friend of Hasan Gero and Wali Kalimu, Mzuzu, 5.10.2013.
[445] Int. Rasck Patel, Respected Founding Member of Hindu Servants Semaj Church, Mzuzu City, 5.10.2013.
[446] Int. Jubea Patel, Church Member at Hindu Servants Semaj Church, Mzuzu City, 5.10.20013.

The groups have no central leadership; however, each group is led by the family head. The language of worship is Hindi.

3.7.27 Masjd Anwarullmadina Mosque

Masjd Anwarullmadina Mosque (commonly known as Vigwagwa Market Mosque) is located south of Vigwagwa Market.

The Vigwagwa Mosque started in 1999. The mosque started with members from various mosques with the idea of having one Central Qudiriyya Mosque parallel to Mzuzu Central Sunni Mosque.[447] The starting of Vigwagwa Mosque was organized by Z. Brothers, Choma, Tawonga and Abdulhamed who, upon looking at the growth of Muslim population in Mzuzu City, felt the need to establish another bigger mosque in order to provide enough space for the growing Muslim population.[448] The above mentioned people handed over their buildings for a mosque and madrassah which were meant for warehouse. The buildings were renovated fit for a Mosque and Madrassah. The Mosque started with 200 people of different races.

The average worship attendance is 400 people, of whom the majority are men. The dominant age group of the mosque is 20 to 45 years. The majority of Mosque members are coming from Mangochi. New members join the Mosque through transfers and conversion. Conversion is done through job opportunities working with Muslim Indians.

The languages of the mosque are Arabic and Chichewa. The leadership of the Mosque is by men.

3.7.28 Mzuzu Seventh-day Adventist Central Church

Mzuzu Seventh-day Adventist Central Church is in Katoto area, located north–west of Katoto Filling Station, next to Harry Guest House.

The church started in 1980 as an outstation of Chasefu Seventh-day Adventist Church. The idea to start a church at Katoto was in consideration of the growth of membership at Katoto and the long distances people were traveling for church services at Chasefu Church in

---

[447] Int. Sheik Anwar, Sheik of Masjd Anwarullmadina Mosque, Mzuzu, 5.10.2013.
[448] Int. Sheik Anwar, Sheik of Masjd Anwarullmadina Mosque, Mzuzu, 5.10.2013.

Katawa.[449] The church started after a 21 days effort done at Katoto Secondary School ground. After the effort, people like; J.G. Mwase, Namwali and Chavunguma Msachi together with 10 other people started the church worshiping at Katoto Secondary School.[450] The church changed its worship place from Katoto Secondary School to Katoto Primary School, and then to Police Hall and finally built their own church where the church is found at present.

The church building has a capacity of 500 people. The church membership is 500 with an average church attendance of 350 people, of whom the majority are women. The dominant age group of the church is 15 to 45 years. The majority of the church members come from Lunjika in Mzimba, Luwazi in Nkhatabay and Nkholongo. New members join the church through transfers, by birth and conversion. Converted members join baptism class before being baptized by water.

The language of the church is Chichewa. The church is led by both sexes; however, men are dominating.

3.7.29 Mzuzu CCAP Church

Mzuzu CCAP Church, commonly known as St Andrew's, is located east of the central Livingstonia CCAP Synod Offices.

The Mzuzu CCAP Church started from Lupaso CCAP Church in 1954. The church started to provide spiritual help to people working under Tung Oil Company. Before 1954, all people in Mzuzu were worshiping at Lupaso CCAP Church. The majority of workers at Tung Oil Estate were CCAP members. It is believed that W.K. Nyirenda, one of the first Christians, asked Lupaso church to consider the growth of membership at Mzuzu and long distances people from Tung Oil Estate in Mzuzu were travelling for church services at Lupaso.[451] Lupaso Church took further the request to Ekwendeni Mission Station for consideration. When the request was accepted, the church started with 45 members at Jombo, where there is

---

[449] Int. S.B. Nyirongo, Church Member at Mzuzu Seventh-day Adventist Central Church, Katoto, 5.10.2013.
[450] Int. Mama Nyirongo, Church Member at Mzuzu Seventh-day Adventist Central Church, Katoto, 5.10.2013.
[451] Int. Opson Thole, Church Member at Mzuzu CCAP Church, Mzuzu, 5.10.2013.

Taifa Market, under a *Mpapa* tree.[452] The church moved from Jombo area to the present-day place due to shortage of space because it was surrounded by the camp of workers of Tung Oil Company and the graveyard to the other side.

Mzuzu CCAP Church became a congregation from Ekwendeni in 1959 with Lupaso and Lusangazi branches. When Mzuzu CCAP Church became a congregation, evangelist Mhlanga, was sent from Ekwendeni to Mzuzu to nurture the new congregation. The first Church Minister to be sent to Mzuzu was Titus Thole who came from Daressalam in Tanzania; however, he died after staying in the congregation for three months.[453] Later Rev. Nkhowani took over the congregation but he too died after three years, he died when he was coming from a church meeting at Kavuzi Church. Mzuzu Church had grown far and wide because of Tung Oil Company which later was changed from Tung Oil Estate to provincial Headquarters. The Tung Oil Estate changed her ownership from commonwealth Development Corporation to Farmers Marketing Board. Today the church is in the centre of Mzuzu city.

The first permanent church building was built in 1963; however, the church building was small and was extended in 1975 by Rev. Y.C. Kaunda. Due to the growing population of Mzuzu City, the church building was felt small again. In 1986, under the leadership of Rev. A.M. Mfuni, the church decided to build a new church which was completed in 2000. The new church building has a capacity of 1600 people. The church has a membership of 2000 with average church attendance of 900 people, of whom the majority are women. The church is dominated by age group of 20 to 50 years. New members join the church through transfers, by birth and conversion. New converts join the church through door to door visitation and open-air rallies. Converted members join baptism class before being baptized by water.

The church is led by both sexes. English and Tumbuka are the common languages.

---

[452] Int. Johnstone Sibande, Worked with Tung Oil Estate in the Early Days, Mzuzu. 5.10.2013.

[453] Int. Rev. M.M.D. Sibande, Former Parish Minister at Mzuzu CCAP Church, Luwinga, 5.16.2013.

3.8 Religious Places in Masasa/Msongwe Ward

3.8.1 Moyale Anglican Church

Moyale Anglican Church is in Moyale area, located inside Moyale Barracks, South of the Administration Building.

The church started in 1992 as an outstation of St Mark's Anglican Church. Church members from Moyale Barracks, Kasiwale, Chinjati and Nindi, asked St Mark's church to consider the growth of membership at Moyale and long distances people were travelling for church services to St Mark's.[454] The St Mark's Church accepted the request and the church started at Moyale with 20 people from Moyale Barracks, Mzuzu Government Secondary School and surrounding areas. The church started while worshiping at Moyale Primary School; later Bishop Biggers built them a church in 2006.

The church has 100 members with an average church attendance of 65 people, of whom the majority are women. The church is dominated by members from Likoma, Nkhota Kota and Mangochi. New members join the church through transfers and by birth.

The church is led by both sexes; however, men are dominating. Language of the church is Chichewa.

3.8.2 St Joseph Roman Catholic Church

St Joseph Roman Catholic Church is in Moyale area, located inside Moyale Barracks, west of the Administration Building.

The church started as an outstation of St Peters Church in 1978, just when Moyale Barracks was starting as a barracks. Moyale Barracks started as a training school in 1967; from that time to 1978 it was a section of St Peters Church.[455] When Moyale Barracks became a barracks, the numbers of church members grew as a result, they asked for an outstation of St Peters Church. Evangelist Mweso and Zulu were among the people who asked St Peters church to give permission to Moyale Section to start an outstation. When permission was granted, the church started with 50 people worshiping in Officers Mess Hall.

---

[454] Int. J. Nindi, Church Member, Moyale Anglican Church, Moyale Barracks, 4.10.2013.
[455] Int. Name withheld, Church Member, St Joseph Roman Catholic Church, Moyale Barracks, 4.10.2013.

The church has 200 members with average church attendance of 140 people, of whom the majority are women. The dominant age group of the church is 25 to 55 years. New members join the church through transfers and by birth.

The church is led by men. The language of the church is Chichewa.

3.8.3 Moyale CCAP Church

Moyale CCAP Church is located inside Moyale Barracks, south–east of the Administration Building.

The church started in 1978 when Moyale Barracks became a Barracks. When Moyale was a training school, church members were worshiping at Mzuzu CCAP Church. Moyale CCAP Church became a church because of the growing number of church members when Moyale Training school became Moyale Barracks.[456] Peter Zako, Ngamuti and Dickson Phiri asked Mzuzu CCAP Church to consider the growth of membership in the barracks. When Mzuzu CCAP Church accepted the request, the church started with 30 people worshiping in the Officers Mess Hall. Later they built their own church initiated by Rev Major Makuni Gondwe.

The church building has a capacity of 400 people. The church membership is 300 with average church attendance of 200 people, of whom the majority are women. The dominant age group of the church is 20 to 45 years. The majority of church members are form Moyale Barracks and nearby areas. New members join the church through transfers and by birth.

The church is led by men. The language of the church is Chichewa.

3.8.4 Mzuzu Government Secondary School CCAP Church

The Mzuzu Government Secondary School CCAP Church is located at Mzuzu Government Secondary School.

The church started in 2006 out of the declaration from the headmaster that all students should be attending church services inside the school campus.[457] Before 2006, all CCAP church members were going to Mzuzu

---

[456] Int. Francis Kasaso, Session Clerk at Moyale CCAP Church, Moyale Barracks, 4.10.2013.
[457] Int. Munyimbili, Vice Chairperson at Mzuzu Government Secondary School CCAP Church, 4.10.2013.

CCAP Church for church services. When the declaration was passed, Mzuzu CCAP Church allowed all members from Mzuzu Government Secondary School to start a worshiping centre under Mzuzu CCAP Church. The church started with 20 people most of them were students, however, Mzengeleza Gondwe and Nathan Mntahli were among elders who started the Church of Mzuzu Government Secondary School. They started while worshiping in a classroom before coming in a Min Hall.

The average church attendance is 200 people during school session and 25 people off school session. The church is dominated by youth of 14 to 20 years of age. New members join the church through transfers.

The leadership of the church is by both sexes. The language of the church is Chichewa.

3.8.5 Msongwe Trinity CCAP Church

Msongwe Trinity CCAP Church is located along State Lodge - Msongwe Water Tanks road, east of Msongwe Primary School.

The church started in 1969 as an outstation of Mzuzu CCAP church. Symon Vilimo Mhoni, Richard Zimba, Ester Manda and R.Z.W. Manda asked Mzuzu Session, moderated by Rev. Chauluma Chimaliro, to consider the growth of membership and long distance people from Msongwe/Kavuzi were travelling to Mzuzu CCAP Church for service of worship.[458] When the permission was granted, the church started with 30 people worshiping under a *Kachere* tree. The church changed from worshiping under a *kachere* tree to Msongwe Primary School. In 1969 and later, the church was covering the whole of Msongwe, Kavuzi and Kanjilirwe areas.[459] It was 2005 when the church started worshiping in a temporary church building before building a permanent one.

---

[458] Int. Austine Msiska, Session Clerk at Msongwe CCAP Church, Msongwe, 6.10.2013.

[459] The present Msongwe area was commonly known as Kaning'ina or Kanjilirwe. The whole of Kanjilirwe, Kavuzi and Msongwe was known as Kanjilirwe and were under Mzuzu CCAP Church, and when Mzuzu CCAP Church became an independent church from Lupaso, the Church was called Kanjilirwe until when Kanjilirwe and Kavuzi became independent from Mzuzu CCAP. Int. Alice Chimaliro, The First Chairperson of Umanyano in Mzuzu CCAP Congregation, Lupaso, 5.10.2013, and Johnstone Sibande, Worked with Tung Oil Estate in the Early Days, Mzuzu. 5.10.2013.

The church building has a capacity of 500 people. The church membership is 400 with average church attendance of 250 people, of whom the majority are women. The dominant age group of the church is 15 to 45 years. New members join the church through transfers and by birth and conversion. Conversion is done through door to door visitation. New converted members join baptism class before water baptism.

The language of the church is Chitumbuka. Church leadership is for both sexes.

3.8.6 Msongwe New Apostolic Church

Msongwe New Apostolic Church is located along State Lodge - Msongwe road, south of Msongwe Water Tanks.

The church started in 1974 with the initiative of a group of Germany missionaries led by Apostle Felenades. The group of Germany missionaries came from Zambia to plant churches in Mzuzu whereby Zolozolo, Msongwe and Masasa were planted with the initiative of the same group of people at the same time.[460] Msongwe New Apostolic Church was started by George Kaira, father of Apostle Kaira. The church started as a fellowship in the house of Harawa. As the number of church members was increasing, the church changed her worshiping place to close to where New State Lodge is.[461] The church moved again from where there is New State Lodge to the present place due to the construction of New State Lodge. The present place was bought from Bible Believers who sold the church and place.

The church has 100 members with average church attendance of 80 people, of whom the majority are men. The majority of church members are coming from Rumphi. New members join the church through transfer and by birth.

The church is led by men. Chitumbuka is the language of the church.

3.8.7 Masasa Assemblies of God Church

Masasa Assemblies of God Church is, located along Masasa to Prison road.

---

[460] Int. Nicely Nyirenda, Church Member at Msongwe New Apostolic Church, Msongwe, 6.10.2013.

[461] Int. Agnes Chirwa, Church Member at Msongwe New Apostolic Church, Msongwe, 6.10.2013.

The church was started in 1990 by American missionaries who came through Katoto Assemblies of God church. The American missionaries organized crusade at Masasa ground for two weeks, the result of the crusade was that many people gave their life to Jesus Christ and the formation of Masasa Church.[462] When the crusade was over, the church was left in the hands of Pastor Chisi to nurture it. The church started with 8 people worshiping in the house of Mayi Kuyokwa until when they built a church.[463]

The church building has a capacity of 150 people. The church membership is 100 with average church attendance of 80 people, of whom the majority are women. The dominant age group of the church is 15 to 35 years. The church is dominated by people from the central and southern regions. New members join the church through transfers and conversion. Conversion is done through door to door evangelism and open-air rallies. New converts join baptism class before being baptized by water.

The language of the church is Chichewa. The church is led by both sexes.

3.8.8 *Masasa Unity Pentecostal Church*

Masasa Unity Pentecostal Church is in Masasa area, located at Masasa Primary School.

The church was started in 2010 by Pastor Alex Msompha who had same disagreements with his supervising minister, Pastor Gondwe, at Masasa Assemblies of God Church. When the disagreements became huge, Pastor Alex Msompha asked Pastor Gondwe to give him permission to start his own church.[464] The permission was granted, the church was started with five families who also left Masasa Assemblies of God Church. The church started as a fellowship worshiping in the house of Pastor Alex Msompha and later went for renting at Masasa Primary School.

The church has 50 members with average church attendance of 30 people, of whom the majority are women. The dominant age group of

---

[462] Int. Lucy Senzani, Church Member, Masasa Assemblies of God Church, Masasa, 6.10.2013.

[463] Int. Nancy Sikulamowa, Church Member, Masasa Assemblies of God Church, Masasa, 6.10.2013.

[464] Int. Pastor Alex Msompha, Church Pastor at Masasa Unity Pentecostal Church, Masasa, 6.10.2013.

the church is 20 to 35 years. The majority of church members are from Central Region. New members join the church through conversion. Conversion is done through open-air and door to door visitation. The converted members join the church without going through baptism, neither class nor water baptism.

The language of the church is Chichewa. The church is led by both sexes.

Chapter Four: Religion in Mzuzu by Numbers

This chapter summarizes and gives an analysis of the data presented in Chapter three as a data base. The chapter starts by presenting statistics on the general overview of places of worship, where it presents church location and type of worship structures, and then it ends up by presenting statistics regarding membership and language of the various religious denominations found in Mzuzu. The statistics are presented as per denominational families. It has been difficult to present statistics as per worship centre because there are 200 plus worship centres captured in chapter three which could have been not easy to write one by one.

4.1 Places of Worship

Places of worship are the community of believers. These are social religious communities where believers meet regularly at a given time for a common purpose in worship; the significance of places of worship is shown through the type of worship centres in terms of structures and of location. Places of worship are major aspects in assessing the life of religious adherents. Activities done in places of worship provide the standard measure of assessing strengths and weaknesses of religions and denominations.

4.1.1 Location

Mzuzu has four main religions and different denominations. The four main religions are African Traditional Religion, Hinduism, Islam and Christianity, each of these has been located in favour of open competition. However, they have been located in different positions; at the centre, country sides, and or evenly distributed. It has to be noted that Christian religion has many denominations located in different locations. Table 4.1 below shows locational characteristics of different religions and denominations.

As shown in the table 4.1 below, most denominations have their churches located in middle and high-density areas. African Traditional Religion and Seventh- day Baptist (CAC, Original and Reform) have the highest figures, 3 and 4 respectively, of their churches in Traditional Housing Areas. Churches with not more than two worship centre are commonly Pentecostal, Charismatic or fellowships. These churches are predominantly located in high and middle density areas.

Table 4-0-1: Location of worship centres

Denomination	Traditional housing areas	Middle Density	High Density	Low Density
Africa International Church	0	2	4	0
African Traditional Religion	3	0	0	0
Anglican Church	1	1	2	1
Assemblies of God	0	6	4	0
Baptist Convention of Malawi	1	2	2	2
Bible Believer	0	1	2	0
CCAP	1	9	6	1
Chipangano	1	1	2	1
Church of Christ	0	1	7	1
Evangelical Baptist Church	0	1	2	0
Fellowships and Churches with not more than two worship Centres	1	6	36	7
Islam	0	4	3	1
Living Waters	1	1	2	1
New Apostolic Church	1	5	3	0
Roman Catholic	1	5	3	3
Seventh- day Adventist	2	6	5	1
Seventh-day Baptist, CAC, Reform, Original	4	1	1	0

4.1.2 Worship Structures

Religions and denominations have worship places where sacred structures are constructed and the function of sacred structures influences the arrangement of those structures across the landscape. Some religions and denominations have relatively large and elaborate structures, while others have more modest ones. The quality of worship structures depends upon the wealth of a particular worship centre. There are some religions and denominations that have no worship structure; instead they are renting ordinary structures for worship purposes. The type of worship structure is measured by worship structural capacity.

Table 4-0-2 : Church Capacity

Denomination	Church Capacity			
	Small	Middle	Rented Building	Big Size
Africa International Church	6	0	0	0
African Traditional Religion	3	0	0	0
Anglican Church	0	3	0	1
Assemblies of God	4	2	3	2
Baptist Convention of Malawi	0	7	0	1
Bible Believer	0	1	1	0
CCAP	1	4	2	10
Chipangano Church	2	3	0	0
Church of Christ	4	2	1	2
Evangelical Baptist Church	0	2	0	1
Fellowships and Churches with not more than two worship Centre	19	3	17	2
Islam	1	3	0	3
Living Waters	3	1	0	1
New Apostolic Church	0	8	0	1
Roman Catholic	1	6	1	4
Seventh-day Baptist, CAC, Reform, Original	0	3	1	0
Seventh- day Adventist	3	7	0	3

In this study worship structures with a seating capacity of less than 100 were classified as small, those with seating capacity between 100 to 250 were classified as medium and those with seating capacity higher than 250 were classified as big size. Regardless of the seating capacity, rented buildings were also classified independently. Worship centres that are in rented houses are regarded as worship centres without building structures of their own as a worship centre; many of these are from Pentecostal and Charismatic denominations found in the category of churches with not more than two worship centres. The figures in the table are presented in real figures.

As shown in the table (4.2) above, many church buildings in Mzuzu belong to the "middle" category. The reason is that many of these churches have medium numbers of church members and these members do not contribute that much wealth towards the church building project. Many of these churches have been strongly built depending upon funding from donors outside the church membership, either by church friends from America or Europe, or by contributions from the national head office. Very few churches have been built by members themselves and most of such churches have not been completed.

Worship centres that have the smallest number of worshippers fall in the category of small size church buildings. These churches have no donor; the construction of the church building is done by the Christians themselves who happen to have small income. Some of the church buildings have been constructed with *vigwagwa* (planks) wall instead of bricks. Such buildings are often temporal and poorly built. The majority of them are located outside the central areas of the city or townships. Such church buildings had no formal procedures on how the land was acquired and the church can be removed at any time. The sizes of church buildings are small because of small number of members and people of low income. To have a church building is an improvement from rented.

4.2 Worship Centres and Membership

Worship centres are composed of believers who by registration become members of a worship centre. Members of worship centres, as a fellowship of believers, meet together regularly at a given place and a given time for a common purpose, so that they form a congregation.

4.2.1 Membership Accession

New members join worship centres through conversion. Conversion is done through open-air rallies, door to door visitation and provision of social services. Conversion is also done through personal witnessing, where members of worship centres share their religious belief to non-members, so that eventually some of them become part of their worship community. Sometimes conversion is the result of marriage. Some people have joined other religions and denominations by following their marriage partners. The converted members became legal members of a worship centre only when they have been baptized in a particular worship centre. The other means of joining a worship centre is through movements of worship members. Members move from one area where they had been already a member of a particular worship centre to a particular worship centre in Mzuzu. When these people are moving, they carry with them a transfer letter. The other means of membership accession is by birth. Children are born and brought up in a particular worship centre where their parents are members.

Table 4-0-3 : Membership Accession

Denomination	Membership Accession %		
	Birth	Transfers	Conversion
Africa International Church	20	50	30
African Traditional Religion	100		
Anglican Church	35	55	10
Assemblies of God	5	35	60
Baptist Convention	25	60	15
Bible Believer	5	45	50
CCAP	30	60	10
Chipangano	20	50	30
Church of Christ	20	50	30
Evangelical Baptist Church	10	25	65
Fellowships and Churches with not more than two worship Centre	2	5	93

	Membership Accession %		
Denomination	Birth	Transfers	Conversion
Islam	40	55	5
Living Waters	5	25	70
New Apostolic Church	35	55	10
Roman Catholic	30	60	10
Seventh day Adventist	30	45	25
Seventh-day Baptist, CAC, Reform, Original	30	50	20

The study in the above table (4.3) sought to know how people join various worship centres. There are three major ways of how people join various worship centres. These are; birth, transfers and conversion. As indicated in the above table, it shows that in the mainstream denominations (CCAP, Roman Catholic, and Anglican), Seventh-day Adventist, Islam and New Apostolic Church, birth and transfers are found to be the main ways through which members get to enter a worship centres. The reason is that these religions and denominations are deeply rooted in various areas as a result they are like traditional religions or denominations. To a larger degree, conversion of members to these religions and denominations is just a matter of coming back to their original religions and denominations. It is noted that conversion is the main way through which members are joining Pentecostal and Charismatic denominations. These denominations seem to be new and they get members from already existing denominations through conversion.

4.2.2 Relationship between Membership and Attendance

The relationship between the enrolled membership in worship centres and attendance drawn from chapter three indicated in the table below, shows that there has been no time when worship has been attended by all members of a particular worship centre at any given time. Members of worship centres meet regularly at their respective worship centres at a given time for worship purpose. However, participation of members has always been represented as less than the total registered number. The difference between membership and attendance in some denominations is bigger than in other denominations.

Table 4-0-4 : Membership and Attendance

	Membership and Attendance		
Denomination	Roll	Attendance	Attendance %
Africa International	785	650	83
Anglican Church	980	695	71
Assemblies of God	1135	1056	93
Baptist Convention	882	750	85
Bible Believer	230	160	70
CCAP	14335	7780	54
Chipangano	410	294	72
Church of Christ	761	581	76
Evangelical Baptist Church	210	105	50
Fellowships and Churches with not more than two worship Centre	2135	1769	83
Islam	2385	2145	90
Living Waters	330	175	53
New Apostolic Church	1140	1020	89
Roman Catholic	4285	2575	60
Seventh-day Baptist, CAC, Reform, Original	601	476	79
Seventh day Adventist	3055	2690	88
		Average	**75**

The table 4.4 above shows the relationship between attendance and the total number of registered members. As the figures show in the table above, mainstream denominations have the lowest percentage of membership attendance, while at the same time; they have the highest numbers of registered members. The lower side of attendance of worship members indicates that worship members are less committed in worship issues than their personal issues. There is no follow up and encouragement to worship members on how they can be regular worshippers. The Pentecostals, Charismatic denominations and Fellowships have the highest percentage of worship attendance, meaning that there is no big difference between the numbers of people attending services of worship and the enrolled number of worship members. The reason is that the numbers of worship members are small, worship members are encouraged through participating in worship rather than just to attend. Many members in these worship centres are taking part in the service of worship as a result they fill obligated not to miss the service. While in Islam, worshippers are obligated by law to pray five times a day.

4.2.3 Women Proportion in Worship Centres

Worship centres are comprised of males and females of various ages. When looking at Worship centres, women are more than men and are actively involved in many activities done at worship centres.

Table 4-0-5 : Gender Participation

Denomination	Gender Participation	
	Female (%)	Male (%)
African Traditional Religion	80	20
Evangelical Baptist Church	75	25
Fellowships and Churches with not more than two worship Centres	75	25
Africa International	72	28
Chipangano	72	28
African International	72	28
Assemblies of God	70	30
Living Waters	70	30
Islam	65	35
Anglican Church	60	40
Baptist Convention	60	40
CCAP	60	40

Denomination	Gender Participation	
	Female (%)	Male (%)
Roman Catholic	60	40
Mboni za Yehova	60	40
Church of Christ	55	45
New Apostolic Church	55	45
Seventh-day Baptist, CAC, Reform, Original	55	45
Seventh-day Adventist	55	45
Bible Believer	50	50
Kubwezeretsa Sabata la Yehova	30	70
	62.55	**37.45**

Table 4.5 above, shows the proportion in percentage of the two genders in worship centres as per denomination and religion. For example, the table shows that African Tradition Religion has more women in her worship centres than men, it is indicated that women have a proportion of 80% while men are at 20 percent. As it can be seen in general for the rest of the denominations, the proportion of women in worship centres is higher than that of men. The reason is that, on average, women are more interested in spiritual matters than men.

Denominations and religions where the numbers of men are outnumbering or equal to women shows that women are not interested to join such denominations. In most cases, women are just forced by their husbands or a person closer to them to join such denominations. In these denominations, women are deprived of activities, choir group or any women's groups; instead men are the ones who do activities while women become spectators.

4.2.4 Language in Services of Worship

Language is one of the cornerstones of religious identity; it enables them to pass on information of salvation to religious adherents, through preaching, teaching, singing and discussions. Language and religion in Mzuzu are serving both to identify and classify individuals within complex societies and to distinguish populations and regions of different tongues and faiths. Language evolves responding to the dynamics of human thoughts, experience and expression of faith. There are three languages commonly used in Mzuzu worship centres, English, Chitumbuka and Chichewa.

Table 4-6: Language of Service

Denomination	Language		
	English	Chitumbuka	Chichewa
Africa International Church	0	6	0
African Traditional Religion	0	3	0
Anglican Church	1	0	4
Assemblies of God	9	0	10
Baptist Convention	1	1	8
Bible Believer	0	0	2
CCAP	15	17	2
Chipangano	0	6	0
Church of Christ	1	7	2
Evangelical Baptist Church	1	0	4
Fellowships and Churches with not more than two worship Centres	30	2	30
Islam	0	0	8
Living Waters	5	0	5
New Apostolic Church	2	6	2
Roman Catholic	3	8	1
Seventh-day Baptist, CAC, Reform, Original	0	2	3
Seventh-day Adventist	3	1	13

Table 4.6 above shows the proportion of denominations using different languages. The languages are shown in real figures. Three major

languages, Chitumbuka, Chichewa and English, were found to be commonly used in various worship centres in Mzuzu. Some denominations use a combination of these languages, while some use one of the three. The figures above show that Chichewa is commonly used many denominations in Mzuzu. The language is commonly used by in the worship service of Pentecostal, Charismatic denominations and Fellowships. The reason is that these denominations originated from a Chichewa speaking background. Most of them have come to Mzuzu from south and central Malawi or with people who have been in south or central Malawi or from people who have done Christian fellowships in secondary schools, colleges, universities and Christian organizations where the main language was Chichewa.

The other finding is that Chitumbuka language is used in the denominations that seem to uphold the culture of Mzuzu. The language is commonly used in the mainstream denominations, African Instituted Churches and African Traditional Religion, where the majority of leadership and worshippers are Tumbuka speakers. The reason is that Chitumbuka is relatively important in Mzuzu because it is the main cultural language widely spoken and heard among the people in northern Malawi. The use of Chitumbuka in the mainstream denominations, African Instituted Churches and African Traditional Religion is a way of preserving the cultural language of Mzuzu. These denominations that are making use of Chitumbuka language in their services of worship are culturally respected as well.

The finding further shows that the English language is dominating in many denominations in Mzuzu as well. The language has fund acceptance in both mainstream churches, Pentecostal and Charismatic denominations. Unlike in the Mainstream churches, Pentecostal and Charismatic denominations use both languages, English and Chichewa, in one service of worship, while in the mainstream churches they use separate services.

Chapter Five: The Geographical Distribution of Religions and Denomination

Religious geographers are naturally interested in the distributional characteristics of religions and denominations in a particular region.[1] To understand the spatial distribution of religions and denominations, one must take in account of the principle of the so-called spheres of influence or fields of operation.[2] By this, religions and denominations have allocated themselves in areas where they are operating. The influence of religions and denominations on the Mzuzu settlement structures can be examined through the criteria religious founders used in locating religions and denominations. The distribution of religions and denominations is based on religious adherents, in terms of population, culture, and social class, home of origin, and geographical factors of the area, such as trade, industries, education and urbanization.[3] The spatial distribution depicted on the denominational maps shows that the Christian religion is dominating among the religions of Mzuzu.

Close observation reveals that religions and denominations in Mzuzu have located themselves in such a way that some religions are found at the centre of the study area, some are found at the country sides of the study area, while others are evenly distributed, covering the whole study area. Mzuzu has multiple religions and denominations; however, there is religious freedom.[4]

5.1 Locational Settlement of Religions and Denominations

Mzuzu has four main religions and different denominations. The four main religions are African Traditional Religion, Hinduism, Islam and Christianity, each of them has been located in favour of open competition. However, they have been located in different positions; at the centre, country sides, or evenly distributed.[5]

---

[1] H.J. de Blij and Peter O. Muller, *Human Geography: Culture, Society and Space,* New York: John Wily and Sons, 1995, p. 300.
[2] Int. R. Mchali, Mzuzu University, Department of Geography, 8.6.2014.
[3] Int. Rev. Dr T.P.K. Nyasulu, Synod Moderator, CCAP Synod of Livingstonia, 9.10.2012.
[4] Int. Sheikh Zambali Juma, Area 1B Mosque, 8.8.2013.
[5] Int. Ngwaza Muwela Mbeya, Muwela Traditional Healer, Dunduzu, 30.8.2013.

5.1.1 African Traditional Religion

African Traditional Religion is a special form of ethnic religion distinguished by their small size, their unique identity with localized cultural groups not yet absorbed into modern society, and their close ties to nature.[6] The religious worship centres are located at the country sides of the study area. The denominational map of African Traditional Religion shows that worship centres are in the remote parts of the study area where people are living in the village or experience mixed life. Worship centres are represented by medicine men/women. The religion cannot be clearly seen in an organized form today, however, the practices and beliefs are still among the people.[7]

African traditional religious centres have never been at the middle of villages; but they had to be away from villages.[8] The map of African Traditional Religion depicts Muwela Traditional Healers Centre at Dunduzu at the edge of the study area, at the same map; it also shows Maria Traditional Healers Centre at the remote area of Sonda. Most of the traditional centres which could have been inside Mzuzu today have moved outside the area. Traditional worship centres which are found inside the study area are commercial and temporary.[9]

Traditionally, African traditional religious centres are located outside the village, a practice that resulted from the ancestral spirits and the concept of moral purity.[10] The reason is that ancestral spirits do not live together with people in the village in order to avoid interferences with people and to make them live a free life.[11] When people need to inquire from the ancestral spirits they have to follow them up where they live or when the spirits are angry with the living, the spirits could come down to them in

---

[6] Jerome B. Fellmann, *Human Geography, Landscape of Human Activity*, New York: McGraw Hill, 1999, p. 162.

[7] For a study of dual religiosity, see; Joyce Mlenga, *An Investigation of Dual Religiosity between Christianity and African Traditional Religion among the Ngonde in Karonga District in Northern Malawi*, PhD Thesis, Department of Theology and Religious Studies, Mzuzu University, 2013.

[8] Int. Maria Sakala, Maria Traditional Temple, Sonda, 28.9.2013.

[9] Int. Maria Sakala, Maria Traditional Temple, Sonda, 28.9.2013.

[10] James N. Amanze, *African Traditional Religion in Malawi, the Case of Bimbi Cult*, Zomba: Kachere, 2002, p. 22.

[11] Int. Rev. Dr S.M. Nyirenda, *Chancellor of Livingstonia University*, Mzuzu, 14.7.2014.

the form of snakes, etc. Worship was done outside the village at a shrine where people could meet with their ancestral spirits who could carry their prayers to the Supreme Being. The other reason why traditional religious centres were outside villages was to maintain the values of moral purity. Traditionally, for example, sexual intercourse and more especially adultery, destroys the values of moral purity,[12] therefore, religious centres were to be located outside the village to keep sexual taboos.

5.1.2 Hindu Religion

The Hindu religion is a religion without an ecclesiastical organization, a common creed or single doctrine; it lacks the kind of bureaucracy that is familiar to Christians and Muslims.[13] The religion is located in a small single geographic area, found at the centre of Mzuzu, where its adherents reside. Its members have no communal place of worship; worship is done in each family except when they have anniversaries. Shrines are found in every family member's house and this brings merit to the family.[14] Hindu families are clustered around Mzuzu main market square; all of them are business people, owning shops. Most Hindu resides behind or above their shops and a few others live in Nkhalapya and Chimaliro areas.[15] Traditionally, Hindu are business people in Mzuzu, each craft and profession is the property of castes.[16] The caste structure of society is an expression of the eternal transmigration of the soul. The castes are subdivided into thousands of *jati* groups defined by geography and occupation. Caste rules define whom you can mingle with, where you can live, what you may wear, eat and drink, and how you can earn your livelihood.

---

[12] James N. Amanze, *African Traditional Religion in Malawi, the Case of Bimbi Cult,* Blantyre, CLAIM - Kachere, 2002, p. 22.

[13] H.J. de Blij and Peter O. Muller, *Human Geography: Culture, Society and Space,* New York: John Wily and Sons, 1995, p. 301.

[14] Int. Jubea Patel, Hindu Religious member, son of Rasck Patel, the founding member of Hindu Religion in Mzuzu, Mzuzu Market, 5.10.2013.

[15] Int. Swanny, One of the pioneers of Hindu Religion in Mzuzu, Mzuzu market, 5.10.2013.

[16] James M. Rubenstein, *The Cultural Landscape. An Introduction to Human Geography,* Miami: Miami University, 1999, p. 175.

Certainly, there are holy men, but they represent literally thousands of gods. Hinduism is polytheistic, fragmented by numerous cults, and without a prescriptive book, such as the Bible or Quran. The religion remains concentrated in a single geographic realm, the religion of its source; it is regarded as the world's oldest organized religion.[17] Hindu religion emphasizes the divinity of the soul and is based on the concepts of reincarnation and passage from one state of existence to another in an unending cycle of birth, death and rebirth in which all living things are caught.[18] One's position in this life is determined by one's *karma*, or deeds and conduct in the previous life. The primary aim of this life is to conform to prescribed social and ritual duties and to the rules of conduct.

5.1.3 Islam

The Islamic religion is distributed around central places of the study area. Worship centres are located at busy exposed places; most of them are around the market square of Mzuzu townships. The religion is strongly represented at the centre of Mzuzu clustered around her three major markets; Hardware or Central, Vigwagwa and National Bank site at Kawuwa market. The three religious centres are Hardware Mosque at Hardware Market, Vigwagwa Mosque at Vigwagwa Market and Kandaha (Hilltop) Mosque at National Bank site. The religious centres' headquarters are Hardware Mosque and Vigwagwa Mosque of Sunni and Qudiriyya respectively.[19] The other two worship centres located at the market squares of Chibavi and Chiputula townships are regarded as full mosques where they do have Friday's communal service of worship.

Madrassas are equally located in all places where Islamic worship is taking place. The headquarters of all Muslim primary education is in Auze Education Trust (Vigwagwa Mosque Madrassa) with classes from beginners up to standard eight.[20] Most of the learners at Vigwagwa Madrassa are coming from other madrassa and are there for further studies. The

---

[17] Int. Rasck Patel, Founding member of Hindu Religion in Mzuzu, Mzuzu Market, 5.10.2013.
[18] James M. Rubenstein, *The Cultural Landscape. An Introduction to Human Geography*, Miami: Miami University, 1999, p. 175.
[19] Int. Sheikh Answar, Masjid Anwarullmadina Mosque, Vigwagwa Market, 5.10.2013.
[20] Int. Samuel Banda, Islamic Religious Member, Chiputula Mosque, 20.8.2013.

school offers free boarding for boys from the whole of the northern region who are in standard five to eight. Most of madrassas in Mzuzu are giving only basic education to learners while Vigwagwa is for both basic and higher primary education. The Islamic religion has another *madrassa*, by the name Maa Hawa Madrassa, near Immigration offices where they provide secondary education to Muslim learners. The school is co-educational with boarding facilities for boys from the whole northern region.

It is believed that Muslim worship centres are located at exposed strategic places of market squire to attract people and make it known to the general public.[21] Mosques are built at an open area, in most cases near busy roads or market squares so that people may easily identify it and or join the religion. The other reason is that most members of the Islamic faith are business people, owning groceries, shops, tailoring shops and other small businesses. This being the case, it becomes easier for them to fulfill the obligation of five daily prayers and Friday communal prayer, more especially for men, when mosques are closer to their working place.[22] The religion of Islam allows any Islamic religious member to worship at any mosque regardless of the area of residence. Muslims belong to any mosque where they feel comfortable.[23] Therefore mosques are built at most convenient places for the benefit of all.

5.1.4 Christian Religion

The Christian Religion is divided into denominational families and different denominations have different characteristics of location. The divisions are presented in the following categories; mainstream churches, African Instituted Churches, Pentecostal and Charismatic Churches, Ministries and Fellowships, and Convents.

(a) Mainstream Denominations

Mainstream denominations have been classified together basing on common characteristics when locating worship centres around Mzuzu. Worship centres of mainstream denominations are located at every corner and location of the study area, basing on population and distance.

---

[21] Int. Sheikh Ibrahim Fikila Banda, Chibavi Mosque, Chibavi, 22.9.2013.

[22] Int. Brother Yusufu Dane, Instructor at Chibavi Chewasene Madrassah, Chibavi, 8.9.2013.

[23] Int. Sheikh Zambili Juma, Area 1B Mosque, 5.8.2013.

The mainstream denominations will include; Church of Central Africa Presbyterian, Roman Catholic, Anglican, Baptist Convention of Malawi, Seventh Day Adventists, and New Apostolic Church. Worship centres of mainstream denominations are strategically located within the residential areas of church members, located on demand delivery.[24] The distribution of worship centres is based on population growth. This being the case worship centres become busy expanding in terms of building bigger churches and or opening new worship centres.

The mainstream denominations have a larger constituency therefore many worship centres, thus reducing distance for their adherents. Worship centres are distributed based on distances that church members travel from their respective homes to a worship centre. Church members are advised to worship at a worship centre within their residential area, most of them go to church on foot, and worship centres are located closer to their homes for easy mobility.[25]

(b) Pentecostal Denominations

Pentecostals are ecstatic denominations; they came from revivals within or outside existing churches.[26] Worship centres in Mzuzu are located in areas of low class residents, dominated by youth membership and people of poor and lower classes. Most denominations are loosely distributed; they have one or two worship centres. Many worship centres have no church structures of their own; they are renting in institutions, like schools, or dwelling houses of their religious leaders or others. For those who have their own church structure, most of them are of bad looking. Worship centres are more owned by a founder or a leader who possesses all resources acquired by the church.[27] Church adherents, most of them, are moving long distances on foot from their respective residential areas to a worship centre. Assemblies of God in Mzuzu is the

---

[24] Int. Bishop Fanuel Magangani, Bishop of the Anglican Church, Northern Diocese of Malawi, Mzuzu, 30.10.2013.

[25] But even in Mainline denominations there is some concerning of boundaries, see; Zeenah Sibande, *Religious Geography: Investigation of Christian Distribution Around CCAP Church Centres in Mzuzu City*, MA Module, Department of Theology and Religious Studies, Mzuzu University, 2013.

[26] Steven Pass, *The Faith Moves South. A History of the Church in Africa*, Zomba: Kachere, 2006, p. 227.

[27] Int. Pastor Belson Mtonga, Kavibale Gospel Pentecostal Church, Kavibale, 25.9.2013.

only Pentecostal denomination that is distributed widely, it has some differences in locational characteristic to other Pentecostal denominations.

Pentecostal worship centres are involved in all aspects of social life and open to supernatural possibilities, stressing the possibilities of empowering against evil powers, which should lead to transformation and freedom from physical and spiritual oppression.[28] They focus on, rather than shy away from, the realm of the Holy Spirit and his powers and gifts, which seem to be dealing with an important area of life of people as can be seen in helping people in a more honest and direct way to cope with the struggles of life which define and circumscribe day to day living for many.[29] Pentecostal worship centres tend to be even more condemnatory of 'compromise with paganism' than the old established churches, and consequently more hostile to those African Instituted Churches which are arrogantly dismissed as pagan.[30] With this background church members have joined these churches to seek freedom from physical and spiritual oppression, which seems to be found in non-Pentecostal Churches. Church founders or leaders, most of them, are people living in desperate life; therefore, it becomes easier for them to mobilize people of the same character.

(c) Charismatic Denominations

Charismatic piety is a quest for deeper Christian life going beyond attending catechism classes, church services, and behaving properly.[31] Charismatic worship centres are less African than the Pentecostal churches, located in middle class societies. Some interdenominational para-church organizations, like Scripture Union, Students Christian Organization of Malawi, and New Life for All provided a breeding ground for Charismatic church distribution. Further developments came from outside Mzuzu where people from abroad and outside Mzuzu have come

---

[28] Int. Jessie Msukwa, Chibavi Agape life International, Mzuzu, 18.9.2013.

[29] Steven Pass, *The Faith Moves South. A History of the Church in Africa*, Zomba: Kachere, 2006, p. 228.

[30] Int. Prophet King Solomon Jere, Church Prophet, Chibavi Enlighten Gathering Ministry, Chibanja, 19. 9. 2013. See also Steven Pass, *The Faith Moves South. A history of the Church in Africa*, Zomba: Kachere, 2006, p. 228.

[31] Steven Pass, *The Faith Moves South. A History of the Church in Africa*, Zomba: Kachere, 2006, p. 232.

to establish Charismatic churches in the name of fellowships or through crusades. Such churches are Living Waters, Calvary Family, and Charismatic Redeemed Ministry International. Those started as a fellowship group by members of existing churches and consolidated into a denomination over the years.

Charismatic worship centres are loosely distributed; most Charismatic denominations have more than one worship centre. Worship centres are dominated by middle class youth membership. Most worship centres have church structures of their own; while some are renting in institutions, like schools and some use the dwelling houses of their religious leaders or others. For those who have their own church structures, some are good looking. Worship centres are often connected to denominational founders or denominational headquarters. Church adherents, most of them, are moving long distances on foot, by cars, taxi or *kabaza* from their respective residential areas to a worship Centre. Worship centres emphasize the spiritual edification, a movement which influences internal revivals.

(d) African Instituted Churches

African Instituted Churches are churches founded in Africa, by Africans and for Africans.[32] They are churches that emerged outside and independent from churches instituted as a result of the work by the missions. African Instituted Churches are located in areas of high density, where people of low income are living. Most worship centres are found at the outskirts of Mzuzu, in places where church adherents are commonly absorbed in village life. Worship centres have church structures usually of poor quality. Church members seem to be lowly educated and influenced by traditional practices.[33] People are free to worship as Africans and they are not bound to missionary church traditions and practices. Denominational worship centres are not closely distributed, most of them are far from each other. Worship centres are not many per denominational family. They are commonly not more than six; usually they are four or five. Church adherents are walking long distances from their respective residential areas to a worship centre.

---

[32] Steven Paas, *The Faith Moves South. A History of the Church in Africa*, Zomba: Kachere, 2006, p. 140.

[33] Int. Aphraim Mkandawire, Church Secretary at Chang'ombe Zion Christian Church, Area 1B, 13.9.2013.

African Instituted Churches in Mzuzu are mainly of two types; the first are those which were founded as a result of a reaction against the evil of humiliation and shame caused by missionaries' disrespect or contempt.[34] They are separated from missionary churches motivated by the desire for leaving leadership in the hands of Africans and free from the questions of doctrine and worship practices.[35] Church of Africa Presbyterian, Chipangano, African National and Last Church of God are good examples of churches founded as a result of a reaction against the evil of humiliation and shame caused by missionaries' disrespect or contempt. The other type is the prophet – healing churches, founded not so much as a reaction against the evil of foreign leadership, but as a reaction against the evils that destroys life, such as illness and infertility.[36] Zion Christian Church is a good example of the prophet – healing church in Mzuzu.

(e) Fellowships and Ministries

Fellowships and Ministries are a part of Christian religion commonly born out of the so-called Born Again movement which is composed of smaller groups to demonstrate spiritual gifts through signs and wonders.[37] Generally, ministries and fellowships are found in every Christian church, working as special Christian groups which deal with the quest for a deeper Christian life, going beyond attending catechism classes and church services. However, the discussion in this paper is particularly on ministries and fellowships existing outside the churches. Such Christian groups are found in areas of high and middle density among low and middle class, especially with young people. Ministries and Fellowship groups are not many per denominational family; they are rarely more than three, usually they are one or two. There are some groups which may have more than two centres per family group name; these are national or international groups, with an organizational hierarchy.[38]

---

[34] Steven Paas, The Faith Moves South. A History of the Church in Africa, Zomba: Kachere, 2006, p. 142.
[35] Ibid.
[36] Steven Paas, The Faith Moves South. A History of the Church in Africa, Zomba: Kachere, 2006, p. 145.
[37] Int. Pastor Job Major Nyirenda, One More Time Christian Movement, Mzilawayingwe, 23.8.2013.
[38] Int. Joseph Kaunda, Church Secretary of Chibavi Emmanuel Pentecostal Movement, Chibavi, 18.9.2013.

These Christian groups are founded or led by active spirit filled church members on interdenominational or denominational basis who feel unsatisfied with the traditional two hours Sunday service of worship a week.

Most of the ministries and fellowship groups do not have their own worship structures; instead they are renting classrooms and halls or use individual members' houses. Those who worship in individual members' houses do that often on a rotational basis. Worship is taking place in the afternoon or evenings at any day during the week and weekends. Well-structured groups with bigger permanent membership tend to worship on Sundays during the time existing churches use to worship, so that they develop into separate churches. Ministries and fellowship groups have loose leadership, usually led by one person, mostly the founder, or coordinator. Members of the groups call themselves born again; most of them are youth because of the nature of how worship is being conducted. Youth like vibrant and energetic worship and it becomes a place where they can spend their time and keep themselves busy, while the elderly find help for their social problems.

(f) Convents

Convents are Christian communities under monastic vows, especially of nuns, from Roman Catholic and Anglican churches. The spatial distribution of convents shows that they are not commonly distributed, they are located in places of high value, in institutions such as schools, hospitals and parishes. The Anglican Church has one convent which was supposed to be at the Diocesan offices but due to insufficient space it went to Luwinga Holy Trinity Church. In the Roman Catholic Church, convents are located at parish headquarters and institutions such as secondary schools and hospitals. They are found in these places for the nuns to perform their duties through such institutions.

Convents in Mzuzu are special communities', part of worship centres, and peaceful and orderly life groups for the nuns from Roman Catholic and Anglican churches.[39] Women, who join such religious groups, adopt the celibate life proposed as the highest ideal of Christian living; they enjoy security, respect and personal freedom given only to grandmothers

---

[39] Steven Paas, *The Faith Moves South. A History of the Church in Africa*, Zomba: Kachere, 2006, p. 209.

in the society.[40] The recruitment of nuns depends upon the need from orders' headquarters.[41] Nuns are not permanent members of a particular local convent; they are subject to transfer, in and out. They live a life of sharing, all what they have belongs to the order.[42] Nuns are well educated, especially in the social field; most of them are school teachers, nurses and community workers.

5.2 Religious Infrastructure and Physical Development

Worship infrastructure is part of the cultural landscape influenced by religions. According to the cultural landscape approach, the variety of worship infrastructures we observe in landscape results from different human actions across the earth's surface.[43] Geographers try to explain why particular human actions tend to produce distinctive cultural landscapes. The fundamental principle underlying the cultural landscape approach is that people are the most important agents of change on the earth's surface. Religions have sacred places where sacred structures are constructed, and the functions of sacred structures influence arrangement of those structures across the landscape. Some religions require a relatively large number of elaborate structures, while others have more modest needs. Interestingly, the quality of worship infrastructure depends upon the wealth of a particular worship centre.

As much as religions are influencing the cultural landscape, religions too are influenced by events and features in the physical environment.[44] Certain features of the landscape are incorporated into the philosophy and rituals of religions and interpreted consistently with religious values. Religions incorporate environmental features differently. The selected features are influenced by distinctive physical conditions on the portion of the earth's surface where the religion originated or diffused. The physical environment influences the organization of religion in three

---

[40] John Waller and Jane Linden, *Mainstream Christianity in Malawi, Zambia and Zimbabwe,* Gweru: Mambo, 1984, p. 108.

[41] Int. Sister Mather Theu, Sister in Charge, St Mary's Luwinga Convent, Luwinga, 21.82013.

[42] Int. Sister Cecilia Chiumia, Marymount Sisters of Holy Rosary, Marymount, 22.8.2014.

[43] James M. Rubenstein, *The Cultural Landscape. An Introduction to Human Geography,* Miami: Miami University, 1999 p. 28.

[44] Ibid., p. 175.

basic ways; natural events, features of the physical environment, and religious organized portions of the earth's surface.

Religious structures in Mzuzu have developed from the component of religious organized portions of the earth's surface. Religious adherents of each religious worship centre have acquired a portion of earth surface in the physical environment where religious infrastructures have been developed. Later, the acquired portions of land have tended to become sacred places where the presence of God is felt.

5.2.1 Christian Sacred Structures

The main Christian sacred structure in Mzuzu is the church building. Church buildings play a more critical role than in other religions, in part because the structure is an expression of religious principles, an environment in the image of God.[45] Mzuzu Christian church buildings are prominent because attendance at a collective service of worship is considered extremely important. The prominence of churches on the landscape of Mzuzu stems from their style of construction and location. Underlying the large number and size of Christian churches is their considerable expense. Because of the importance of a place of worship, Christians have contributed much wealth to the construction and maintenance of churches. A wealthy congregation may build an elaborate structure designed by an architect to provide an environment compatible with the religion's doctrines and rituals.[46]

Since the Christian religion is divided into many denominations in Mzuzu, no single style of church construction dominates. Church buildings reflect both the cultural values of the denominations and the religions' architectural heritage.[47] Mainstream church buildings have good looking and permanent structures with bigger sizes reflecting a conception of a church as an assembly hall for the congregation. Availability of building materials also influences church appearances. Church of Central Africa Presbyterian church buildings are the biggest structures compared to other denominations of the mainstream churches in Mzuzu because of bigger church membership and wealthy contributions of church

---

[45] Ibid., p. 183.
[46] Int. Rev H.M. Nkhoma, Former General Secretary of CCAP Synod of Livingstonia, Mzuzu, 8.7.2014.
[47] Int. Rev. Dr S.M. Nyirenda, Chancellor of the University of Livingstonia, Mzuzu, 8.7.2014.

members towards church projects.[48] For example, Mchengautuwa CCAP Church was constructed with funding from her church members. The church has an average capacity of 1600 people, while the total membership is 2100.

Figure 5.1 : Mchengautuwa CCAP Church Building

Chisomo Baptist Convention Church has a good church structure, built equal to Mainstream Churches. The Church building has a permanent structure built with funding from her church members. Church buildings of this nature are not common to non-mainline denominations, as most of them depend upon donor funding.

Figure: 5.2 Chisomo Baptist Convention Church

---

[48] Int. Rev. L.N. Nyondo, General Secretary, CCAP Synod of Livingstonia, Mzuzu, 8.7.2014.

Church buildings of other denominations often have poor looking church structures compared to the mainstream churches. Church buildings that have a well-built church with permanent structure, depended upon funding from donors of the church in Europe or America. Such churches are located at the centre of Mzuzu City and most of them are denominational or regional headquarters. These churches are bigger in size and with more membership compared to others of the same type. The majority of membership is those with higher social status who often come from long distances. A good example of such church buildings are those located behind the regional police station, along Jomo Kenyatta and Nkhatabay roads. Mzuzu Central New Apostolic Church is one of the church buildings around the area. The church was built with funding from Germany with the idea to build a Regional New Apostolic Church for Northern Malawi. When the church construction work had been done, the building was handed over to local people as a regional church. The average church attendance is 400 people, who come from different locations, while church capacity is 650 people.

Figure 5.3 : Mzuzu Central New Apostolic Church

Other such churches are located opposite Grand Palace Hotel behind Sky Ways Private Secondary School at Chithila area along Mzuzu – Lilongwe road. One of the churches is Katoto Calvary Family Church.

Katoto Calvary Family Church has been built with funding from the National Office, which is receiving funding from partner churches and organizations in America and Europe. The church has 100 members and it is a regional church. The other church along the area is Christ Citadel International.

Figure 5.4: Katoto Calvary Family Church

Figure: 5.5 :: Christ Citadel Church

Christ Citadel is the only church of this denomination in Mzuzu. They received funding for church construction from the National Office in Lilongwe and from church friends in America. The church has 60 members.

Many church buildings of different denominations have been built with local funding. Most of them are small in size and poorly built. The majority of these churches are located outside the central areas of the city or townships. An example of these churches is Chiputula African National Church. The church has 130 members; most of them are people of small income.

Figure 5.6 : Chiputula African National Church (Locally funded church buildings)

The church has no donor; the construction of the church was done by Christians themselves.

Other Christian churches have been constructed with *vigwagwa* (planks) walls instead of bricks walls. Such buildings are often temporary and poorly built. The majority of them are located outside the central areas

Figure 5.6 : Disciple Faith Mission (a locally funded church building)

of the city or Townships. Such church buildings have no formal procedures on how the land was acquired and the church can be removed any time. The sizes of church buildings are small because of small sized membership and people of low income. An example of such churches is Disciple Faith Mission located at Chibavi. The church has 60 members and started as a fellowship worshiping in the house of Isaac Banda founder of the church.

When more members started joining the fellowship, it became a church and moved from the house of Isaac Banda to rent a class room at Chibavi Community Day Secondary School. It was from there at Chibavi Community Day Secondary School where they found a piece of land where they have constructed a vigwagwa church.

Some Christian churches have no church buildings at all. They are renting from schools, available halls and even meet in individual dwelling houses. These borrowed buildings serve their normal purpose all days and become sacred during worship hours. Usually when new churches are being introduced, it becomes difficult for them to start with their own church building; instead they start by congregating in rented or borrowed buildings. Later, a new church builds a church building when it has been fully established. Christians of Zolozolo Power Ministry of the Living God Church are using the house of Daniel Kamanga for worship.

Figure 5.7 Zolozolo Power Ministry of the Living God Church, Worshiping in the house of Daniel Kamanga

The church has 20 members, started by Daniel Kamanga in 1994. The church cannot afford to rent a private building because the income is small and it has a small number of people who live on limited resources as a result, up to now, they are still worshiping in the house of the owner of the church.

Figure 5.8 Royal Private Secondary School

However, same churches have had little capacity to build their own church buildings and have remained in rented or borrowed buildings. Due to limitation of rentable halls and dwelling houses, many churches are congregating in school buildings. Almost in all government and private schools, except in CCAP, Roman Catholics and Seventh-day schools, there are worship centres for Christian churches. Some schools are accommodating many churches to the extent that all classes are being occupied by different churches. Royal Private Secondary School is accommodating six different churches while Njelenjele Private Secondary School is accommodating seven.

5.2.2 Islamic Places of Worship

Mosques are organized around a central courtyard - traditionally open-air, although it may be enclosed in harsher climates.[49] The pulpit is placed at the end of the courtyard facing Mecca, the direction to which all Muslims pray. Surrounding the courtyard is a cloister used for schools and non-religious activities. A distinctive feature of the mosque is the minaret, a tower where a man known as a muezzin summons people to worship, however, these days almost invariably represented by a loudspeaker.

Most mosques in Mzuzu are of small size, mostly because of limited numbers of Muslims who attend services of worship.[50] The other reason is that most worshippers are found in town busy with their businesses and it becomes easier for them to worship at the Central Mosque at Hardware market and Masjid Anwarullmadina at Vigwagwa market. The

---

[49] James M. Rubenstein, *The Cultural Landscape. An Introduction to Human Geography,* Miami: Miami University, 1999, p. 183.
[50] Int. Sheik Zambili Juma, Area 1B Mosque, 8.8.2013.

two are the largest mosques with a bigger capacity of worshippers. Some of the mosques are temporarily built with *Vigwagwa* walls instead of brick walls, e.g. Area 1B and Masasa Mosques.

Figure 5.9 Mzuzu Central Mosque

Mosques in Mzuzu have been built with funding from well-wishers and money from Malawi government, a compensation fund for the destruction of some mosques in 1999 by the general public resulted from the winning of the united Democratic Front (UDF) General elections of 1999. The example of a Mosque built with funding from well-wishers is Mzuzu Central Mosque. At first the mosque was built by Wali Karim and Hasan Gero, both Malawians of Indian origin as Muslims doing business

Figure 5.9 Hilltop Kandaha Mosque

in Mzuzu. They employed their own builders and used their own building materials. When the mosque was built, the building was handed over to the Muslim community as a sacred structure. Since the first building was small and with the growing number of Muslims around town, the building has undergone a series of expansions to the present day when it can accommodate 700 worshippers. Masjid Anwarullmadina was built through renovating a handed over structure to the Muslim community for worship purposes. The building belonged to Z. Brothers who originally built it as warehouses for their businesses. The renovation modified the buildings for the purpose of mosque and madrassa. The mosque has a capacity of 500 peoples while the madrassa has six classes.

The compensation fund for the damage of mosques in Mzuzu targeted to rebuild five mosques damaged at Chibavi, Ching'ambo and upper Chasefu areas. The damage was done simultaneously on the same day in three major areas of the north namely Mzuzu, Rumphi and Mzimba, and the total estimated cost of repairing/rebuilding for the damaged mosques was estimated at U$ 450,000.[51] The compensation fund in Mzuzu was beyond the estimated cost of damage whereby it necessitated those controlling the funds to build three improved mosques and two additional ones. The three mosques were Chibavi Chewasene, Chibavi Central, and Ching'ambo. Hilltop Kandaha and Chiputula mosques were not part of the damaged mosques, however,

Figure 5.10 : Masasa Mosque

---

[51] Ibrahim Milazi, The Burning of Mosques in the North: Is it the Beginning or Climax of Political Fanaticism or Christian Fundamentalism in Malawi? *Religion in Malawi*, No. 9, 1999, p. 42.

they benefitted from the funding. These mosques have a capacity of 100 people.

Mosques like Area 1B, Masasa are built with *vigwagwa* (planks). Such mosques have a capacity of 20 people.

Mosques are built divided into two courtyards; one for men, the other is for women. The division is strictly observed during times of worship as neither sex is supposed to go to each other's section.[52] There are no chairs in mosques, worshippers worship while kneeling or seated on the floor.

5.2.3 Hindu Places of Worship

Hindu worship centre serves as a home to one or more gods, although a particular god may have more than one worship centre.[53] The size of a worship centre is determined by local family preferences and commitment of resources rather than standards imposed by religious doctrines. There is no specific structural building like a Hindu temple in Mzuzu; each member uses the dwelling house for worship. Hindu members decorate their houses, especially rooms where Hindu worship is taking place, in a way temples are being decorated.

The Hindu religion is lacking a communal temple in Mzuzu because the location of a temple in Hindu religion is very important. Temples should be located where there will be minimal disruption of the natural landscape. The temple should be in a comfortable position under a large shady tree and near water, where possible, because many gods will not venture far from water and because water has a holy function in Hinduism.[54] The other reason is that temples are traditionally built ranging from small village temples to structures so large and elaborate that they are virtually holy cities. This being the case, family members' houses act as small village temples and because the Hindu population is too small to build a large elaborate temple for communal festivals, so that communal festivals are held in hired halls or in open areas.

Traditionally, worship is done in a small village temple while large temples are used for communal festivals. The typical Hindu temple

---

[52] Int. Sheik Ibrahim Sikila Banda, Chibavi Central Mosque, 22.9.2014.
[53] James M. Rubenstein, *The Cultural Landscape. An Introduction to Human Geography,* Miami: Miami University, 1999, p. 184.
[54] Int. Rasck Patel, Founder of Hindu Religion in Mzuzu, Mzuzu, 5.10.2013.

contains a small dimly lit interior room where a symbolic artefact or some other image of a god rests. The remainder of the temple may be devoted to space for ritual processions. Because congregational worship is not part of Hinduism, the temple does not need a large interior space filled with seats.[55] The site of the temple is demarcated by a wall and may also contain a structure for a caretaker and a pool for ritual baths.

5.2.4 African Traditional Religious Shrines

African traditional religious worship structures take the form of shrines. Traditional religious shrines are structures where rituals are performed, worship is done by medicine men/ women at a shrine, while sometimes such people have no shrine structure, and hence worship is done on the bare ground or in the house of a medicine man/woman.

African traditional religious shrines in Mzuzu are small in size built with local materials. Most of them are grass thatched. The construction of a shrine is done by the owner, medicine man/woman, since these traditional worship centres do not have permanent members apart from the medicine men/women and their assistants.[56] Most worship is done in the open or in the dwelling houses of medicine men/women for it becomes difficult for them to build a shrine since they have small income and are not permanent at one place; they like to move from place to place. One example of an African traditional religious shrine building is Muwela Traditional Healer Centre. The shrine was built by Ngwazi

Figure 5.11: Muwela Traditional Religious Shrine

---

[55] Int. Joshua Patel, Hindu Religious Member, Mzuzu, 5.10.2013.
[56] Int. Justina Maria Sakala, The Owner of Maria Temple, Sonda, 25.9.2013.

Muwela Mbeya, the owner of the shrine, with his own money at his own home. The shrine has a capacity to accommodate 50 people.

5.3 Geographical Origin of Members

Different religions and denominations have come to Mzuzu from different areas to which each religious adherent is connected in one way or the other.[57] Adherents have joined worship centres equal to what they have been brought up at their home area or family, so that those who join other religions and denominations have been termed rebellious children.[58]

When people are coming to Mzuzu, they make sure that they find a worship centre equal to what they have at home. Chipangano Church originated from Phiri in Nkhata Bay and the majority of her members are coming from west of Nkhata Bay Boma, Phiri, Mzenga and Kavuzi areas. When people from these areas and other places who belong to Chipangano Church come to Mzuzu, automatically, they join Chipangano and most of them reside in Masasa Township. The majority of Seventh-day Adventist members are coming from Nkholongo, Lunjika and Luwazi areas. Those who belong to the Seventh-day Adventist Church from these areas and others when coming to Mzuzu look for this church. Muslims in Mzuzu are predominantly coming from Nkhotakota, Mangochi, Machinga and Zomba. When Islamic members from these areas and elsewhere come to Mzuzu, they join Islamic worship centres of Hardware Mosque, Vigwagwa Mosque, Hilltop and others.

When the religion or denomination of origin of a member is not found, the majority of them do not worship until others initiate them to start their own worship centre which could be found in their home area.[59] Chiputula St Michael's Lutheran Church of Central Africa was started by members of the Lutheran Church of Central Africa who had joined the church elsewhere before coming to Mzuzu. When these members came to Mzuzu, they found that the church was not there and they could not worship anywhere until when Rev. R.G. Cooks mobilized them to start a church. Rev. Cooks had heard about Harawa, a Lutheran from

---

[57] Int. Rev. B.C. Kaonga Parish Minister, Mchengautuwa CCAP, Mchengautuwa. 10.10.2014.
[58] Int. Hanna Kamoto, Luwinga Methodist Church, Viyele, 1. 10.2013.
[59] Int. Gogo Ester Jere, Wife to Pastor L.H.K. Banda, Founder of Chiputula Cavalry Family Church, 20.8.2013.

Mpherembe that he became a member while at Mpherembe but was not worshiping in Mzuzu. Cooks came to Harawa at Mzilawayingwe in Mzuzu and convinced him to start a Lutheran Church. The two evangelized in the city, and when Cooks was leaving Mzuzu, Harawa took over the initiative and visited door to door to find church members who had joined the church before coming to Mzuzu. Later, the group of people became big enough that they became the Lutheran Church of Central Africa - Mzuzu.

Some religions and denominations are nick-named after a tribe or place of members' origin; such associational names have come because the majority of such religious adherents come from such places.[60] The Anglican church of the northern diocese is nick- named Likoma Church because, historically, the church came from Likoma and the majority of her members come from Likoma.[61] The said associational names identify worship centres with people of a particular area of religious origin; similarly, the Islamic religion is associated with the Yao tribe of Mangochi and Machinga where they are commonly found. Yao people are the majority of Muslims in Mzuzu; hence it is called *Yao religion*.[62] The other example is the Seventh - day Adventist Church; the church is associated with Lunjika, Lwazi or Nkholongo areas where the majority of adherents are coming from.

Most religions and denominations have a specific geographical background of their religious adherents. The area of origin of a religious worship centre has an influence when prospective members want to come up with a decision of joining a particular religion or denominational worship centre.

5.4 Religious Membership

Religious Worship centres are composed of believers who, by registration, become members of that worship centre. Members of worship centres, as a fellowship of believers, meet together regularly at a given place and a given time for a common purpose,[63] as such they form

---

[60] Int. Archdeacon, Fr. James K. Chifisi, Parish Minister, St. Marks Anglican Church, Kaning'ina, 7.10.2013.

[61] Int. Fr. Arthur Chitowe, Chaplain at St Mary's Convent, Luwinga. 11.8.2011.

[62] Int. Samuel Banda, One of the first members of Islamic religion in Mzuzu, Chiputula Mosque, 20.8.20112.

[63] Hans Küng, *The Church,* Wellwood: Kent, 1986, p. 85.

a community of worshiping believers. Congregational worship is the fellowship of believers; it is also, in spite of mistaken religious-sociological ideas, the foundation and creation of God's kingdom, the one who calls them.[64] Membership in religious worship centres is not based on worship centres found in their residential area. Members are free to belong to any religious worship centre regardless of area of residence and distance. The belief is that a person belongs to a worship centre of his or her religion. What comes first in the mind of a person before choosing a worship centre is religion, then after that comes denomination and lastly choice of a worship centre.

There is a general movement of members from the supposed residential religious worship centres to a worship centres far from their residential areas.[65] Members from the respective religions are leaving worship centres next to their home for worship centres far from their homes. Some members even walk long distances from their residential areas to a worship centre of their choice, Burton Kaminja Nyirenda and his wife of the Baptist Convection of Malawi had to walk 16 km to and from a worship centre at Dunduzu to his residential area leaving behind many worship centres of different religions and even of his own denomination.[66]

5.4.1 Factors Influencing Membership in Worship Centres

There are certain factors which influence people when deciding to become members of a particular religion, denomination and worship centre. Such factors are quite strong to drive a person when choosing where to belong.

5.4.1.1 Cultural Religion

Some religions seem to be cultural whereby a person feels obligated to join a religion and worship centre of his/her culture. Such religions look like acculturated, i.e. family, area and region, and forces subsequent

---

[64] Ibid, p. 86.

[65] Zeenah Sibande, Religious Geography: *Investigation of Christian Distribution Around CCAP Church Centres in Mzuzu City*, MA Module, Mzuzu University, 2013, p. 29.

[66] Hany Longwe, *Christians by Grace. Baptist by Choice, A History of the Baptist Convention of Malawi*, Zomba: Kachere, 2012, p. 81.

generation to belong to a religion of their parents joined by birth.[67] African Traditional religion is one of such religions whose adherents join by birth. Members of African Traditional Religion are known when they are in crisis and situations forces them to join a traditional religious worship centre.

Mzuzu being a cosmopolitan city her citizens have come with different cultural religions from their respective home of origin. The Anglican Church is dominated by people from Likoma and some parts of Nkhotakota. The Anglican Church seems to be a traditional and cultural denomination of people from Likoma, no wonder Mzuzu Anglican worship centres are denominated by people from Likoma. When these people have come to Mzuzu, they look for Anglican worship centres no matter how far it might be.

5.4.1.2 Social Status

Some people have joined certain religions, denominations and worship centres based on social status. Some people, when they consider their wealth, education, honour and location of residence feel to belong to a religion, denomination and worship centre which could be equal to their social status regardless of distance.[68] For example, people from Chimaliro, Fairclough, Kaning'ina and Marymount would rather worship at Mzuzu CCAP, St Andrews Church than going to Zolozolo and Katawa,[69] or some from Chibanja area are worshiping at Mzuzu Baptist Convention Church instead of going to Chibavi Baptist Convention Church. Some people who belong to high social status have joined certain worship centres with lower social status where people of their status are few or none and have gained honour and respect.[70] For example, some people from Hilltop are worshiping at Viyele and Mchengautuwa CCAP prayer houses respectively. Such people travel by car.

---

[67] A speech made by M'mbelwa (IV) at Njuyu during the celebrations of 100 years of Njuyu Station since its establishment, 2004.

[68] Int. Sigman Chilambo, Church Elder at Viyele CCAP, Viyele, 20.6.2013.

[69] Zeenah Sibande, Religious Geography: *Investigation of Christian Distribution around CCAP Church Centres in Mzuzu City*, MA Module, Mzuzu University, 2013, p. 30.

[70] Int. Sigman Chirambo, Church Elder, Viyele CCAP, Viyele, 20.6.2013.

5.4.1.3 Social Services

Some people feel obligated to be members of a particular worship centre because of the provision of social services.[71] The African Evangelical Church of Malawi started at Luwinga through the provision of relief maize to people who were badly affected by hunger in 1991. The relief maize mobilized many people who joined the fellowship supported by revivals organized by Rev. Gregory, a missionary from the United Kingdom, so that eventually a church was established. In general, there are several social services which worship centres do provide to their members and the community at large, i.e. cheering the sick, visiting the bereaved, provision of needs; when these have been carefully done at a particular worship centre; people became tempted to join it. However, Klaus Fiedler says that in spite of such obvious profits, healing churches love the tendency to remain small.

5.4.1.4 Spiritual Gifts

People may affiliate themselves to a worship centre where they feel that they are offered spiritual help. People are hungry for the provisions of the Holy Spirit and feel obligated to join a worship centre where there is such provision. Members are looking for healing, deliverance, prophecy and provisions of social life, like wealth, employment etc.[72] God's Will Church of Pastor Frank Zebrone started with the vision from God to deliver people from spiritual and physical oppressions. People at God's Will Church are following Pastor Frank Zebrone who seems to have the gifts of the Holy Spirit of healing, prophecy, deliverance and provisions of social life required by many people.

5.4.1.5 Personal Relations and Friendship

Some people have joined certain religions, denominations and worship centres following their personal relations. The decision of belonging is influenced by friends, of course depending upon the type of relationship, i.e. spouses, parents, head of the village and or home mate.[73] Nkholongo

---

[71] Int. Pastor Christopher Mwalweni, African Evangelical Church of Malawi, 21.8.2013.

[72] Int. Father Rev A. Chitome, Chaplain at St Mary's Convent, Luwinga, 6.4.2014.

[73] Int. Rev B.C. Kawonga, Parish Minister at Mchengautuwa CCAP, Mchengautuwa, 27.6.2014.

Church of Christ started under the initiative of Mr. Manda who was an old man and unable to attend services of worship at Chamalaza. The church started at his home village and being the head of family, he mobilized the whole village to join his church.

Some churches have been started by a certain member of a family, i.e. parents, child or home mate, and then the whole family, relatives or friends have joined it. This has depended upon the trust which family, relatives and friends have in each other. Lupaso Full Gospel Church of God started by Mr. Kabichi, who later was joined by his family, relatives and friends. Sometimes a person joins a particular church by following a partner in marriage. The Roman Catholic Church has many members who have joined the church through marriage. When a member of the Roman Catholic marries a non-Catholic, for the church to recognize and allow the officiation of the marriage, they are requested to join the Catholic Church.[74]

5.5 Membership and Attendance at a Worship centre

When looking at the statistical estimated fingers on membership and attendance in chapter four which has drawn its figures from chapter three, it shows that there has been no time when worship has been attended by all members of a particular worship centre at a particular time.

The congregational worship, as a fellowship of believers, meets regularly at a given place and a given time for a common purpose. However, participation of members at a worship centre has always been less than the total registered number. The difference between membership and attendance in some denominations is bigger than in others. There are different reasons why not all registered members of a particular worship Centre attend worship services together at a particular worship time. Some of the reasons are as follows:

5.5.1 Lack of Commitment

Some religious adherents in Mzuzu are lazy in attending regular services of worship. They are lacking commitment to religious issues, to them to be a member is when you have registered a name in a nominal roll book

---

[74] Int. Bonaventura Mvula, Church Member at St Peters, Chiputula, 23.8.2013.

of a worship centre.[75] Mrs. Agnes Longwe, a member at Lupaso CCAP Church, has no time for attending regular services of worship; she attends worship when there are special occasions, or when she feels she has time. Services of worship are not a priority to her, what she wants is to be a church member so that she has the right to benefit from all privileges accorded to a member, more especially in times of need, like sickness and death.[76] The absenteeism of such members from regular services of worship will reduce the number of members who attend services of worship compared to the total number on the nominal roll.

Mr. Kawonga and his family, a teacher at Lupaso Day Secondary School, registered their names at Luwinga Evangelical Baptist Church in order to benefit from privileges accorded to its members. The worship centre was providing a scholarship fund to its members so that many people joined the Church and benefited from the fund. Kawonga was given a scholarship for BA and Master's Degrees and studied at African Bible College. He and his family were going for worship when scholarships were available; when these were over they could not go for worship. The church does not give scholarships any more today; worship attendance has reduced to 10 members from 150 at the beginning.

5.5.2 Social Commitment

Some members in Mzuzu are too committed with social issues to the extent that they find it difficult to attend services of worship regularly. Members are affected with social problems which become a reason to make them fail to attend services of worship.[77] Members of worship centres in Mzuzu are often affected with sickness or deaths of family members, relatives or people within the society. When they are occupied with these problems, they find it difficult to leave behind the problem and attend services of worship. Lucy Nyirenda, Mrs. Mtawali, Church Elder at Katawa CCAP Church went to London for three months, October to December, where she was nursing her daughter who was expectant. John Nyirenda was not attending services of worship at Chibavi CCAP

---

[75] Int. Rev. A.M. Phiri, Moderator of CCAP Mzuzu Presbytery, St Andrews Church, 8.7.2013.

[76] Int. Ethel Singini, Chairperson of Lupaso CCAP Women Guild, Lupaso, 29.7.2013.

[77] Int. Pastor Tony Nyirenda, Mzuzu International Pentecostal Holiness Church, 3.10.2013.

Church for two consecutive months while nursing the sickness of his brother in-law who was admitted at Mzuzu Central Hospital and also when attending to funerals of his relatives. Hanna Kamoto of Luwinga United Methodist Church was not attending services of worship for two months when she fell sick in March and April 2014.

Apart from the above-mentioned problems, there are various social commitments which religious adherents become affected with, which make them fail to attend services of worship. Some of these commitments are weddings and political meetings. Mrs. Phiri, a member and deacon at Lupaso CCAP, took five months without going to church doing political rallies during the campaign period of the general election of 2014.

5.5.2.1 Long Distances and Travel

Most worship centres in Mzuzu are far from residential areas so that members require proper arrangements in terms of transport. For example, the majority of members at Mzuzu International Pentecostal Holiness Church walk on foot; some come by car and others on bicycles. When those who travel by car or bicycle have problems with their means of transport, they decide not to go for the service of worship and for those who walk on foot fail to attend worship when they started preparing for the service of worship late.[78] While those who go by public transport like minibus, taxis, and *kabaza (*bicycle taxi) fail to go to attend services of worship when they do not have transport money or when transport is unavailable. Some members are old and find it difficult to walk long distances on foot in order for them to attend regular services of worship.

Luwinga United Methodist is another example of a worship centre experiencing poor attendance because of distances to residential areas of her members. The United Methodist worship centre at Luwinga is the only centre the whole of Mzuzu; therefore, it becomes difficult for those living outside Luwinga to attend worship regular. The registered number is 150 members while average attendance is 70 members.

---

[78] Int. Ludalinga Khonje, Luwinga Grace Community Pentecostal Church, 27.7.2013.

5.5.2.2 Employment and School

Mzuzu is a cosmopolitan city; people come from different areas, often for employment and school. Most people in Mzuzu are looking for money, employed by different employment agencies, while others are self-employed. Time pressure for employees is very high; some people work from Monday to Sunday in their offices or outside by attending workshops, trainings, seminars and others. This makes members busy and makes them fail to attend regularly services of worship.[79] Some members are students from various schools; during examinations or when they are occupied with assignments they fail to find time for worship.

At Viyele CCAP Church many members are employees and students and sometimes, when they are busy at work and or at school, worship attendance drops. When CCAP members from Mzuzu University are on holiday, worship attendance reduces heavily. The average attendance when schools are in session is 2100, but when university students are on holiday, it reduces to 1700 members.

5.5.2.3 Financial Struggle

Residents of Mzuzu are economically pressed with escalating costs of living, causing a challenge to earn a living. Religious members are facing challenges when dividing their earnings to meet both social and religious requirements, in a way, some become inactive in attending worship services when they are left without money for religious contributions. Religious worship centres require their members to come with something during the service of worship; dole, tithe, fundraising and various other contributions. This makes some members helpless; as a result, they fail to attend services of worship when they do not have money.

Redeemed Christian Church of God, Upper Chasefu worship centre, is so demanding that when members have nothing to give, they become ashamed and stays home. Members are asked one by one to go forward and give after a preacher has preached on giving and when someone has not gone forward he/she is asked by deacons why he/she has failed to do so. When members have nothing to give they do not come for the service

---

[79] Int. Pastor Gertrude Mhlanga, Dunduzu Jesus Missionary Church, 20.8.2013.

of worship.[80] It happens sometimes that members may have dole, a usual contribution, but they do not have other contributions, they do not come for the service of worship because of these other contributions. Those who do not give tithe for several months become irregular in attending worship. Mchengautuwa CCAP Church has a system of purging off her members on nominal roll who are not giving tithe or monthly pledges for six months. In July 2012, 120 people were purged from the nominal roll. When people know that they have taken time without giving monthly pledges they became irregular in attending worship while waiting to be purged from the roll book.

When Lupaso CCAP Worship Centre has organized a fundraising on a particular Sunday, worship attendance drops because people excuse themselves that they do not have anything to give, hence they may be ashamed when they go and attend worship while they do not have anything to give. The normal average worship attendance is 350, but when it comes to a fundraising day, the number drops to 200. The overemphasis on giving at Chibavi Enlightened Gathering Ministry has reduced the attendance of her members. The worship centre is too demanding, any service done to her member is paid for. This made worship attendance drop from 300 members in the early days to 20 members recently.

5.5.2.4 *Conflicts and Disagreements*

It is obvious in Mzuzu that when there are conflicts and disagreements worship attendance dwindle. Members do run away from attending services of worship because of conflicts among members. As group members work together, they also build expectations of one another.[81] Conflicts over roles and responsibilities occur because of different expectations. Many problems occur simply because people are not clear about what they expect of each other. Besides different expectations overlapping roles and responsibilities create tension, especially when two or more members see themselves as equal for the same tasks.[82] Roles overlaps, although not inherently bad, have a potential for conflict

---

[80] Int. Peter Chawawa, Church Elder, Redeemed Christian Church of God, Upper Chasefu, 21.8.2013.

[81] Anthony D'Souza, *Leadership. A Trilogy on Leadership and Effective Management*, Limuru: Paulines, 1994. p. 73.

[82] Ibid.

as long as they exist, conflicts sometimes arise because of personal clashes. Religious members misunderstand each other; instead of solving the problem some resolve it by not attending worship. When worship centres have conflicts and disagreements, many adherents resolve that by not attending services of worship until peace prevails.

Lupaso Good News Revival worship centre survived through conflicts and disagreements among members which has been reducing attendance. The worship centre has been experiencing leadership struggles, first between Pastor Justine Jungwana and Pastor Sharpsharp Banda, secondly between Pastor Justine Jungwana and Pastor Elias Soko. Though the early conflicting leaders left the worship centre, still there has been a leadership struggle to date. Lupaso Good News Revival has 60 members while average attendance is 20. Mzuzu CCAP Worship Centre dropped in attendance of her members due to disagreements that arose in the Church choir. The conflict was big enough to the extent that the group got divided into two groups. The Kirk Session banned the new group from singing; this did not please members of the church, attendance dropped to 1500 members out of 2500 registered members. The issue was resolved when the new group was accepted as one of the church choirs. Conflicts sometimes arise when there is competition over Spiritual gifts. Some people do not like to recognize Spiritual gifts of others, when someone seems to have such gifts the one in charge of a worship centre tries to surprise him or her and when there is resistance they end up by splitting.

5.5.2.5 Lack of Social Services

Worship centres in Mzuzu provide social services to their members like cheering the sick, visiting the bereaved, and other social services. When these are not satisfactorily done, adherents become discouraged and irregular in attending services of worship. In 1990 members of Luwinga Church of the Nazarene became irregular in attending because of insufficient provision of social services. The church stopped giving her members second hand clothes, organizing football teams for the youth, cheering the sick and visiting the bereaved because they stopped receiving such gifts from Walter Meyer due to mismanagement of what they were receiving. It was the expectation of members to be provided with social services, when these were not duly met members became inactive and irregular in attending services of worship.[83]

Mzuzu Winners Chapel at the time when it was starting had more attendance than today due to the provision of social services. The worship centre was providing handouts and transport to her members who attended services of worship every time. When these provisions stopped, the attendance dropped immediately from 520 to 140. The worship Centre at Hilltop is still experiencing low attendance to date; the attendance is less than 100 people.

5.5.2.6 Physical Geographical Aspects

Weather and some physical conditions have contributed to inadequate attendance of worship services in Mzuzu. For example, rivers and poor road network, poor or no bridges have made people fail to connect properly from different areas. Kang'ona and Kanyika rivers are giving problems to people who are members of Lupaso Assemblies of God who are coming from Kang'ona area and want to attend service of worship at Lupaso when rivers are full. The rivers have no bridges and there is a poor road network. Members who travel by car use long routes to access to bridges while those who walk on foot become unhappy to cross rivers without proper bridges.[84] This sometimes causes attendance to drop to 30 out of 71 members.

The other example could be weather conditions; Mzuzu is cold and rainy which sometimes makes members unable to attend services of worship. The weather at Kaning'ina and Chimaliro causes some members of City Chipangano Church to fail to go out for services of worship. When it is too cold or rainy, worship attendance drops to 40 out of 110 members. Ching'ambo Churches of Christ is experiencing the same problem of poor attendance when the weather conditions are bad. Ching'ambo area is a wetland with poor roads and bridges. When the weather condition is bad, rainy or cold, worship at Ching'ambo Churches of Christ drops, sometimes from the total number of 55 members to 15.

---

[83] Int Rev. Voster T. K. Mhango, Parish Minister, Luwinga Nazarene Church, 8.8.2013.

[84] Int. Bonaventura Mvula, St Peter's Roman Catholic Parish, 23.9.2013.

Chapter Six: Religious Worship Places as Social Centres

Congregational worship in worship centres is the fellowship of believers, a religious sociological community. This being the case the community of believers' in worship centres meets regularly at a given place and at given times for a common purpose.[1] In other words while I see faith as the centre of all religion, this section shows the social aspects of religion. The significance of worship centres is shown through the performance of church members, as social groupings, in worship centres. Worship centres are major aspects in assessing the life of religions and denominations. Activities done in worship centres provide the standard measure of assessing strengths and weaknesses of religions and denominations.

6.1 Social Groups

Worship centres are composed of males and females of different age groups. Mzuzu worship centres are primarily seen as a spiritual movement. The secret behind being religious centres is the combination of spiritual and social factors or to be more precise, combination of the spiritual and social needs of the people. Most people in the area encounter almost insurmountable problems. The stabilizing kinship codes and tribal mores no longer function in a heterogeneous mass society, resulting in social isolation or degeneracy.[2] This means that worship centres are new models and criteria needed for a meaningful existence. Religious worship centres emerge as reorientation communities offering security and a chance of reintegration, a new home providing anchorage in a harsh, competitive world.[3] Mzuzu worship centres as social groups provide the following to membership:

6.1.1 Brotherhood

Individuals who have a place in worship centres are encouraged to regard each other as kin. In this way new family ties are created taking

---

[1] Hans Küng, *The Church*, Wellwood: Kent. 1986, p. 85.

[2] M.L. Daneel, *Missiology. Christian Theology of Africa (Mission as Liberation: Third World Theologies),* Pretoria: University of South Africa, 1989, p. 64.

[3] Int. Catherine Mhoni, Church Member, Zolozolo West Chipangano Church, Mzuzu, 12.9.2013.

the place of the traditional extended family one has lost touch with.[4] The bond of relationship becomes very strong and meaningful, something beyond blood relationship. The family of Gray Mwanza and Fumu Mvula, both from Mchengautuwa CCAP Church are so close to each other. The two have known each other from Mchengautuwa CCAP Madodana Choir where both of them are members. The relationship is very strong to the extent that Gray Mwanza has given Fumu Mvula his own plot where Fumu Mvula has built his house. Such relationships are common in worship centres; worship centres have created these relationships where people are helping each other like brethren.

6.1.2 Social Interaction

Scope is provided for the formation of new friendships. In a metropolitan way of life, there is a need for an intimate circle which forms the basis for a new life and helps the individuals to cope with day to day problems.[5] Worship centres become the nucleus of a new circle of friends. Two married women at Lupaso created a good social interaction both from Lupaso CCAP Church, Umanyano. The other woman and her husband came from Mzimba to Lupaso, while at Lupaso, the family experienced a difficult situation to the extent that the marriage was about to break. The family lost their first-born daughter, and also the husband was going around with a girlfriend, a nearby neighbour. The woman who was found at Lupaso used to counsel the woman from Mzuzu on how she can get back her lost husband and at the same time on how she can accept the death of her daughter. Through social relationship and counselling the family of the woman from Mzuzu has managed to cope with the situation and it is strong again.

6.1.3 Protection

In an insecure and sometimes threatening situation, worship centres become a new home to stay. Religious leaders provide needed counsel and assistance with regard to business affairs, job opportunities and allied matters. Again, on the background of the traditional world view, which presupposes continual interaction between the empirical and the

---

[4] Int. Closby Kamanga, Church Member, Chibavi Baptist Church, Chibavi, 20.9.13.

[5] Int. Christina Standfore, Church Member, Chibavi Bible Believers, Chibavi, 20.9.13.

spirit world, religious leaders in worship centres provide a simple but convincing frame of reference in which God's spirit acts as an informative, protective force in the callous urban environment. Ching'ambo Free Methodist Church is grouping Christians together every Thursdays on career guidance. Pastor Mwiza Msiska discovered that Christians in his church had problems of unemployment; this prompted him and his wife to start an employment club where he could be giving counsel to Christians on how they can be self-reliant. The employment club is teaching Christians skills like Knitting, baking *mandasi* and tailoring. Through this many Christians at Free Methodist Church are self-employed and are assisting each other in many threatening situations.

6.1.4 Social Guidance

In the absence of centralized authorities which maintain traditional codes, religious leaders of worship centres step in as substitutes. Codes of marriage, family commitments, entertainment, use of alcohol, sex and so on, are worked out and strictly enforced by religious councils. Thus, religious leaders of worship centres take the place of traditional headmen and worship centres become a new tribe. The Seventh-day Adventist Church is teaching her members in every Sabbath on how they ought to behave as Christians in marriage, family and other social issues. Christians are grouped together in small groups basing on age. Different age groups have different needs whereby subjects are taught differently in order to meet the varying needs of her Christians. Katawa Assemblies of God Church organizes premarital and post marital seminars for her Christians three times a year. These seminars are of a great help to Katawa Assemblies of God Christians in the sense that Christians have strong families.

6.1.5 Information and Assistance

In the centres of worship members are given useful information on job opportunities, accommodation and transport. Some people have found a job through information given to Christians while at church. Gift Mlute from Mzuzu CCAP Church is working as a messenger with University of Livingstonia. He got the information about the job opportunity at the university during a church service. Apart from spiritual support, there is also material assistance, for instance food and domestic help in times of illness and funerals; women's organizations concentrate on assisting those in trouble.[6] Luwinga African Evangelical Church of Malawi had many members in 1991 when the church was giving relief maize to people who had no food. The relief maize was assisting people who were affected by draught in 1991. Through this many people joined the church and the total number of Christians went up to 2500, however, when the church stopped giving relief maize, the number of Christians dropped to 25. The holistic way of helping people becomes a major attraction, causing socially alienated city dwellers to join religious groupings.

The overall image that emerges in society gives hope to worship centres that actualize a theology of fellowship by way of new social structures and behavioral codes that support members in stressful situations marked by insecurity, alienation and isolation. Material and spiritual frames of reference, adapted by the social environment, give meaning and hope to an otherwise disorienting and emotionally debilitating urban existence.

6.2 Worship Participation by Age

The participants in worship services and other activities in worship centres are people of different age groups. When looking at activities done in religious worship centres, it shows that youth are more active than adults. Youth of different ages have more activities in worship centres than adults. Worship centres are filled in large numbers by youth of different age groups; youth are more involved in physical work, choir groups, teaching Sunday school classes and fellowships. Adults are good at church leadership and preaching.

6.2.1 Youth Participation

Services of worship in Mzuzu worship centres are attended by more young people of both sexes than adults. Children of Sunday school age, 5 to 14 years, and youth of 15 to 39 years of age are considered to be more in all worship centres than adults from 40 and above. This reflects the situation of the society as a whole. Although youth are many in worship centres, leadership and preaching are dominated by adults with the view that religion is a major part of their lives. Adults found fullness of life in worship centres and that is why leadership is actively done by them in order to protect their places in the church.

---

[6] Int. Agnes Nhlema, Mzuzu Presbytery Women's Coordinator, Mzuzu, 15.11.2012.

Pentecostal and Charismatic Churches have a higher percentage of youth than the mainstream churches. Most members (in some denominations all of them) are youth who sometimes are people of below 35 years of age. In such cases all activities found in worship centres are done by the youth. Kaviwale Gospel Pentecostal Worship Centre has the highest number of youth aged below 35 years; most of them are people of school age and few are economically productive, who could take responsibility for the consequences of their actions.[7] The worship centre has 52 members of which 50 are people of below 35 years. Lupaso Full Gospel Church of God has 30 members, 20 of them are youth below 30 years. Area 1B Charismatic Redeemed Ministries and International Church has 40 members of which 35 are people of below 35 years of age. In such cases leadership and preaching are done by a religious leader or the owner of the church while all other activities found in the worship centre are done by youth.

Youthful age in the mainstream churches is outnumbering adults. Mainstream churches have more youth below 40 years, however, children below 14 years normally do not worship together with people of above their age unless those in choir groups because most of them are attending Sunday school lessons at the same time when worship is taking place. Viyele CCAP Church has more youth than adults, most of them are students from Mzuzu University and other surrounding schools, and many are of the economically productive age group. St Joseph Roman Catholic Church is dominated by youth below 40 years. Most of these are students from various schools while some are working. Youth in the Mainstream churches are commonly used in choir groups and for physical work at worship centres. Youth at Msongwe CCAP Church are the ones who clear the surroundings at the church. At one time they were asked to dig a toilet and construct a temporary kitchen at a new Manse when they were about to welcome a new minister, Rev N.G. Hara. Youth at Mzuzu CCAP, St Andrews Church, were the ones who pulled down the old manse and cleared the ground before the church contractor started constructing the new manse.

Children and youth are more participating in religious worship centres than full grown youth or emerging adults. Mchengautuwa CCAP Church

---

[7] Int. Pastor Belson Mtonga, Kaviwale Gospel Pentecostal Church, Kaviwale, 25.9. 2013. /John. W. Santrock, Life-Span Development, Texas: McGraw Hill, 2009, p. 439.

at one time had a youth choir by the name Church Choir under the leadership of Gwaziwe Shumba. The choir was very strong when choir members were not full-grown youth; however, when choir members became emerging adults, the choir started losing its members and it became weak, eventually it stopped singing. The reason was that most members had developed an independent mind, making their own decisions, rather than depending on parental guidance. Youth of under age are oriented and mobilized to worship centres, commonly, by female parents on two reasons:

6.2.2 Tender Love and Care

Naturally women spend more time with children at home; the indoors home is female space while males are associated with the outdoors.[8] With this children and youth are close to the natural love and care of female parents and are driven by female parents' wishes. Because of the closeness of female parents to their children, the majority of female parents at Katawa CCAP Church are the ones who bring their children for infant baptism. Sometimes male parents do accompany their wives at baptism; however, children remain under the care of female parents. Rev. Makuni Gondwe of Katawa CCAP informed the church that when both parents have come for their child's baptism, the male parent should be the one giving the child to him for baptism. Interestingly, when both parents go forward to baptize a child, a child is carried by the female parent and when they are about to hand over to a minister, a husband takes over the responsibility from the wife of handing over the child to the minister and after baptism he receive the child back and passes it on to his wife. Even at Sunday school classes, children are coming to Sunday school under the influence and escort of female parents. The background of female parents' closeness to their children encourages children to listen more to female parents and to respond positively when they are asked to go to worship centres.

6.2.3 Worship Services are more Attended by Women

Services of worship are predominantly attended by women who are actively accompanied by their children. Mothers feel proud to be accompanied by their children when going to church. Children attend

---

[8] H.J. de Blij and Peter O. Muller, *Human Geography: Culture, Society and Space,* New York: John Wily and Sons, 1995, p. 206.

worship services in large numbers under the influence of female parents. Worship services which are attended by more men than women have low numbers of children and youth. Kubwezeretsa Sabata la Yehova, one of the very few male dominated churches, has 35 members, 22 of them are men, 8 are women and 5 are youth. The church has no member who is below 18 years. Most women are not interested to join the church and those who are in the church are following their husbands. Women are not interested to bring their children because in most cases worship is done during the night, wearing sack cloth and without shoes. Mothers are not encouraged by the conditions of the church to bring their children to the worship centre; as a result, they are left behind or sent to other worship centres.

6.2.4 Adult Participation

Most adults in Mzuzu seem to be religious and consider religion as a major part of their life. Worship centres consider them with high respect as people of full knowledge and responsibility in religious matters, which they are slowly transmitting to the growing generation. The age of religious significance begins in the late 40s and increases in the late 50s, and females are more interested and active in both organized and personal forms of religious worship than males.

Of the adults who show strong beliefs in God and actively participate in worship, most of them are not interested in Pentecostal and Charismatic worship. When one attends Pentecostal and Charismatic worships, it will be discovered that the majority of them are youth. Enlightened Christian Gathering Ministry was joined by many people, both adults and youth, from mainstream churches. While there, slowly, adults felt out of place, as such they moved out and rejoined mainstream worship centres in the name of going back to their parental churches. Mama Joyce Chinkhuntha abandoned Lupaso CCAP Church as a deacon together with her two grown up daughters and joined God's Will Church. After six months, Joyce Chinkhuntha came back to Lupaso CCAP Church leaving behind her two daughters. Mr. Kalumbi, former Principal at Livingstonia University, Laws Campus, left CCAP and joined one of the Charismatic churches, Enlightened Christian Gathering Ministry. Before he died he rejoined CCAP as his mother church.

Adults in mainstream worship centres are always in conflict with the youths who are bringing in Pentecostal and Charismatic elements of worship. CCAP Churches were or are in conflicts between youths and adults because youths wanted an inclusion of Pentecostal elements in worship, while adults were not interested to do so. The Church has accepted the request of the youths by giving them a separate service by the name of 'contemporary service', which is allowing them to incorporate Pentecostal elements in worship. The service is largely attended by the youth with few adults, women in particular.

Adults, especially men, have a strong desire and will to take up religious leadership, in order to protect their membership in religious places which can be lost when leadership can be in the hands of youth. The Parish Minister at Chibavi CCAP Church has internal conflicts with adults, who seem to be losing leadership positions and membership as well because the minister is in favour of the youth. The minister favours the youth because they are less critical then adults. The participation of adults, especially men, has been reduced because the minister has succeeded in giving most of the prominent leadership positions of the church to the youth. Adults feel out of place in the church and are not participating in totality. They complained to the minister, through John Nyirenda, that he has to consider them because their religiosity is linked to health, in the sense that it lowers incidence of depression in life. Worship in adults is related to a sense of well-being and can provide for some important psychological needs in helping them to prepare for impending death, finding and maintaining a sense of meaning and significance in life, and accepting the inevitable losses to old age.

6.3 The Role of Women in Worship Centres

This section will provide information on the position of women in worship centres. The discussions will centre on women participation and leadership in worship centres.

6.3.1 Women Participation at Worship Centres

Worship centres are comprised of males and females of various ages. When looking at Worship centres' participation, women participate more than men. Women are the majority in worship centres and are actively involved in many activities done at worship centres. They are much involved in social work and day to day church activities like cleaning the church and the surrounding. Area 1B International Pentecostal Church has 20 members, 19 of them are women and one is a man. Chibavi Ephata Ministry has 30 members of which 20 are female and 10 are male.

Women are actively involved in forming church groups. Mchengautuwa CCAP Church has 15 choir groups, out of which six are for women only, eight of them are for both men and women, while women are still dominating. Church activities in worship centres are commonly done by women like cheering the sick, visiting the bereaved and cooking and ushering food at church meetings.

Table 6-0-1: Gender Participation

Denomination	Gender Participation	
	Female (%)	Male (%)
African International Church	72	28
Anglican Church	60	40
Assemblies of God	70	30
Baptist Convention of Malawi	60	40
Bible Believer	50	50
CCAP	60	40
Chipangano Church	72	28
Church of Christ	55	45
Evangelical Baptist Church	60	40
Fellowships and Churches with one Worship Centre	75	25
Islam	65	35
Living Waters	70	30
New Apostolic Church	55	45
Roman Catholic Church	60	40
Seventh-day Baptist, CAC, Reform, Original	55	45
Seventh-day Adventist	55	45
African Traditional Religion	80	20
Kubwezeretsa Sabata La Yehova	30	70
Mboni za Yehova	60	40
African International	72	28
	63.55	37.45

Table 6.1 above shows the gender participation in worship centres as per denomination and religion. The table shows that in African Traditional Religion and Fellowships and Churches with not more than two Worship Centres has the heights participation of women than men. It indicates that women have a proportion of 80% and 20% men in the African Traditional Religion and 75% women while men have 25% in Fellowships and Churches with not more than two Worship Centres. The reason is that in most of these worship centres there is a practice of healing and deliverance where women respond more quickly to such issues than men. Naturally the concerns for health issues and other problems for women differ from those of men, as a result women respond quickly in larger numbers to such issues than men. The above reason does also apply to worship centres belonging to Pentecostal and Charismatic denominations. There is another indication in the table of a higher women participation than men in the African Instituted Churches. The table shows that women have a proportion of 72% while men have 28%. The reason is that, in most of these worship centres, church members are living a polygamous life where a man marries two or more women and he joins a particular worship centre with all of them.

The table gives an average gender participation of 62.55% for women and 37.45% for men. However, I have noticed that the Kubwezeretsa Sabata la Yehova has more men participation than women. The table shows that men have a proportion of 70% to 30% of women. The reason for the lower participation of women is that women are not interested in joining the church; they are just forced by their husbands or a person closer to them. The church does not give women opportunity to do activities in the church, all activities are being done by men themselves, the church does not allow choir groups, and church members are not allowed to wear shoes and are asked to dress in sack cloth while entering into the church.

Apart from the reasons given above, there are other reasons why women are leading in numbers and participation in worship centres than men. Reasons for the difference in 'sex ratio'[9] could be the following:

---

[9] Sex ratio is the number of males per females within the total population and it varies among countries depending on the particular birth and death rates. James M. Rubenstein, *The Cultural Landscape. An Introduction to Human Geography,* Miami: Miami University, 1999, p. 66.

6.3.2 Females are more than Males

Naturally, women in Malawi, including Mzuzu, are more than men. The composition of the population indicates that 48% are men and 52% are women.[10] This shows that already women have advantages in numbers whose figures are to the higher side than men which at the end together with some other reasons make worship centres to have 37.45% men and 62.55% women. Birth rate and death rate records at Nkholongo Seventh-day Adventist Clinic show that slightly more males than females are being born but males have higher death rates than females. The higher mortality rate of males from child birth to adulthood is one of the reasons which partly explain the lower percentage of males' participation in worship. The composition of men and women at Nkholongo Seventh-day Adventist Church shows that 100 are men and 200 are women. The records show that women outlive men on the average for about four years; however, the difference varies spatially.[11] Dr Ruth Leger Sivard noted that the widening gap resulted not only from medical and other advantages associated with socio-economic progress; also women seem to have been less inclined to adopt some of the unhealthy habits often associated with social influence; cigarette smoking, in particular, but also the excess consumption of food and alcohol, fast driving (high accident rates), high levels of stress. However, writes Sivard, the increased stress on women trying to deal with competing demands of the home and work places plus life style changes associated with modern times may in time erode the gender longevity gap.[12]

Although during lifetimes, woman's health problems and concerns differ from those of men, pregnancy and childbirth confront women with high health risks. Inadequate medical care, an excessive number of pregnancies and malnutrition are among the leading causes of maternal deaths. In addition, the other fact is that an estimated number of women die each year due to illegal abortions and yet we are reminded that men face nothing comparable during equivalent years of their lives. Under all these circumstances it is remarkable that women's life expectancy

---

[10] *A Students' Handbook for Population Education in Malawi*, Domasi: Malawi Institute of Education, 1998, p. 38.

[11] H.J. de Blij and Peter O. Muller, *Human Geography: Culture, Society and Space,* New York: John Wily and Sons, 1995, p. 302.

[12] Ruth Leger Sivard, *Women: A World Survey*, Washington DC: World Priorities, 1985, p. 386.

exceeds that of men, a situation that results in the words of Dr Sivard who says that they are 'genetically programmed to have a lower mortality rate than men'.[13] This is one of the reasons which make women to be more in worship centres than man.

6.3.3 Social Groupings

Women living in the city need an intimate circle of life which form the basis of life and help the individual to cope with day to day problems.[14] Unlike men, women are facing many challenges of life, whereby, for them to make decisions they need to be taught or learn from others, in so doing they become attracted to join communities where they can be helped. Women in the Baptist Convention Churches in Mzuzu, more particular at Chibavi, have a women organization called Umodzi wa Amayi a Baptist. Often, Umodzi is referred to by other names as Umanyano, Mvano and Chigwirizano in other churches like CCAP Synod of Livingstonia, Blantyre Synod and Churches of Christ.[15] More women have joined Chibavi Baptist Umodzi wa Amayi group as a group that offers security and chances of reintegration, a new home providing anchorage in a harsh competitive world.[16] The aim of the group is to preach Christ to others; the group fulfills this aim through Bible Study, preaching, giving and sharing, fellowship, prayer and training. As more women are being interested in joining the group, women membership increases while men feel independently safer than women.

Women organizations attract more women who became members' of worship centres than men. The overall image of women in worship places is the theology of fellowship by way of social structures and behavioral codes that support members in stressful situations marked by insecurity and isolation. Mzuzu being an urban area, material and spiritual frames of references, adapted to the industrial environment,

---

[13] Ibid.

[14] M.L. Daneel, *Missiology, Christian Theology of Africa (Mission as Liberation: Third World Theologies)*, Pretoria: University of South Africa, 1989, p. 64.

[15] Rachel NyaGondwe Banda, *Women of Bible and Culture. Baptist Convention Women in Southern Malawi*, Zomba: Kachere, 2005, p. 92.

[16] Hopelessness and despair in women living in isolated life may cause a short circuit in moral development when confronted by hardships in life. Mary Kumwanje Safe-Motherhood, University of Malawi, College of Medicine. Open Discussion, Mangochi, 6.9.2014.

give meaning and hope to an otherwise disorienting and emotionally debilitating urban existence.[17]

6.3.4 Adaptability to Healing and Deliverance

Ndumanene Silungwe, a Technical Psychologist at St John of God College of Health Science, said that naturally during lifetimes, the concerns for health issues and other problems for women differ from those of men, as a result women are always quick to issues of healing and deliverance.[18] More women than men have joined worship centres in order to find solutions for the concerns of health and other problems which confront them. Pastor Isaac of Holy Spirit Channel International Church started his church at Viyele in 2012 through the gift of healing and deliverance. Mrs. Rev. Chipeta from Chikangawa, having become convinced that Pastor Isaac has gifts of healing and deliverance, introduced him to Mrs. Rev. Victoria Nyirenda, who had a sick son. Mrs. Rev. Chipeta was convinced that Pastor Isaac had a gift of healing and deliverance when he prayed for her sick daughter who seemed to have been healed at that time. Mrs. Rev. Victoria Nyirenda invited Pastor Isaac to her house to pray for a sick son and the family. After prayers, she was convinced of the gift and she started going round calling family friends and others to join them in prayers which were taking place at her house. Men and women were coming to attend these prayers; however, most men were in doubts about what they were hearing from their wives or other women about Pastor Isaac's gift of healing and deliverance. Although many men were reluctant to join Pastor Isaac's ministry, many women joined the ministry, by the time when the ministry was changing worship place from Mrs. Nyirenda's house to where they wanted to build the church; they were 50 women and three men. Today, the number of women has dropped to 17 while the number of men increased to five.

Women were coming to Pastor Isaac in large numbers with their own problems which needed the help of what they were hearing of healing and deliverance. That is one reason why women are in the majority in

---

[17] Women put more value on Church groups and activities than male counterparts. The use of religion is a way of coping with stress and becomes a source of strength. Edrine Sibande, Ministry of Health, Nkhota-kota District Hospital, Safe-Motherhood. Open Discussion, 6.9.2-14.

[18] Open discussion, when he was responding to a question on why women are found in the majority in Prophet Healing Churches, Mchengautuwa CCAP Church during rally, 19.10.2013.

religious worship centres and are more actively participating than men. Men show, on average, less interest in spiritual matters.

6.3.5 Protection and Social Guidance

Women, who by nature take the indoors home as their space, need protection and support from other quarters unlike men who seem to live in the outdoors. Chithira Peace Ministry Church organizes women seminars three times a year with the view of equipping women members with skills in social guidance and protection. The guest speaker at one of the seminars on 30 September 2013 was the wife of Pastor Vweza Banda of Peace Ministry Church; the speaker advised women that in such insecure social and threatening situations of individualistic city life, religious places become a place which provides the needed counsel and assistance as an allied body. Worship centres provide social guidance to women in matters regarding day to day living, i.e. marriages, family commitments, entertainment, sex, funerals and domestic help in time of illness. The social help in matters of day to day living is a major attraction to the majority of women at Chithira Peace Ministries who seem to be socially alien in urban centres.

Worship centres with women organizations provide social encouragement to women, a help which cannot be found elsewhere, this makes more women than men to join and fully participate in worship centres.

6.3.6 Position of Women in Leadership

The leadership of Mzuzu religious worship centres is constructed in a hierarchical order where the top most authority level is dominated by men although the majority of the members are women. The system seems to support and reinforce the traditional gender-based roles, ignoring the central authority of religious leadership of women in the same traditional culture where women were considered top in religious leadership.[19] Thus, worship centres select from the word of God and African culture those elements that confirm exclusion of women from top management when men are present. Religious authorities in Mzuzu seem to show that men, women and youth are not partners in top

---

[19] Isabel Apawo Phiri, *Women, Presbyterianism and Patriarchy, Religious Experience of Chew Women in Central Malawi*; Blantyre: CLAIM Kachere, 2000, p. 30.

leadership.[20] Women are actively participating in leadership when it comes to women organizations, i.e. women's guild, or choir groups, although final authority will come from men. The type of leadership presented here is centred on executive administration or top authority, i.e. religious leader, pastor or administrative secretary, of a religious centre, not on general leadership of sub-committees or ministries.

Although religions and denominations have little regard for women leadership, the approach to it is different. Some religions and denominations are strictly not allowing women leadership in the presence of men while some do allow them, though with limited support. Women in the religions and denominations seem to be almost living in a different world from that of men.

6.4. Religions and Denominations whose Women are not Participating in Leadership

6.4.1 Islamic Religion

The Islamic religion is absolutely strict that women are not allowed to lead any function in the presence of men. The religion does not even allow women to worship together with men in the same room.[21] Mosques are divided into two rooms, the front room, where there is a provision of space for a preacher, is for men and the room behind is for women. Women or men are strictly not allowed to enter into each other's room, in the service of worship, women are only hearers of the voice of a preacher, but they cannot see him. Preaching is only done by a male person, no woman is allowed to lead the service of worship in the presence of men, but she is during women's meetings. Muslim women are denied the right of leadership right from preaching to the general administration in the presence of men.

---

[20] Here women demand that the church return to Christlike understanding of authority and ministry, so that women and men may become partners in authority. Women's demands for inclusiveness in ecclesial ministry and authority is search for human development, search for wholeness. Isabel Apawo Phiri, *Women, Presbyterianism and Patriarchy. Religious Experience of Chew Women in Central Malawi*; Blantyre: CLAIM-Kachere, 2000.

[21] Int. Sheik Ibrahim Fikila Banda, Sheik at Chibavi Mosque, Chibavi, 22.9.2013.

6.4.2 Hindu Religion

Hindu religion in Mzuzu, like the Islamic religion, does not give the right of leadership to women; however, the difference is that worship is done in the same room. Women are not supposed to lead a service of worship; they are requested to remain quiet in the presence of men.[22] The one who leads the service of worship and is responsible for general administration is the male head of the family.

6.4.3 Christian Religion

The Christian religion is divided into two: those who deny women leadership and those who allow it. For example, Church of Christ, New Apostolic Church, Bible Believers, and others are not allowing women leadership in the presence of men. Grace Chipeta, deaconess and secretary at Church Square Section, at Mchengautuwa CCAP Church was once a member of the New Apostolic Church at Mphaka Worship Centre. She withdrew her membership when she was silenced and condemned publicly during a service of worship when she attempted to read Scriptures in the service in the church. She was warned that women are advised to remain quiet in the presence of men in the church. They are not allowed to speak, if they want to inquire about anything, they are advised to ask their husbands at home for it is disgraceful for a woman to speak in the church. She was further told that women are not allowed to lead a service of worship, even at home, when men are present. Salome Nyirenda, former member at Jomo Road Church of Christ joined CCAP, now at Mchengautuwa CCAP as vice Chairperson at Sector 12, because she was crushed by her pastor in the church to remain quiet before men, when she wanted to comment on church announcements which were concerning women. She was told that women's subordination is divinely sanctioned.[23] The creation story in Genesis is taken as the biblical foundation for the subordination of women, it is interpreted that the woman was created from man, after man and for man's advantage. Genesis 3:16 is taken as the divine law that a man is the head of a woman; therefore, she should not lead in the presence of men for she is

---

[22] Int. Rasck Patel, Founding Member of Hindu Religion in Mzuzu, Mzuzu, 3.10.2013.
[23] Int. Pastor Longstar Mlotha, Pastor at Jomo Road Church of Christ, Mzuzu, 3.10.2013.

supposed to remain quiet before the head. However, Genesis 3: 16 does not represent the divine order but shows the consequence of sin.[24]

There are other Christian denominations that seem to be not seriously debating the denial of women leadership; however, the practice shows that women are not given full opportunity of leadership. Denominations like the Anglican Church, Baptist Church, Roman Catholics and others do not debate seriously on women leadership, however, women are not given full recognition. Ching'ambo Church of Christ relay upon women leadership indirectly. The church has more women than men; women under the leadership of Violet Kamphukusi are the ones who go out for pastoral visitation and open-air preaching. Women are running a maize mill which is the main source of income to the church. They are given the right to preach in the presence of men apart from eldership, deacons and other leadership roles. However, they are not allowed to be pastors or priests and or administrative secretaries. They are allowed to take lesser administrative roles while those considered to be high are men's responsibilities.[25]

Women sometimes are considering themselves inferior before men. For example, Area 1B International Pentecostal is a worship centre where all are women except one, there are 20 women and one man. In principle, the top most leader is a woman, Bishop Gertrude Mhlanga, assisted by a male pastor, Petros Ziyendani, however, practically, the whole administration is done by a male pastor. Pastor Petros Ziyendani is the one who coordinates all Programmes at the worship centre; nothing can be done without his approval.

6.4.4 Those who Allow Women in Leadership

Some Christian denominations are giving equal opportunities of leadership to men and women. Apart from being deacons, elders, and preachers, some women are holding the top most authority of the church like being pastors and administrative secretaries. Such denominations like CCAP Synod of Livingstonia believe that both men and women are equal before God and they have equal ability to lead

---

[24] Janet Kholowa and Klaus Fiedler, *In the Beginning God Created them Equal*, Blantyre: CLAIM-Kachere, 2003, p. 27.

[25] Int. Violet Kamphukusi, Ching'ambo Churches of Church, Mzuzu, 12.9.2013.

God's people since leadership is a gift from God.[26] CCAP Synod of Livingstonia acknowledges the biological differences between men and women, but the differences cannot be convincing reasons to deny women the right of leadership. They recognize the traditional way of making decisions at village level, traditionally, men cannot carry out any decision without the approval of the women, otherwise the decision will be proven to be futile. In African Traditional Religion, God uses both men and women as his mediums of communication. For example, in the Chewa Traditional Religion God worked through Makewana, a female medium.[27]

Zolozolo CCAP had a female Parish Minister, Rev. Agnes Nyondo, who worked with them from 2008 to 2012. She came to Zolozolo on Synod transfer from Ekwendeni Hospital, where she had been hospital chaplain, now she has been transferred to St Paul's CCAP Church in Lilongwe. Rev. Margret Kalimanjira was another female CCAP Parish Minister at Msongwe Church. She came to Msongwe from Zomba Theological College in 2011 and was transferred to Phiri CCAP Church in Nkhata Bay in 2014. These women worked very hard in their respective churches in administering the sacraments, leading Kirk sessions, preaching and day to day administration. Pastor Miriam Nyirenda was a Pastor at Dunduzu Chekina Assemblies of God Church from 2008 to 2013, currently; she has been transferred to Lusangazi Road Block Assemblies of God Church. She came to Dunduzu when the church was experiencing a leadership crisis resulting in splits. The major contribution she made at Dunduzu Chekina Assemblies of God Church was to bring peace and unity among conflicting men over leadership. Her leadership, pastoral visitation, preaching and love of people united the splitting church.

Apart from parish ministers, women are also holding top leadership positions in worship centres. Anita Shaba is session clerk at Viyele CCAP. She has been session clerk for two consecutive terms of four years from 2009 to date. She is also a member of the Synod Executive Committee and chairperson of the Synod Lay Leadership Committee. During her

---

[26] Int. Rev. D.F. Chipofya, Synod Moderator, Speech at Farewell Ceremony of Rev Mrs M. Kalimanjira, Msongwe CCAP Church, Mzuzu, 9.10.2014.

[27] The roles of women were very clear and acceptable at territorial rain shrines, women, known as spirit wives were controllers of these shrines. They were receiving messages from god and were being communicating to communities when they were in a state of ecstasy.

term of office, the church has been building a new church, bigger than the old one, which is at roofing stage. Stella Mwangonde is Session clerk at Mzuzu CCAP (St Andrew's) Church. In her time the church has constructed a wall fence around the church premises and they have built a manse. Unius Moyo has been session clerk at Kachere CCAP Church from 2013. She took leadership when the church had financial problems. Due to her financial management skills, the church has improved her financial standards. Some women are holding senior leadership positions like deputy session clerks, session treasurers and recording secretaries. Lizzie Mwambazi is Deputy Session Clerk at Katawa CCAP Church. Elise Chiumia is Session Treasurer at Lupaso CCAP Church. Although some denominations give equal opportunities of leadership to men and women in the church, some women are shy to take up positions before men.[28] Joyce Trinidade, one of the first converts at Mzuzu Pentecostal Church, was offered the opportunity to become an assistant pastor. She refused the offer because she was shy to speak before men; instead, the offer went to Trevour Mwambila, who later became an assistant pastor.

---

[28] Int. Rev. D.F. Chipofya, Synod Moderator, Speech at Farewell Ceremony of Rev Mrs M. Kalimajira, Msongwe CCAP Church, Mzuzu, 9.10.2014.

Table 6.2: Women in Leadership

Number	Denomination	Restricting	Accepting	Numbers in Leadership
1	Africa International Church	Yes	No	0
2	Anglican Church	No	Yes	0
3	Assemblies of God	No	Yes	5
4	Baptist Convention of Malawi	No	Yes	0
5	Bible Believer	Yes	No	0
6	CCAP	No	Yes	15
7	Chipangano Church	Yes	No	0
8	Church of Christ	Yes	No	0
9	Evangelical Baptist Church	No	Yes	0
10	Fellowships and Churches with one worship Centre	No	Yes	7
11	Islam	Yes	No	0
12	Living Waters	No	Yes	2
13	New Apostolic Church	Yes	No	0
14	Roman Catholic	Yes	No	0
15	Seventh-day Baptist, CAC, Reform, Original	Yes	No	0
16	Seventh-day Adventist	Yes	No	0
17	African Traditional Religion	No	Yes	1
	Percentage of Restricting/Acceptance	**52.90%**	**47.10%**	

As shown in the table 6.1 above, 52.9% are denominations which do not give women the right to leadership. The denominations restrict rights to women leadership in the presence of men. These denominations are at the column of restrictive where they are indicated yes. The other column in the middle of the table indicates acceptance is for those denominations which give women the right to leadership equal to men, the table indicates 47.10%. Although these denominations accept women leadership, some of them are not practicing it. 37.50% are denominations which do not give women the opportunity to lead in their worship centres. 62.50% are denominations which give women the opportunity to lead in their worship centres. Denominations where women are leading in worship centres have given women very limited opportunity, in most cases only 1% has been given to women leadership. For example, in the CCAP worship centres 1% of the total leadership is given to women in practice.

6.5 Language

Language is one of the cornerstones of religious identity, of cultural unity and of community cohesion.[29] Webster's Dictionary defines language as a systematic means of communicating ideas or feelings by the use of conventionalized signs, gestures, marks or especially articulate vocal sounds. Sound communication is the crucial part in doing religion in Mzuzu; all communication is done in articulate vocal sounds and gestures. Language is important to religion as a means of everyday life; it enables them to pass on information of salvation to religious adherents, through preaching, teaching, singing, counselling and discussions.

Language and religion in Mzuzu are prominent threads in the tapestry of culture serving both to identify and classify individuals within complex societies and to distinguish populations and regions of different tongues and faiths.[30] It is the means of transmission of culture and the medium through which its beliefs and standards are expressed. Hindu Religion is communicated through the Hindi language; therefore, if one joins the religion one has to embrace Hindu culture transmitted through language. Language responds to the dynamics of human thought, experience and expression and to the exchange and borrowing ever more common in a closely integrated world.[31]

Language may be rigorously defended and preserved as an essential element of cultural or religious identity or abandoned in the search for acceptance into a new society. To trace their diffusion, adaptations and

---

[29] Int. Bishop Fanuel Magangani, Bishop of Anglican Church of the Northern Diocese, Mzuzu 3.10.2013.

[30] Ibid.

[31] Jeremia D. Fellmann, *Human Geography: Landscape of Human Activities*, New York: McGraw Hill, 1999, p. 140.

disappearances is to understand part of the evolving course of historical cultural geography. The English language unites people of different cultural strata in Christian religion in Mzuzu in search for acceptance into a new society. *ChiNgoni*, the dominant language among the Ngoni of Mzimba and Mzuzu in the old years has been abandoned by all religions in Mzuzu because the language has been swallowed up by *Chitumbuka*. Chichewa is a new language in Mzuzu being accepted because Mzuzu has become a mixed society dominated by Tumbuka speaking people. Religions as well as languages in Mzuzu are dynamic, sweeping across national linguistic and cultural boundaries by conversion and conviction.

6.5.1 Dominant Languages in Worship Centres

Mzuzu worship centres have different religions and denominations; each of them has one or two dominant languages depending upon historical, cultural and geographical background. The commonest languages are: Chitumbuka, Chichewa and English, however, there are some minority languages like Yao and Arabic which are used in Islam, while Hindi is the dominant language in Hindu religion. The idea of having a common language is to have a systematic method of communicating ideas, altitudes or intent of salvation through the use of mutually understood sound words and gestures.[32] Through language, Mzuzu religious adherents communicate to each other messages of salvation with mutual comprehension.[33] Let us look at the three dominant languages.

Table 6.2 below shows the three dominant languages found in worship centres in Mzuzu. The table shows that most of Fellowships, Pentecostal and Charismatic worship centres use both languages, English and Chichewa, in one service. Normally they have one service of worship where English and Chichewa are used through an interpreter; they speak in English and interpreted in Chichewa. The Mainstream churches and few others have divided their services of worship into two, the English service and either Chitumbuka or Chichewa. In the CCAP worship centres, English is dominating in many worship centres and most of the attendants are the youth. African Instituted Churches have one service of worship dominated by the Chitumbuka language.

---

[32] Int. Pastor Danwell Masamba, Katoto Assemblies of God Church, Katoto, 30.9.2013.
[33] Int. R. Mshali, Lecturer, Mzuzu University, Department of Geography, lecture notes. 16.6.2014.

Table 6 3: Three Dominant Languages and Attendance

Denomination	Language and Attendance					
	English	Attendance %	Chitumbuka	Attendance %	Chichewa	Attendance %
African International Church			6	100		
Anglican Church	1	20			4	80
Assemblies of God Church	9	45			10	55
Baptist Convention of Malawi	1	20	1	20	8	60
Bible Believer					2	100
CCAP	15	50	17	40	2	10
Chipangano Church			6	100		
Church of Christ	1	10	7	70	2	20
Evangelical Baptist Church	1	20			4	80
Fellowships and Churches with one Worship Centre	30	40	2	20	30	40
Islam					8	100
Living Waters	5	50			5	50
New Apostolic Church	2	20	6	60	2	20
Roman Catholic	3	30	8	60	1	10
Seventh-day Baptist, CAC, Reform, Original			2	40	3	60
Seventh-day Adventist	3	20			13	80
African Traditional Religion			2	100		

6.5.3 Chitumbuka

Chitumbuka is the dominant cultural language in Mzuzu. The language is relatively important as it is the main cultural language widely spoken and heard among the people in northern Malawi.[34] Mzuzu being part of northern Malawi is a Chitumbuka speaking area, as a result most worship centres which have northern region influence communicate in Chitumbuka. The language is commonly used in the mainstream denominations, African Instituted Churches and African Traditional Religion, where the majority of leadership and worshipers are Tumbuka speakers.

In the mainstream denominations of Roman Catholic and CCAP Synod of Livingstonia, Chitumbuka plays a major role in worship centres. Worship centres might have one or two to three services of worship on a Sunday; however, the Tumbuka service of worship is accorded high respect by calling it the general service of worship, where most prominent church leadership attend.[35] The service starts at 9 o'clock for those who have a Tumbuka service only or soon after the English service. The Tumbuka service is commonly attended by the elderly who feel comfortable to worship in the local language.

6.5.4 Chichewa

Chichewa is a migrant language which came from central and southern Malawi. The language has migrated to Mzuzu and found a place in religious worship centres by the majority of Chewa speakers from Chewa speaking regions that have moved to Mzuzu with Chichewa as their standard means of communication.[36] The other means through which Chichewa has been transmitted to Mzuzu is through assimilation and learning, Tumbuka speakers have learnt Chichewa through schools and contacts with Chewa speakers in Mzuzu or elsewhere.[37]

Chichewa is commonly used in Pentecostal and charismatic worship centres because they originate from a Chichewa speaking background.

---

[34] Int. Sigman Chilambo, Church Elder, Viyele CCAP Church, 10.8.2014.

[35] Int. Frank Changwe, Church Elder, Mchengautuwa CCAP Church, Mchengautuwa. 15.1.2015.

[36] Int. Ranker Kumwenda, Katoto Cavalry Family Church. Chithira. 30.9.2013.

[37] Int. Pastor Chipulapula, Chisomo Baptist Convention Church, Hilltop. 2.10.2013.

Most of these worship centres have come to Mzuzu from south and central Malawi or with people who have been in south or central Malawi or from people who have been in Christian fellowships in Secondary Schools, Colleges, Universities and Christian Organizations where the main language is Chichewa. Katawa Assembles of God Church started with individual members of Assembles of God from Lilongwe and Blantyre who came to reside in Mzuzu. The Church started as a fellowship among these individuals with Chichewa speaking background and has remained a Chichewa speaking church. Mzuzu Pentecostal Church was started by Pastor Samuel Banda who was sent from Lilongwe by the Pentecostal Church Head Office. He started the church with a Chichewa speaking background as a fellowship in his house and it is still a Chichewa speaking church. Pastor Msikiti was sent from Lilongwe to start International Pentecostal Holiness Church in Mzuzu. He started the church from the background of Chichewa speaking, which has remained to date. Chiputula Ambassadors for Christ Ministries started by 14 members, all of them were members of Scripture Union and while at secondary school were members of Student Christian Organization of Malawi. The language used in the ministry is Chichewa inherited from the two Christian organizations where it is commonly used.

Chichewa language in Mzuzu is also dominantly used in religions and denominations whose origin and the majority of her religious adherents come from a Chichewa speaking background. The Anglican Church came to Mzuzu from Likoma, a Chewa speaking area and the majority of her members come from Likoma and Nkhotakota, Chewa speaking regions. Rev. Fr. Kamanga, Parish Priest at Luwinga Holy Trinity Anglican Church, is a Tonga by tribe. By virtue of being an Anglican Priest he is forced to speak Chichewa although he is not a good Chichewa speaker. Fr. Kamanga has no option because the majority of Anglican Church members are Chichewa speakers, singing, liturgy and other literature are in Chichewa. The Seventh-day Adventist Church equally originated from a Chichewa speaking background. Spoken words, singing, literature and liturgy are in Chichewa. Although the church might have other literature in English, but when it comes to teaching it has to be in Chichewa. Mr. Ndovi, an adult class teacher at Mchengautuwa Seventh-day Adventist Church is a Ngonde, he speaks and understands well Chitumbuka and English, and his teaching materials for adult classes are in English. One day he was found teaching his class in English and Chitumbuka, the church leadership stopped him and he was ordered to translate his teachings into Chichewa immediately and be able to teach in Chichewa.

6.5.5 English

English is another major language which is being used in worship centres of Mzuzu, which has been migrated to Mzuzu as a result of colonization.[38] When Malawi became a British colony, English was introduced as a high premium language and became the medium of education, administration, trade and commerce. English became a prestigious language acquired through schools, daily contact and business or social necessity, gradually lower social strata of society were absorbed into the expanding pool of language adopters.[39]

The language is commonly used in mainstream churches, Pentecostal and Charismatic churches, and is not found in African Instituted Churches, African Traditional Religion, Islamic and Hindu religions. The CCAP Synod of Livingstonia worship centres in Mzuzu, one of the Mainstream denominations, have full Sunday services of worship in English where spoken words, singing and liturgy are done in English. At Mzuzu CCAP Church English service starts at 7 o'clock to 9 o'clock. The service is attended by some who are not comfortable with Chitumbuka language; however, the majority of the attendants are the youth and those who want to attend Sunday service first before going to other day's engagements. The service is brief compared to the Chitumbuka service where leaders of the service become very free expressing themselves in their mothers' language.

In the Pentecostal and Charismatic denominations, English is combined with Chichewa or Chitumbuka in one service, spoken words and singing is done interchangeably, Chichewa or English or Chitumbuka. A preacher at Redeemed Christian Church of God at Katawa preaches in English while an interpreter interprets into Chichewa. Or sometimes a member in the congregation may speak in Chichewa or Chitumbuka and an interpreter interprets it into English. Liturgy, songs and scriptural readings are done interchangeably, Chichewa or English. People view the practice of interpretation as originated from where the preacher does not know the local language of his or her congregation or the congregation does not

---

[38] Int. Mama Rose Ziba, First Female Cabinet Minister of Malawi in MCP Government, Kaning'ina, 3.6.2013.

[39] Int. Rev H.M. Nkhoma, Former General Secretary, CCAP Synod of Livingstonia. 16.1.2015.

understand the preacher's language.[40] This practice seems to have become the tradition of the Pentecostal and Charismatic Churches.

6.5.6 Language Influences Worship

Language is one of the aspects influencing religious adherents on where and how to worship and help to shape the belief system of a worshipper and transmit it to succeeding generations; however, it distinguishes people and groups. Religious adherents will register their names to a worship Centre where they will be conversant with a spoken language, no member of a worship Centre can remain where they do not understand the language because serious issues are discussed in a language you understand.[41]

Language has influenced worship by being adopted in worship centres. Mzuzu being mixed, worship centres have adopted languages which could group different tribes together in worship. In the CCAP Synod of Livingstonia worship centres, Chitumbuka was the only language used in worship. When the number of people from different tribes who joined Mzuzu CCAP worship centre was increasing, the centre introduced an English service, which made many people to attend worship services including those who were not CCAP members, people like Mpachika and Zuwa, members of Church of the Nazarene whose church was not yet introduced. All CCAP worship centres in Mzuzu today are having English services, a case which was not there before. The service is being attended by more people than the Chitumbuka service, more especially in worship centres of Katawa, Mzuzu, Viyele, Mchengautuwa, Chiputula, Zolozolo and Chibavi. Churches which started from a Chichewa speaking background have included Chitumbuka in their services of worship. Mchengautuwa Seventh-day Adventist Church, a Chichewa speaking church, is using Chitumbuka interchangeably with Chichewa. This is because the majority of Church members are Tumbuka speakers who do not understand Chichewa.

6.6 Culture of Healing and Deliverance in Worship Centres

People of Mzuzu are coming from a religious cultural background where each and every one is aware of the existence of God as the creator and

---

[40] Similar to what Dr Hastings Kamuzu Banda, Former president of Malawi, was doing when addressing Malawians during his rallies.
[41] Int. Rev A.G Mhone, Parish Minister, Limphasa CCAP Church 30.11.2014

sustainer. The concept of God among them is as old as their cultural background, going back to the time when they became aware that they were mere creatures in the complexity of all created things. The awareness makes people inwardly dependent on a creator God, who is beyond and yet within their immediate surroundings, a being that they have to honour, worship and depend upon for their very existence.[42]

Traditionally, God the creator was not to be approached directly but through intermediaries, the spirits.[43] It is believed that the spirits were making the will of God known to religious leaders through draughts, epidemics and other ecological crises. Religious leaders were being possessed by the spirits and then were able to utter God's will and help those in suffering.

The traditional background has special significance for religious distribution among people in Mzuzu. Religions and denominations have emulated the roles of the spirits, but now the Holy Spirit is helping people through prophecy, healing and deliverance. Religious adherents have a common belief that religious leaders have the power of the Holy Spirit that enables them to heal, deliver and prophecy. Religious adherences feel unfortunate to preachers who seems lacking the gifts of the Holy Spirit of healing, prophecy and deliverance.

The physician Luke wrote in his gospel that healing has a higher purpose than physical restoration (Luke 17, 11-19). To return to Jesus with body, soul and spirit is the intention of the healer and the healing. The practice of healing in churches seems to have replaced the traditional religious healers like prophets (*nchimi*) and medicine men. People with all kinds of illnesses and problems are brought to worshiping centres for healing and

---

[42] The people of Mzuzu have a common expression of 'God knows' or 'God Almighty' when something bad or good happens to them. The expression of 'God knows' is when a certain person has caused harm to somebody. The victim has the feeling that God is aware of all what has happened and He has an appropriate solution. While the expression of 'God Almighty' usually means that somebody has achieved something beyond his or her imagination and it has been achieved through the work of God Himself. The expressions are making God to be the owner of creation and the sustainer.

[43] Whatever Science may do to prove the existence or non – existence of the spirits one thing is undeniable for African peoples is that spirits are a reality which must be reckoned with, whether it is clear, blurred or confused reality. John Mbiti, *African Religions and Philosophy*, London and Nairobi; Heinemann, 1969, p. 91.

deliverance. Worshiping centres, more especially from Pentecostals and Charismatic denominations, are as good as local clinics. Persons, including members from other religions or denominations, are coming to Pentecostal and Charismatic worship centres with problems for prayers almost in every Sunday service and or middle week prayer. Conversion or baptism is made on demand when one has been helped. A close association of the command to heal the sick reiterates the attitude of the traditional belief that diseases are caused by the evil spirits - not a blessing or a fate sent by God.[44] There have been some cases where religious leaders have promised to pray for those who have problems or delays in conception until the baby is born.[45]

Healing does not always happen. Not everybody who comes for healing can be healed and even those who can be healed are not immune to sickness for the rest of their lives, as important as the factual healing is, there is another element even more decisive in the process. A call to come forward and be prayed for moves a sick person into an atmosphere of concrete spiritual expectation. An encounter with God is offered, a non - sacramental link to the spiritual world. This is a mystical experience linked with freedom of expression and manifestation. Since the Holy Spirit has taken over some of the functions of the traditional beliefs of spirits, this does not mean that He has thereby become the traditional spirits, but rather that the Holy Spirit has become in the context a counsellor and guide as portrayed in the scriptures.[46]

6.6.1 Prophecy

The practice of healing goes with the practice of prophecy. The practice of prophetical diagnosis seems to have replaced the traditional diviners. Prophecies may be concerned with telling the unknown future that surrounds a person. The diagnosis is a search for the evils that destroy life, such as illness, infertility, unemployment or other misfortunes. According to African Traditional Religion, evils are misfortunes caused by disgruntled spirits, sorcery and witchcraft.[47] With this background the

---

[44] Ulf Strohbehn, *Pentecostalism in Malawi, A History of the Apostolic Faith Mission in Malawi*, Zomba: Kachere, 2005, p. 56.

[45] Int. Lanes Kaunda, Church Elder, Lusangazi CCAP, 2.6.2014.

[46] Int. Gladess Maganga, Church Member, Chibavi Providence Industrial Mission, Chibavi, 19.9.2013.

[47] Int. Justina Maria Sakala. Maria Traditional Healer, Sonda, 28.9.2013.

concept has been shifted from the traditional healers, who had been unable to have victory over these powers, to Christian prophets, whose powers are originated in Jesus Christ. Prophecy is commonly done in Charismatic and Pentecostal denominations by religious leaders who call themselves Prophets or Major Prophets. Shepherd Bushiri of Enlightened Christian Gathering is one of the notable prophets in Mzuzu. The prophet calls himself Major Prophet while his juniors are Minor Prophets.[48]

6.6.2 Healing and Deliverance

Deliverance is an inward psychological healing of a disordered person possessed with evil spirits. The belief is that evil spirits produce demons that enter into persons and torment them; however, the belief has been shifted to the understanding that evil spirits are fallen angels. The teaching is that the possessed persons need to be delivered for them to have a complete healing.

Pastor Frank Zebrone of God's Will Church has a mission from God to heal and deliver people from physical and spiritual bondage. Healing and deliverance prayers are conducted to deliver people from demonic possession. Many people are coming to God's Will Church that have been trapped in habits of serious sin, they are unable to break from until the Holy Spirit sets them free. Victims of demonic possessions are said to have been snatched away suddenly and dramatically from immorality, drunkenness, drug addiction, prostitution and every disorder and degradation to which human nature is liable.[49] Deliverance has released people from psychological bonds and set them free to effectively serve God in the complete and joyous freedom of the Holy Spirit.

Healing and Deliverance prayers conducted at Chibavi Ephata Church are done by religious leaders who sometimes use Biblical verses to counsel the victims. Sufferers are taught biblical texts to make them aware of the kind of their bondage and an assurance for healing to induce willingness to be set free, although sometimes a person may have struggled for years.[50] For example, such are people who have tried to give up the habit of smoking but had been unable on their own. Verses used during

---

[48] Bushiri now lives in South Africa and his congregation in Malawi has been declining. See chapter 3.
[49] Int. Pastor Mc Evans Gondwe, Sonda Assemblies of God Church, Sonda, 26.9.13.
[50] Int. Funny Singini, Sonda Christ Rock Church, Sonda, 20.9.2013.

deliverance are like: Isaiah 42:22 " But this is the type of people who have been plundered and looted, all of them trapped in a pit or hidden away in prison with no one to say, send them back." They also use John 14:6, where Jesus says; "I am the way and the truth and the life, no one comes to the father except through me."

The religious culture of people in the area has been seen leading the wave of spatial distribution of religions and denominations. The cultural practices might be different from one tradition to the other; however, all of them are characterized by two urgent quests: a desire to demonstrate the presence of the ancestral spirits, and a desire to directly address problems and frustrations of human life.[51] The spatial religious distribution arose from the desire of God's power amidst human misery. As such, spatial distribution comes from a lively apprehension for the priorities of many anxious people. Religious life is characterized by prophecy, healing, divination, and revelation. They have a strict and precise order, with a detailed code of regulations, exhortations, and prohibitions, often under a charismatic leader and with much congregational participation.

6.7 Geography of Conflicts and Splits in Worship Centres

Mzuzu worship centres are experiencing conflicts and splits every day. Conflicts are common in every worship centre while splits due to conflicts are commonly found in Pentecostal and Charismatic churches. The positive side of conflicts and splits is that it is one of the causative agents of the diffusion of worship centres in Mzuzu.

6.7.1 Conflicts and Disagreements

When group members work together, they build expectations of one another.[52] Conflicts over roles and responsibilities occur because of different expectations. Many problems occur simply because people are not clear about what they expect of each other. Besides, different expectations and overlapping roles and responsibilities create tension, especially when two or more members see themselves as equal for the

---

[51] Int. Ngwaza Muwele Mbaya, Muwela Traditional Healer Temple, Dunduzu, 30.8.2013.

[52] Anthony D'Souza, *Leadership. A Trilogy on Leadership and Effective Management*, Paulines: Limuru, 1994, p. 73.

same task.⁵³ Role overlaps, although not inherently bad, have a potential for conflict as long as they exist, conflicts sometimes arise because of personal clashes. Conflict disagreements are found in all worship centres, the difference is that some are severe to the extent that it becomes difficult to resolve them, hence they reduce worship attendance.

Homebound Assemblies of God Church survived through alleged conflicts and disagreements among members because of the marriage of Pastor Lukhele. Pastor Lukhele, who was an assistant pastor at Rumphi, married a daughter of Pastor Shakespeare Mvalo, pastor at Luwinga Assemblies of God. Pastor Mvalo thought to open a worship centre out of his church for his son in-law to have a reason to come to Mzuzu. Instead of opening one worship centre, he opened two of them, Homebound and Viyele. Pastor Lukhele was posted at Homebound Church. Many members at Homebound Church were not happy to have Pastor Lukhele as their pastor, when they discovered that his father in-law had created Homebound Church for him. The conflict was severe to the extent that many members stopped attending services of worship at Homebound. The situation was normalized when Pastor Lukhele was transferred to Viyele Assemblies of God Church.⁵⁴

Mzuzu International Pentecostal Church had a severe conflict over disagreements between members following Bishop Msikiti and those supporting National Head Office. Bishop Msikiti was enquiring from National Head Office on why churches in the north were not supported the way other churches were supported in the centre and south. The response which came from the Head Office was a shout at Bishop Msikiti in the presence of church members. Through this, the church got divided in a way that many supported Bishop Msikiti, while few supported the National Office. The situation was severe. Peace came to the church only when Bishop Msikiti was dismissed from the Church and was declared no longer to be a pastor of International Pentecostal Church.⁵⁵

---

⁵³ Ibid.
⁵⁴ Int. Ludalingwa Khonje, Former Member of Luwinga Assemblies of God, Luwinga, 27.7.2013.
⁵⁵ Int. Chricy Msikiti, Wife to Pastor Msikiti, Pentecost Christ Church International, Mzilawayingwe, 23.8.2013.

6.7.2 Splits

When conflicts and disagreements have failed to reach a compromise, it is obvious that the result becomes splits. Splits due to conflicts are commonly found in Pentecostal and Charismatic denominations. Most of these churches in Mzuzu have no clear roles and responsibilities that could govern people working together on the managerial level. Oftentimes individuals in these churches have power and leadership struggles. Competition on Spiritual gifts of healing, deliverance and prophecy is one reasons causing conflicts and splits in worship centres as well. When worship centres have conflicts and disagreements and have failed to reach a compromise, the result is a split so that peace prevails.

Dunduzu Assemblies of God Church originated from leadership struggles. At first the church started as Dunduzu Pentecostal Assemblies of Jesus Christ under the leadership of Bishop Thunga. Suddenly the church was caught in a leadership struggle between Bishop Thunga and Elias Soko, who wanted to be a pastor of that church. The conflicts were severe to the point that the church divided into two parts; Dunduzu Pentecostal Assemblies of Jesus Christ which later became Living Waters and Kalibu kwa Yesu under the leadership of Elias Soko. Dunduzu Assemblies of God Church came as a break away from Kalimbu kwa Yesu Church. Conflicts rose again among Christians of Kalimbu kwa Yesu Church over the alleged mismanagement of funds given by American missionaries for building a church at Lupaso. Pastor Elias was accused of having built his own house instead of the church. Clashes rose between Pastor Elias and Yohani Gondwe, who also became pastor of the other group. The new group took the church back to Dunduzu area where they asked Assemblies of God Luwinga Church to take over the church. Today the church is Dunduzu Assemblies of God. Out of this struggle, five churches have emerged.[56]

Mzuzu Pentecostal Church had a conflict during her early days of existence. The conflict was between Pastor Samuel Banda and Pastor Nepard, a missionary. The conflicts arose because of competing gifts of the Holy Spirit. The church was in love with Pastor Samuel Banda who had a gift of healing and deliverance. Pastor Nepard, who came from Lilongwe, was sent to support the growth of the church. While here Pastor Nepard was not happy to see how people loved Pastor Samuel Banda, he asked Christians to focus their attention on him in order for

---

[56] Int. Thomas Gondwe, Pastor of Lupaso Kalimbu Kwa Yesu, Lupaso, 26.82013.

him to help them in developing the church. The conflict between the two pastors was severe and made Pastor Samuel Banda to start his own church by the name Pentecostal Christian Church. Many people followed Pastor Samuel Banda.

6.8 Interreligious Relations

Despite conflicts and splits of religious worship centres, Mzuzu religions and denominations have religious tolerance which enhances the spatial distribution of religions and denominations. Mzuzu is a God-fearing city which gives freedom of worship to her citizens and invites people of other religions or denominations to establish their own religions or denominations.[57] The practice is that all religions and denominations have freedom to establish a worship centre at any place that seems good to them with an assurance to work amongst the residents of the area and beyond without any difficulties. Religious centres of different religions and denominations in some areas have been distributed in a clustered manner and are living together without any interference to each other. Good examples of such clusters are churches found along Nkhata Bay - Kenyatta roads behind Mzuzu Regional Police Station and Malawi Broadcasting Corporation station area, and also churches clustered around at Chithila area near Toyota Malawi and Grand Palace Hotel. Religious tolerance is achieved in the sense that her citizens are peace loving people where there is no civil rivalry. There is no tribe which is above the other, whereby each tribe accepts each other the way it is.[58] Tribes have one common law which is respect to each other. On the same note, Mzuzu is dominated by the youthful productive age group which has loose connections with tribal ties, most of them are educated citizens, born and brought up from different places and busy with particular occupations i.e.; employment, education and business.[59] Citizens are mindful of their own business, hence promoting peace and tranquility in the area.

The other point which helps to achieve religious tolerance is lack of centralized authority among the ethnic groups. Mzuzu has several ethnic

---

[57] Honourable Khumbo H. Kachale, Vice President of the Republic of Malawi, Speech at Kataba CCAP Church Silver Jubilee Celebrations 23.12.2013.
[58] Int. Wayinga Singini, Group Village headman, Lupaso, 6.4.2013.
[59] Int. Opson Thole, Mzuzu Museum, Department of Culture and Heritage, Mzuzu, 4.4.2014.

groups who have no centralized authority of their own groupings. Citizens of the area have no substantial roots which can make them claim for a rightful authority; those who seem to be traditional chiefs are as good as area chairpersons, since they have no traditional background connecting them to the area.[60] Luwinga Singini and Mafuta Kaunda are the ones who can fairly be treated as traditional chiefs, however, they do not have full control over the whole region, and their legitimacy was overtaken by Tung Oil Estate.[61] The estate transformed the way of life people used to live in the area from ethnic traditional life to monetary urbanized life. Mzuzu has different tribal traditions, however the common denominator of all traditions is monetary urbanized life. People have come to Mzuzu for money.[62]

The type of settlement pattern is another factor which promotes religious tolerance in Mzuzu. The settlement pattern is based on social economical class regardless of tribe, race or ethnic boundaries. People of different tribes, races and nationalities are mixed together in their residential area based on social economic class. Many people are living in rented houses and those who have their own house bought a plot from city council or fellow residents. This means that the settlement pattern does not allow people of a particular tribe to live together in a tribal or clan pattern where they can practice their own traditional way of life and have a centralized type of authority.[63] Normally, the classification of settlement pattern is in such a way that those who live in low density area have high income, in the middle density area have middle income, and in the high-density area have low income.[64]

---

[60] Int. Opson Thole, Museum, Department of Culture and Heritages, Mzuzu, 4.4.2013.

[61] Int. Wayinga Singini, Group Village Headman, Lupaso, 6.4,2013.

[62] Int. John Nyirenda, Session Clerk, Chibavi CCAP, Chibavi 5.9.2013.

[63] Int. Opson Thole, Museum, Department of Culture and Heritage, Mzuzu, 4.4.2013.

[64] Of late it has been discovered that the classification of settlement pattern of Mzuzu seems not to be followed. Many people who seem to be living in the low density are found in the middle density, while some in middle class are living in the high density. Three reasons for the practice are: Security from theft and robbery. The second reason is that they are running away from high rental costs. The third reason is that there is no proper policy from the city which could guide people when building houses. The majority of people are living in high density areas.

6.8.1 *Respect and Value*

The Religious Tolerance can also be measured basing on respect and value Mzuzu citizens are giving to religions. Religions in Mzuzu are accorded high respect in the sense that they are a help in times of need. Committed and nominal members view religion as the only hope when they are in trouble. All religions have similar respect by citizens regardless of where one belongs.[65]

Religious significance in the lives and thoughts of people is indisputable. Respondents insistently asserted that religions are the only means of communication between God on the one hand and people on the other. Religion helps people to formulate and awaken sentiments of dependence on God.[66] Through religions mortal people transcend beyond themselves to the spiritual realm of God who governs the destiny of their lives by supplying their material and spiritual needs.

The significance of religion is at the heart of every citizen of Mzuzu.[67] Those who seem forgetful are reminded and encouraged by their families, friends, religious leaders and traditional leaders at different avenues. One day, among several village headmen, Village Headman Hardson Singini at a funeral advised people around to worship God in different religions and denominations surrounding their residential areas. He condemned those who value material possession more than God. He said that money, education and wealth cannot give life, life and material possessions come from God, what is required is to stand firm before God and prostrate in prayers in worship places.[68] He concluded his speech by asking those present at the funeral, who were not worshipping, to find a worship centre of their choice. These are some of the speeches which encourage and remind people to value and respect religion in order for them to have better life on earth.

---

[65] Int. Ngwaza Muwela Mbeya, Muwele Traditional Healers Temple, Mzuzu, 30.8.2013

[66] Int. Florah Ngulube, Ngoni Christian Women Counselor, Mzuzu, 10.10. 2011.

[67] Int. Thomas Gondwe, Church Coordinator of the Northern Region of Good News Revivals, 29.7.2013.

[68] Hardson Singini, Village Headman, Speech at Funeral Ceremony, Lupaso, 6.9.2012.

Chapter Seven: Religious Social Ministries in Mzuzu

While worship is the central theme of religion, there are some religious social ministries where worship is done irregularly but they are important arms of religions. Such ministries are undoubtedly the most universally appreciated religious contributions to Mzuzu citizens. The concept of these ministries is to seek to extend the work of religions to all areas of life beyond spiritual matters.

Religious geographers accept the concept that religions have to apply to the whole person. While the improvement of a person's social living standards cannot, in itself, make a person whole, this task is nevertheless the concern of religions because a person is not divisible. Religious social ministries can be a means to transform a person's social living and they try to help people to discover in themselves that they have a great power to make progress.[1] Human transformation should help people acquire attitudes of self-determination, self-reliance, dignity, achievement, maturity, sharing, unity and community building.

7.1 The Significance of Religions in the Development of Education

The significance of the religious contribution in the development of education in Mzuzu is undisputable. The introduction and development of the Mzuzu educational work with particular reference to its spatial distribution is the work of religions. Religions are the most important partner agencies with government in doing educational work in Mzuzu. The assessment shows that their contribution to the education sector is undoubtedly the most universally appreciated to Malawian citizens and government over the past century to date. It is therefore without doubt that the religious contribution in education plays a dominant role in laying the foundation in transformation of people politically, culturally, economically and intellectually.[2] Such education in Mzuzu is a much-needed help, contributed by religions, in the social and economic development of Malawi and Mzuzu in particular.

---

[1] Int. Rev. H.M. Nkhoma, Former General Secretary, CCAP Synod of Livingstonia, Mzuzu, 18.12.2014.

[2] Int. Rev. Dr S.M Nyirenda, Chancellor of University of Livingstonia, Mzuzu, 18.12.2014.

The educational work in Mzuzu was first introduced by religions before the Malawi government took an initial role.[3] Religions considered education to be a means of distributing their faith, as it is said that those who hold the school hold the country hold its religion and hold its future.[4] Religions have a big share in the establishment of education in Mzuzu, both in quality and numbers. The 2013 Mzuzu Presbytery Education Report of the CCAP Synod of Livingstonia shows that religions had 18 primary schools, four secondary schools and four higher academic Institutions by 2013. It is in the recent years when the Malawi Government became serious in developing education in Mzuzu, more especially when the government put restrictive rules restraining religions from opening grant aided schools. Before the Malawi Government became independent, the Government then in power had a problem in the organized system of education.[5] One of the problems in the educational system was government failure through the Department of Education to muster full awareness of the way education actually operated in the hands of so many providers.[6] From 1964 the Malawi Government has not only recognized the responsibility it has to Mzuzu society in the field of education, but it has also a responsibility in activities of education as such.[7]

7.1.1 The Genesis of the System of Formal Education

In the pre-colonial era society imparted traditional education to their young ones through informal education. The exception was the initiation schools in which young people were prepared for adult life. The essentially informal character of traditional African upbringing did not mean that it was less effective, although this was usually overlooked by many early educationalists. It was effective in providing members of society with the abilities necessary in the natural and social environment of the time. What clearly differentiated it from the education the newly arrived Europeans were offering was the lack of any form of writing.

---

[3] Int. Mrs. Sichinga, Former District Education Manager, Mzuzu, 28.1.2015.

[4] This was a popular saying of Dr Robert Laws, used at graduation ceremonies (Rev. Dr S.M. Nyirenda's Memories).

[5] J. Coolen, *The History of Mzuzu Diocese*, Mzuzu, 1989, p. 117.

[6] Isaac Chikwekwere Lamba, *Contradictions in Post- War Education Policy Formulation and Application in Colonial Malawi 1945 – 1961, A Historical Study of the Dynamics of Colonial Survival*, Zomba: Kachere; 2010, p. 45.

[7] J. Coolen, *The History of Mzuzu Diocese*, Mzuzu, 1989, p. 117.

One of the early missionaries' tasks in education was thus to learn the language of the people of the area and to put it down in writing so that they could open schools in which reading and writing, first in the native language and then in English, could be taught. In the early years of the missionaries only few schools were established. This is because the population of Mzuzu at that time was small and also because formal education was alien to Africans who initially often did not see the worth of reading and writing. Children were only sent to school if they were not needed for work in house or fields.

The first school was established at Kaning'ina in 1878 by the Livingstonia Mission in an attempt to find a new station in the inland.[8] William Koyi and Alexander Riddel were the ones who started the Mission station and school. The school started as a missionary activity at Kaning'ina initiated by missionaries at Cape Maclear. The Kaning'ina Mission was established between Ngoni and Tonga tribes; however, the school was largely attended by the Tonga.[9] The school building was used as church on Sundays. After eleven months, the school together with the whole mission centre was withdrawn to Bandawe, from where, after two years, it was reestablished at Njuyu. The closure of the mission centre was due to the act that it was on no man's land, where missionaries feared to be involved in village disputes with no local authorities around them.

The Livingstonia Mission came back to Mzuzu with a school from Ekwendeni in 1905. They established a village school as well as a church at Mganthira in the village of Mafuta Kaunda. Mganthira School provided education to villages around Mganthira, Mafuta Kaunda, Luwinga Singini and Chigweli, who was at Majiga around Choma Livestock. The growing population of young people at Mganthira attracted Rev. Dr Elmslie, in charge of Ekwendeni Mission Station, to start a school at the area.[10] The

---

[8] John McCracken, *Politics and Christianity in Malawi 1879-1940, The Impact of Livingstonia Mission in the Northern Province,* Blantyre: CLAIM-Kachere, 2008, p 89.

[9] In contrast to the southern Malawi situation where the first proper school at Cape Maclear was regularly attended in 1879, three years after its foundation, by only some 30-40 mission dependents, Tonga land rapidly became the scene of extraordinary educational enthusiasm, John McCracken, *Politics and Christianity in Malawi 1879-1940, The Impact of Livingstonia Mission in the Northern Province,* Zomba: Kachere, 2008, p. 113.

[10] Int. Chisowa Chiumia, Secretary of Group Village Headman Chigweli, 20.12.2013.

school started as a village school with one teacher from Ekwendeni Mission who was teacher as well as evangelist. Slowly, the school grew; another teacher from Ekwendeni joined the school. The school went on very well, many pupils attended the school, and one of the students at this school was Spanock Kaunda, who later worked with Commonwealth Development Cooperation at the Tung plantation as a captain and time keeper.[11] However, the school did not last long as it was closed for two reasons. The first reason was that during the First World War, the school was used as a centre for recruiting soldiers for the Kings African Rifles. This did not please village headman Mafuta Kaunda, whose people were not coming back from the war; as a result, he set on fire the school so that the place should no longer be a centre for recruiting soldiers.[12] When the district commissioner from Mzimba heard about this, he ordered a temporary closure of the school. The second reason was the coming of the Tung Plantation in Mzuzu. In 1924 Mganthira area became the proposed area for Tung Oil Estate. The three villages which were around this area were asked to move out of the area and find a place of settlement elsewhere.[13] In 1930 the three villages moved out of Mganthira area and found settlements in the neighbouring areas; Luwinga Singini went to Lupaso, Chingweli went to Chingweli and Mafuta Kaunda to Msongwe. The movement of these villages made the Ekwendeni Mission, in charge of the Mganthira School, to close the school permanently and open another one at Lupaso where Luwinga Singini had made his village.

7.1.2 Primary Education from the 1930s to Date

7.1.2.1 Lupaso Primary School

The year of 1930 brought some changes in the education system in Mzuzu. The movement of Luwinga Singini from Mganthira to Lupaso had positive effects on the primary education system in Mzuzu. The move made Mzuzu to have the first permanent primary school, established at Lupaso in 1930. Lupaso Primary School came from Mganthira after the closure of Mganthira Village School due to the moving out of villages at Mganthira area. The School came to Lupaso while following Luwinga

---

[11] Int. Spanock Kaunda, Former Student at Mganthira School, 12.5.2013.
[12] Int. Posepose Nyirenda, Adviser of Group Village Headman Wayinga Singini, Lupaso, 18.12.2014.
[13] Int. Chipwafu Singini, Inkosana Luwinga Singini, Luwinga, 18.12.2014.

Singini, who settled at Lupaso area.[14] Lupaso Primary School provided education to Lupaso and the surrounding areas: Nkholongo, Doloba, Dunduzu and Msiro. In the beginning, the school had a large geographical catchment area, later in the years the school catchment area has been reduced to the surrounding areas of present day Lupaso. The school started as a village school; later it became a junior primary school until after 1960 when it became a full primary school. When the school was a village school, students that did well after village school were sent to Ekwendeni Mission School for primary education, and when it became a junior primary school, those who did well at junior school were sent to Mzuzu Primary School for senior primary school education.[15] John Kamoto Nhlama was among the first early head teachers at Lupaso Primary School. Agnes Kaunda was the first female teacher who happened to come from Lupaso area and a former student at Lupaso School. The school has produced many students throughout its years of existence whereby many of them were highly qualified who some of them have been working in high positions in Malawi and elsewhere.[16] Some of the students who have gone through this school are; Dr Boyson Moyo, Lecturer at Lilongwe University of Agriculture and Natural Resources,[17] John Wesley Nyirenda, retired Regional Health Director and Rev. G.J. Msowoya, Parish Minister in the CCAP Synod of Livingstonia.

7.1.2.2 Nkholongo Seventh-day Adventist Primary School

After the establishment of Lupaso Primary School, Nkhorongo Seventh-day Adventist Primary School was established at a distance of 2 km from the present day Lupaso Primary School. The school started as a private school at first, owned by Ephraim Chibambo, in 1942.[18] Ephraim Chibambo had been a teacher at Ekwendeni Mission School. While there he stopped teaching with the idea of starting his own church and school.

---

[14] Int. Wayinga Singini, Group Village Headman, Lupaso 18.12.2014.

[15] Int. Rev. G.J. Msowoya, Former Student at Lupaso School, Lupaso, 15.9.2012.

[16] School Assessment Report, presented to School Management Committee, Lupaso, 15.9.2012.

[17] Boyson Henry Zondiwe Moyo, *Agriculture and Environment for Developing Countries*, Mzuzu: Mzuni Press, 2014.

[18] Int. Palangu Mhangu, one of the Early Students at Nkholongo Primary School, Nkholongo, 20.12.2014.

He managed to start the school with 16 pupils.[19] The classroom served two purposes, Sunday to Friday it was used for learning purposes while church services were held on Saturdays. The church and school, which Ephraim Chibambo started at Nkholongo, was called Truthful Seekers. In 1945, Ephraim Chibambo surrendered the school and the church to the Seventh-day Adventist Church through Pastor Davie William Ludlow, who was in-charge of Luwazi Mission. The school had many pupils from the surrounding areas of Nkhamba, Kafwiri, Doromba, and Nkhorongo. Many of the students who went through this school belong to the Seventh-day Adventist Church; the school has been able to produce good students, who, after finishing school, have worked in various fields within and outside Malawi.[20] Some of the students who went through this school are A. Longwe, Regional Road Traffic Supervisor (North), and Pastor Maona Ngwira, Retired Seventh-day Adventist Pastor.

7.1.2.3 *Mzuzu CCAP Primary School*

The beginning of Mzuzu CCAP Primary School is connected with the establishment of the Tung Oil Estate in Mzuzu.[21] This estate was established soon after World War II, which in turn brought many families who came to work in the estate and eventually settle in Mzuzu. The Colonial Development Corporation in conjunction with the colonial government opened a school at Mganthira near where Mzuzu Technical College is situated. Later the school moved to a new site near where McConnell store is located today. There again the school only survived from 1948 to 1953 and then it was closed. The closure of the school did not please the citizens of Mzuzu who thought to pressurize Ekwendeni CCAP Mission Station to open a school in Mzuzu. The Head of Station at Ekwendeni CCAP Mission, Rev. P.C. Mzembe, upon realizing the urgent need for more education facilities and being anxious to maintain the Christian influence of the church among the rising generation, wished to open a grant aided school in Mzuzu.[22] The vision he held with firm

---

[19] Int. Doctor Munthali, First Student at Nkholongo Primary School, Nkholongo, 20.12.2014.
[20] Pastor Maona Ngwira's Report, presented to Education Department of Nkholongo Seventh-day Adventist, 10.11. 2010.
[21] N.A. Luwe, The Establishment of Mzuzu CCAP Full Primary School. Historical Pamphlet of Mzuzu CCAP Primary School
[22] Int. A.G. Chimaliro, First Head Teacher of Mzuzu CCAP Full Primary School, Choma, 19.12.2014.

resolution, in spite of the fact that the then secretary for education, Rev D.F.N. Crawford, had reservations concerning such a plan. In 1954, Ekwendeni school management decided to close Choma School because of low enrollment. Following the initiative of Rev P.C. Mzembe, they suggested that Choma School funding be transferred to open a new school in Mzuzu. The Department of School at Ekwendeni Mission Station approved the idea and hence Mzuzu School was opened on 1st October 1954.

The school was first situated near the present day Jombo Rest House; her walls are still standing and are being used by the police as a cadet force office. The school moved from Jumbo site to the present site near the main church due to insufficient area for a sporting field. In 1958 the school became a full primary school and was the first among all schools present at that time around Mzuzu, so all other schools at that time became feeder schools to Mzuzu Full Primary School. The school has produced many students who many of them have been working in various parts of the World. Some of the people who have gone through the corridors of this school include; Mary Waya - famous Malawi National Netball player, and Dr Kennedy Nkhoma - Doctor in Nursing at Mzuzu Central Hospital.

7.1.2.4 *Lunyangwa Girls and St Peters Catholic Primary Schools*

The St Peters and Lunyangwa Girls primary schools are to be commented on concurrently as both are Catholic Schools. The formation of these schools was that at first the school was Lunyangwa Primary School, co-educational, formally started by Bishop St Denis in 1955. The school started almost at the same time when Mzuzu Primary School was being started. When the school was being started, Bishop Denis made a successful campaign in persuading many Mzuzu children to join the school. The Bishop used to give children little gifts and lively jokes which made many children to join his school.[23]

The Girls' Primary School, which later became Lunyangwa Girls' Primary School, started where Marymount Secondary School is presently situated. The school was started by the Missionary Sisters of the Immaculate Conception as a girls' school. Many girls were not interested

---

[23] Int. Innocent Nkhata, Former Education Secretary-Mzuzu Diocese Mzuzu, 13.1.2015.

to go uphill to Marymount; as a result, the school had low attendance.[24] The reason was that the school at Marymount was somehow separated from the residential areas where pupils were coming from. Many pupils were coming from Katawa, Chasefu, Chiputula and Mzilawayingwe. The situation prompted Bishop Louis Jobidon to order the school to come down to where Lunyangwa School was situated. When the school come down to Lunyangwa co-educational primary school, the school management together with the Sisters of the Immaculate Conception split it into two separate entities, co-education and girls, within the same distance. The girls who came with the school from Marymount remained a separate girls' school. The schools at first were called by the same name, Lunyangwa, but later the girls' school was called Lunyangwa Girls Primary School while the co-education school became St Peter's Primary School. Since then, Lunyangwa has remained a girls' school while St Peter's is a co-educational school.

While religions are striving to open up more primary schools with the idea to meet the growing need of primary education in Mzuzu, the Malawi Government is reluctant to allow religions to open new grant aided schools. Because of this, religions have started opening private primary schools. Some of these schools are:

7.1.2.5 Katawa CCAP Private Primary School

Katawa CCAP Private Primary School is a day school targeting the young generation in Katawa and surrounding areas. The school started in 2000 as Early Childhood Development Centre (nursery school) when Rev. M.M.D. Sibande was the parish minister of Katawa CCAP Church. The performance of pupils was attractive so that Katawa Session made a proposal to open a grant aided primary school.[25] Katawa Session sent a proposal of her intention to Synod Education Department, who is responsible for forwarding proposals to the District Education Manager for the government to take action. At this time the leadership of the church was under Rev. M.K. Chilongo, parish minister, and Selfridge Ng'ambi, Session Clerk, while at Synod Education Department was Rev. Mezuwa Banda, Education Secretary, and the District Education Manager was Mrs. Joyce Sichinga. The response from the government did not

---

[24] Int. Bonvential Mvula, Former Head Teacher - St. Peter's Primary School, Chiputula, 23.8.2015.

[25] Int. Rev. M.K. Chilongo, Founder of Katawa Primary School and Former Parish Minister of Katawa CCAP Church, Mzuzu, 20.2.2015.

allow Katawa Session to open the proposed school because of logistical problems from the government.[26]

The response from the government did not please the Katawa Session considering the need for a primary school. The need for a primary school came about because of the performance of children at the nursery school and the growing population of children around the area. Because of this, the Katawa Session painfully agreed to start a private primary school. The school started in 2006 with standard one, gradually the school has grown to standard eight. Katawa School started with three teachers; Mr. Kayange, Mrs. Chisenga and Mrs. Mwandosha, all of them retired from government teaching. The first head teacher was Kayange and the present one is Bonavential Mvula. The total number of teachers is 12 with the enrolment number of 40 pupils per class. The school has a good pass rate at Malawi Primary School Leaving Certificate, standard eight, where students are selected to various secondary schools.[27]

Education at Katawa Primary School is not for free, each student pays K 20,000 a term for both junior and senior classes. The school fee is used for teachers' salaries and general administration. Money for bigger projects i.e. building classrooms and other funding comes from Katawa CCAP Session. Currently the session is building toilets.

7.1.2.6 Auze Education Trust

Auze Education Trust is a Private Muslim Boarding Primary School situated near Vigwagwa Market Mosque. The school started in 2003 with standards 3 – 7 with the aim of educating a young Muslim generation in both spiritual and social aspects. The school started from the buildings of Z. Brothers, Choma, Tawonga and Abdul Muhammad who handed over their buildings meant for business warehouses to religious use. The buildings were renovated to meet the purpose of mosque and school. The idea for a school originated from those who handed over their buildings for the school who thought to create a future for young Muslims who, after attending madrassa, seemed to have nowhere to go.[28] The school started to create room for further and secular studies for Muslim children who graduated from elementary Muslim education done in mosques.

---

[26] Int. Selfridge Ng'ambi, Former Session Clerk, Mzuzu, 20.2.2015.
[27] Annual School Report to Katawa Session, December, 2014.
[28] Int. Name withheld, 14.1.2015.

The school is a Boys' Boarding Primary School enrolling students from the whole of the northern region and some parts of the central region. The target group is Muslim boys who have done elementary Muslim studies and who are willing to go out to promote the Islamic faith after primary education.[29] The boarding school is from standard five to eight. Learners are studying two types of studies, Islamic studies and secular studies. The school has eight teachers together with sheiks and the head teacher, a retired teacher from Zambia. Students do not pay anything; the whole responsibility for paying teachers and administration costs is carried by the mosque leadership.

Many students who have graduated from this school are now Sheiks in different mosques. Some of them are Sheik Mayinda Yusuf -- Head Sheik at Enukweni Mosque, Sheik Uthman - Head Sheik at Chibavi Mosque, while some are teachers at the same school like Yasini Milazi and Uthman.

Primary education was the beginning of formal education in Mzuzu. Religions were the first to introduce formal education started with village

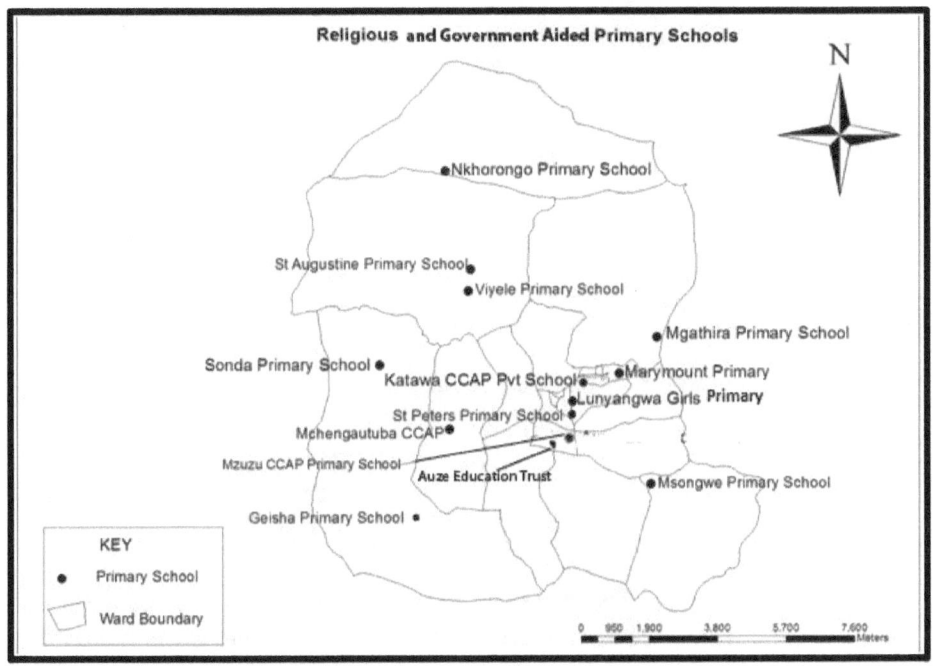

Figure 7.1: Religious private and government aided primary schools

---

[29] Int. Name withheld, 14.1.2015.

school, junior schools, and gradually have grown into full primary school, with junior and senior classes. Mzuzu CCAP School was the first primary school to become a full primary school while others were junior schools. All junior primary schools; Lupaso, Lunyangwa and Kambulufu (Zolozolo) were feeder schools to Mzuzu Primary school until when they became full primary schools. Most primary schools today have grown from single class to two or more classes, while each class is having more than 60 pupils. The numbers of pupils in all schools have been significantly increasing from the day of inception of formal education to date; this therefore, has made religions to open more schools with the view of accommodating the growing population of Mzuzu. Most of the primary schools started by the initiative of religions are now government grant aided schools, however some are religious private primary schools. Figure 7.1 is a Map showing religious private primary schools and religious government aided primary schools.

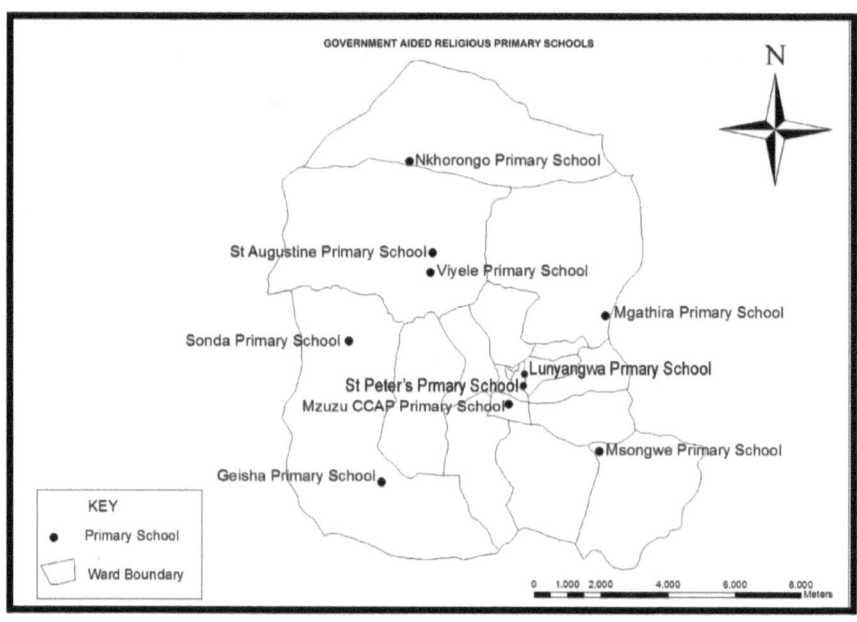

Figure 7.2: Map showing government aided religious primary schools

There are 14 primary schools in Mzuzu which belong to religions. Some of these schools have been covered in the research while some have not been covered but are presented in the religious primary school map (Figure 7.2). There are four private primary schools which belong to religions as shown in figure 7.3. In these schools, The CCAP Synod of

Livingstonia has many primary schools, second Roman Catholics, and then Seventh-day Adventists and Islam. The CCAP schools are; Mzuzu, Lupaso, Geisha, Msongwe, Zolozolo, Matope, Viyele, Katawa and Mchengautuwa. Roman Catholic Schools are; St Peter's, Lunyangwa Girls,

Nambo, Sonda, Mganthira, St Augustine and Marymount. Seventh-day Adventist has one school, Nkholongo. Auze Education Trust is the only Islamic school in Mzuzu).

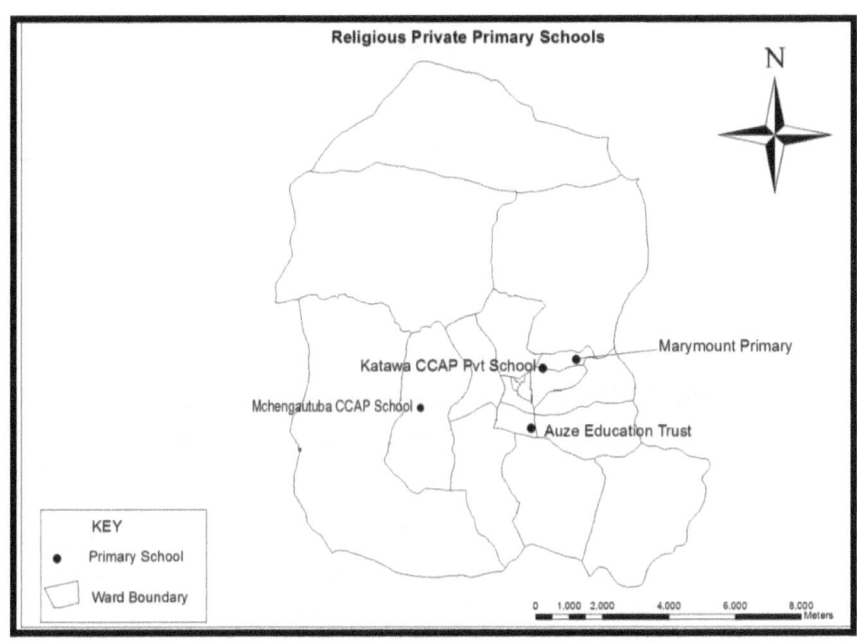

Figure 7.3: Map showing religious private primary schools

7.1.3 Secondary Education

The efforts religions made in educating children in Mzuzu as is the case with primary education is also the same with secondary education.[30] Religions have strong passion for secondary education. The idea was to help primary pupils who qualified for secondary school education but were unable to go for further education because secondary schools were far from Mzuzu. During the colonial government and soon after independence, travelling was a problem in Malawi, there was a poor

---

[30] Int. Innocent Nkhata, Former Education Secretary-Mzuzu Diocese Mzuzu, 13.1.2015.

road network in the northern region and in the country as a whole. The northern region had no public road transport, only the lake, as a result travelling was by foot, through traditional paths. At that time, secondary education in the North was attended at CCAP Secondary Schools, Ekwendeni, Loudon and Livingstonia, Roman Catholic Secondary School at Karonga and Nkhata Bay, and Mzuzu, a government secondary school. All of these schools were junior secondary schools. Looking at the nature of travelling and distance, many parents whose children were selected for secondary education, especially girls, were unable to let them go. The other challenge was the low-income level of many families, it seems that many parents at that time could not afford to send their children to study far from their homes because they could not afford to give their children the required resources for their education since they were living on low income levels and that was even worse with long distances.

7.1.3.1 Marymount Secondary School

When Mzuzu Government Secondary School was instituted as the first secondary school in Mzuzu, it was found that almost all students were boys. This did not please the Sisters of the Immaculate Conception, who asked Monsignor St Denis to give them land where they could build a girls' secondary school in Mzuzu.[31] St Denis asked the Colonial Administration to give him a plot in Mzuzu where he could build a hospital and a girls' secondary school. The plot was given by the Colonial Administration, at where Marymount Secondary School is situated, after when St Denis had bought a plot at Limphasa Rice Scheme project in Nkhatabay, a land abandoned by Commonwealth Development Corporation.[32] In order for St Denis to have the European population on his side, he accepted the request to have a convent primary school for the education of European children at Marymount from where Marymount Secondary School developed.[33]

The request from the Sisters of the Immaculate Conception to start a girls' secondary school at Marymount Convent Primary School coincided with the order by Bishop Louis Jobidon to split Karonga Secondary School

---

[31] Int. John Richard Banda, Head teacher Marymount Secondary School, Mzuzu 13.1.2015.

[32] J. Coolen, The *History of Mzuzu Diocese*, Mzuzu, 1989, p. 67.

[33] Cecilia Mzumara, *Fostering Girl Child Education in Malawi, Case Study of Marymount Girls' Secondary School and the Missionary Sisters of the Immaculate Conception in Malawi*, Balaka: Montfort Media, 2012, p. 33.

into boys' and girls' secondary schools. Karonga Secondary School was co-educational, the school needed renovation and expansion since it was accommodating both primary and secondary school pupils. It was then decided that a boys' secondary school be built in Karonga by the name Chaminade and a separate girls' secondary school be built in Mzuzu at Marymount by the name Marymount. The decision was further reinforced after the British Government offered a substantial grant to the Catholic Mission after insistent pleas by St Denis. On 19 March, 1960, Miss Moore, the Education Inspector for the North, granted permission to start the construction of the school. On 29th January 1963, Marymount Secondary School was opened with Forms I, 2 and 3.

The first intake was 60 pupils drawn from almost all Junior Secondary Schools in the country for forms 2 and 3, while form 1 was from various primary schools.[34] The first headmistress was Sr. Jacqueline Bastien who came with her students from St. Mary's in Karonga. The other three teachers were Sisters Suzanne Rinfret, Helene Labelle, and Doris Twyman. The first Malawian teacher to come to the school was Mr. Kumwenda, a Malawi Young Pioneer, who taught agriculture and physical education in 1965. The number of teachers kept increasing as the school progressed. The Sisters chose 'Work with Joy' as the motto of the school.[35]

Marymount Secondary School became a private secondary school, independent from the government, soon after multiparty system of government. The immediate reason which made the Diocesan authorities to privatize the school was the going down of the standard of education in government and grant aided schools.[36] The other reason was that many Roman Catholics were complaining that their daughters were not selected to Catholic grant aided schools, Marymount and Nkhamenya Girls, in Mzuzu Diocese.[37] The school has maintained her

---

[34] J. Coolen, *The History of Mzuzu Diocese*, Mzuzu, 1989, p. 84.

[35] The emblem of Marymount Girls Secondary School was designed by Sr. Doris Twyman. She taught for 25 years at Marymount and she was the Provincial of the MIC Sisters, Malawi and Zambia.

[36] Int. Innocent Nkhata, Former Education Secretary - Mzuzu Diocese, Mzuzu, 13.1.2015.

[37] Cecilia Mzumara, *Fostering Girl Child Education in Malawi, Case Study of Marymount Girls Secondary School and the Missionary Sisters of the Immaculate Conception in Malawi*, Balaka: Montfort Media, 2012, p. 53.

vision to be the best school in providing quality education in Malawi. In 1979, the School was visited by Mr. Dick Matenje, Minister of Education, who reminded students of their luck to receive their education at Marymount with teachers who were dedicated to their work.[38] The number of graduates has risen tremendously over the years; many of them have acquired various professions.[39] Some of these graduates are; Mary Nangwale – Former Inspector General of Police, Rosemary Mkandawire – Chief Executive of Toyota Malawi and Theresa Mbisa – the first Malawian female medical doctor who graduated in 1970 from a University in Canada.

7.1.3.2 St Peter's Day Secondary School

The Roman Catholic denomination has a will in promoting secondary education in Mzuzu. Apart from Marymount Secondary School, the church has opened a new co-educational private day secondary school by the name St Peter's Day Secondary School. The school was started in 2001 by St Peter's parish, which contributed enough money to start the school. The school started with junior classes before it became a full secondary school. Sundress Kamuzu Banda, Deputy Head teacher from 2001 to 2013, was one of the first two teachers who started the school. St Peter's Secondary School is providing education to people around Mzuzu, and the first fruits of the school have gone out of Mzuzu to various Universities and some are working within Malawi.[40] Some of the students who have gone through this school are Charles Chatchela Nkhwanya - working in Blantyre, Restone Thole - Lecturer at Skyway University in Mzuzu. Since the school is a day school and is taking students from all over Mzuzu, there is a problem of late coming of some students who are coming from long distances and to those who cannot afford to pay for their own transport when coming to school; therefore, the school is organizing to have a bus which will help to ease mobility of students from various locations.

---

[38] Mary Immaculate Conception Chronicles, 9 May, 1979.

[39] Cecilia Mzumara, *Fostering Girl Child Education in Malawi, Case Study of Marymount Girls Secondary School and the Missionary Sisters of the Immaculate Conception in Malawi*, Balaka: Montfort Media, 2012, p. 53.

[40] Int. Sandres Kamuzu Banda, St Peters Day Secondary School Teacher, Mzuzu, 14.1.2015.

7.1.3.3 Katawa Seventh-day Adventist Day Secondary School

Katawa Seventh-day Adventist Secondary School is the third religious secondary school in Mzuzu, started in 2014. The school is not known in terms of performance as it has just started, however, it has attracted many students. Katawa Seventh-day Adventist Church constructed the school with funding from friends from America. The school has started with junior classes. The aim of the Church is to help in providing space in secondary education, quality education and Christian values for the youth in post primary education.

7.1.3.4 Maa Hawa Madrassa

Maa Hawa Madrassa is a private Muslim secondary school with boarding facilities for boys, started in 2013. The school is co-educational and started from the buildings of Anur Patel, the owner of the school. Anur Patel decided to have a private secondary school to help pupils who have done free primary education and are able to go for secondary education, but do not have school fees.[41] The school is targeting Muslim communities from the Northern Region of Malawi.[42] Anur Patel is a businessman in Mzuzu who had no knowledge on how to start and run a school. When his idea of opening a school matured, he went to the Association of Sunni Madrassa where he was advised on how he can start a boarding secondary school. When he fulfilled all what was required to be done by the Association of Sunni Madrassa, the association recommended him to start the school.

The school started on 1st July 2013 with form one for boys and girls respectively. At present there are two classes, forms one and two with the total number of 96 students. There are plans to add two more classes to reach form four in the next two academic years. The learning environment is that boys have their own classes, separated from girls' classes, though in the same building. Largely the school is for Muslims; however, those who are non-Muslims are allowed to join the school as long as they follow the rules and regulations of Islam.[43]

---

[41] Int. Haji Alie, The Principal, Maa Hawa Madrasa Private Muslim Secondary School, Mzuzu, 7.6.2015.

[42] Ibid.

[43] Int. Mr. Kamanga, Maa Hawa Madrasa Private Muslim Secondary School Administrator, Mzuzu, 6.6.2015.

Maa Hawa Madrassa offers free secondary education, however, those who can, are requested to pay a commitment fee of MK 5,000. The commitment fee will be reduced to MK 1,400 by next school session. The school administration is done by Principal, Haji Alie, while running costs are the responsibility of the owner of the school, Anur Patel. Anur Patel is responsible for boys' boarding cost, lunch for boys and girls, library, administrative cost and salaries for teachers. There are six teachers of whom four are Christians and two are Muslims. Among these teachers, one is a lady by the name of Lillian Msiska, Bachelor of Arts in Social Studies. She is also responsible for girls' welfare.

Students at the school are learning two types of studies, Islamic studies and secular studies. The idea is that students should have wider opportunities after finishing their school. After form four those interested in secular education will proceed to secular universities, while those interested in Islamic studies will go and study Islamic studies at Islamic University in Lilongwe.

The Roman Catholic Church (Mzuzu Diocese) is considered to be the leading denomination in secondary education in Mzuzu. Many students who go for post primary education seem to be scrambling for space, as a result, most government and private secondary schools in Mzuzu offer day and evening classes with a high enrollment rate compared to the capacity of their schools in order to meet the increasing demand for space. However, many of these private schools have less qualified teachers and limited space, while teachers in government schools are busy with evening classes and other private teachings while putting aside their normal duties.[44] This being the case it seems that education offered by religions has the best quality in Mzuzu, where one of such schools is Marymount Secondary School.[45] Figure 7.4 below shows the location of religious secondary schools.

---

[44] Int. Rev B.C. Kawonga, Manager of Schools-CCAP Mzuzu Presbytery, Mzuzu, 20.12.2015.

[45] The Form Four results and University selection at Marymount Secondary School show that education offered at religious schools is of the best quality. The 2009 Form Four results show that Marymount had the best results in Malawi and Mzuzu in particular. Number of students in class was 164 and number passed was 162, representing a pass rate of 98.7% and University selection was 93 students (Cecilia Mzumara, *Fostering Girl Child Education in Malawi, Case Study of Marymount Girls Secondary School and the Missionary*

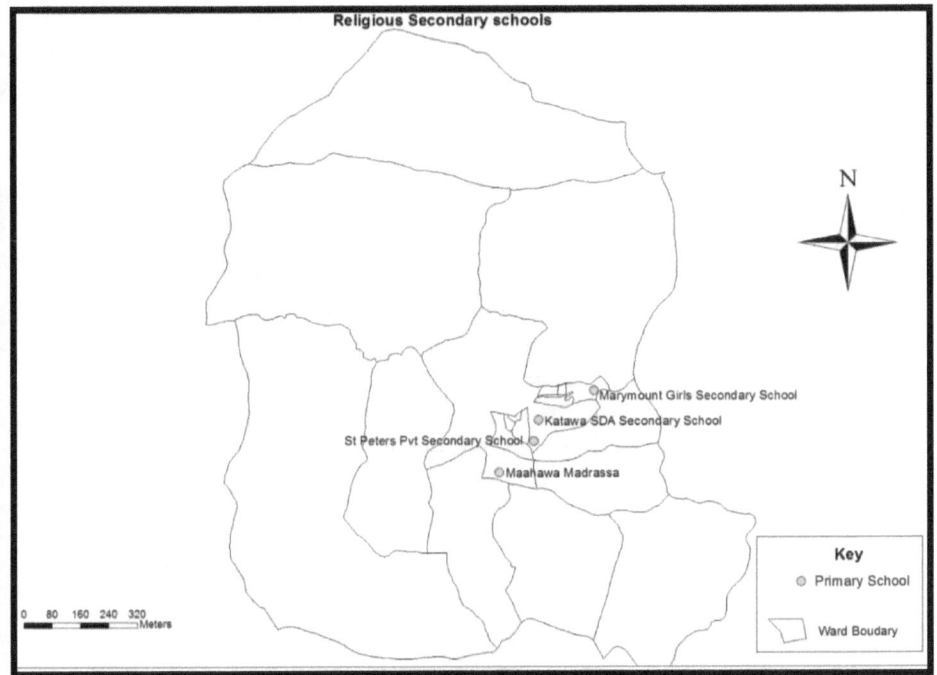

Figure 7.4: Map showing religious secondary Schools

7.1.4 Higher Learning Institutions

Religions in Mzuzu have a strong influence on higher learning education that started with an institution of technical studies in 1963. The Roman Catholic Church has a strong passion for higher education, more than any other denomination in Mzuzu. The institutions of higher learning have been developed to help those who have finished secondary education and now are ready to give their contributions with a particular profession in the development of the nation.

7.1.4.1 Mzuzu Technical College

The first institution of higher learning in Mzuzu was instituted by the Roman Catholic Church in 1963 when Banga Trade School was moved from Nkhata Bay to Mzuzu where Bro. John Bertoni built the present

---

Sisters of the Immaculate Conception in Malawi, Balaka: Montfort Media, 2012, p. 64.)

Technical College.[46] The Trade School moved to Mzuzu because Mzuzu became a regional administrative centre for the north which eventually made it to develop into an urban area from where there could be provisions for industrial development, i.e. electricity. The other reason was that Mzuzu became the Diocesan centre for the Roman Catholic Church in the north, whereby it required these institutions to be closer to the diocese for it to show that it is the headquarters of the church.[47]

Bro. Charles Wolan was the first Principal of the Trade School in Mzuzu in 1963. Initially, however, it was during the time of Bro. Charles Lukes' principalship, from 1963 to 1966, when the Mzuzu Trade School developed into a Technical College. The Trade School developed into a Technical College when the Marist Brothers took over the running of the School and when the Beit Trust gave a substantial grant towards the building of this new College which became ready for occupation in 1968.[48] The Marist Brothers left the College in the hands of layman, assisted by Malawian staff, in 1974.

The Mzuzu Technical College started by offering Carpentry, Joinery and Bricklaying courses. In 1975 the Polytechnic introduced night classes for Commercial and Crafts subjects. Further, the Malawi Government upgraded the College into a big Technical Institution and additional subjects were introduced, i.e. commercial and motor mechanic courses. Due to high demand in the industrial world, they have increased the number of courses to ten. Courses offered are; Automobile, Accounting, Secretarial Studies, Marketing, Electrical Installation, HIV/AIDS Management, Rural and Community Development and I.C.T. The Institution has achieved to provide skilled personnel to the nation,[49] some of those who have gone through this college are; Mrs. M. Nthambazale- Credit Manager at New Building Society (NBS Bank) - Mzuzu Branch, Mr. M. Banda, Service Manager, Toyota Malawi, Mzuzu Branch.

---

[46] J. Coolen, *The History of Mzuzu Diocese*, Mzuzu, 1989, p. 69.
[47] Int. Lusayo Mukhondya, Mzuzu Technical College Boarding Master, Mzuzu, 13.1.2015.
[48] J. Coolen, *The History of Mzuzu Diocese*, Mzuzu, 1989, p .69.
[49] Int. John Kondowe, Principle of Mzuzu Technical College, Mzuzu, 13. 1. 2015.

7.1.4.2 St John's College of Nursing

The institution is a member of the Christian Health Association of Malawi. It was started in 1963 by three sisters of the Mary Medical Missionaries with the aim of training Malawian nurses who could work at St John's Hospital since at that time all nurses at St John's hospital were whites. Sisters Gemma Breslin, Maria Goretti O'Connor and Edelweir of Mary Medical Missionaries worked after establishing St John's Hospital in 1962, on the establishment of St John's College of Nursing. The first class of a two years programme started with a Midwifery Course. The class had five female students who, after graduation, became nurses at St John's Hospital. Later in 1964, the College started another two years programme of Enrolled Nursing with eight female students who, after finishing the course, became nurses of St John's Hospital.

The College started by training nurses to work at St John's Hospital only, however, the Government then asked the college authorities to consider training nurses who could work in all hospitals in Malawi.[50] Basing on this plea, the college authorities considered the request and started offering nursing courses to the general public. St John's College of Nursing started with a Midwifery course and later added an Enrolled Nursing course; hence it became the first Nursing College to offer both Midwifery and Enrolled Nursing in Malawi.[51] All through, the College has been enrolling female students only until in the 2000s, when it became co-educational. The change coincided with the change of courses from Enrolled Nursing and Midwifery to Diploma in Nursing and Midwifery Technician. The College has 300 students with a ratio of 1/3 males to 2/3 females.

St John's College of Nursing has started offering her courses to both residential and non-residential students in order to meet the increasing demand of nurses in Malawian hospitals. The increased number of students has caused a problem of where to do practical work, because space at St John's Hospital became insufficient. The problem has forced the college authorities to be distributing students on practical work to hospitals around and beyond Mzuzu, where again the problem of transport and accommodation has surfaced. However, the college has managed to produce well qualified nurses as a contribution to health

---

[50] Int. Alice Ngulube, Former Staff-Cashier, St John's Nursing College, 15.1.2015.

[51] Int. Walwani Mbakaya, Deputy Principal Tutor at St John's Nursing College, Mzuzu, 14.7.2015.

services in Malawi. The assessment from hospitals around Mzuzu done through interviews show that nurses trained at this college proved to be the best nurses in discipline as well as performance.[52] Some of the students who have gone through this college include; Lily Thindwa- Principal of St John's College of Nursing, and Lilian Chirwa – Head of Health Department at Mzuzu City Council, Nyuma Luhanga Working with the University of North Carolina at Bwaila Clinic.

7.1.4.3 St John of God College of Health Sciences

The college was started by Brothers from the Order of St John of God in 2003 with the aim of helping the nation in capacity building for psycho-social counselling. The college was started to train people in sick-social counseling, but later it was extended to psychiatric counselling.[53] The college contributes to the development of health professionals in Malawi and the sub region through provision of training in the following;[54] Bachelor of Science Degree in Mental Health and Psychiatrics, Bachelor of Science Degree in Clinical Medicine (Mental Health) and University Diploma in Counselling.

In 2004 the college started offering a Bachelor of Science Degree in Mental Health and Psychiatric Nursing and in 2007 it went on to offer Bachelor of Science Degree in Clinical Medicine (Mental Health). These Programmes are affiliated to the University of Malawi-Kamuzu College of Nursing and Chancellor College Faculty of Social Sciences respectively. The Clinical Medicine is affiliated to Mzuzu University. St John of God College of Health Science strives to be a centre of excellence in education, training, and research for the enhancement of quality of mental health services in Malawi and the sub region.[55] Many people have studied under this College and some of them are; Juliet Mphande - Matron at Zomba Mental Central Hospital and Rev. William Muyila – Livingstonia Synod Mental Counsellor.

---

[52] Int. Mama Mphande, Matron at Mzuzu Central Hospital, Mzuzu 13.7.2015. A survey done by Walwani Mbakaya, Deputy Principal Tutor at St John's Nursing College, Mzuzu, 05.1.2015.

[53] www.sjog. mw/college. html, 13.3.2015.

[54] Application Form for the 2015 Intake, St John's Nursing College, Mzuzu, 13.3.2015.

[55] www.sjog. mw/college. html, 13.3.2015.

7.1.4.4 St John of God Institute of Vocational Training

St John of God Institute of Vocational Training started in Mzuzu with the order of St John of God Brothers. The vocational training is for people recuperating from mental illness and for people with disabilities or other special needs.[56] It started in 2004 as a day care centre, an extension of St John of God Mental Hospital Service, where patients suffering from mental illness were receiving skill - based training (carpentry, brick laying, cooking, etc). The institution started from within St John of God Mental Hospital and has so far opened three sites, Masasa, Kaviwale and Ching'ambo and is hoping to open another site at Chibavi.

The aim of the institution is to enhance quality life for all based on Mathew 4:23, 25:34-46, Luke 10:25-37, to provide a community based mental health service with rehabilitation Programmes for adults and children with disabilities, drop in centre for vulnerable children found in the streets, special education for children with learning disabilities, psychological and pastoral care to prisoners at Mzuzu Prison, a college of Health Sciences for the training of psychiatric nurses, clinicians and professional counsellors.

The institution does assessment, advice and counselling for all who come, while vocational training through a range of skilled based Programmes is secondary.[57] Graduates for this institution are trained in Carpentry and Joinery, Home Management, Horticulture, Brick Laying, Tailoring and Textile, Computer Studies, Education Resource Centre, Entrepreneurship, Internal and External Training Placements, Personal and Social Development, Life Skills and Pastoral Care. The centre is accredited by TEVETA. Many people have benefited from the institution either by self-employment or are employed by certain companies.[58] Job Enterprise is carrying out their contracts. Since 2004, the enterprise is carrying out contracts in areas like Mzuzu University ground maintenance, Ekwendeni Nursing School, Karonga District Hospital, St John's Nursing School, ESCOM Mzuzu, Mzuzu Central Hospital, Malawi Blood Transfusion Service and Toyota Malawi -Mzuzu. Some individuals who have benefited from this vocational institution include; Samson Phiri- Self Employed brick layer- Mzuzu, Hanet Ndovi - Self-employed-

---

[56] wwwsjog.mw/vocationaltraining.html, 13.3.2015.
[57] Int. Mwawi Ng'oma, Director of Programmes at St John of God, Mzuzu, 14.1.2015. Opera: 14, 12.3.2015.
[58] www.sjog/jobenterprise.html. 13.3.2015.

Tailoring and Textile in Mzuzu market and Saulos Nyirenda - Tutor in Carpentry and Joinery at St John of God Vocational School.

Oswald Mhango is in charge of St John of God Vocational School working under the management of the Director of Programmes, Mwawi Ng'oma. All Programmes at the institution are under the management of St John of God Mental Hospital through the office of Director of Programmes.

7.1.5 Theology and Religious Studies

7.1.5.1 Theological Education by Extension (Northern Region)

Theological Education by Extension in Malawi is divided into three regions and in the north the Head Office is in Mzuzu. The regional offices are for coordination purposes while decisions and running of the institution is done by the National Office in Zomba. The Regional Office in the North came to Mzuzu from Ekwendeni, when Ekwendeni Offices were closed. The opening of these offices in Mzuzu was to find a central place and a place of their own since at Ekwendeni they were renting from offices belonging to the Lay Training Centre of the CCAP Synod of Livingstonia.[59] The Regional Office in Mzuzu started in 2010; it started from Mzuzu CCAP Congregation offices at the bell tower. The first Regional Director in Mzuzu was Rev. Been Mwakasungula. It was through him when the offices were moved from Mzuzu CCAP Congregation to where they are situated at present at Hilltop.

Theological Education by Extension in Malawi has been offering Diploma and Certificate in Theology as one of the participating colleges of the Board for Theological Studies of the University of Malawi since 1997. The Institution uses a mixture of distance learning and face to face teaching called blended learning. Students receive course designed self-study workbooks. Additionally, they attend monthly seminars on a Saturday in designated centres. In this way Theological Education by Extension is able to offer the best of both worlds: the flexibility of independent self-study, lively personal interactions with experienced theological lecturers and fruitful times of fellowship with other distance learning students.[60] Many people have benefited from the institution; many of them are secondary

---

[59] Int. Rev. C. Kapombe Mwale, Director (North) of Theological Education by Extension in Malawi, Mzuzu, 18.1.2015.
[60] Student Admission Forms for the Academic Year of 2013/2014, Zomba, 12.7.2013.

school teachers while some are church ministers. Examples are Bishop Fanuel Magangani - Bishop of the Anglican Church, Diocese of Northern Malawi, and B.M. Mwandira - Northern Region Inspector of Schools.

7.1.5.2 Department of Theology and Religious Studies at Mzuzu University

The University is owned by the state and it is offering Bachelor's, Master's and Doctorate degrees in Theology and Religious Studies. The university was started in 1998 by a decree from former president of the republic of Malawi Dr Bakili Muluzi with the idea to have a university in the north.[61] Theology and religious studies started in 1998 as a section in the Department of Education. Other sections in the department were History and Geography. The Theology and Religious Studies section was offering courses to the level of Bachelors of Arts (Education) and was started with one student. In 2001 another student joined the course. In 2007 the three sections of the humanities department (History, Geography and TRS) attained the status of fully-fledged departments. The section of Theology and Religious Studies started offering Bachelors of Arts in Theology and Religious Studies. The Section became the Department of Theology and Religious Studies in order to respond to the demand for qualified theologians to work in church, Faith based organizations, NGOs and Government departments.

In 2007 the first orientation workshop for MA and PhD Programmes was held, effectively launching the post graduate Programmes. The post-graduate programme had a good beginning and the current Post-graduate Coordinator is Prof. Klaus Fiedler. The Department has produced many graduates, some of whom are school teachers and others are church leaders. The postgraduate programme has produced eight PhDs; among them are Dr Moses Mlenga, Dr Joyce Mlenga - Principal and Dean of Education at University of Livingstonia respectively, and 20 MAs to people like Towera Chione Mwase, Douglas Chipofya - teacher and parish minister respectively. Bishop Fanuel Magangani, Bishop of Anglican Church of the Northern Diocese of Malawi was among students awarded with BA degrees.

Religions have a strong influence in producing a learned generation who are contributing towards the development of the Malawi nation. This is

---

[61] Int. Posepose Nyirenda, Former United Democratic Front Regional Executive Member, Mzuzu. 20.12.2014.

due to their passion in education from the time of inception to date. If one considers educated people of the nation and follows their educational background, it will be discovered that a good proportion of them have done their education through religious institutions in one way or the other.[62] It is discovered that Roman Catholic Church has done more in the secondary and tertiary education than any other denomination in Mzuzu. The CCAP synod of Livingstonia has done well in primary education in Mzuzu. All religions that are offering education in Mzuzu have no restrictions on who may attend their education.

It is evident to judge that various success rates reflect content and quality of respective education offered to various people. The quality of education is significant in explaining the rise of persons to national prominence. The role of religions in the formation of educated people must be viewed in the context of rapid changes in the political and economic spheres which is taking place in the country. In many cases the education provides the catalyst for change, rather than being the direct cause of change. Figure 7.5 is showing the location of the afore discussed institutions of higher learning.

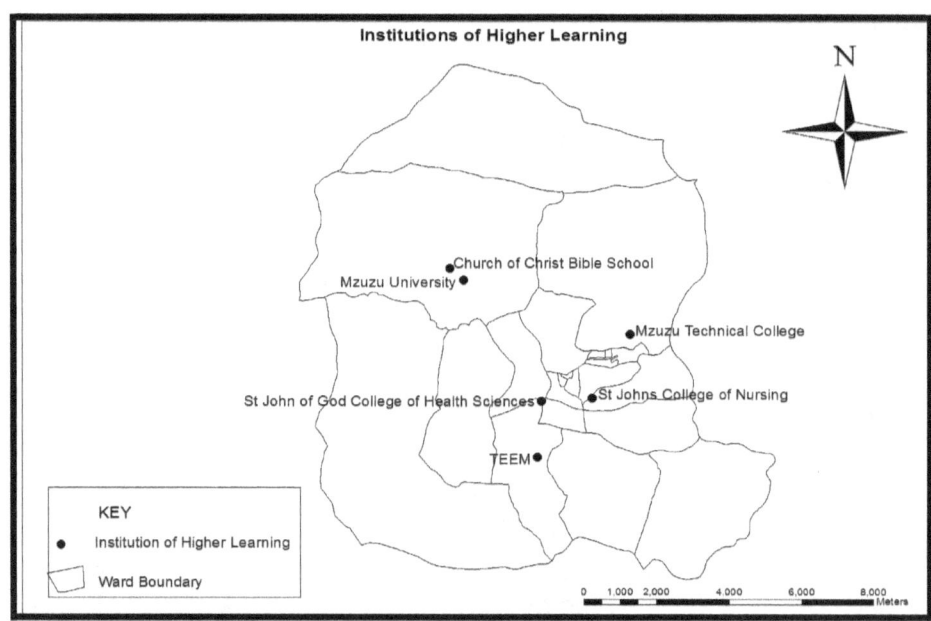

Figure 7.5: Institutions of Higher Learning

---

[62] Int. Restone Nyasulu, Primary Education Advisor of Mzuzu City, Mzuzu, 18.1.2015.

7.2 Contribution of Religions to Medical Care

As with education, health services have been and remain one of the two most important secular activities of religions. Religion and health services are traditionally bound together, thus it is seen as quite fitting that religions which propagate new faith and spiritual healing have also to heal physical sicknesses. If one examines the present-day distribution of medical care facilities in Mzuzu, you will be surprised to see that the difference between private and public hospitals is very high. Government hospitals are best in terms of equipment and qualified personnel but are considered to be worse service providers than private hospitals.[63] There are two types of private hospitals; individual people's hospitals and religious hospitals. Between the two, religious hospitals are well attended by patients because of fair prices, better equipment and specialized personnel. Religious hospitals have a long-time history as the best medical service providers who, before the institution of Mzuzu Central Hospital, were taken as referral hospitals. Roman Catholic hospitals are considered to be leading service providers in Mzuzu.

7.2.1 Spatial Distribution of Religious Medical Care

There was a time when Mzuzu had no medical service provider, for those who could afford were going to hospitals like Ekwendeni Mission hospital, Mzimba and Nkhata Bay, which was known as John Lengi. The first medical care centre was a small dispensary established by the colonial government at Kaning'ina, which was situated next to the Tourist Lodge. The clinic was small in terms of size and capacity compared to the growing population of the area which became a regional administrative centre. There was a good effort offered by Christians at government dispensary so that there was that need to expand medical services because at that time the clinic succeeded in gaining trust from the local population to introduce western medicine.[64] This being the case the gap

---

[63] The general outcry of patients seems to be disappointment with services in government hospitals. People are complaining that every time you go there, the hospital has no drugs and you are asked to buy your own, there is no patient-clinician relationship and they do not mind of time when to start work but only when to knock off. -- I have no way to check the facticity of such claims. They are given here as relating widespread sentiments.

[64] Int. Mrs. Mphande, Matron at Mzuzu Central Hospital and former Regional Nurse Officer, 20.1.2014.

was felt by religious organization and the first religious hospital was St John's Hospital.

7.2.2 St John's Hospital

St John's Hospital is a 215 bed Mission Hospital. The hospital was established in 1962 by the Catholic Sisters of Mary Medical Missionaries from Ireland.[65] When Bishop Louis Jobidon became Bishop of Mzuzu Diocese, he was saddened when he saw the gap between medical services provided at the government dispensary and the required services to the general public.[66] He then asked the Sisters of Mary Medical Missionaries in Ireland to come to Mzuzu and help to establish a hospital, the Bishop knew these sisters from Chala in Tanganyika where they had a hospital.[67] The Sisters of Mary Medical Missionaries came to Mzuzu in 1961 to start working on the project and in 1962 they opened up St John's Hospital at the place where St John's Hospital is situated today. The hospital played a vital role in health delivery within Mzuzu and the whole of Northern Malawi.

The hospital started as a small health unit, although it was bigger than the government dispensary. It had three wings, an Outpatient Department (OPD), Maternity and 15 beds for medical and maternal admissions. The provision of Medical Services to patients has been based on cost sharing; patients at the beginning of the Hospital were being charged one penny for outpatient and three pence for admission.[68] The coming of St John's Hospital was a relief to medical services in Mzuzu. From the humble beginnings of a health unit St John's has since been developed into a 225 beds capacity hospital. People from different parts of the northern region were coming to the hospital; today the catchment area has been reduced to the whole of Mzuzu City, Chikangawa and Usisya. The Sisters of Mary Medical Missionaries handed over the hospital to the Roman Catholic Church, Mzuzu Diocese in 2001. The hospital is registered under CHAM where financial assistance for salaries of medical practitioners comes from. The hospital management is responsible for support staff, buying of drugs and infrastructural

---

[65] www.Datanauts.co.uk, 13.3.2015.
[66] Int. Alice Ngulube, Cashier at St John's Hospital, Mzuzu, 13.1.2015.
[67] J. Coolen, *The History of Mzuzu Diocese*, Mzuzu, 1989, p. 104.
[68] St. John's Hospital Annual Report, July 2004 to June 2005 and July 2005 to June 2006.

development. Most doctors and senior nurses in the past were coming from Europe, for example; Dr Albert Naminga from Holland and Sister Martina from Ireland, while at the moment all medical staff are Malawians. However, the performance of the hospital has gone down compared to when the hospital was being run by Mary Medical Missionaries.[69]

7.2.3 Nkhorongo Seventh-day Adventist Hospital

Nkholongo Hospital belongs to the Seventh-day Adventist Church, started by missionaries in 1979. The hospital started when chiefs from around Nkhorongo area requested a health centre from Nkhorongo Seventh-day Adventist Church. At that time people from Nkhorongo and surrounding areas were walking long distances to access medical services. People were going to St John's Hospital, Kaning'ina Dispensary and or Ekwendeni Mission Hospital, where distance to these places was almost the same and patients could not afford going there since they were walking on foot.[70] The hospital started with one Medical Assistant, H.M. Sibakwe, and two other members of staff in a boys' quarter belonging to Christian Service Committee. The hospital is basically serving out patients. It covers areas like Biya, Choma, Nkholongo, Chigwere, Lupaso, Dunduzu and Andreya Moyo. Medical services offered at the hospital are not free; patients are charged for the service given.

7.2.4 St John of God Mental Hospital

St John of God Hospital is a Mental Hospital started in 1994 by the Order of St John of God under the management of Brother Aidan Clohessy. The hospital is largely dealing with outpatients; admission is done only when the hospital management sees a need for admission.[71] There are 12 outreach clinics and the hospital also provides mental health care for Mzuzu Prison. The Hospital started through Bishop Mukasa Zuza, who convinced the Brothers of St John of God to start mental health services in Mzuzu. Before 1994, patients suffering from mental illness from Northern Malawi were referred to Zomba Mental Hospital. This was a

---

[69] Int. Mrs. Chinkono, St. John's Hospital Administrator, and Simwanza, Chief Clinic Offer, St. John's Hospital, 23.6.2015.

[70] Int. Doctor Munthali, One of the first Students at Nkholongo Primary School. 20.12.2014.

[71] www.intercare.org.uk/health-centre/Malawi/st-john-of-god-mzuzu, 12.3.15.

challenge to many families due to poor financial status and long distance. As a result, many patients were kept at home untreated and were becoming problems.[72] The other reason was that HIV and AIDS related problems accelerated mental illness whereby a mental hospital was a need at Mzuzu and in Northern Malawi as a whole.

Mental services at St John of God hospital are a help to people around Mzuzu, part of the central region and the whole of the northern region. Mental illness is treated at St John of God Hospital, the only mental hospital in the North of Malawi and it has the only psychiatrist in the whole of the country.[73] The hospital has outpatient treatment and admission at a cost. The Government of Malawi provides funding for salaries for medical practitioners and medicine for inpatients but not for outpatients who represent 78% of the total pharmacy budget.[74] Patients go to St John of God Mental hospital as referrals from hospitals and or direct from home.[75] The hospital has two separate premises, admission situated close to St John's Hospital and outpatient which is next to St John of God College of Mental Health. Admission is done at the House of Hospitality; patients with acute symptoms of mental illness are referred to stay for a short period and are then discharged.[76]

7.2.5 Private Seventh-day Adventist Clinics

The Seventh-day Adventist Church has one private clinic owned by an individual church member in Mzuzu. Kandindindi Clinic is a private clinic belonging to Shadreck Kamanga, a Seventh-day Adventist Church member. The clinic started in 1998. It is serving outpatients within the catchment area of Mzuzu. This private clinic has been accorded with special recognition in this paper because, although it is owned by individual church members, the clinic has been organized under the

---

[72] Int. Mwawi Ng'oma, Director of Programs at St John of God Director of Programs, Mzuzu, 14.1.2015.
[73] www.intercare.org.uk/health-centre/Malawi/st-john-of-god-mzuzu, 12.3.15.
[74] Ibid.
[75] Int. Zione Mgala, Director at St John of God House of Hospitality (Admission), Mzuzu, 14.1.2015.
[76] http://www.sjog. mw// hospitality. html, 13.3.2015.

principles of the Seventh-day Adventist Church.[77] The other reason is that the clinic is one of the first individual private clinics in Mzuzu that has existed to date.

Shadreck Kamanga, the owner of Kandindindi Clinic, was born and brought up a Seventh-day Adventist. He did his course of clinical medicine at Malamulo Hospital. He has worked with Seventh-day Adventist Hospitals, Luwazi, Lunjika, Nkholongo, until his retirement. It was at Nkholongo where he decided to start his own clinic at Chibanja. He retired prematurely as a Seventh-day Adventist medical worker at Nkholongo Hospital because of continuous attacks by armed robbers at Nkholongo Hospital where he was in charge.[78] This background makes Kandindindi Clinic to look like a clinic belonging to the Seventh-day Adventist Church.

The distribution of religious medical services in Mzuzu has been of great help to the citizens of Mzuzu and the northern region. For a long time, the government had no hospital in Mzuzu, apart from the dispensary at Katoto, which could help the growing population of Mzuzu. It is also discovered that many times services at government hospitals are compromised and insufficient, patients are ordered to buy drugs for themselves. Religious hospitals bridge the gap for the growing need of health services which government hospitals alone are failing to meet for the growing population. The relationship between government and religious hospital is good whereby patients from religious hospitals can be referred to Central Hospital and vice versa without difficulties. Government through CHAM is paying salaries for religious hospital medical personnel which help to subsidize the cost of treatment for the general public.

7.3 Religious Human Rights

Religious human rights contribute to the creation of a vibrant and God-fearing society that upholds the fundamental principles of human rights,

---

[77] For a study of the Seventh-day Adventist Health Management see: Frank Chirwa, *Theology of Health in the Seventh- day Adventist Church. A Quest for Abundant Life in Jesus,* PhD Module, Mzuzu University, 2010.

[78] Int. Pastor Maona Ngwira, Retired Pastor of Seventh-day Adventist Church and Group Village Headman at Nkholongo Nkhamba Area, Nkholongo, 17. 10.2015.

good governance and democracy.[79] Religious institutions of the human rights campaign want to ensure that all human beings enjoy human rights and freedoms. Respect and observance of human rights are intended to achieve equality, non-discrimination, human dignity, freedom, justice and peace. Chapter four of the constitution of Malawi states that the inherent dignity and worth of each human being requires that the state and all persons shall recognize and protect fundamental human rights and afford the fullest protection to the rights and views of all individual groups and minorities, whether or not they are entitled to vote.[80] Church and Society of the CCAP Synod of Livingstonia and Catholic Commission of Justice and Peace of the Roman Catholic Church of Mzuzu Diocese are religious institutions who advocate for respect of Human Rights.

Figure 7.6: Map showing location of religious hospitals

---

[79] Int. Rev. Maurice Munthali, Former Deputy General Secretary -- CCAP Synod of Livingstonia, 10.12.2014.
[80] *Building an Informed Nation, a Handbook for Civic Education on Good Governance and Human Rights, Democracy Consolidation programme*, Montfort, 2000, p. 105.

7.3.1 Church and Society

Church and Society of the CCAP Synod of Livingstonia is situated where the Synod secretariat offices are situated. The institution started as a committee in 1992 under the Synod secretariat comprising of clergy and church elders. The rule of law and respect of human rights were almost non-existent at that time.[81] The committee was therefore established in order to break the silence by fighting for human rights, good governance and democracy. The committee continued working in the background until 1999, when it broadened its scope and established itself as a department working in the areas of advocacy, civic education, research and consultancy. The aim of the institution is to have a just and peaceful society that respects human rights. The current Director of the Institution is Moses Mkandawire.

The Department of Church and Society is reaching out to the society with different Programmes, currently they are working on the following Programmes. The first is Education and Training, on this programme they are conducting seminars, workshops and structured short courses in order to mainstream human rights, democracy and good governance. The other area is Research and Monitoring; they are conducting research on human rights, democracy and good governance in order to determine the extent of problems to be addressed. The findings are used to develop strategic plans for the implementation of projects. They are also involved in peace building, whereby they provide a forum for mediation in order to manage and resolve conflicts.

In order for the Church and Society Department to achieve her Programmes she is networking with other institutions as follows; the Malawi Electoral Support Network (MESN) which discusses issues of election. The group comprises of civil society and other service providers accredited by the Malawi Electoral Commission. The institution is coordinating activities on economic governance under the Malawi Economic Justice Network (MEJN). It is coordinating civil society organizations on issues of corruption under the Anti-corruption Bureau. It is coordinating and chairing SADC civil and political rights network under the Human Rights Trust of Southern Africa. The institution is also networking with governance institutions on issues of human rights, good governance and democracy.

---

[81] Int. Moses Mkandawire, Church and Society Director, Mzuzu, 23.1.2015.

On the issue of mediation, the institution is remembered in Mzuzu on how it handled the aftermath of the 20 July, 2011 demonstrations. The Director of the institution, Moses Mkandawire together with Rev Maurice Munthali, Synod Deputy General Secretary together with Rev. Zeenah Sibande, Mzuzu Presbytery Clerk took the responsibility in negotiating with the Government to bury honourably 20 bodies of people killed during the demonstrations. The mediation was somehow slippy, however, it went on successfully, the government accepted the request to give the remains of those killed by Malawi police to deceased relatives and be buried honourably at the same grave yard while the CCAP Synod of Livingstonia led the burial service of worship.[82]

7.3.2 Catholic Commission for Justice and Peace

Mzuzu Catholic Commission for Justice and Peace belongs to the Roman Catholic Church - Mzuzu Diocese. The institution started in 2000 as a Diocesan committee with the aim of advocacy in good governance, rule of law and human rights. When awareness of issues of human rights, good governance and rule of law were growing in the society, the diocese decided to establish an institution responsible for good governance on a day to day basis.[83] The Catholic Commission for Justice and Peace was created to promote awareness on human rights, justice and peace in the communities the church serves in order to create a God fearing, just and peaceful Malawian society that promotes integral development and lasting peace that will contribute to the common effort of the Episcopal Conference of Malawi and the whole church goals.[84] The CCJP, as a Catholic organization, is guided by the social teachings of the Catholic Church. This is in line with the church's doctrines. This institution attempts to operate in a multi-faith setting, however, the Catholic principles are not compromised.[85] The offices are situated at Mchengautuwa, next to the bishop's residence. The current Director of the Institution is Alnord Msimuko.

---

[82] Int. Rev. Maurice Munthali, Former Deputy General Secretary, CCAP Synod of Livingstonia, 10.12.2014.

[83] Int. Pauline Kawonga, Field Officer for Catholic Commission for Justice and Peace, Mzuzu, 18.1.2015.

[84] CCJP/ Episcopal Conference of Malawi, Opera: 3, 29.4.2015.

[85] Ndongolera C.W. Mwangupili, *Ngoni and CCJP Approaches to Reconciliation in Katete Parish*, MA, Mzuzu University, 2011.

The institution is carrying out duties in the whole of Mzuzu Diocese, and Mzuzu in particular, in the following Programmes; the General Election Procedures - it civic educates citizens to realize that they have a representative form of democracy that requires them to choose their representatives. The parliamentary liaison committee bridges the gap between parliamentarians and constituency in terms of vote civic education. The other service is called Action for Better Service Delivery - where the institution is educating local communities about their responsibilities in taking part in developing and submitting developmental project proposals to the relevant authorities for their areas. The fruit of this project is what took place at St Augustine, where the community, through funding from City Assembly, managed to build a bridge at Kanyika stream.[86] The Institution is responsible for the promotion of Economic Governance, Capacity Building and Advocacy.

In the area of socio economic justice and advocacy, the institution is facilitating dialogue on extractive industry between Kanyika Community in Mzimba District, Malawi Government and Global Metal and Mining Company. The Kanyika Community has expressed concern over the delay by both the Government and the Mining Company in compensating and relocating the community to another place from the mining area. 244 families have been affected by the relocation process after the Government of Malawi granted an exploration license to the Mining Company at Kanyika. The exploitation of these resources does not only negatively affect the wellbeing of the local community of the respective areas, but for the whole nation. Because of this, Mzuzu Catholic Commission for Justice and Peace has decided to capacitate the Kanyika Community Members (rights holders) to defend and claim their rights.[87] The Institution strives to advance truth and justice through a project called Transparency Initiative with our Natural Resources that aims at ensuring that all people of Malawi benefit from the commercialization of the country's natural resources.

---

[86] Int. Pauline Kawonga, Field Officer for Catholic Commission for Justice and Peace, Mzuzu, 18.1.2015.

[87] Malawi: CCJP Facilitates Dialogue on Extractive Industries/ AMECEA NEWS - LOG - Opera: 47, 29.4.2015.

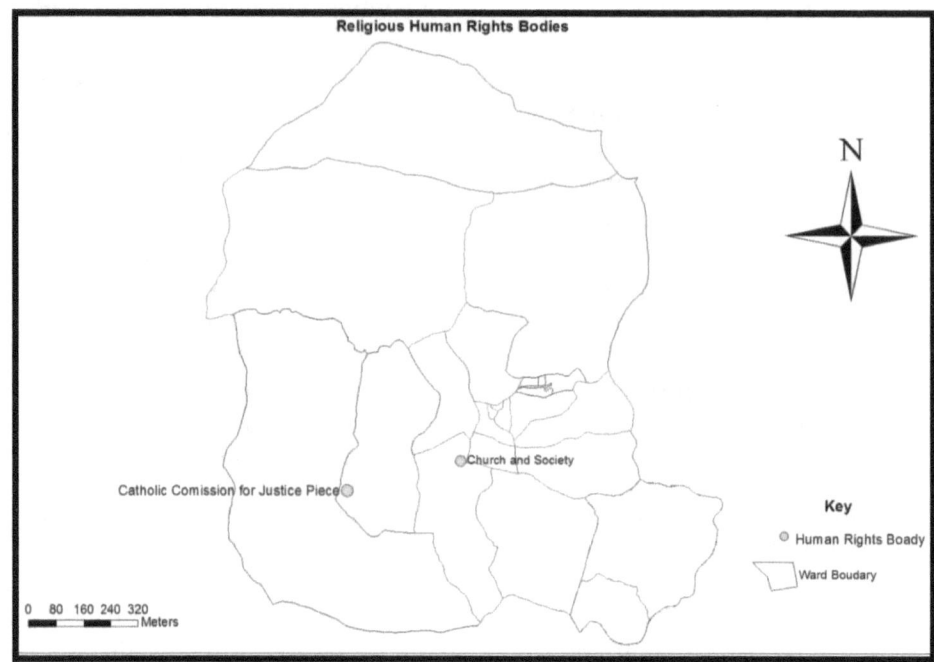

Figure 7.7: Map showing location of religious human rights bodies.

Religious human rights institutions promote human rights issues in Mzuzu. The institutions teachers that Human Rights are entitlements that a person demands from birth, it does not need to fulfill any condition in order for a person to have them. All human rights are based on a common foundation often referred to as the fundamental principles of human rights. Religious human rights institutions see to it that fundamental principles of human rights in Mzuzu are equally distributed to all citizens of Mzuzu. The fundamental principles of human rights include human dignity, equality, and non-discrimination, participation and inclusion, and accountability. Religious human rights institutions in Mzuzu have classified human rights issues in three categories; civil and political rights, economic, social and cultural rights, and solidarity rights. Human rights institutions in Mzuzu fight against infringements of human rights caused by a law passed by parliament or the executive arm of government and customary laws. Religious human rights institutions in Mzuzu are aware that there is a direct relationship between human rights and good governance. The two affect each other in Mzuzu; good governance creates the environment in which human rights can be effectively protected. It also provides the tools by which human rights are promoted and enforced.

7.4 The Influence of Religions on Mass Communication

Religions believe that information is power. People need information and knowledge in order to make informed decision. Religions feel that they have the duty to serve their faithfuls and the nation at large by communicating the joyful message of Christianity, reconciliation, hope, heeling and emphasizing Christian values for the building up of families and promoting social harmony diversity on basis of Christian love.[88] Therefore religions have opened radio stations where community and national needs, achievements and aspirations are articulated and promoted with the view of influencing change and nation building.[89] The influence which religious radios have on the community of Mzuzu through education, entertainment, informed and advanced skill development has helped the community to make informed decisions in matters of faith, culture and social development. There are two radio stations belonging to CCAP Livingstonia Synod and the Roman Catholic Church, respectively.

7.4.1 *Voice of Livingstonia Radio*

Voice of Livingstonia Radio belongs to CCAP Synod of Livingstonia and is situated close to St Andrews CCAP Church in Mzuzu. The idea of having a radio within the CCAP Livingstonia Synod was first muted by Ekwendeni Mission Hospital with the view to broadcast news, stories and Programmes related to Health, HIV and AIDS and women's issues to communities around the area. As the Malawi Communication Regulatory Authority dilly dallied in issuing a broadcasting license, the Synod secretariat took over the radio project, discussing with the government until when the broadcasting license was given. The radio is serving Mzuzu community on religious issues, socio-economic, political and other issues that affect people within the Synod and beyond.[90] In September 2012 MACRA granted Voice of Livingstonia a broadcasting license and it started with a coverage of 73 km^2 in Mzuzu and surrounding areas in the Northern Region of Malawi. However, today, the Radio covers also some parts of Lilongwe and Blantyre Districts in the Central and Southern

---

[88] Int. Bishop Joseph Mkasa Zuza, Mzuzu Diocese Bishop, 17.11.2014.
[89] Int. Rev. L.N. Nyondo, CCAP Synod of Livingstonia- General Secretary, 20.11.2014.
[90] Int. Rev. L.N. Nyondo, CCAP Synod of Livingstonia- General Secretary, 20.11.2014.

Regions of Malawi, respectively. Most of the workers working at the Radio Station are volunteers. The Director of Voice of Livingstonia Radio is Jessie Puwapuwa while Menard Mtemang'ombe is Business Manager.

Voice of Livingstonia Radio is a community radio, serving its faithful and the general public around her coverage area in all aspects of human life. By communicating the joyful message of Christianity, reconciliation, hope, healing and Christian values for the building up of families and promoting social harmony in diversity on the basis of Christian love, the radio assists in promoting economic, cultural and social development for the benefit of the people of the area of operation. The core values of the radio are; integrity-where it is accountable, reliable, honest, trustworthy, devoted and truthful radio station aspiring to proclaim the word of God seeking to serve and encourage both faithful and non-faithful in understanding their God-given purpose in life through prayer, humility and compassion for all. Unity - the radio is an extension of the CCAP Synod of Livingstonia, providing a mouth piece for communication as well as providing means by which various parts of the body of Christ can connect with each other, focusing on shared beliefs rather than differences. Excellence- the radio is committed to operate with the highest degree of professionalism, endeavoring to be the benchmark of this kind of ministry.[91]

The Voice of Livingstonia Radio Programmes are focused on two areas; spiritual growth- with focus on mission and evangelism, and edutainment - with the focus on education, health, HIV/AIDS, governance, food security and climate change. Some of the popular Programmes on the radio station are Salaula,[92] Family Half Hour[93] and Wanambumba[94] aired at respective times.

---

[91] The statement made by Rev. Douglas Chipofya, Moderator of the CCAP Synod of Livingstonia, in his speech at the Appraisal Ceremony Award where Voice of Livingstonia Radio was accorded the best performer of the year of 2014 of all CCAP Synod of Livingstonia Departments, 11.12.2014.

[92] Salaula is a radio programme where the radio is advertising different types of businesses. Salaula is a one-hour programme, starting from 7 o'clock to 8 o'clock in the evening from Monday to Saturday.

[93] Responsible for Family Half Hour are Joyce and Moses Mlenga, who received there PhDs from Mzuzu University in 2013 (Joyce Mlenga, *An Investigation of Dual Religiosity between Christianity and African Traditional Religion among the Ngonde in Karonga District in Northern Malawi*, PhD, Mzuzu University, 2013:

7.4.2 Radio Tigabane

Radio Tigabane belongs to the Roman Catholic Diocese of Mzuzu. It is situated west of St John's Hospital next to St Peters Day Secondary School. The radio station was started in 2005 facilitated by Fr. Eugen Ng'oma who had acquired experience in radio communication. Fr. Eugen Ng'oma studied radio communication in Rome, after his studies he worked with Amaseya Radio in Kenya. It was from this background that he came up with a radio station project proposal to the Bishop of the Diocese who later approved it, hence the beginning of Tigabane Radio station. Tigabane Radio Station started airing Programmes for two hours a day within a small coverage area, starting with Mzuzu, Jenda, Lundazi and a few other areas within the radius. All radio Programmes were Catholic in nature divided into two parts; spiritual music and spiritual reflection. Today the Radio Station covers the whole of Mzuzu Diocese and also some parts of the central region. It is airing a variety of Programmes to her faithful. Most of the workers at the Radio Station are working on a voluntary basis. The current Director of Tigabane Radio Station is Eugen Ng'oma, while Sister Bernadetta Munyenyembe is Programme Manager.

Radio Tigabane is a Community Radio targeting Roman Catholic faithful, however, the general public benefits from her Programmes. The aim of the radio is to reach out to the Roman Catholic faithful in areas where it is geographically difficult to reach out with the Christian message. Further, the radio is concerned to reach out to her listening communities with holistic information - by broadcasting information which is not only for devotional use but also to empower people through cultural and social development information.[95] Some of the favoured Programmes on

---

Moses Mlenga, *Polygamy and the Synod of Livingstonia in the Northern Malawi: Biblical, Moral and Missiological Implications*, PhD, Mzuzu University, 2013.

[94] Wanambumba radio programme is an hour long programme being aired every morning from 8 o'clock to 9 o'clock Monday to Friday. The programme teaches women on how they are supposed to live as women in their families and communities.

[95] Int. Sister Bernadetta Munyenyembe, Programme Manager at Tigabane Radio. 13.1.2015.

Radio Tigabane are; Kauzganga Drama Programme, Family Planning, Bank M'khonde and Chuma Chili Mdongo.[96]

7.4.3 Radio ABC (Mzuzu Sub-Station)

Radio ABC belongs to African Bible College, it is a support ministry of the African Bible College. The Mzuzu Radio ABC is situated at Luwinga, a sub-station of Lilongwe Radio ABC. The radio in Mzuzu started in 2001 by Moses Mlenga, former student of African Bible College. Initially, Lilongwe Radio ABC wanted to open a sub-station in Blantyre before Mzuzu, the decision was changed by Mr Munthali, the Managing Director of Lilongwe African Bible College Radio.[97] Mr Munthali proposed to Dr Jack Chinchen that it would be an ideal to start a radio station in Mzuzu than Blantyre because Mzuzu had no private radio station unlike in Blantyre. The Mzuzu community had no opportunity to be reached out with spiritual radio Programmes, only through selected times at MBC Radio. When Dr Chinchen was convinced with the proposal, he ordered Moses Mlenga, graduating student at African Bible College on radio communication, to start a radio sub-station in Mzuzu.

When Moses Mlenga came to Mzuzu in 2001, he started Radio ABC at Luwinga, 100 metres South of Luwinga Holy Trinity Anglican Church. During the initial stage of the beginning of Radio ABC in Mzuzu, the station had one member of staff, Moses Mlenga. Moses Mlenga asked permission from the Managing Director of African Bible College to allow him to incorporate his wife, Joyce Mlenga, who was teaching at Katoto Secondary School, former student of African Bible College, to become one of the members of staff.[98] The Managing Director of African Bible College accepted the request and the radio station had two members of staff. At present the Mlenga's have left the radio station for other employments. The radio has two other new permanent staff and three volunteers.

---

[96] Bank M'khonde and Chuma Chili Mdongo: Bank M'khonde is a business programme where Radio Tigabane is giving skills to people on how they can run their businesses. The programme focuses on small scale business. Chuma Chili Mdongo is an Agricultural programme; the radio is giving skills to small scale farmers on how they can benefit from farming.

[97] Int. Brinal Kumwenda, Mzuzu Sub-station Radio ABC Manager, Mzuzu, 15.12.2015.

[98] Int. Moses Mlenga, Former Mzuzu Sub-station Radio ABC Manager, Principal of Livingstonia University, Laws Campus, 18.12.2016.

The Mzuzu Radio ABC Sub-station is working under Lilongwe Radio Station; it has one transmission, licence and broadcasting station with Lilongwe Radio Station. The radio is a community radio targeting to serve the general public of Mzuzu community with spiritual, health and socio-economic radio Programmes. The radio is evangelistic in nature. Some of the favoured Programmes are; Arise Nations, a drama programme, Ticheze a Chinyamata and Kuyimbila Mulungu.

Religious radios in Mzuzu have a bigger reception than State owned radios. Most people like to listen to Gospel Music and spiritual reflection, which religious radios do provide to their listening communities. In so doing, listening communities are able to listen to their Programmes whose information focuses on cultural and social development. The core idea of religious radios is to reach out to their communities with a wholistic message so that people should be able to make informed decisions. Figure 7.8 below shows the location of these religious media houses.

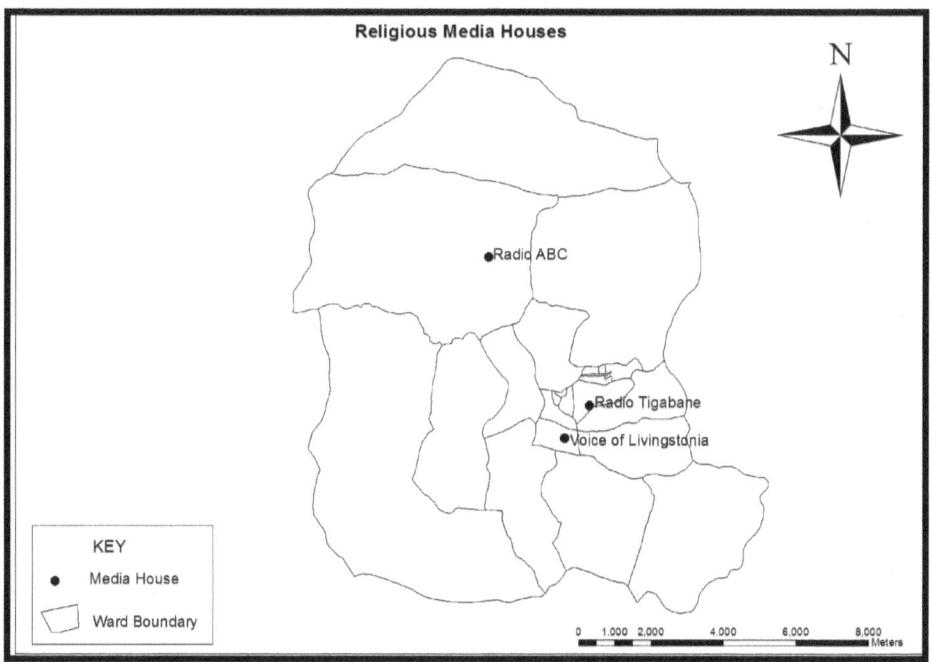

Figure 7.8: Map showing location of religious media houses

Religious social ministries are a help to religions and denominations in matters of faith. They are tools in reaching out to communities. Religious social ministries are an aid in the holistic transformation of a person. Spiritual transformation and social transformation make a whole person.

Chapter Eight: Conclusion and Recommendations

Mzuzu is a religious City dominated by the Christian religion followed by Islam and Hinduism to a minor degree. Traditionally, almost all people in Mzuzu belonged to African Traditional Religion without regular worship and being non-congregational. Some religions like Bahai and Rastafarianism have no organized presence in Mzuzu; however, members of such religions are living in the City.

The Christian religion has been divided into different denominations with real differences without a call for unity. The major divisions of the religion are Reformation Churches[1] (the churches from the Reformation are often called Mainline Churches), Restorationist, Evangelical, Pentecostal, and Charismatic. The religion has different denominations and numerous worship centres. It is noted that the Mainline Churches have been distributed far and wide, in almost every location of Mzuzu; CCAP for example, is the largest denomination in Mzuzu followed by the Roman Catholic.[2] The Assemblies of God Church is the largest distributed of all Pentecostal and Charismatic denominations while these other denominations have been largely represented by one to two but not more than five churches.[3] The non-Christian religions are not widely divided compared to Christian religions. In the Islamic religion, there are

---

[1] Denominations that underwent reformation include: Presbyterian, Anglican and Roman Catholic. Klaus Fiedler has problems in dating the Roman Catholic reformation; however, he features a few examples of Catholic reformation. Contarini (later Cardinal) experienced his conversion (along similar lines as Martin Luther) in 1511. In 1517 the Oratory of Divine Love was founded in Rome (one of their innovative methods of evangelization were stage plays and the music of Palestrina), in 1522 Ignatius of Loyola found Christ, and the first Reform Pope Paul III (1534 -1549) in 1545 called for the Council of Trent (1545 - 1547, 1551 - 1552, 1562 - 1563), and in 1536 Terasa of Avila became a Carmelite nun. - For a good overview see: Robert D. Linder, 'The Catholic Reformation' in: Tim Dowley (ed), Oxford: Betania, Sydney: Lion, 1990, pp. 410 -428, Klaus Fiedler, *Mission as the Theology of the Church, An Argument from Malawi*, Mzuzu: Mzuni Press, 2015, p. 19.

[2] The study shows that there are 19 worship centres belonging to CCAP and 10 to Roman Catholics.

[3] There are 11 worship centres belonging to Assemblies of God, as the largest denomination of all Pentecostal and Charismatic denominations shown in the study.

two divisions, Qudiriyya and Sunni, but the divisions are not clearly seen by an outsider.

8.1 Important Observation: Rural Expansion

It has been observed that worship centres in rural areas are not expanding compared to urban areas. The African Independent Churches are the most favoured churches in rural areas; however, they are not growing by opening more worship centres but by membership. Although these churches are seen to be growing by membership, they are outnumbered by membership from the mainstream churches. Mainstream churches have more membership because many people seem to be attracted by the location of worship places which have a special role as service centres in these neglected parts of the city.[4] Many of the places have schools (Sonda CCAP School and Church, Nkhorongo Seventh-day Adventist School and Church, Kanthete Roman Catholic School and Church) and hospitals (Nkholongo Seventh day Adventist Hospital and Church). These places on their own do attract people as social places, and people feel proud to be associated with them.

It might be seen surprising that some denominations saw their role primarily to work among the urban population and found it difficult to extend their work to rural areas; realizing that Mzuzu is both rural and urban.[5] Mzuzu Zone under consideration extends for a radius of 9.5 km from the Central Business District.[6] Such denominations like Pentecostal, and Charismatic and religions like Islam and Hinduism have no influence in rural areas. Hindu religion is ethnic, it has no member in the rural areas; the religion is among the Hindus who are residing around Mzuzu Central Business District, most of them are business people. Islam has no worship centre in the rural areas of Mzuzu. They may have members of Islamic faith in rural areas, but the majority of them are living in urban areas and their worship centres are located around busy market places. Many Muslims are business people who, throughout the day, are found in market areas.

---

[4] Int. Moses Mtambo, Social Development Officer of Mzuzu City, 23.11.2015.

[5] Int. Pastor Mwakiwinga, Pastor at Chithira Pentecostal Miracle Working Church, Chithila, 20.12.2015.

[6] Central Business District refers to the core business area of Mzuzu consisting of shops, banks, and the Government Administrative Buildings.

Pentecostal and Charismatic denominations seem to favour educated young people who are rarely found in rural areas.[7] The churches of these denominations are not commonly found in the rural areas, and those who are found in such areas are located in areas where many of them cannot grow. The churches are located in areas where they cannot find people with the ability to speak or understand English and most of them are not Chichewa speakers. When a Pentecostal or Charismatic church starts in rural areas, they fail to grow because most of the people around the area are not educated and people become embarrassed to be spoken to in English or Chichewa.[8] The majority of people living in the rural areas are elderly and Chitumbuka speakers. These people find it difficult to hear the word of God in a foreign language, English or Chichewa. Many Pentecostal and Charismatic churches in the rural areas are safe supported whereby members of such churches in the rural areas find it difficult to support these churches, financially, as a result leaders or founders of such churches decide to abandon the church and go to urban areas where they can be supported. Sometimes church members are the ones who abandon the church when their expectations are not met. Through this, membership diminishes little by little till it closes down.

Mainline churches, being CCAP and Roman Catholic, are strategically positioned in both rural and urban areas, and are expanding steadily in all areas. People from the rural areas love these churches because worship centres are found everywhere. Mainline churches value the people they are serving by adopting the language of the people and with decentralized leadership, churches are governed by local people themselves.[9] Church growth is felt by the people themselves and the decision to open a new church is done by themselves. In so doing church members feel that they belong to the church which is theirs, hence expansion becomes easier even in the rural areas. Expansion in rural areas is gradual because the areas are sparsely populated. It happens that people in rural areas of Mzuzu are running away from these areas

---

[7] Pentecostal and Charismatic Services of worship are being conducted in English and Chichewa which the majority of people in the rural areas cannot understand, and many of them are elderly, who do not follow well the worship practices.

[8] Int. Robert Chaula, Church Elder at Kaviwale CCAP Church, Kaviwale, 5.12.2015.

[9] Int. Mrs. M. Ndovi, Church Member, Mchengautuwa Seventh-day Adventist Church, Mchengautuwa, 5.12.2015.

either by going into the urban areas to look for paying jobs or business or by going further to rural areas when the town advances to their areas.[10] As a result, rural areas have limited number of citizens.

8.2 Developments during the Study Period (2013 to 2015)

During the time I conducted the research (from 2013 to December, 2015), a lot more has happened in the study area. It is not possible in this chapter to give detailed account of the developments which religions and denominations have experienced throughout the study period, from 2013 to 2015, so I am going to present a general observation with selected example of worship centres which could give a true reflection of what has happened in worship centres in the study area.

8.2.1 Church Growth

Many worship centres have grown by membership while at the same time some have diminished. Chithira Peace Ministries has managed to increase her membership after a time when her membership went down. In 2013, church membership diminished because the presiding pastor Alick Vwaza Banda abandoned the parish for America in 2012.[11] In 2013, the church had 90 members with an average church attendance of 70. Pastor Alick Vwaza Banda came back from America in 2014. When church members heard about the coming back of their pastor, they started joining the church again. Today the church has 200 members with an average church attendance of 140 people.

The Mzuzu Winners Chapel is another church which has experienced change within the study period. In 2013, the church was led by Pastor Kent from Nigeria and Pastor Mwale as assistant pastor. People favoured the administration of Pastor Mwale which made them to ask Pastor Kent to leave the place.[12] The church was divided between those who were in support of Pastor Kent and of Pastor Mwale. The wrangle became bigger to the extent that the church got split into two groups. The first group remained at Hilltop Church with Pastor Kent, while the second group

---

[10] Int. Vincent Nzima, Lands Department of Malawi Government, Mzuzu. 10.12.2015.

[11] Int. Daniel Nyirenda, next door neighbor to Chithira Peace Ministries Church, Chithira, 10.12.2015.

[12] Int. Martin Magawa, former member of Winners Chapel, Mchengautuwa, 15.12.2015.

went to Chenda Hotel Hall, where the church originally had started from before going to Hilltop. In 2014, Pastor Kent was promoted, he became head of Winners Chapel Church, and he was transferred to the National Office in Lilongwe. His promotion resolved the disputes; the two groups merged together worshiping at Hilltop Church under the leadership of Pastor Mwale. Church membership has grown from 120 to 220 with an average church attendance of 160.

8.2.2 Birth of New Churches

While some churches are growing, some new churches are being born in the study area. One of the churches which have come to Mzuzu is the CCAP Nkhoma Synod. The CCAP Nkhoma Synod has come to Mzuzu from Lilongwe in the central region.[13] The church was started in Mzuzu in 2014 by Mr. and Mrs. Merina Chikuse, who had come to Mzuzu from Lilongwe in 2013; Mr. Chikuse is working with ADMARC at Mzuzu Regional Office, while the wife is a teacher at Katoto Secondary School. During their early days in Mzuzu, the two joined Mzuzu CCAP Church (St Andrews). While there they became disappointed with the way worship was being conducted. They were not happy to worship in Chitumbuka. The two were further disappointed with the English service when preachers sometimes could add Chitumbuka in the sermons or to hear choirs singing in Chitumbuka in the service.[14] They were against anybody speaking Chitumbuka in their presence at Mzuzu CCAP Church; hence they decided to introduce CCAP Nkhoma Synod Church where they could be free from Chitumbuka.[15]

Mr. and Mrs. Chikuse reported their intention of starting the church to the General Secretary Rev. Kachipapa Banda, who, after meeting with

---

[13] The establishment of a Nkhoma Congregation is part of the larger border dispute between Livingstonia and Nkhoma Synods. For a full treatment see Rhodian Munyenyembe, PhD, Free State University, 2016. For experiences on the opposite side see Samson Kaonga, *A History of the Birth and Growth of Livingstonia Synod's Congregation in Kasungu District in the context of the Border Dispute with Nkhoma Synod (2005-2012)*, BA, Mzuzu University, 2012.

[14] Mrs. Merina Chikuse, Mzuzu CCAP Nkhoma Synod Church, discussions with fellow teachers at Katoto Secondary School while trying to convince them to join Mzuzu CCAP Nkhoma Synod Church, Katoto Secondary School, 2014.

[15] Mrs Chisemphere, Church Member, Mzuzu CCAP Nkhoma Synod Church, discussions with fellow members from Nkhoma Synod worshiping at Mchengautuwa CCAP Church, Mchengautuwa, 2015.

the CCAP Nkhoma Synod Executive Members, supported the idea. The church started in 2014 with 15 people worshiping at Katoto Secondary School Hall. Mr. and Mrs. Chikuse started the church through persuading people from the central region, particularly CCAP Nkhoma Synod members, who at that time were belonging to other churches.[16] They visited people house to house asking them to leave their various churches and start CCAP Nkhoma Synod Church. The other means they used in persuading people to join their church was through handouts, they were giving out women guild uniforms for free to all who were showing interest to join their church. When membership started becoming bigger, they bought a piece of land behind ADMARC Regional Offices to the east and Grand Palace Hotel and Toyota Malawi to the north, where they have built a *vigwagwa* church structure. The church has 130 members with an average church attendance of 70 people. The church building has a capacity of 100 people. Some of the prominent members of the church are Mr. and Mrs. Chikuse, Chisemphale, Sapuwa and Steven Potani. The church had many members at the beginning, but some withdrew when they were asked to contribute MK 10,000 towards the church building project.[17] When the church administration realized the withdrawal of some church members because of church building project contribution, they withdrew the request and saved church membership.[18] The church is being served by a visiting minister from Jenda CCAP Nkhoma Synod Church for sacraments and Kirk sessions.

8.2.3 Churches that are Diminishing in Size

While some churches are growing and new ones are coming, there are some who are diminishing in size. God's Will Church at Mchengautuwa is one of the churches whose membership has gone down during the time of research, 2013 to 2015. One of the reasons is the split which

---

[16] Rev. Dr Kawale was visited by Mr. and Mrs. Chikuse, trying to persuade him to join Mzuzu CCAP Nkhoma Synod. He publicly addressed the Mzuzu CCAP Church of the Synod of Livingstonia, where he belongs, that he has no intention to join Mzuzu CCAP Nkhoma Synod Church. He said that his church is Mzuzu CCAP of the Synod of Livingstonia while here in Mzuzu.

[17] Int. Mr. Sapuwa, church member at Mzuzu CCAP Nkhoma Synod Church, Mchengautuwa, 17.11.2015.

[18] Mrs. Chisemphere, church member, Mzuzu CCAP Nkhoma Synod Church, discussions with fellow members from Nkhoma Synod worshiping at Mchengautuwa CCAP Church, Mchengautuwa, 2015.

happened in 2013. The split happened because Pastor Frank Zebrone was failing to divide well church finances among church founders. The church had been founded by Pastor Frank Zebrone and Pastor Phiri. The two entered into a dispute when Pastor Phiri discovered that church funds were not shared properly, as Pastor Zebrone was taking to himself almost all church funds without a share for Phiri.[19] The issue was discussed between the two but they failed to come to an agreement, as a result the church split into two.[20] Pastor Zebrone continued with the church, while pastor Phiri started his own church within Mchengautuwa. Many members remained with Zebrone, while others went away together with Pastor Phiri. People followed Pastor Phiri because he is a more gifted preacher compared to Pastor Zebrone.[21] The other reason why membership has decreased is that people are not receiving healing and deliverance miracles as they did before. People were used to go to God's Will Church to receive healing and deliverance miracles, and since these things are not happening as before, many members have stopped going to the church and they have started going back to their original churches and or joined other churches.[22] Because of these, church attendance at God's Will has dropped from 700 people in 2013 to 350 people in 2015.

The other example of a church which has lost membership is Chibavi Cornerstone Presbyterian Church. The church has suffered loss of membership because members of the church heard Pastor Winston Timchindike Banda wanting to go back to CCAP, his original church.[23] One day Pastor Winston Timchindike Banda said, in the hearing of his church members of Cornerstone Presbyterian Church, that when he would die the CCAP Church will bury him.[24] That disappointed many members, who

---

[19] Int Brenda Nhlanga, former church member, God's Will Church, Mchengautuwa, 26.12.2015.
[20] Int. Boniface Ngwira, former church member of God's Will Church, Mchengautuwa, 26.12.2015.
[21] Alfred Milanzi, former church member at God's Will Church, Mchengautuwa, 26.12.2015.
[22] Int Brenda Nhlanga, former church member, God's Will Church, Mchengautuwa, 26.12.2015.
[23] Int. Evangelist Njwaziwe Shumba, former church member of Chibavi Presbyterian Church, Mchengautuwa, 30.11.2015.
[24] Pastor Winston Timchindike Banda at the fundraising wedding anniversary organized by Men's Guild of the CCAP Mzuzu Presbytery held at Katawa CCAP

concluded that Pastor Banda is waiting for the appointed time to abandon the church; therefore, church members should be the ones leaving the church one by one before Pastor Banda. The average church attendance has dropped by 205 (from 50 people in 2013 to 40 in 2015).

8.2.4 Church Buildings

During the study period, religions and denominations have not stopped building churches. Various church building projects were taking place in worship centres; there were activities like, renovating church buildings extending church buildings and building new ones. Churches like Chibavi Holy Cross Pentecostal, Chibavi Bible Believers and Kaviwale CCAP embarked on extending church buildings. Chibavi Holy Cross Pentecostal Church and Kaviwale CCAP Church had *vigwagwa* walls, while today they are being extending by constructing brick walls outside the *vigwagwa* walls. Kaviwale Church is at roofing level while Chibavi Holy Cross

Figure 8.1 : Chibavi Holy Cross Pentecostal Church

Figire 8.2 : Chibavi Bible Beliavers Church

Church publically said that he is a member of CCAP Men's guild. He therefore appealed to CCAP Men's Guild members to recognize him as a follow member although he belongs to the other church and they have to remember to bury him, Kataba CCAP Church, 15.8.2015.

Pentecostal Church is at foundation level. Both of these projects are funded by local people.

Figure 8.3 : Kaviwale CCAP Church (insert: old structure inside)

While some other church buildings are being renovated and some are expanding, there are some church buildings which are diminishing in size and value. Such churches seem to have been abandoned by their church members. Kaviwale African National Church is one of the examples of such churches. Church services at this church are not well attended by her members, many church members are not coming for church service because of internal disputes. The church seems to have been deserted by her members hence there is little or no care of the church building.

Figure 8.4: image Kaviwale African National Church

While some other church buildings are diminishing in seize and value, some new church buildings are being built. Pentecostal Miracle Working God Church is a newly built church, constructed within the study period. The Pentecostal Miracle Working God Church, under the leadership of pastor Mwakiwinga, broke away from Mzuzu Pentecostal Church in 2012. They stated the church while congregating at Katoto Secondary School Main Hall. Sooner or later, they started building a church at Chithira area opposite Grand Palace Hotel. They started building the church in 2013 with local funding and donations from America. The congregation has stopped worshiping at Katoto Secondary School Hall because of their own church.

Figure 8.5 : Image for Pentecostal Miracle Working God Church

8.3 Future Expectations

Looking at the way religions and denominations are being organized, through my research period, the following are my expectations.

8.3.1 Expansion of Religions and Denominations

Mzuzu is a growing city where many people together with their religions and denominations are coming to stay. There are possibilities that Bahai and Rastafarianism religions will be the first new religions to come, the city has members of such religions but they are yet to have an organized form of worship. Pentecostal and Charismatic denominations are being born every day, at the same time, others are dying out. Mzuzu will have more worship places belonging to Pentecostal and Charismatic denominations than any other religions and denominations. Although these denominations will have numerous worship places, church membership will not be there for a long time, they will go back to their original denominations. Church members are not fixed as compared to other religions and denominations, they are mobile, and every day are leaving their churches for other churches and finally going back to their original churches, more especially to the mainline churches.[25]

Mzuzu will have more worship centres in the years to come because of population growth and conversions. While the city population increases, church membership increases as well, church membership increases through new born babies in the religious families, transfers and conversions.

8.3.2 Position of Women

There are possibilities that more women will be given positions in the church, although many denominations have come to the conclusion that a woman must keep her mouth shut in church (but she may sing), or that she may not teach men or that she may not exercise authority over men. Just as the religions and denominations hold to this tradition in the same context, it obviously pleases the Holy Spirit to give women many gifts and tasks, responsibilities and privileges to use them in the church. The research shows that churches which give women opportunity to participate fully in the church, equal to men, have grown more than those who have restrictions. Women as well as men work according to the gifts of the Holy Spirit and are equally good preachers, teachers and organizers. Many people have been saved through the works of women in the church.[26] Slowly churches have started using the gifts of Holy Spirit given to women in the church for the glory of God and church development; sooner or later this will be realized by many religions and denominations.

---

[25] Nelia Manda and Josephine Gondwe testified before Chibavi CCAP Discipline Committee that they are coming back to Chibavi CCAP Church because in all churches they were joining, they were unable to get the satisfaction they wanted from these churches. They were confused with the way worship was being conducted; Chibavi CCAP Discipline Committee Report, 26.12.2015.

[26] See Klaus Fiedler, *Missions as the Theology of the Church. An Argument from Malawi*, Mzuzu: Mzuni Press, 2015, p. 51.

8.3.3 Language

Language in Mzuzu is dynamic, influenced by migration and formal education, and I think Mzuzu religions and denominations will be dominated by three languages; Chitumbuka, Chichewa and English. The way these languages are being used in worship centres today will change, taking the form of mainline churches. Each of the three languages will have its own service of worship; there will be no mixture of languages in one service, i.e. English with Chichewa or Chitumbuka interpretation. There will be an English service of worship where the majority of worshippers will be English speakers and a Chitumbuka service of worship as the local language of the city, or Chichewa where the majority of worshippers will be Chichewa speakers. The current system in some churches that are using English with Chichewa interpretation is not pleasing many worshippers, who slowly are complaining about the system.[27] Some churches that are using Chichewa in their services where the majority of worshippers are Chitumbuka speakers have started discussing to translate the liturgy into Chitumbuka.[28]

8.4 Recommendations

I have observed that religions and denominations that are rigid in practice and procedures lose membership. I think, therefore, that if religions and denominations can be flexible in practice and procedures they will maintain membership. For example, the CCAP Synod of Livingstone has a higher membership compared to any other religions

---

[27] Brenda Nhlanga and Alfred Milanzi testified before Mchengautuwa CCAP Discipline Committee that they are coming back to Mchengautuwa CCAP Church because in all churches they were joining, they were unable to get the sermon since they were being confused by the system as they could preach in English with Chichewa translation, Mchengautuwa CCAP Discipline Committee Report, 26.12.2015.

[28] Bishop Fanuel Magangani proposed to the Anglican Synod of the Northern Diocese of Malawi to set a committee that will look into the translation of the Anglican liturgy from Chichewa into Chitumbuka, Int. Rev. Fr. Auther Chitowe, Anglican Priest of the Northern Diocese of Malawi, 10.11.2015. Seventh-day Adventist Church in the North has plans under way to translate the liturgy into Chitumbuka, Int. Mr. Ndovi Mchengautuwa Seventh-day Adventist Church member, 2.12.2015.

and denomination in Mzuzu because of the flexibility of her practices and procedures.[29]

Religions and denominations should think of promoting Chitumbuka, a local language in Mzuzu. All religions and denominations should consider Chitumbuka first when choosing languages for worship because the majority of worshippers are Chitumbuka speakers. English language should be given worship services only when worship centres have many English Speakers. The Chichewa language as well should have worship services only when worshippers at a worship centre have more speakers of Chichewa than Chitumbuka.

As the city of Mzuzu is growing, there is need that religions and denominations should expand as well. Churches should stop from splitting by quarrels but should grow by normal expansion basing on population and distance. When they split, they should have the same denominational name.

Religions and denominations should think seriously on the position of women in the church. Women should be given equal opportunity with men, since women are in the majority in worship centres and are predominantly active in worship centres as well.

---

[29] The 2012 CCAP Synod of Livingstonia Strategic Report, Mzuzu Presbytery, Viyele Congregation, 20.10.2012.

Bibliography

Oral Sources

Answar, Sheikh, Masjid Anwarullmadina Mosque, Vigwagwa Market, 5.10.2013.

Banda, Fikila, Ibrahim, Sheik at Chibavi Mosque, Chibavi, 22.9.2013.

Banda, Richard, John, Head Teacher Marymount Secondary School, 13.1.2015.

Banda, S. Kamuzu, Sandres, Teacher at St Peters Day Secondary School, 18.1.2015.

Banda, Samuel, One of the first Muslims in Mzuzu, Chiputula Mosque, 20.8.20112.

Boniface, Ngwira, Former Church Member of God's Will Church, 26.12.2015.

Changwe, Frank, Church Elder, Mchengautuwa CCAP Church, Mchengautuwa, 15.1.2015.

Chaula, Robert, Church Elder at Kaviwale CCAP Church, 5.12.2015.

Chawawa, Peter, Church Elder, Redeemed Christian Church of God, Upper Chasefu, 21.8.2013.

Chifisi, James, Kennan, Archdeacon, Vicar General of Anglican Diocese of Northern Malawi, Mzuzu, 3.10.2013.

Chikuse, Merina Mrs., Mzuzu CCAP Nkhoma Synod Church, 2014.

Chilambo, Sigman, Church Elder, Viyele CCAP, Viyele, 20.6.2013.

Chimaliro, A.G., First Head Teacher of Mzuzu CCAP Full Primary School, 19.12.2014.

Chipofya, D.F., Rev., Synod Moderator, Speech at Farewell Ceremony of Rev Mrs. M. Kalimanjira, Msongwe CCAP Church, Mzuzu, 9.10.2014.

Chisemphere, Mrs., Church Member of Mzuzu CCAP Nkhoma Synod Church, 2015.

Chisomo, Chipulapula, Pastor, Baptist Convention Church, Hilltop, 2.10.2013.

Chitowe, Auther, Rev., Fr., Anglican Priest of the Northern Diocese of Malawi, 10.11.2015.

Chiumia, Cecilia, Sister, Marymount Sisters of Holy Rosary, Marymount, 22.8.2014.

Dane, Yusufu, Brother, Instructor at Chibavi Chewasene Madrassa, Chibavi, 8.9.2013.

Gondwe, Mc Evans, Pastor, Sonda Assemblies of God Church, 26.9.2013.

Gondwe, Thomas, Church Coordinator of the Northern Region of Good News Revival, 29.7.2013.

Jere, Ester, Gogo, Wife of Pastor L.H.K. Banda, Founder of Chiputula Cavalry Family Church, 20.8.2013.

Jere, Solomon, King, Prophet, Church Prophet, Chibavi Enlightened Gathering Ministry, Chibanja, 19.9.2013.
Juma, Zambali, Sheikh, Area 1B Mosque, 5.8.2013.
Kachale, H., Khumbo, Honourable, Vice President of the Republic of Malawi, 23.12.2013
Kamanga, Daniel, Pastor, Pastor of Ching'ambo Word of Faith Temple International, 10.9.2013.
Kamoto, Hanna, Luwinga Methodist Church, Viyele, 1.10.2013.
Kamphukusi, Violet, Ching'ambo Churches of Church, Mzuzu, 12.9.2013.
Kanenga, Closby, Church Member of Chibavi Baptist Church, 20.9.2013.
Kaunda, Joseph, Church Secretary of Chibavi Emmanuel Pentecostal Movement, Chibavi, 18.9.2011.
Kaunda, Laness, Church Elder, Lusangazi CCAP, 2.6.2014.
Kawonga, B.C., Rev., Parish Minister, Mchengautuwa CCAP, Mchengautuwa, 10.10.2014.
Kawonga, Pauline, Field officer, Catholic Commission for Justice and Peace, 13.1.2015.
Khonje, Ludalinga, Luwinga Grace Community Pentecostal Church, 27.7.2013.
Kumwanje, Mary, Safe-Motherhood, University of Malawi, College of Medicine, Open Discussion, Mangochi, 6.9.2014.
Kumwenda, Ranker, Katoto Calvary Family Church. Chithira, 30.9.2013.
Maganga, Gladess, Church Member, Chibavi Providence Industrial Mission, Chibavi, 19.9.2013.
Magangani, Fanuel, Bishop, Bishop of the Anglican Church, Northern Diocese of Malawi, Mzuzu, 30.10.2013.
Magawa, Martin, former member of Winners Chapel Church, 15.12.2015.
Masamba, Danwell, Pastor, Katoto Assemblies of God Church, Katoto, 30.9.2013.
Mbeya, Muwela, Ngwazi, Muwela Traditional Healer, Dunduzu, 30.8.2013.
Mchali, R., Mzuzu University, Department of Geography, 8.6.2014.
Mhango, T. K., Voster, Rev., Parish Minister, Luwinga Nazarene Church, 8.8.2013.
Mhlanga, Gertrude, Pastor, Dunduzu Jesus Missionary Church, 20.8.2013.
Mhone, A.G., Rev., Parish Minister, Limphasa CCAP Church 30.11.2014.
Mhoni, Catherine, Church Member, Zolozolo West Chipangano Church, Mzuzu, 12.9.2013.
Milanzi, Alfred, former church member at God's Will Church, 26.12.2015.
Mkandawire, Aphraim, Church Secretary, Ching'ambo Zion Christian Church, 13.9.2013.
Msowoya, Silvester, Prophet, Chibavi Come to Jesus Ministry, Mzuzu, 19.9.2013.
Mkandawire, Moses, Director of Church and Society, 23.1.2015.

Mlotha, Longstar, Pastor at Jomo Road Church of Christ, Mzuzu, 3.10.2013.

Mnthali, Doctor, one of the first members of Nkholongo Seventh – day Adventist Church, Nkholongo, 28.8.2013.

Mphande, Mrs., Matron-Mzuzu Central Hospital, 13.7.2014.

Mshali, Rodney, Lecturer at Mzuzu University, Department of Geography, lecture notes, 16.6.2014.

Msikiti, Chrisy, Wife to Pastor Msikiti, Pentecost Christ Church International, Mzilawayingwe, 23.8.2013.

Msukwa, Jessie, Chibavi Agape Life International, Mzuzu, 18.9.2013.

Mtambo, Moses, Social Development Officer of Mzuzu City, 23.11.2015.

Mtonga, Belson, Pastor, Kavibale Gospel Pentecostal Church, Kaviwale, 25.9.2013.

Mukhondya, Lusayo, Mzuzu Technical College- Boarding Master, 13.1.2015.

Munthali, Docter, One of the First Students at Nkholongo Primary School, 20.12.2014.

Munthali, H.H. working with H.H. Wholesalers, Mzuzu, 5.10.2013.

Munthali, Maurice, Rev., Former Deputy General Secretary-CCAP Synod of Livingstonia, 10.12.2014.

Munyenyembe, Bernadetta, Sister, Programme Manager-Tigabane Radio, 15.1.2015.

Muyila, Rev., Student at St John of God College, 23.2.2015.

Mvula, Bonvential, Former Head teacher at St Peters Primary School, 13.01.2014.

Mwakiwinga, Pastor, Chithira Pentecostal Miracle Working Church, 20.12.2015.

Mwale, J.P.V., Rev., Deputy General Secretary CCAP Synod of Livingstonia, Mzuzu, 3.10.2013.

Mwale, Kapombe, C., Theological Education by Extension of Malawi Director (North), 18.1.2015.

Mwalweni, Christopher, Pastor, African Evangelical Church of Malawi, 21.8.2013.

Ndovi, M., Mchengautuwa Seventh-day Adventist Church member, 2.12.2015.

Ndovi, M., Mrs., Mchengautuwa Seventh- day Adventist Church, 5.12.2015.

Ng'ambi, Selfridge, Session Clerk, Katawa CCAP, 21.8.2013.

Ngulube, Alice, Former Cashier at St John's Nursing College, 15.01.2015.

Ngulube, Florah, Church Elder and Ngoni Women Christian Councellor, Mzalangwe CCAP, 21.3.2013.

Nhlanga, Brenda, Former church member, God's Will Church, 26.12.2015.

Nhlema, Agnes, Mzuzu Presbytery Women's Coordinator, Mzuzu, 15.11.2012.

Nkhata, Innocent, Former Education Secretary-Mzuzu Diocese Mzuzu, 13.1.2015.

Nkhoma, H.M., Rev., Former General Secretary, CCAP Synod of Livingstonia, 8.7.2014, 18.12.2014, 16.1.2015.

Nyasulu T.P.K. Dr, Rev., Synod Moderator, CCAP Synod of Livingstonia, 9.10.2012.

Nyasulu, Restone, Primary Education Advisor - Mzuzu City, 18.1.2015.

Nyirenda, Daniel, next door neighbour to Chithira Peace Ministries Church, 10.12.2015.

Nyirenda, John, Session Clerk, Chibavi CCAP, Chibavi, 5.9.2013.

Nyirenda, M.B.D., Mrs., Nurse at St John's Hospital, Mzuzu, 13.1.2015.

Nyirenda, Major Job, Pastor, One More Time Christian Movement, Mzilawayingwe, 23.8.2013.

Nyirenda, Posepose, Former United Democratic Front Regional Executive Member, 20.12.2015.

Nyirenda, S.M., Dr, Rev., Chancellor of Livingstonia University, Mzuzu, 14.7.2014.

Nyirenda, Tony, Pastor, Mzuzu International Pentecostal Holiness Church, 3.10.2013.

Nyondo, L.N., Dr Rev., General Secretary, CCAP Synod of Livingstonia, Mzuzu, 12.4.2013, 8.7.2014, 20.11.2014.

Nzima, Vincent, Lands Department of Malawi Government, Mzuzu, 10.12.2015.

Patel, Jubea, Hindu Religious member, son of Rasck Patel, the founding member of Hindu Religion in Mzuzu, 5.10.2013.

Patel, Rasck, Founding member of Hindu Religion in Mzuzu, Mzuzu, 3.10.2013.

Phiri, A.M., Rev., Moderator of CCAP Mzuzu Presbytery, St Andrews Church, 8.7.2013.

Phiri, Juliet, Mrs., Former student at St John of God College of Health Science, and Nurse at Zomba Mental Hospital, 13.11.2013.

Puwapuwa, Jessie, Director, Voice of Livingstonia Radio, 13.1.2015.

Sakala, Maria, Maria Traditional Temple, Sonda, 28.9.2013.

Sapuwa, Mr., Church Member at Mzuzu CCAP Nkhoma Synod Church, 17.11.2015.

Shumba, Njwaziwe, Evangelist, Former Member of Chibavi Presbyterian Church, 30.11.2015.

Sibande, Edrine, Ministry of Health, Nkhota-kota District Hospital, Safe-Motherhood. Open Discussion, 6.9.2014.

Sichinga, Mrs, Former District Education Manager, Mzuzu, 25.1.2015.

Singini, Ethel, Chairperson of Lupaso CCAP Women Guild, Lupaso, 29.7.2013.

Singini, Funny, Sonda Christ Rock Church, Sonda, 20.9.2013.

Singini, Hardson, Village Headman, Speech at Funeral Ceremony, 6.9.2012.

Singini, Luwinga, Inkosana, Senior Group Village Headman, Luwinga, 6.4.2013.

Singini, Wayinga, Group Village Headman, Lupaso, 6.4.2013.

Standfore, Christina, Church Member, Chibavi Bible Believer, Chibavi, 20.9.2013.

Swanny, Classic, One of the pioneers of Hindu Religion in Mzuzu, Mzuzu market, 5.10.2013.

Theu, Mather, Sister, Sister in Charge, St Mary's Luwinga Convent, Luwinga, 21.82013.

Thole, Opson, Mzuzu Museum Office, Department of Culture and Heritage, 4.4.2013

Ziba, Rose, First Female Cabinet Minister of Malawian MCP Government, Kaning'ina. 3.6.2013.

Zuza Mkasa Joseph, Bishop-Mzuzu Diocese, 17.11.2014.

Published Sources

A Students' Handbook for Population Education in Malawi, Domasi: Malawi Institute of Education, 1998.

Amanze, James, *African Traditional Religion in Malawi. The Case of Bimbi Cult*, Blantyre: CLAIM- Kachere, 2002.

Banda, Rachel NyaGondwe, *Women of Bible and Culture. Baptist Convention Women in Southern Malawi*, Zomba: Kachere, 2005.

Bryant, A.T., *The Zulu People,* Pietermaritzburg, 1949.

Building an Informed Nation. A Handbook for Civic Education on Good Governance and Human Rights, Democracy Consolidation Programme, Balaka: Montfort, 2000.

Coolen, J., *The History of Mzuzu Diocese*, Mzuzu, 1989.

D'Souza, Anthony, *Leadership. A Trilogy on Leadership and Effective Management*, Paulines: Limuru, 1994.

Daneel, M.L., *Missiology (B.Th.), Christian Theology of Africa*, Pretoria: University of South Africa, 1989.

Daneel, M.L., *Missiology. Christian Theology of Africa (Mission as Liberation: Third World Theologies)*, Pretoria: University of South Africa, 1989.

de Blij, H.J. and Peter O. Muller, *Human Geography: Culture, Society and Space*, New York: John Wily and Sons, 1995.

Elmslie, W.A., *Among the Wild Ngoni*, Edinburgh, 1899.

Fellmann, Jerome, *Human Geography: Landscapes of Human Activity*, New York: McGraw Hill, 1999.

Fiedler, Klaus, *Missions as the Theology of the Church. An Argument from Malawi*, Mzuzu: Mzuni Press, 2015.

Fraser, Donald, *The Autobiography of an African*, London, 1925.

Gehman, Richard J, *African Traditional Religion in Biblical Perspective*, Nairobi, 1993.

Henkel, Reinhard, *Christian Missions in Africa. A Social Geographical Study of the Impact of their Activities in Zambia,* Berlin: Reimer, 1989.

Kholowa, Janet and Klaus Fiedler, *In the Beginning God Created them Equal,* Blantyre: CLAIM-Kachere, 2003, p. 27.

Kohl, Willemijn van, "Ummah in Zomba: Transnational Influences in Reformist Muslims in Malawi", *Religion in Malawi,* Nov. 2010 – Nov. 2011.

Kong, Lily, "Religious Schools for Spirit (f)or Nation," *Environment and Planning. Society and Space.* 2005.

Küng, Hans, *The Church,* Wellwood: Kent, 1986.

Lamba, Isaac Chikwekwere, *Contradictions in Post-War Education Policy Formulation and Application in Colonial Malawi 1945 – 1961. A Historical Study of the Dynamics of Colonial Survival,* Zomba: Kachere; 2010.

Levine, Gregory J., *On the Geography of Religion,* St Kingston, 1986.

Linder, Robert, 'The Catholic Reformation' in: Tim Dowley (ed), Oxford, Betania, Sydney: Lion, 1990, pp. 410 -428.

Longwe, Hany, *Christian by Grace – Baptists by Choice, A History of the Baptist Convention of Malawi,* Mzuzu: Mzuni Press, 2011.

Luwe, N.A., *The Establishment of Mzuzu CCAP Full Primary School.* Historical Pamphlet of Mzuzu CCAP Primary School.

Mbiti, John, *African Religions and Philosophy,* London and Nairobi; Heinemann, 1969.

McCracken, John, *Politics and Christianity in Malawi 1875 – 1940. The Impact of the Livingstonia Mission in the Northern Province,* Blantyre: CLAIM-Kachere, 2008.

Milazi, Ibrahim, "The Burning of Mosques in the North: Is it the Beginning or Climax of Political Fanaticism or Christian Fundamentalism in Malawi?" *Religion in Malawi,* No. 9, November, 1999.

Mzumara, Cecilia, *Fostering Girl Child Education in Malawi, Case Study of Marymount Girls Secondary School and the Missionary Sisters of the Immaculate Conception in Malawi,* Balaka: Montfort Media, 2012.

Paas, Steven, *The Faith Moves South. A History of the Church in Africa,* Zomba: Kachere, 2006.

Park, Chris and J. Hinnells (eds), *Religion and Geography, Companion to the Study of Religion,* London: Routledge, 2004.

Phiri, Isabel, Apawo, *Women, Presbyterianism and Patriarchy, Religious Experience of Chew Women in Central Malawi,* Blantyre: CLAIM-Kachere, 2000.

Rubenstein, James M., *The Cultural Landscape, An Introduction to Human Geography,* Miami: Miami University, 1999.

Santrock, John W., *Life-Span Development,* Texas: McGraw Hill, 2009.

Sivard, Ruth Leger, *Women: A World Survey*, Washington DC: World Priorities, 1985.

Strohbehn, Ulf, *Pentecostalism in Malawi, A History of the Apostolic Faith Mission in Malawi*, Zomba: Kachere, 2005.

Strohbehn, Ulf, *The Zionist Churches in Malawi. History – Theology – Anthropology*, Mzuzu: Mzuni Press, 2016.

Thompson, T. Jack, *Christianity in Northern Malawi: Donald Fraser's Missionary Methods and Ngoni Culture*. Leiden, New York: Brill, 1995.

Thompson, T. Jack, *Ngoni, Xhosa and Scot, Religion and Culture in Malawi*, Zomba: Kachere, 2007.

Waller, John and Jane Linden, *Mainstream Christianity in Malawi, Zambia and Zimbabwe,* Gweru: Mambo, 1984.

Unpublished Sources

Banda, Macleard, The Remnant and its Mission. An Investigation into the Interaction of the Seventh-day Adventist Church with Society in Malawi, PhD, Mzuzu University, 2014.

Banda, Oswald Jimmy, The Role of women in the Anglican Diocese of the Northern Malawi, MA, Mzuzu University, 2013.

Bula, Amos, The Development of Seventh-day Adventist Luwazi Mission since its Establishment in 1928 up until 2003, Mzuni Document, Department of Theology and Religious Studies, Mzuzu University.

CCAP Mzuzu Presbytery Minutes, 2012.

CCAP Synod of Livingstonia Strategic Report, Mzuzu Presbytery, 20.10.2012.

Chibavi CCAP Discipline Committee Report, 26.12.2015.

Chirwa, Frank, *Theology of Health in the Seventh- day Adventist Church. A quest for Abundant Life in Jesus,* PhD Module, Mzuni, 2010.

Democracy Consolidation Program. *Building an Informed Nation; a Handbook for Civic Education on Governance and Human Rights,* Montfort Press, 2004.

Gadama, Richard, Impact of Zionist Church Teachings and Practices on Human Welfare: A Case study of Kaole (Mayani) Zionist Church, Mzuni Document, Department of Theology and Religious Studies, Mzuzu University.

Gadama, Richard, The Bible Believers in Malawi: History, Teaching and Practices (1979-2011), MA Dissertation, Department of Theology and Religious Studies, Mzuzu University, 2012.

Gondwe, Wezi, *A History of the Last Church of God and His Christ in Malawi from 1914 to 2015*, MA Dissertation, Department of Theology and Religious Studies, Mzuzu University, 2015.

Gondwe, Wezi, *The Last Church of God and His Christ: Histories of Four Congregations in Nkhata bay District,* Mzuni Document, Department of Theology and Religious Studies, Mzuzu University.

Kaonga, Samson, *A History of the Birth and Growth of Livingstonia Synod's Congregation in Kasungu District in the context of the Border Dispute with Nkhoma Synod (2005-2012)*, BA, Mzuzu University, 2012.

Mchengautuwa CCAP Discipline Committee Report, 26.12.2015.

Mlenga, Joyce, *An Investigation of Dual Religiosity between Christianity and African Tradition Religion Among the Ngonde in Karonga District in The Northern Malawi*, PhD, Mzuzu University, 2013

Mlenga, Moses, *Polygamy and the Synod of Livingstonia in the Northern Malawi: Biblical, Moral and Missiological Implications*, PhD, Mzuzu University, 2013.

Mphande, C.Z., Some Aspects of the History of the Tonga up to 1934, Dissertation, Department of Humanities, Chancellor College, University of Malawi, 1968/69, p. 4.

Mwangupili, Ndongolera C.W., *Ngoni and CCJP Approaches to Reconciliation in Katete Parish*, MA, Mzuzu University, 2011.

Mzuzu Urban Profile Final Review 2008- 2009, Mzuzu City, 2009.

Nyangu, Austine, A History of Zakumwamba Ministry and its Impact on the CCAP in Malawi, Mzuni Document (BA), Department of Theology and Religion Studies, Mzuzu University.

Population and Housing Census, NSO, Zomba, 2005.

Rhodian Munyenyembe, The Church of Central Africa Presbyterian (CCAP). Its History as a Federative Denomination (1924-2015), Free State University, 2016.

Sibande, Zeenah, Religious Geography: Investigation of Christian Distribution around CCAP Church Centres in Mzuzu City, MA Module, Department of Theology and Religious Studies, Mzuzu University, 2013.

St John's Hospital Annual Report, From July 2004 to June 2005 and July 2005 to June 2006, 2006.

Theological Education by Extension in Malawi Admission Forms for the Academic Year of 2013/2014, Zomba, 12.7.2013.

Internet/Websites

Wikipedia org/wiki/Religion and Geography, 15.10.2012.

Religion and Geography, http/en, Wikipedia org /wiki, 10.15.2012.

Dissertations/Modules

Mphande, C.Z., *Some Aspects of the History of the Tonga up to 1934*, Dissertation, Department of Humanities, Chancellor College, University of Malawi 1968/69.

Nkhoma, D.I., the *Northern Ngoni; a Political System*, Dissertation, Department of Humanities, Chancellor College, University of Malawi, 1968/67.

Sibande, Zeenah, Religious Geography: Investigation of Christian Distribution around CCAP church centres in Mzuzu City, MA Module, Department of Theology and Religious Studies, Mzuzu University, 2001.

Kaonga, Samson, A History of the Birth and Growth of Livingstonia Synod's Congregation in Kasungu District in the context of the Border Dispute with Nkhoma Synod (2005-2012), BA, Mzuzu University, 2012.

Rhodian Munyenyembe, The Church of Central Africa Presbyterian (CCAP). Its History as a Federative Denomination (1924-2015), Free State University, 2016.

Appendices

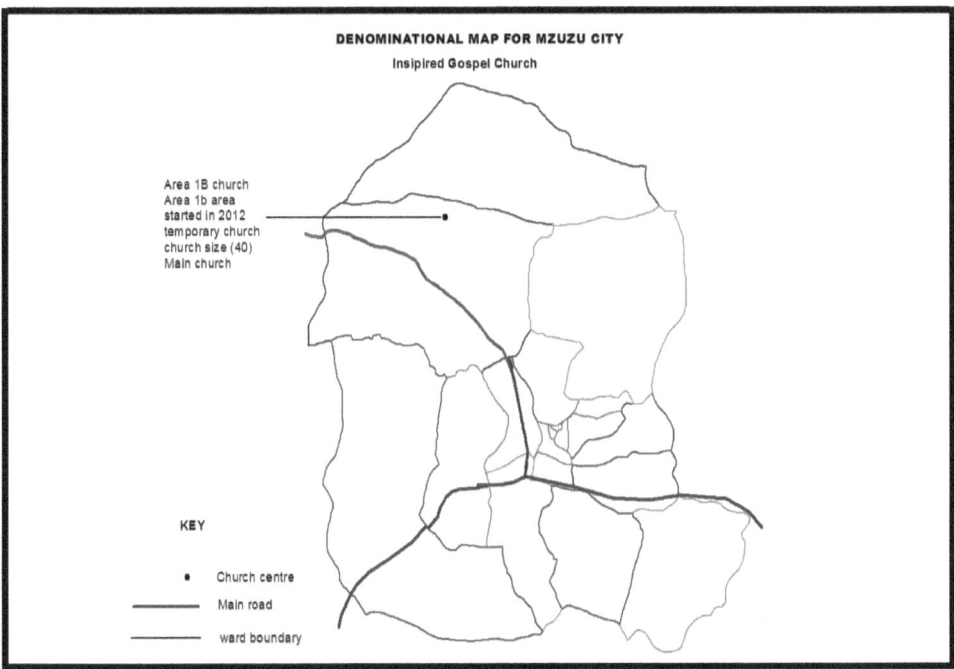

A 1

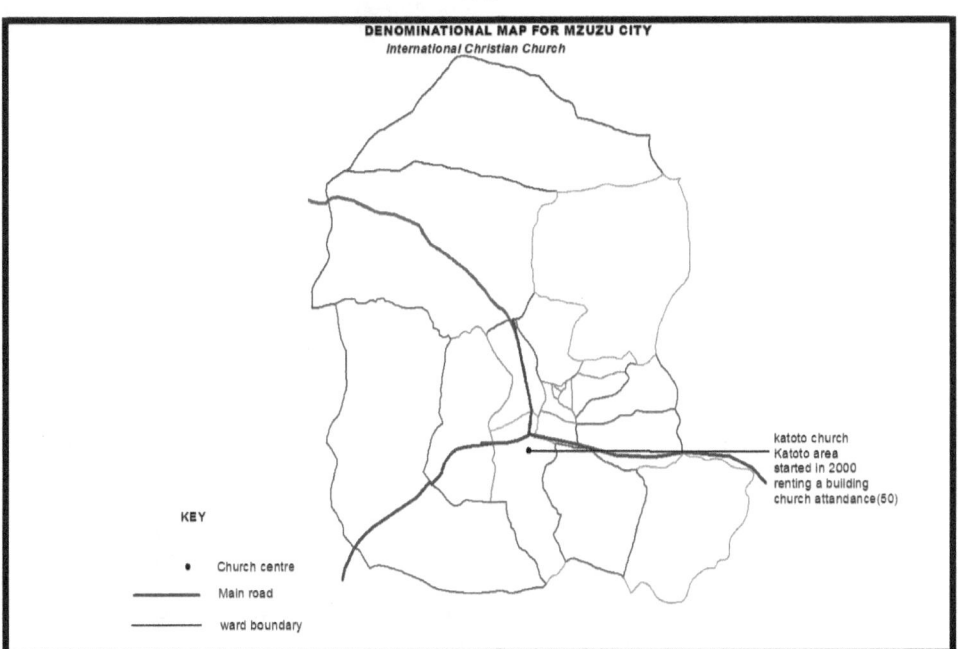

A 2

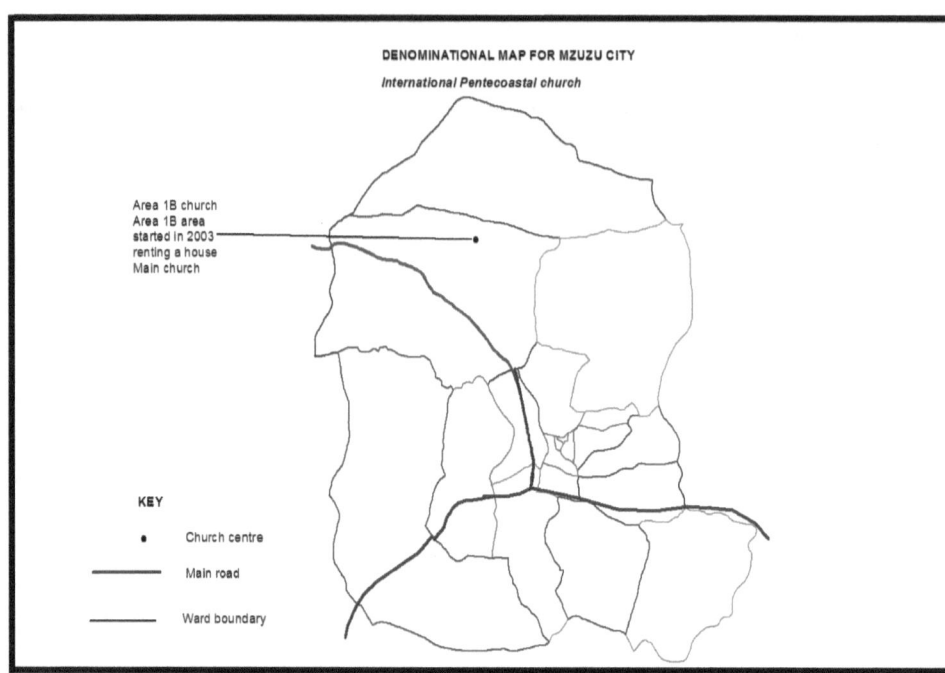

A-3

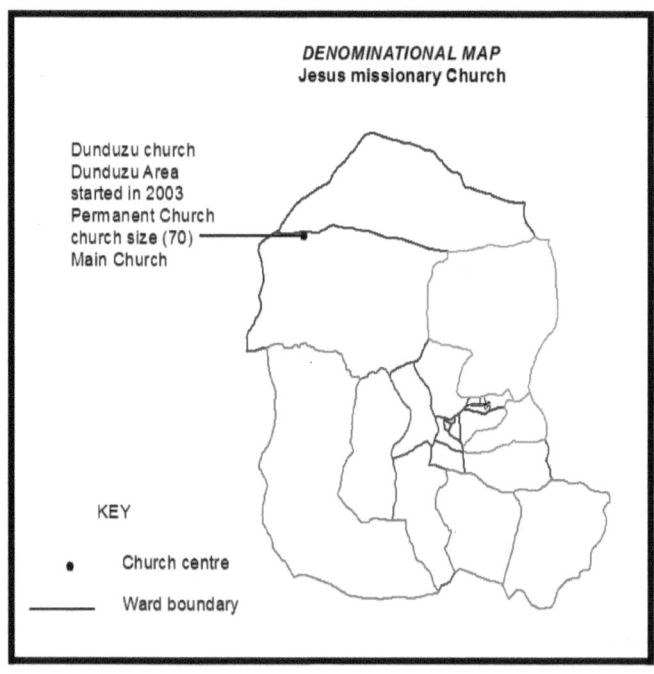

A-4

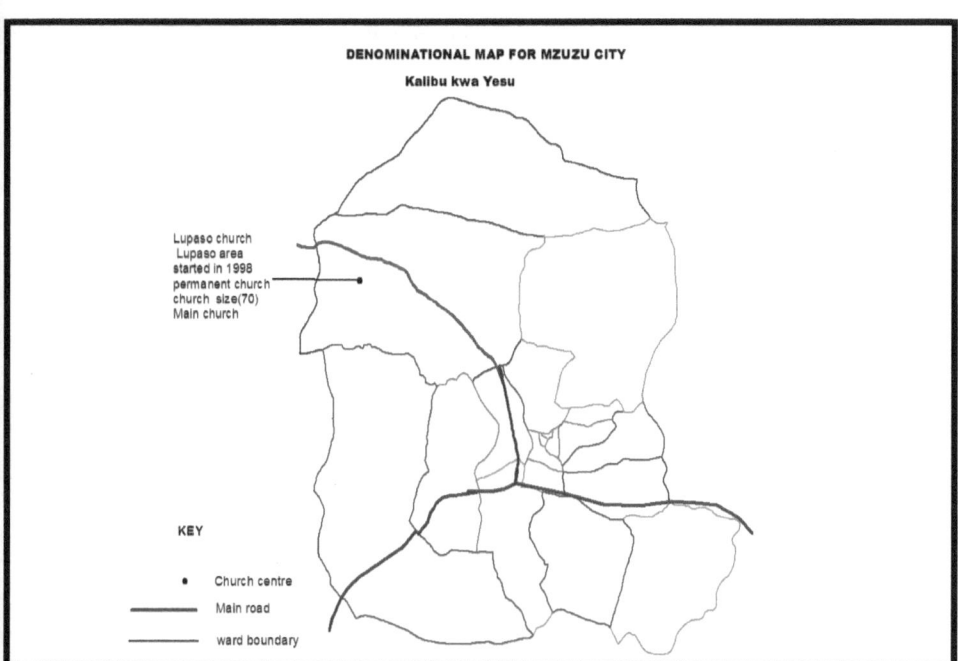

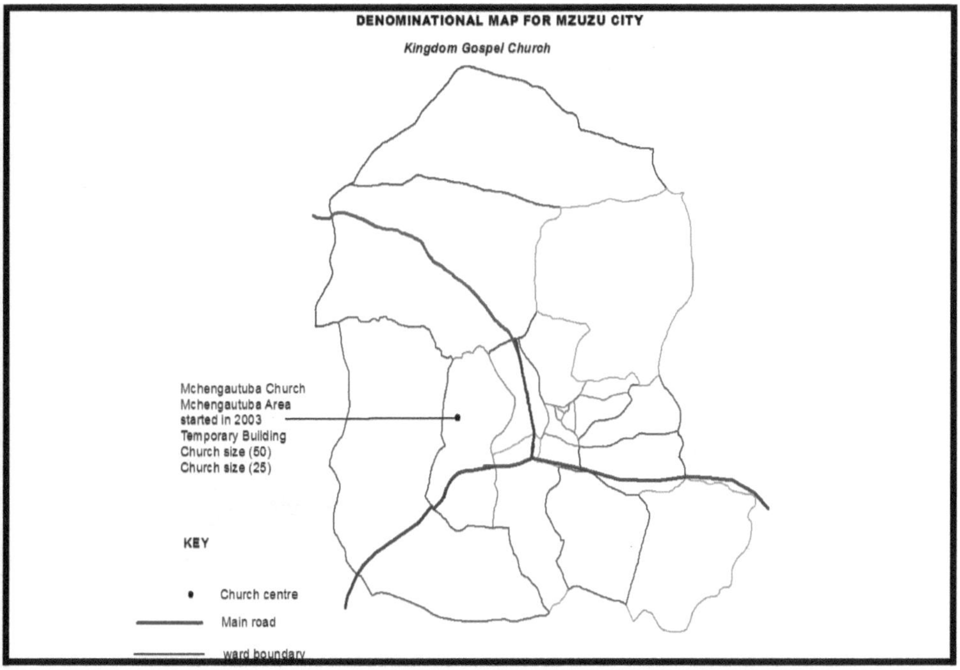

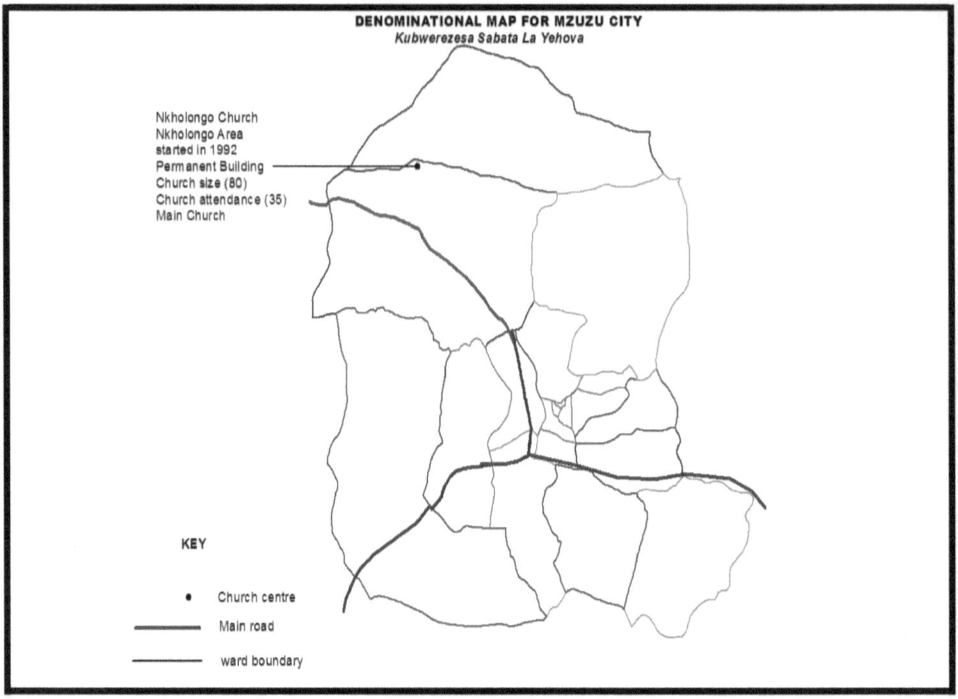

DENOMINATIONAL MAP FOR MZUZU CITY
Kubwerezesa Sabata La Yehova

Nkholongo Church
Nkholongo Area
started in 1992
Permanent Building
Church size (80)
Church attendance (35)
Main Church

KEY
- Church centre
- Main road
- ward boundary

A-7

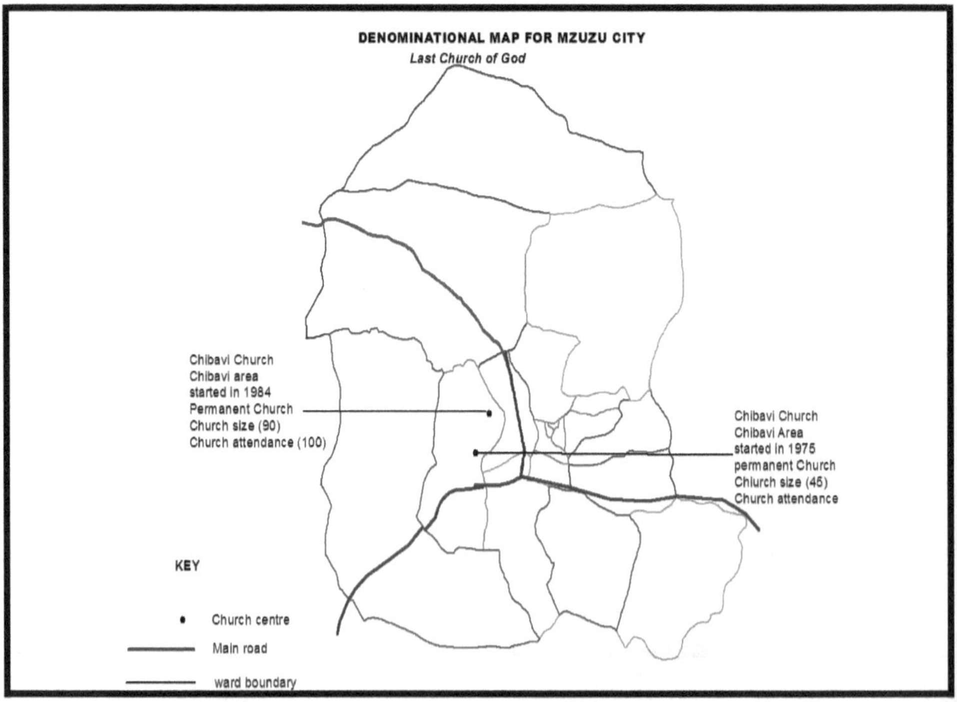

DENOMINATIONAL MAP FOR MZUZU CITY
Last Church of God

Chibavi Church
Chibavi area
started in 1984
Permanent Church
Church size (90)
Church attendance (100)

Chibavi Church
Chibavi Area
started in 1975
permanent Church
Chiurch size (45)
Church attendance

KEY
- Church centre
- Main road
- ward boundary

A-8

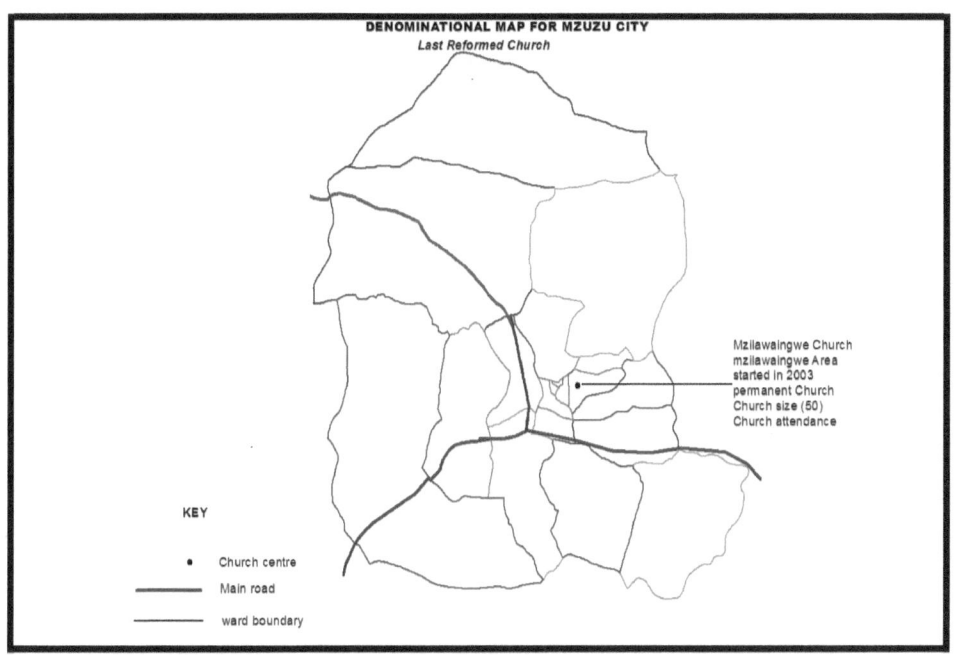

A-9

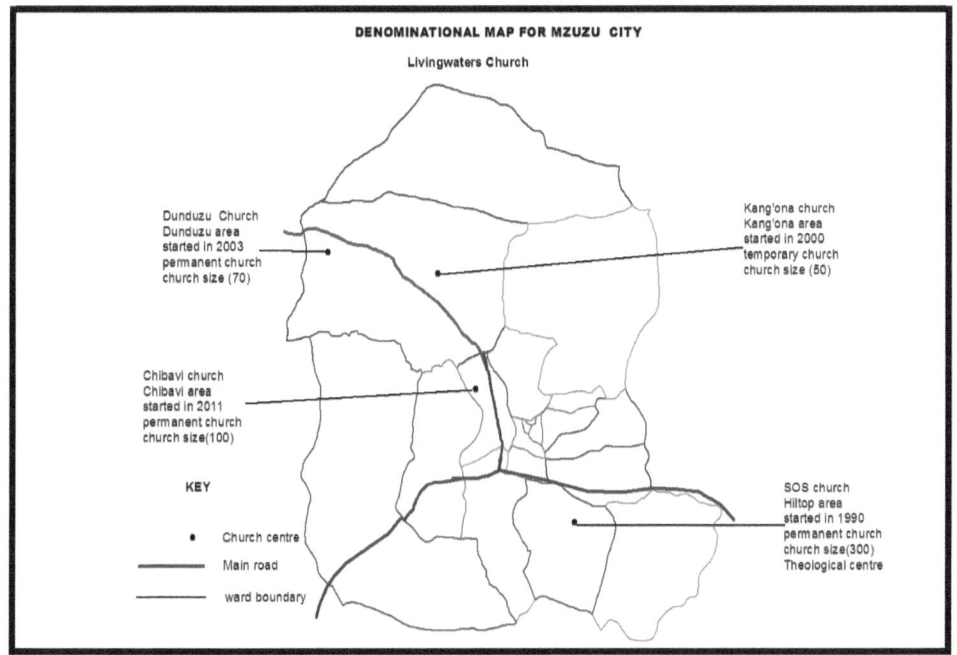

A-10

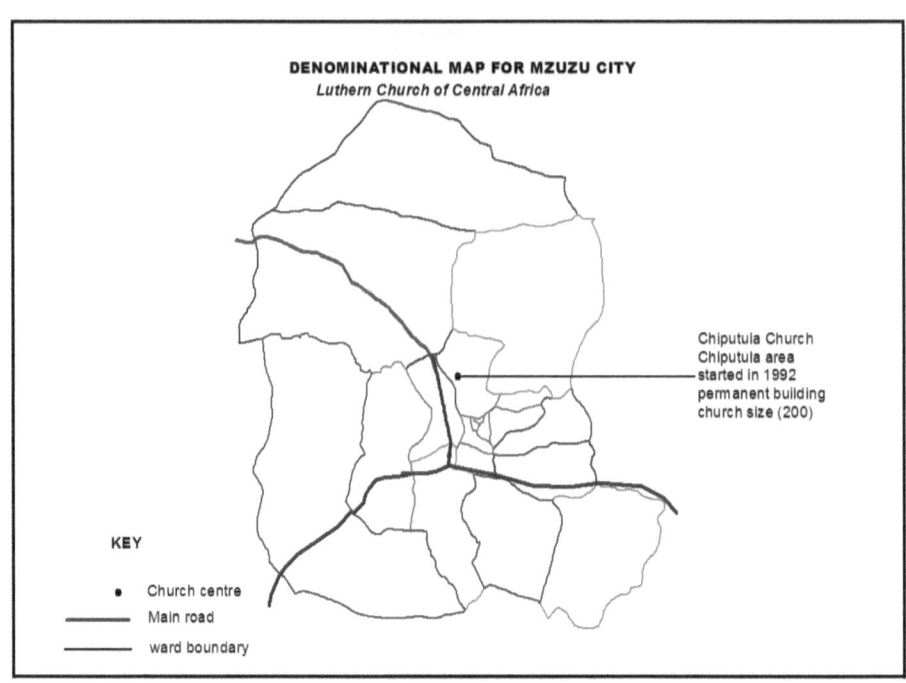

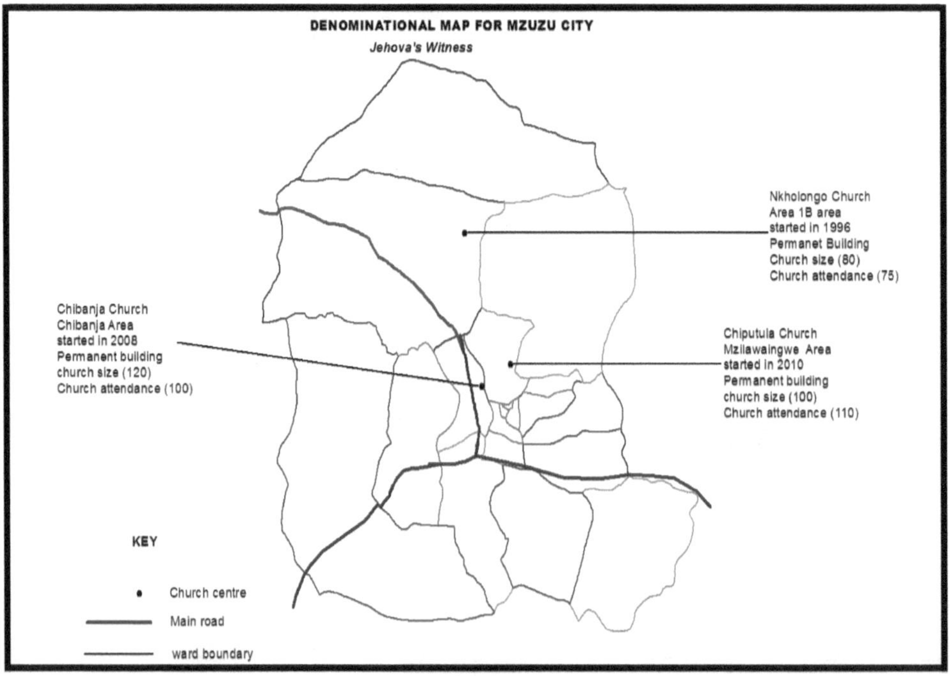

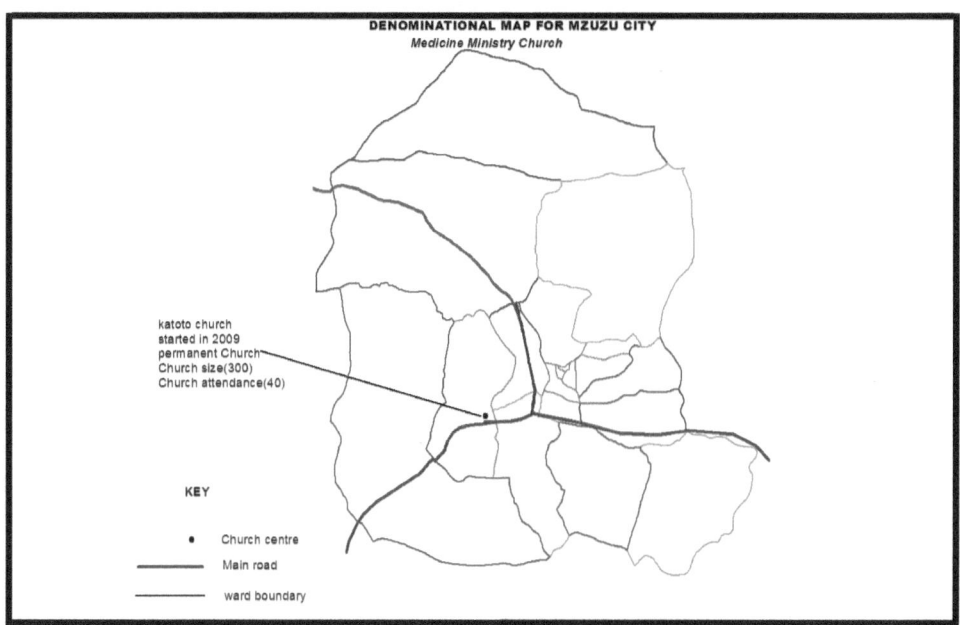

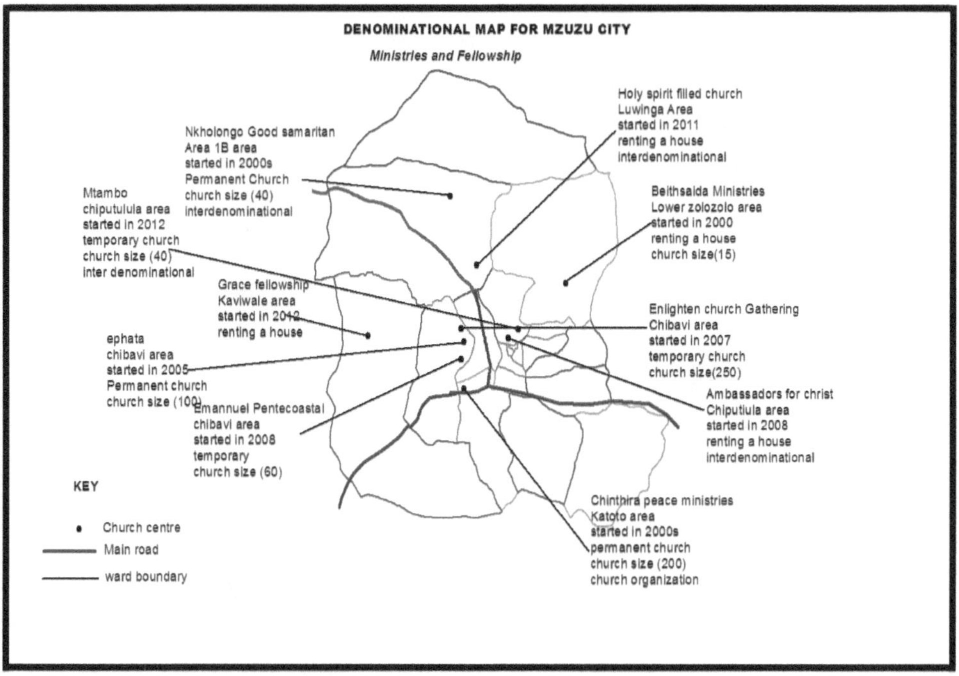

DENOMINATIONAL MAP FOR MZUZU CITY
Moravian Church
Chibanja Church
Chibanja Area
started in 2002
permanent Church
church size (200)
Church attandance (70)
Main Church
KEY
Church centre
Main road
ward boundary

A-15

DENOMINATIONAL MAP FOR MZUZU CITY
Mosques
Area 1B mosque
Area 1B area
started in 2009
Temporary Building
capacity(60)
attendance (50)
Chibavi central Mosque
Chibavi area
started in2005
Permanent building
capacity (100)
attendance (70)
Central Mosque
Ching'ambo Mosque
Ching'ambo area
strted in 2005
Permanent building
capacity(60)
attendance (30)
Chinsewre
Chibavi area
started in 1999
Permanent building
capacity(70)
attendance (55)
Chiputula Mosque
Chuputula Area
started in 2012
Permanent structure
capacity (70)
attendance (70)
Mzuzu central
Hardware MArket
started in 1960
Permanent building
Capacity (700)
attendance (500)
Masjd anwarulimachine
Vigwagwa Market area
started in 1999
Permanent building
capacity (400)
Attendance (500)
Hilltop kandahha
Hilltop Area
started in 1999
Permanent building
capacity (120)
attendance (60)
KEY
Church centre
Main road
ward boundary

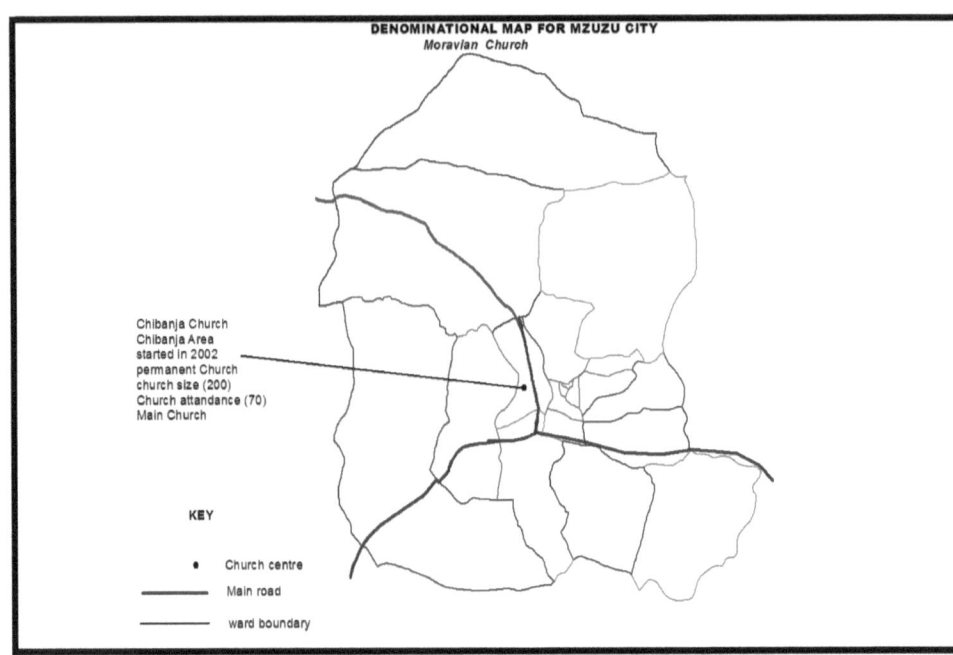

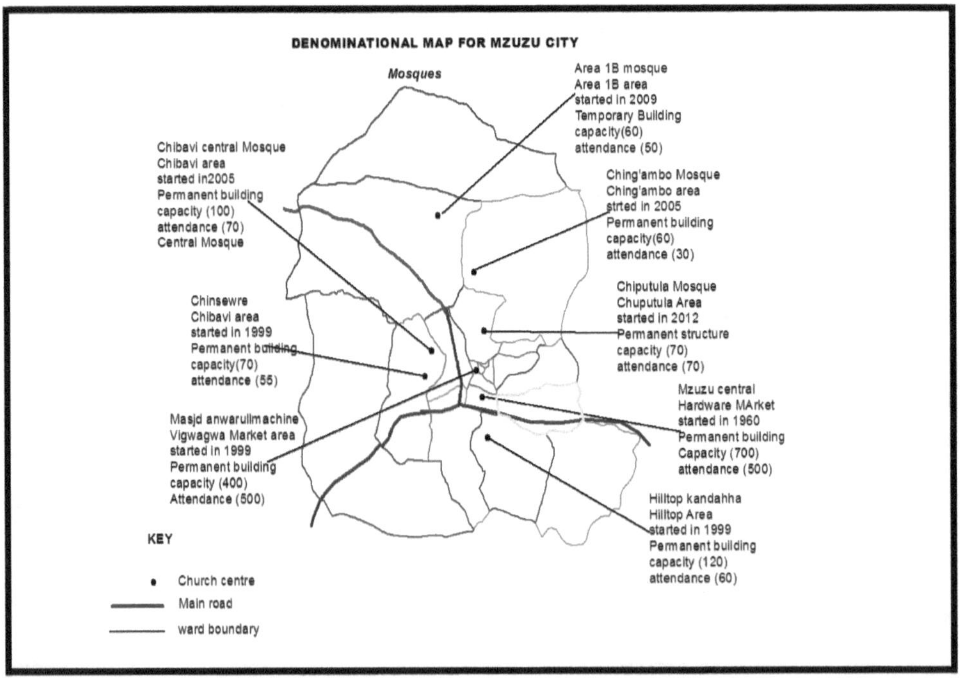

A-16

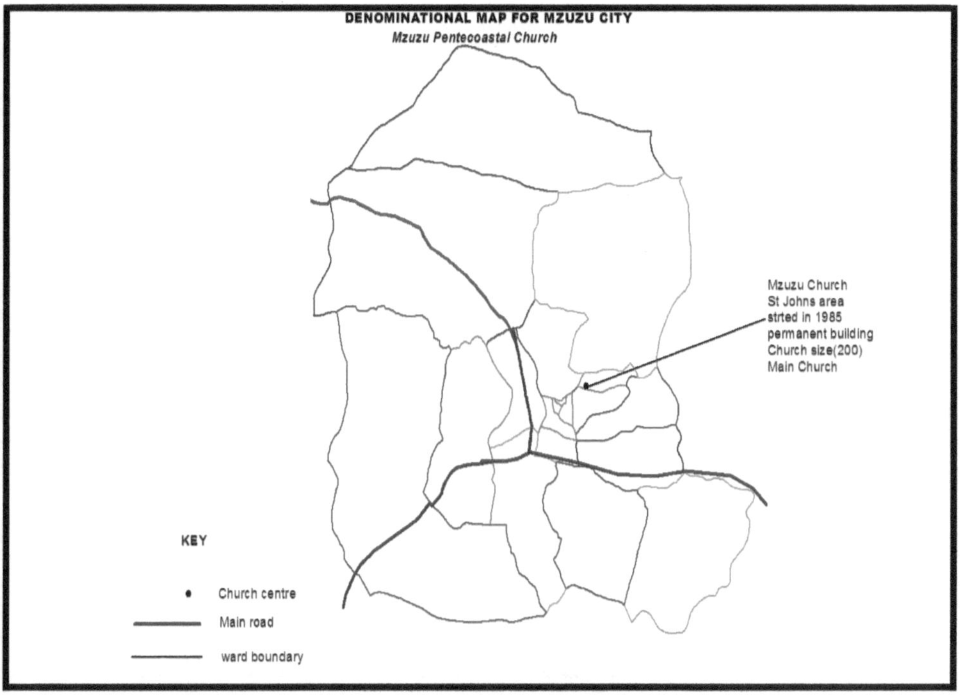

DENOMINATIONAL MAP FOR MZUZU CITY
Mzuzu Pentecoastal Church

Mzuzu Church
St Johns area
strted in 1985
permanent building
Church size(200)
Main Church

KEY
- Church centre
— Main road
— ward boundary

A-17

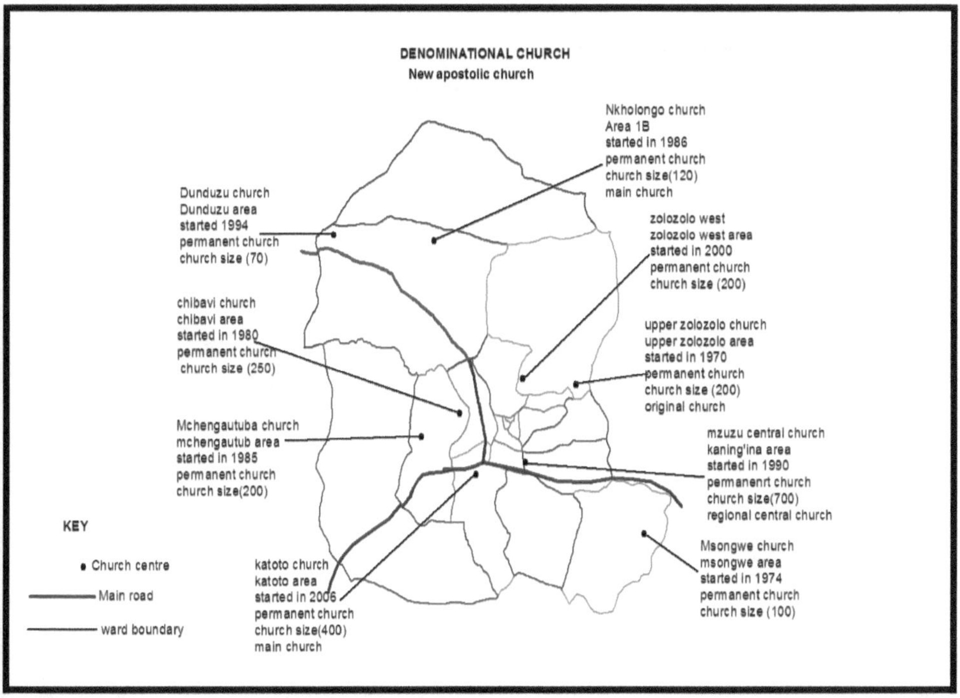

DENOMINATIONAL CHURCH
New apostolic church

Nkholongo church
Area 1B
started in 1986
permanent church
church size(120)
main church

Dunduzu church
Dunduzu area
started 1994
permanent church
church size (70)

zolozolo west
zolozolo west area
started in 2000
permanent church
church size (200)

chibavi church
chibavi area
started in 1980
permanent church
church size (250)

upper zolozolo church
upper zolozolo area
started in 1970
permanent church
church size (200)
original church

Mchengautuba church
mchengautub area
started in 1985
permanent church
church size(200)

mzuzu central church
kaning'ina area
started in 1990
permanenrt church
church size(700)
regional central church

KEY
- Church centre
— Main road
— ward boundary

katoto church
katoto area
started in 2006
permanent church
church size(400)
main church

Msongwe church
msongwe area
started in 1974
permanent church
church size (100)

A 18

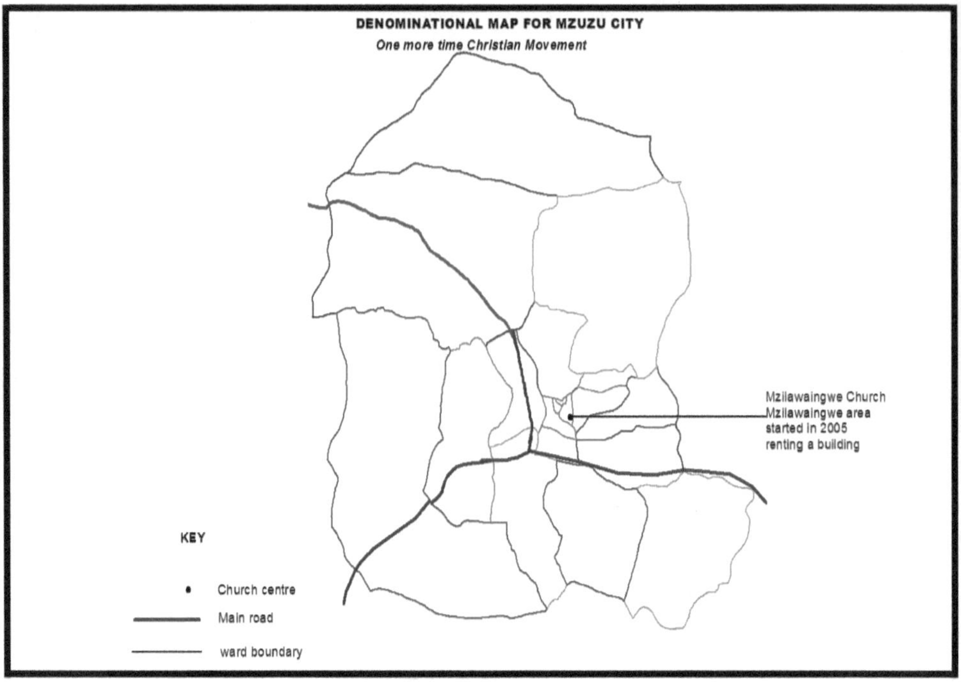

DENOMINATIONAL MAP FOR MZUZU CITY
One more time Christian Movement

Mzilawaingwe Church
Mzilawaingwe area
started in 2005
renting a building

KEY
• Church centre
— Main road
— ward boundary

A-19

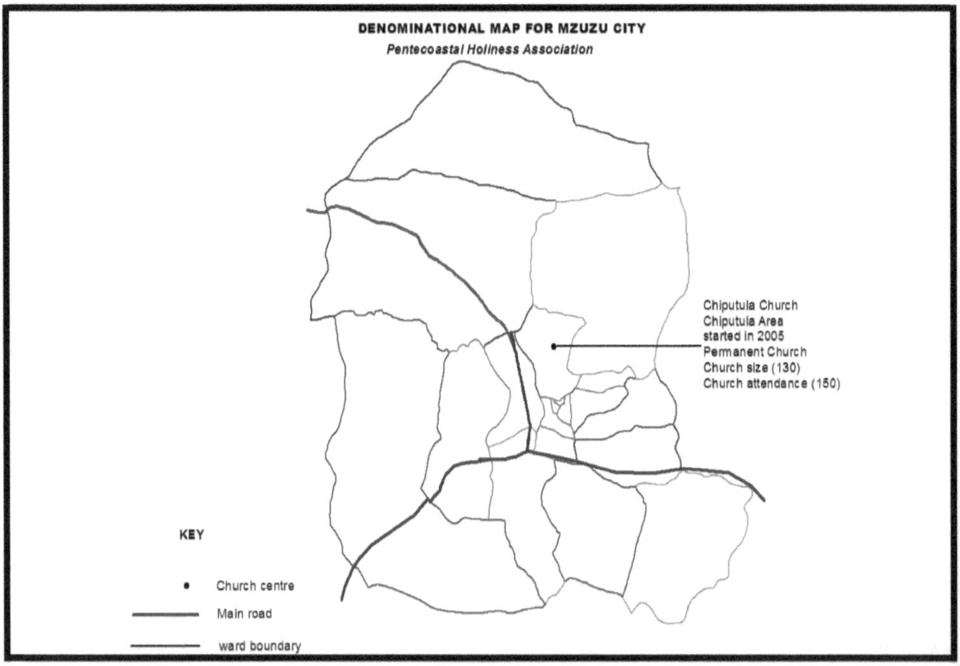

DENOMINATIONAL MAP FOR MZUZU CITY
Pentecoastal Holiness Association

Chiputula Church
Chiputula Area
started in 2005
Permanent Church
Church size (130)
Church attendance (150)

KEY
• Church centre
— Main road
— ward boundary

A-20

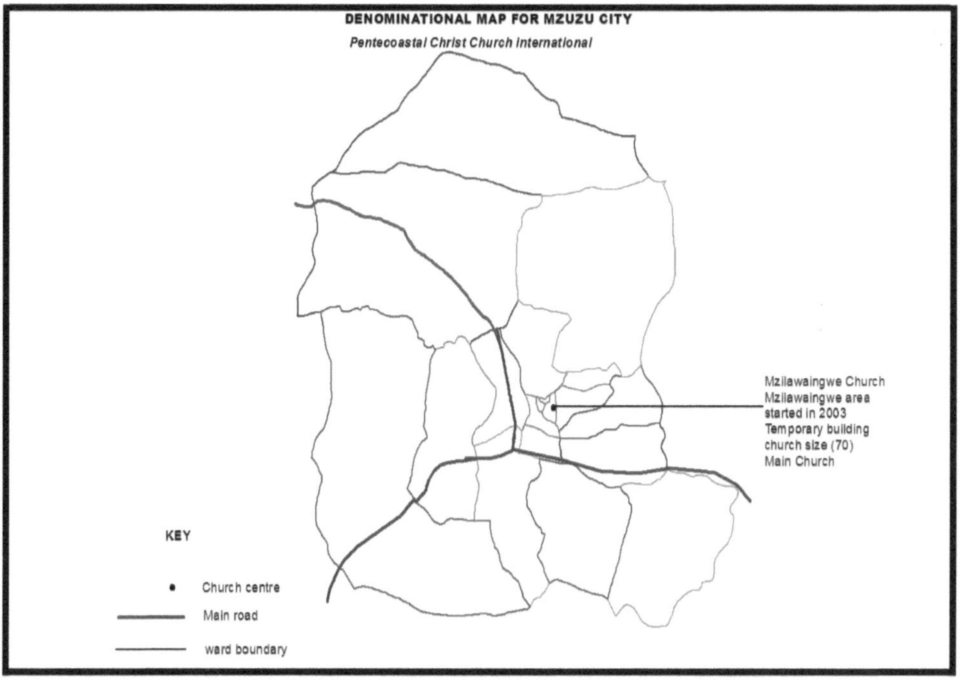

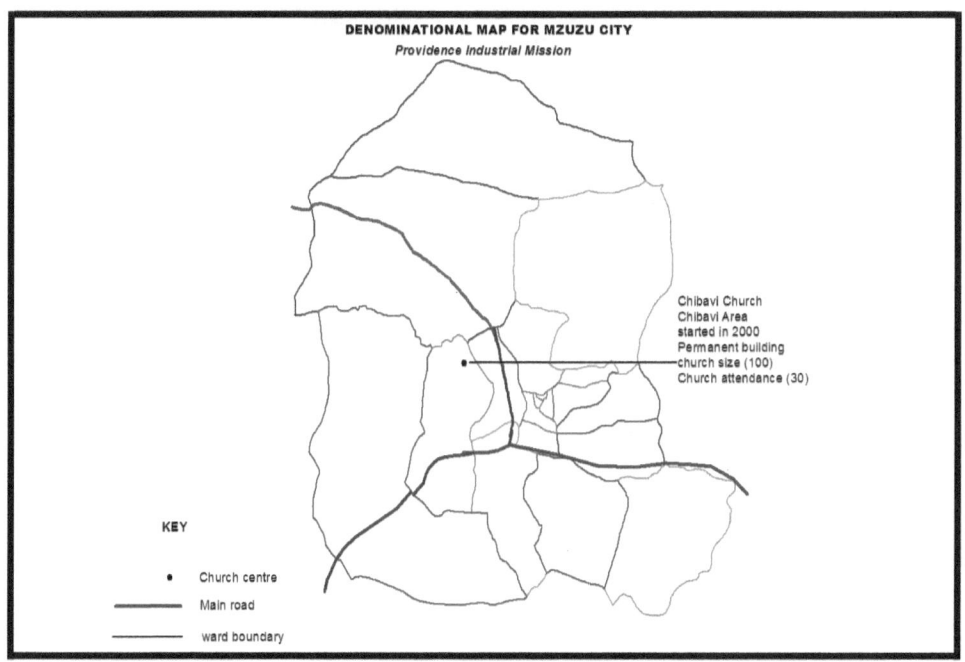

A-21

A-22

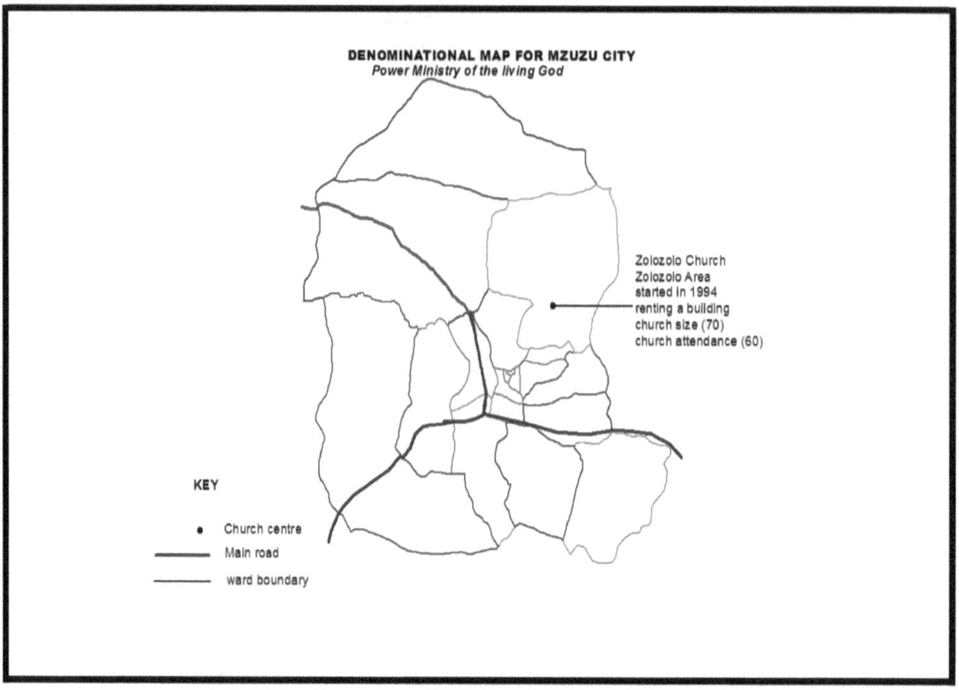

DENOMINATIONAL MAP FOR MZUZU CITY
Power Ministry of the living God

Zolozolo Church
Zolozolo Area
started in 1994
renting a building
church size (70)
church attendance (60)

KEY
- Church centre
- Main road
- ward boundary

A-23

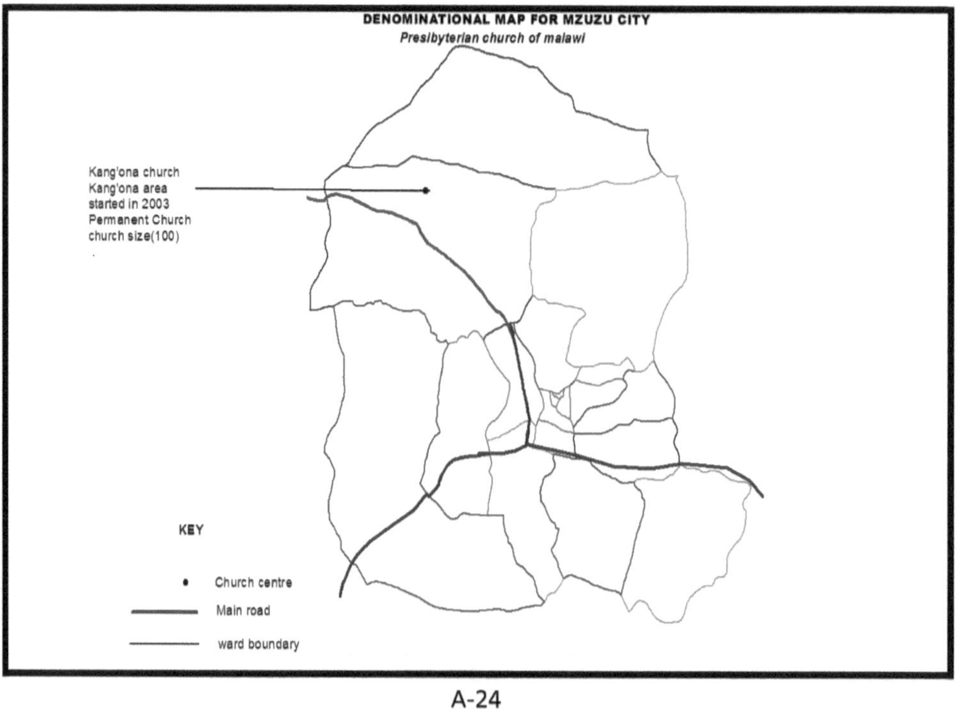

DENOMINATIONAL MAP FOR MZUZU CITY
Presbyterian church of malawi

Kang'ona church
Kang'ona area
started in 2003
Permanent Church
church size (100)

KEY
- Church centre
- Main road
- ward boundary

A-24

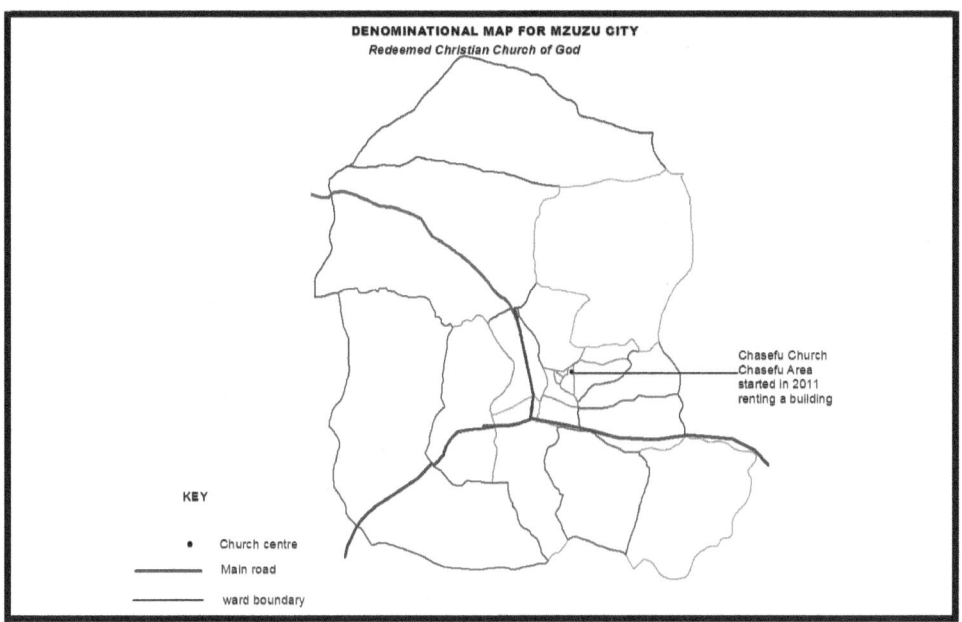

A-25

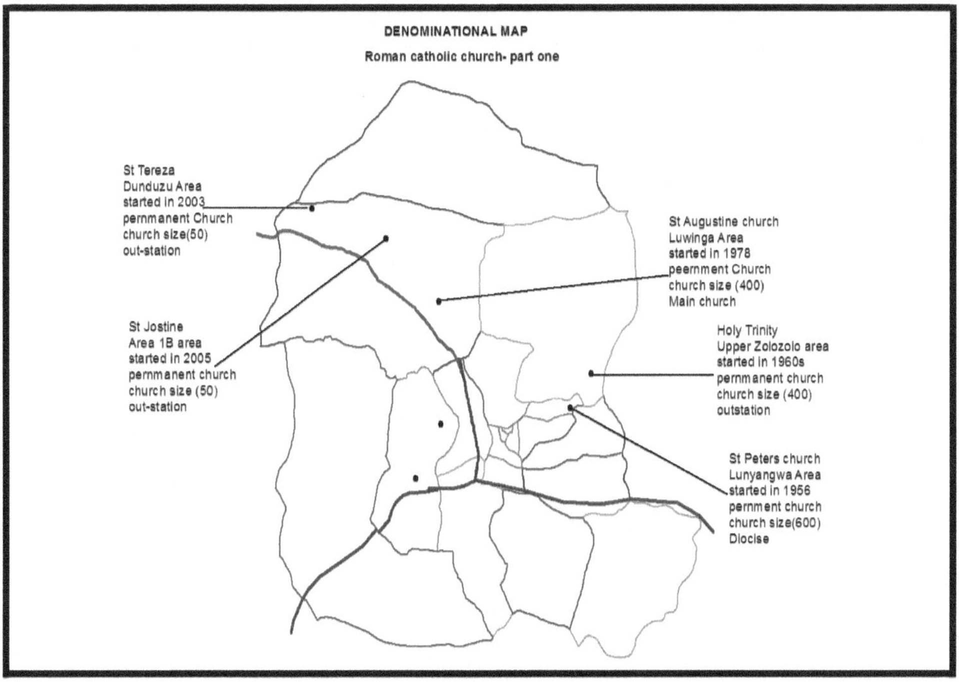

A-26a

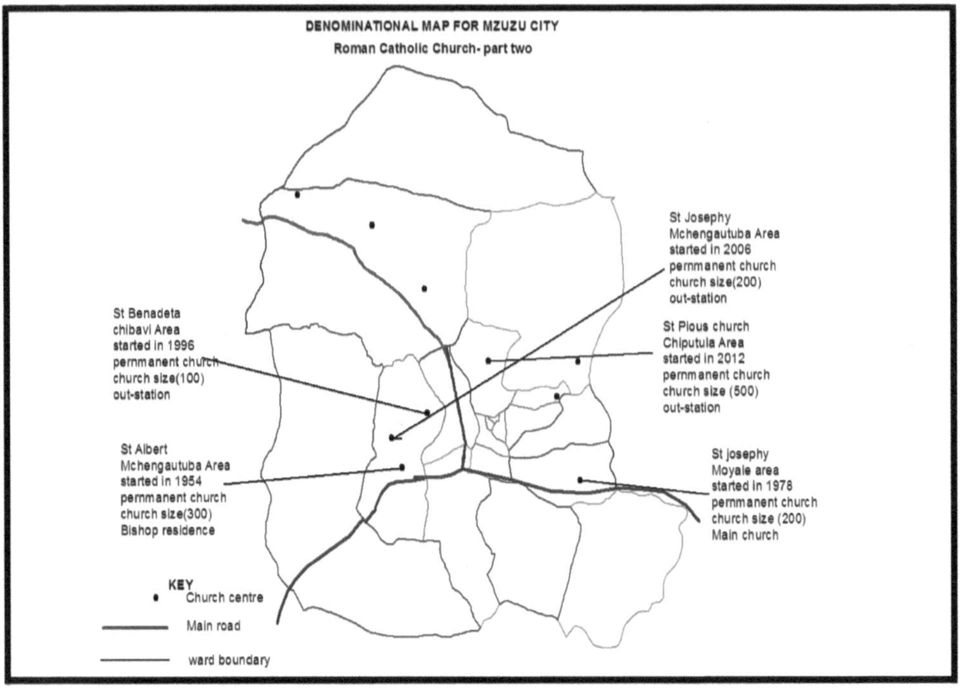

DENOMINATIONAL MAP FOR MZUZU CITY
Roman Catholic Church- part two

St Josephy
Mchengautuba Area
started in 2006
permanent church
church size(200)
out-station

St Benadeta
chibavi Area
started in 1996
permanent church
church size(100)
out-station

St Pious church
Chiputula Area
started in 2012
permanent church
church size (500)
out-station

St Albert
Mchengautuba Area
started in 1954
permanent church
church size(300)
Bishop residence

St josephy
Moyale area
started in 1978
permanent church
church size (200)
Main church

KEY
● Church centre
— Main road
— ward boundary

A-26b

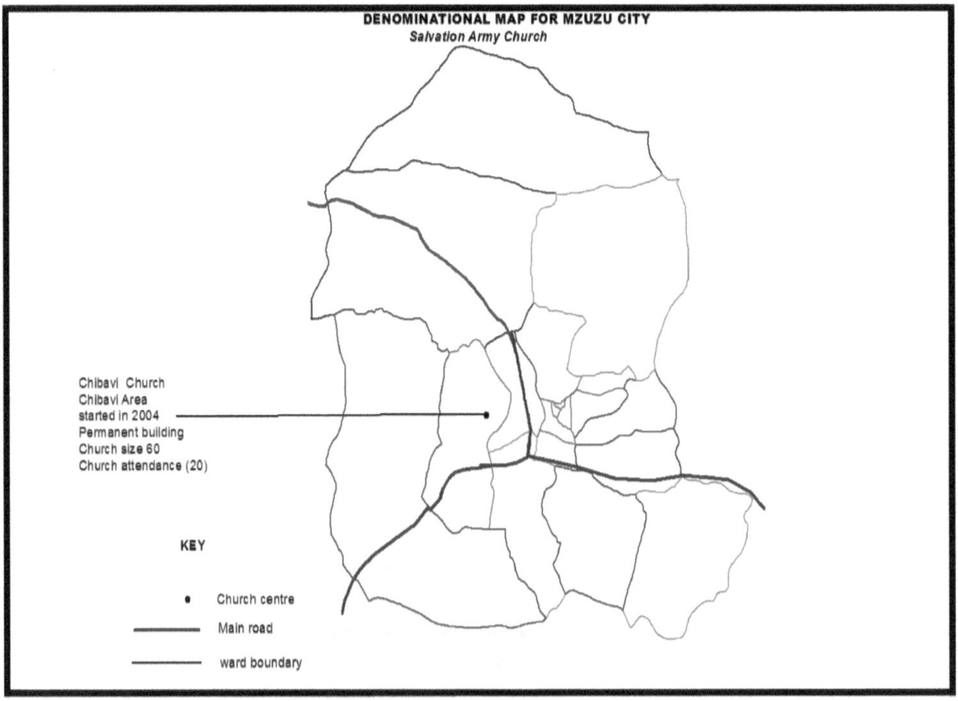

DENOMINATIONAL MAP FOR MZUZU CITY
Salvation Army Church

Chibavi Church
Chibavi Area
started in 2004
Permanent building
Church size 60
Church attendance (20)

KEY
● Church centre
— Main road
— ward boundary

A-27

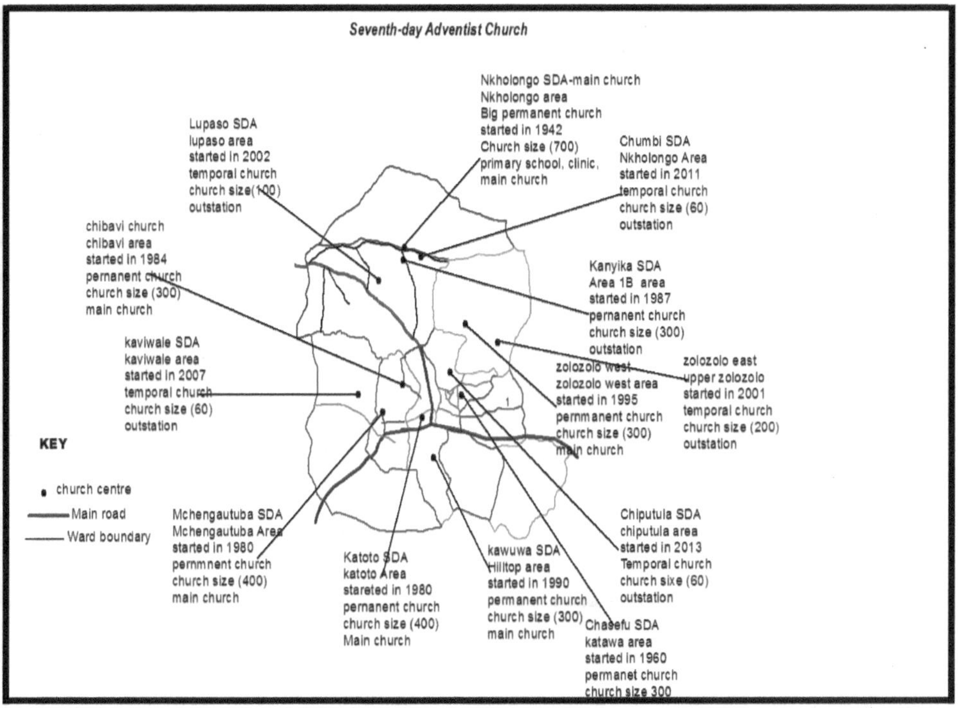

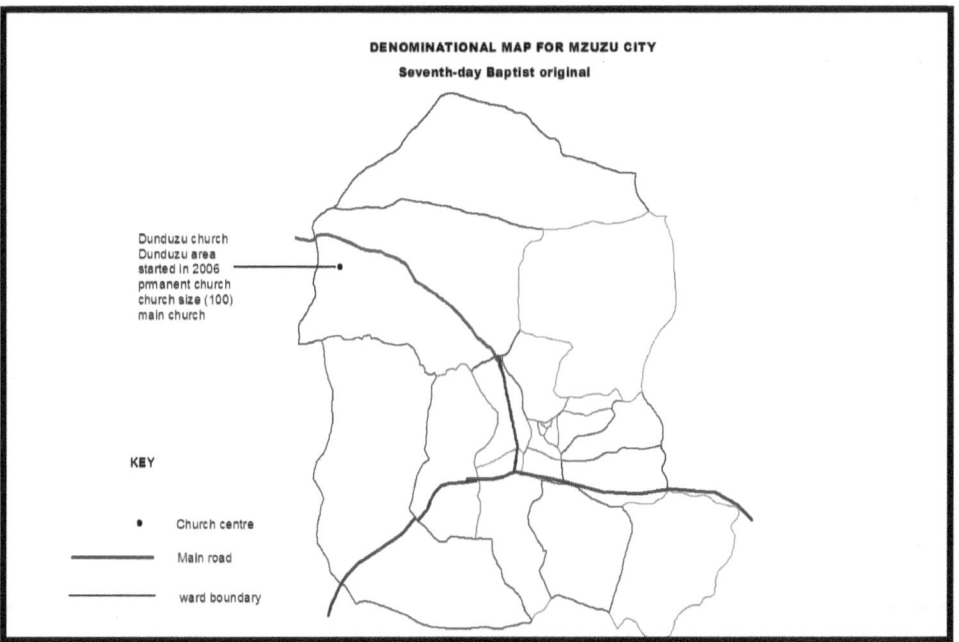

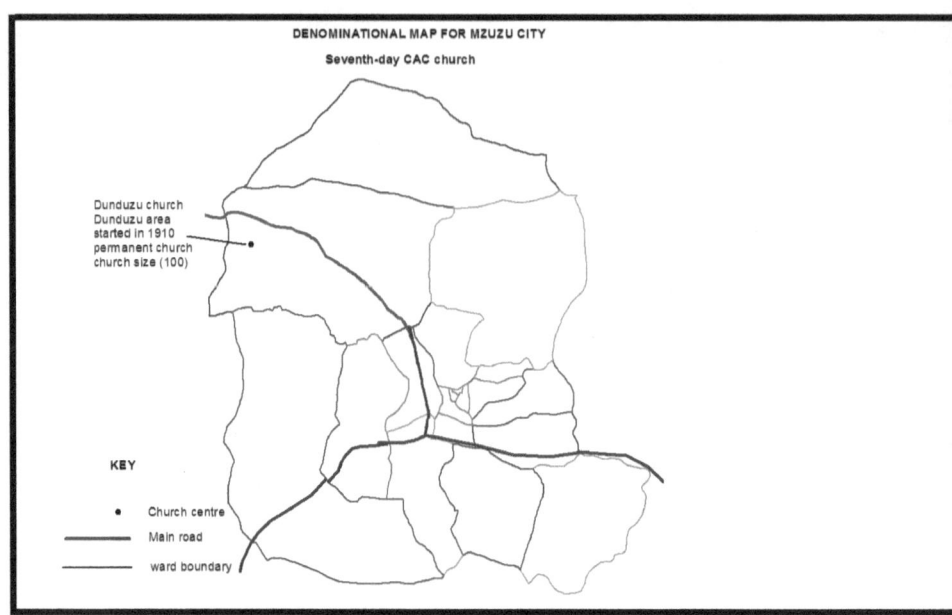

A-30

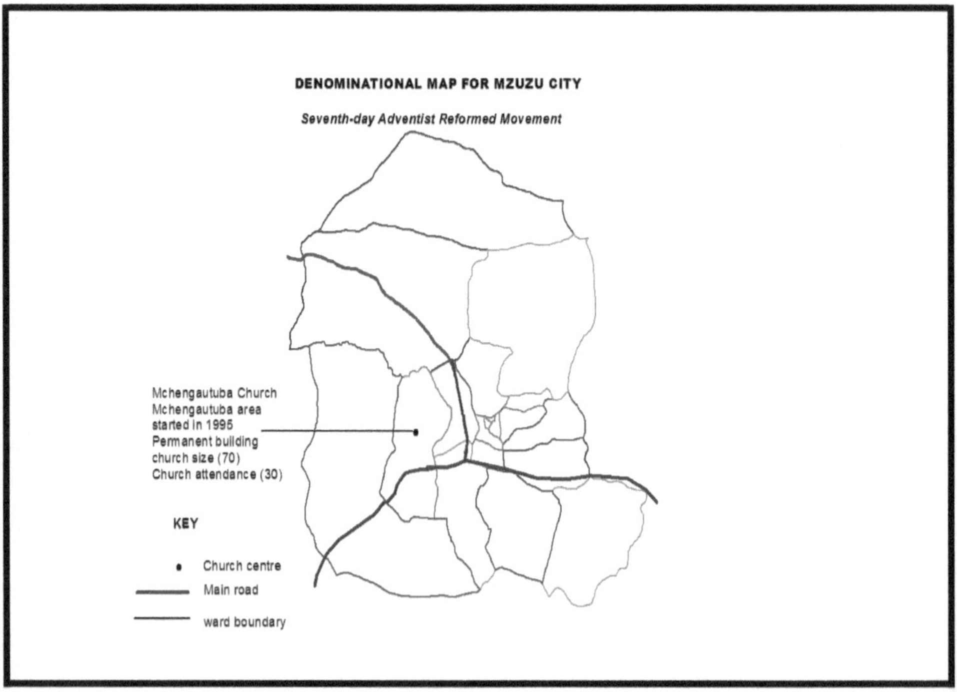

A-31

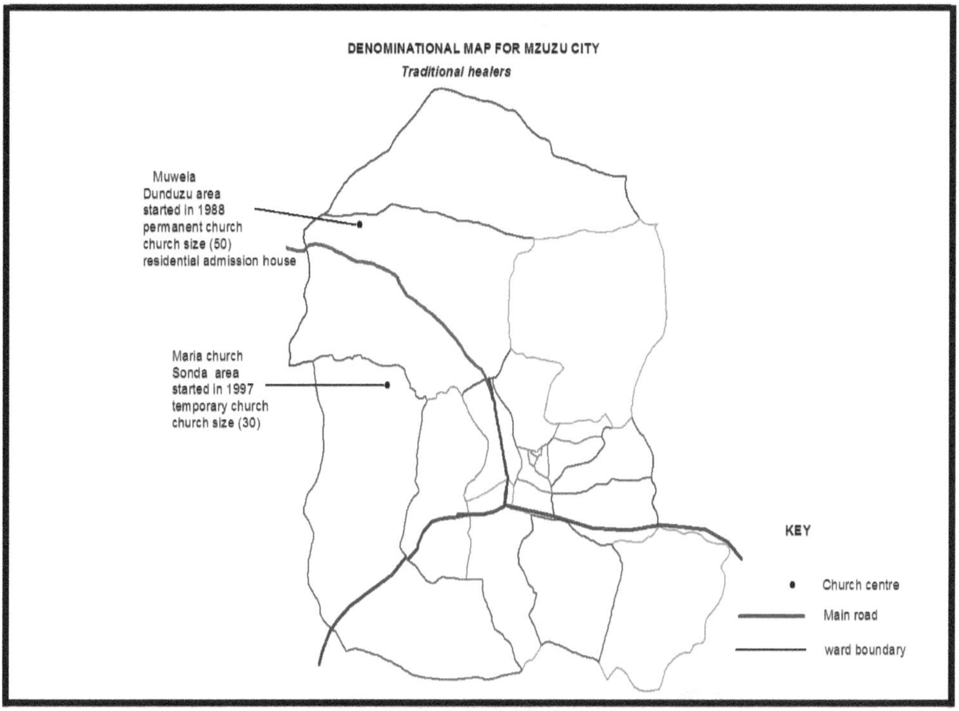

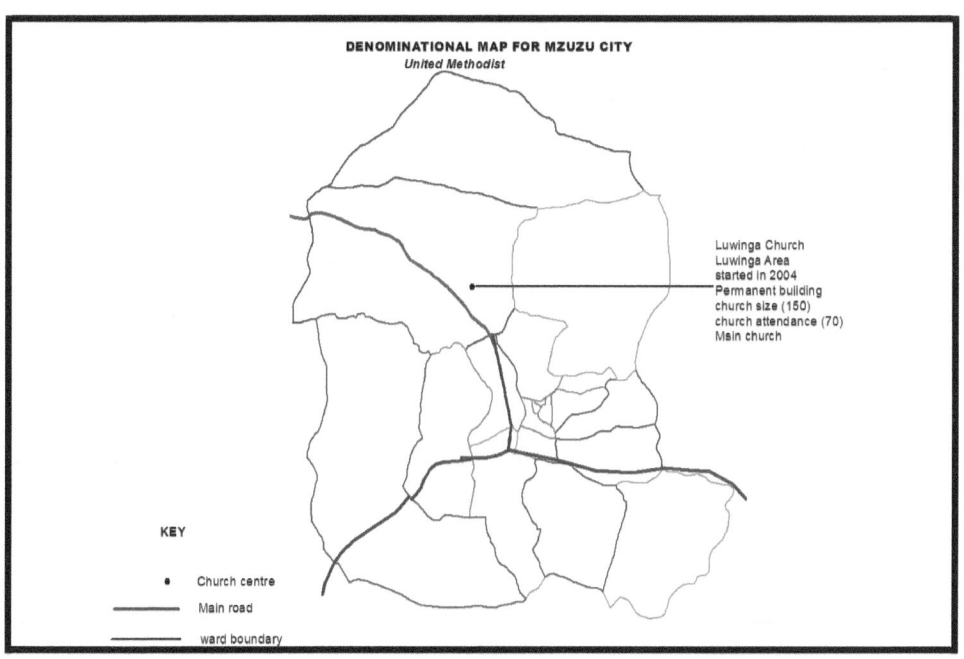

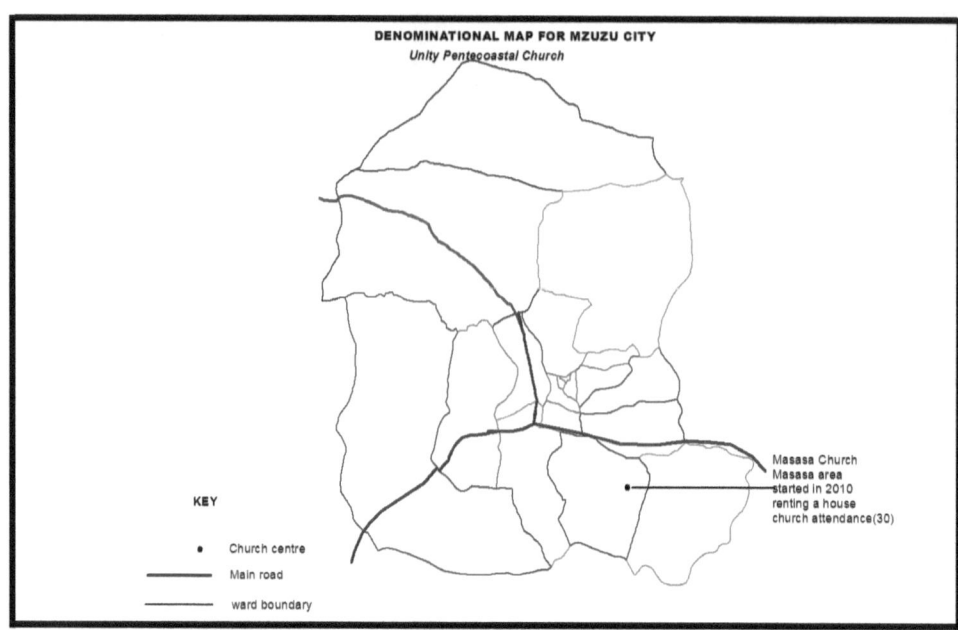

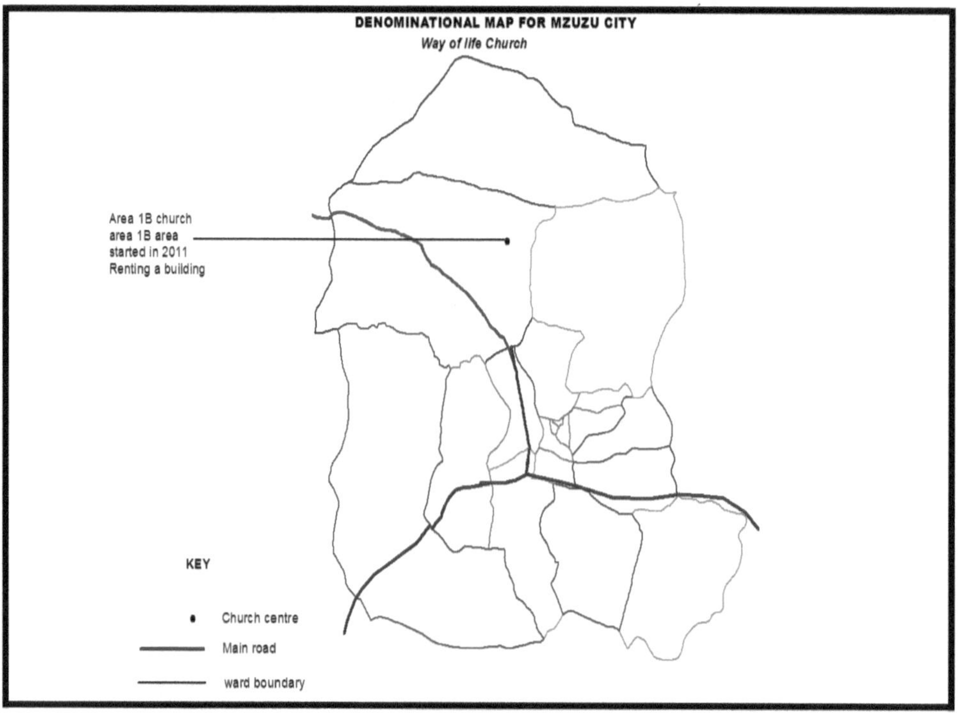

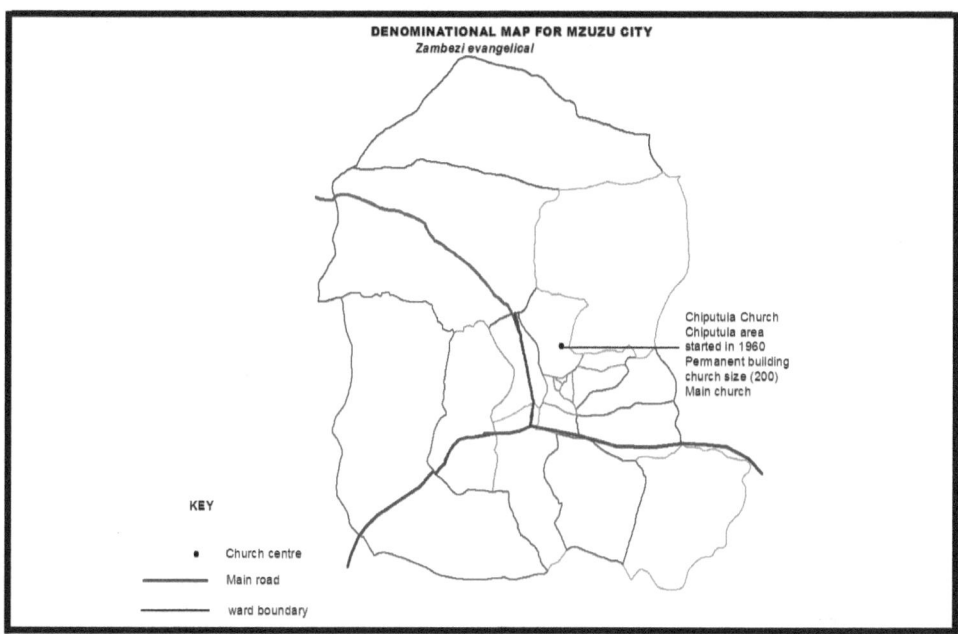

A-35

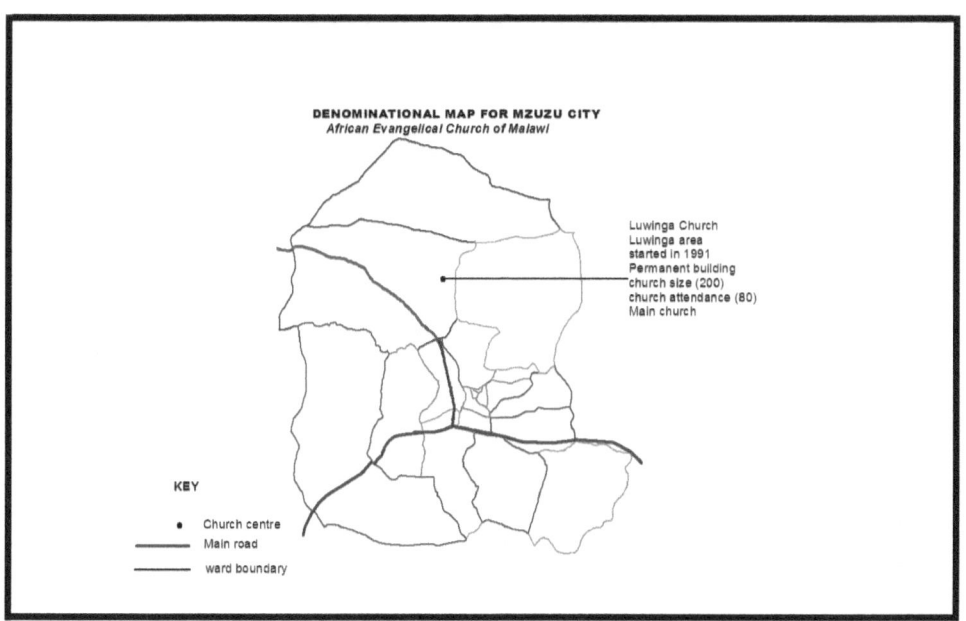

A-36

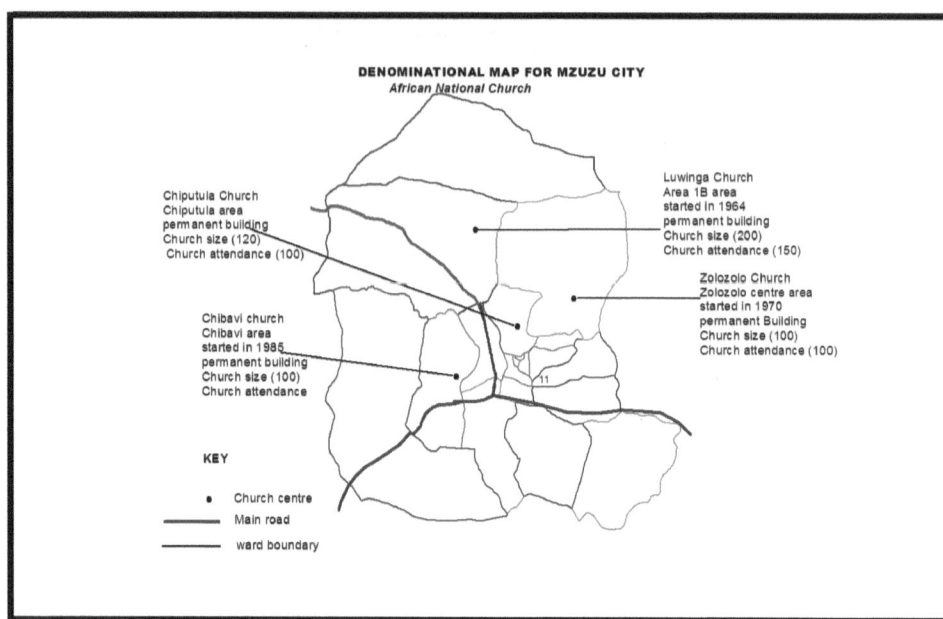

A-37

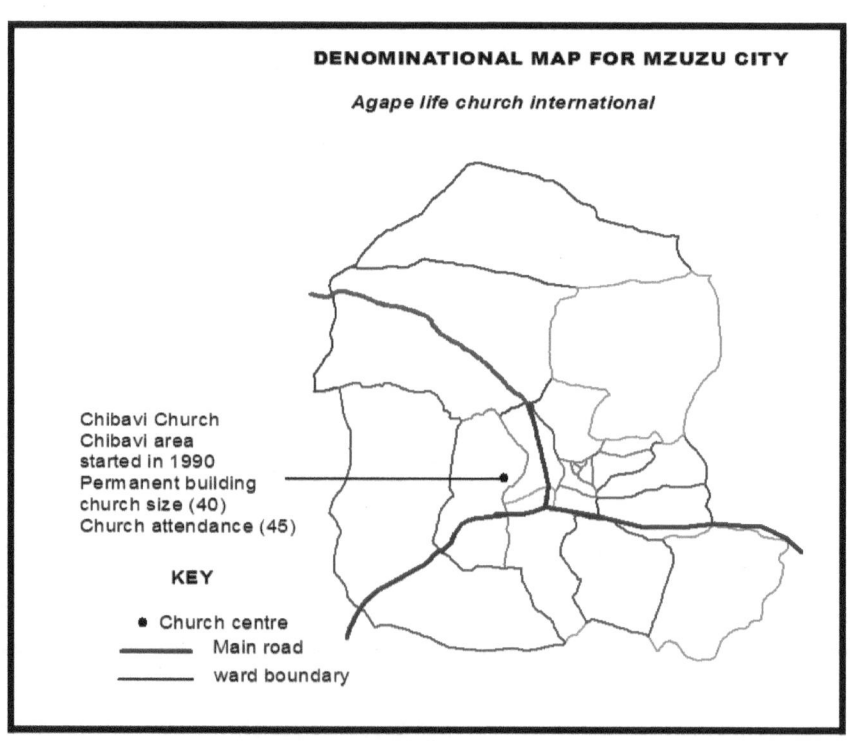

A-39

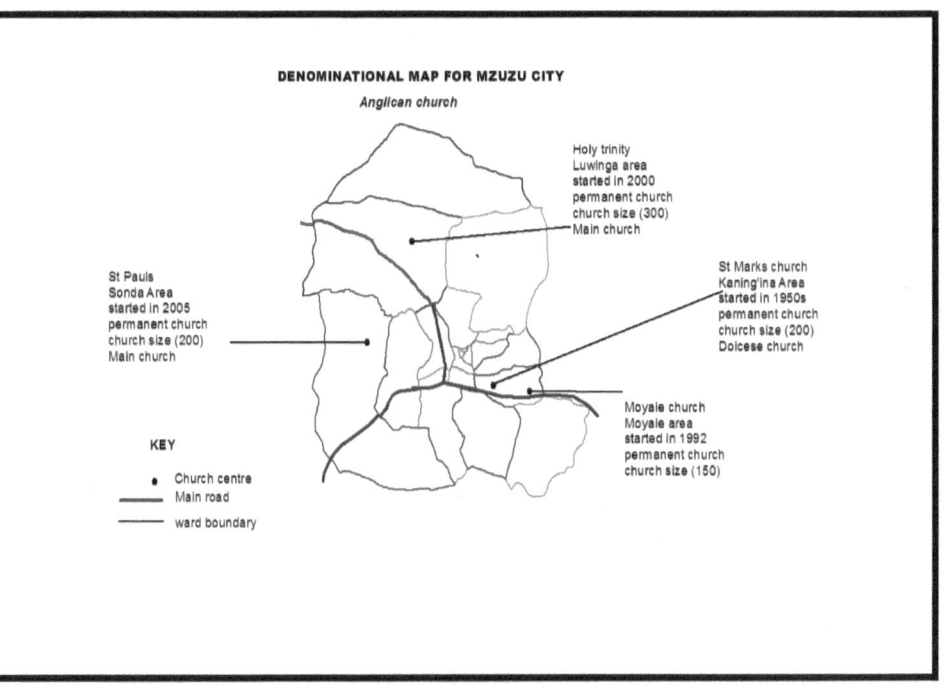

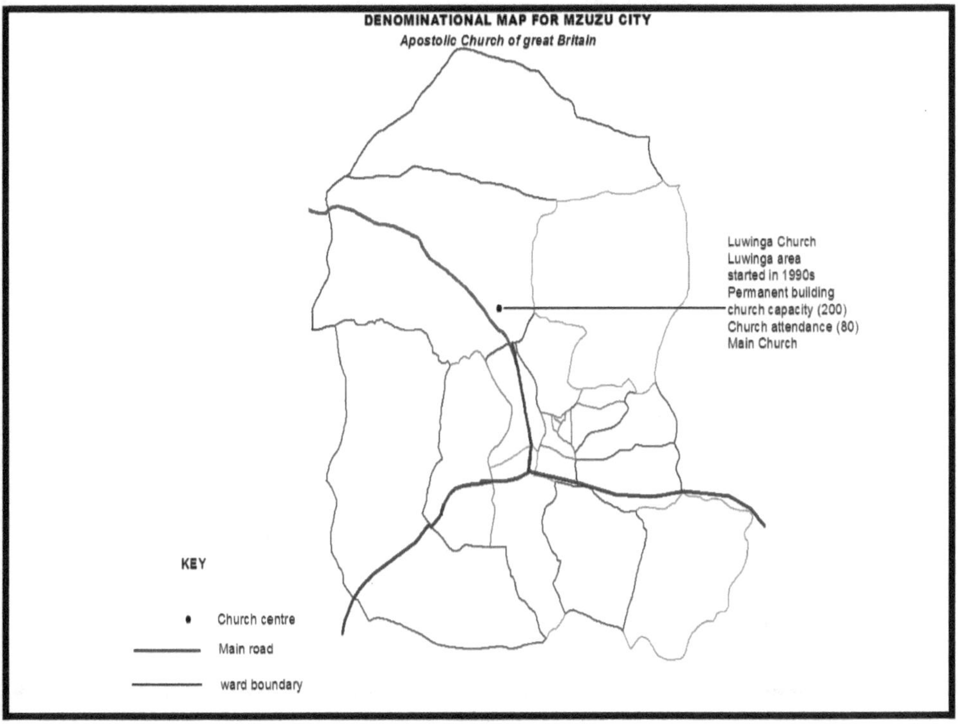

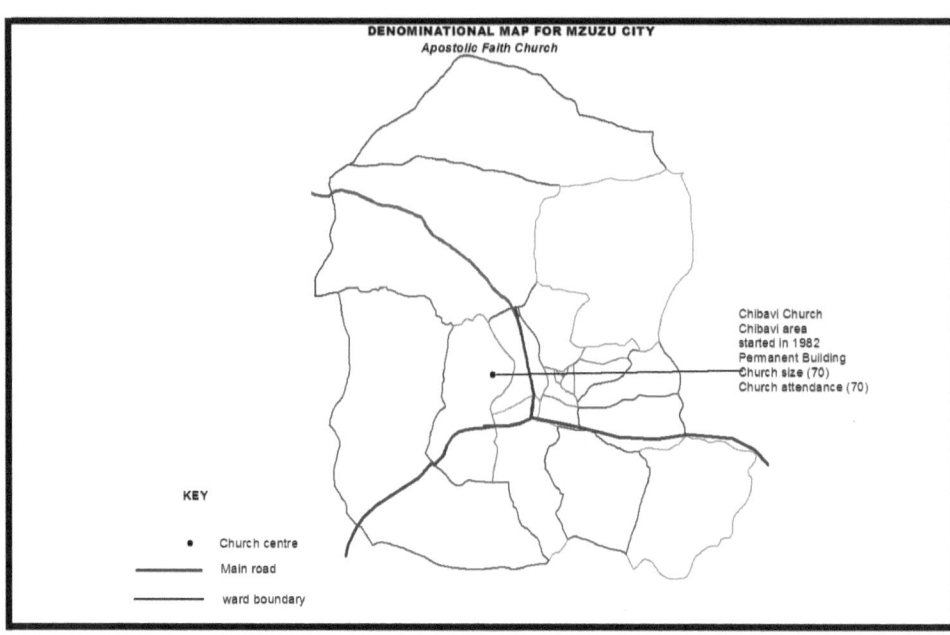

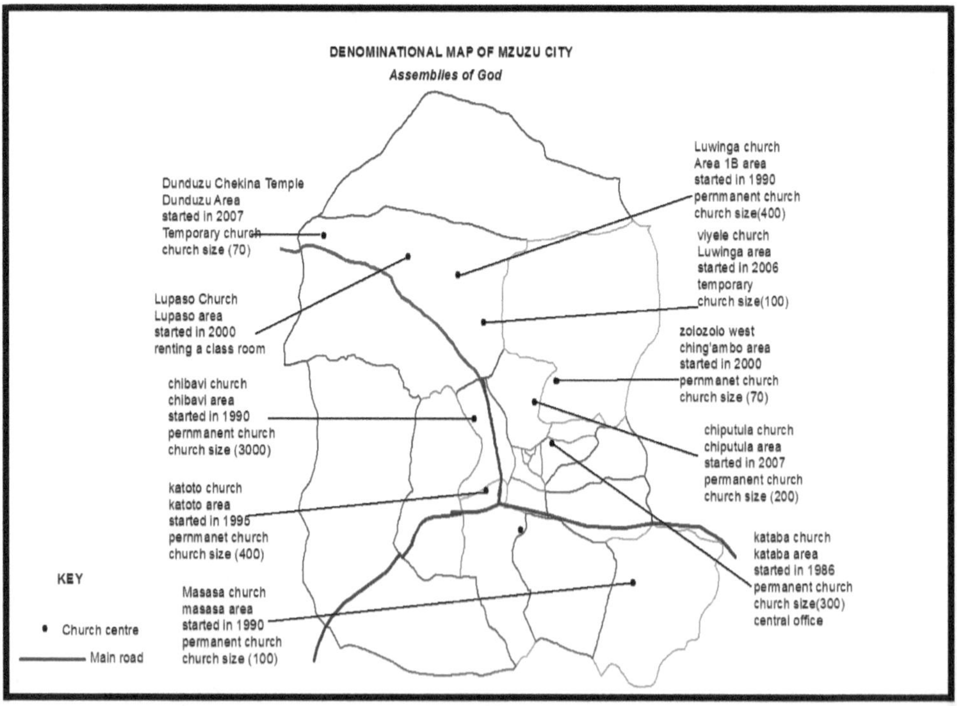

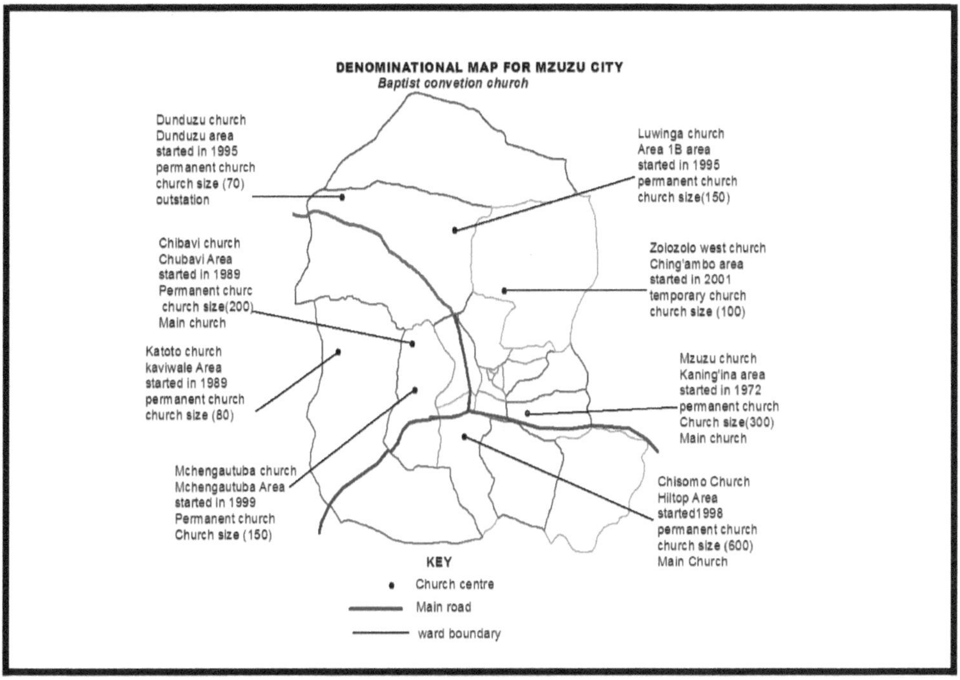

DENOMINATIONAL MAP FOR MZUZU CITY
Baptist convention church

Dunduzu church
Dunduzu area
started in 1995
permanent church
church size (70)
outstation

Luwinga church
Area 1B area
started in 1995
permanent church
church size (150)

Chibavi church
Chubavi Area
started in 1989
Permanent church
church size (200)
Main church

Zolozolo west church
Ching'ambo area
started in 2001
temporary church
church size (100)

Katoto church
kaviwale Area
started in 1989
permanent church
church size (80)

Mzuzu church
Kaning'ina area
started in 1972
permanent church
Church size (300)
Main church

Mchengautuba church
Mchengautuba Area
started in 1999
Permanent church
Church size (150)

Chisomo Church
Hilltop Area
started 1998
permanent church
church size (600)
Main Church

KEY
• Church centre
― Main road
― ward boundary

A-44

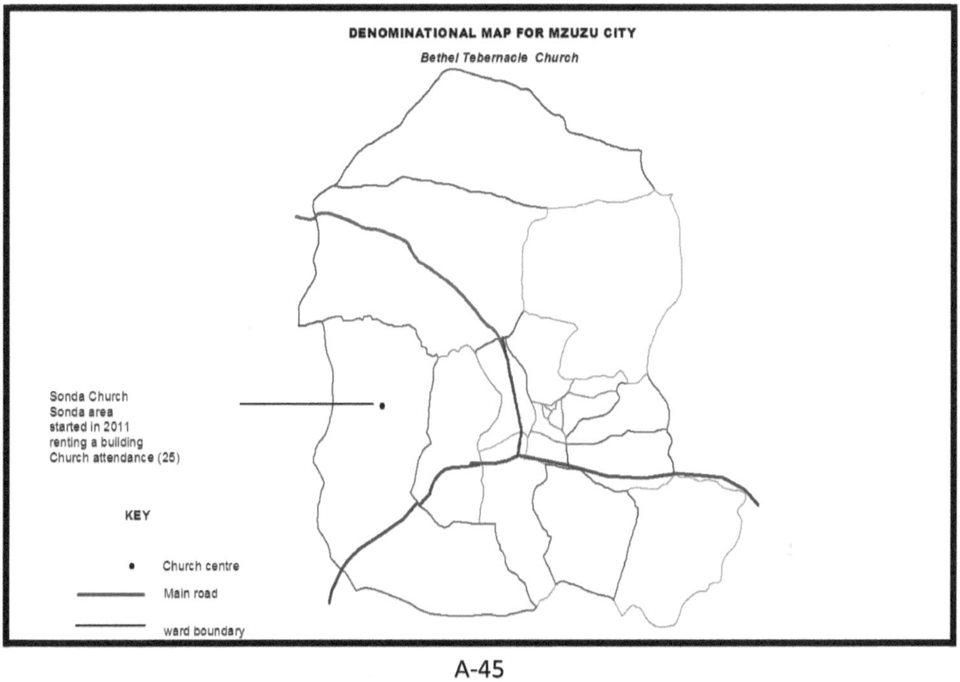

DENOMINATIONAL MAP FOR MZUZU CITY
Bethel Tebernacle Church

Sonda Church
Sonda area
started in 2011
renting a building
Church attendance (25)

KEY
• Church centre
― Main road
― ward boundary

A-45

387

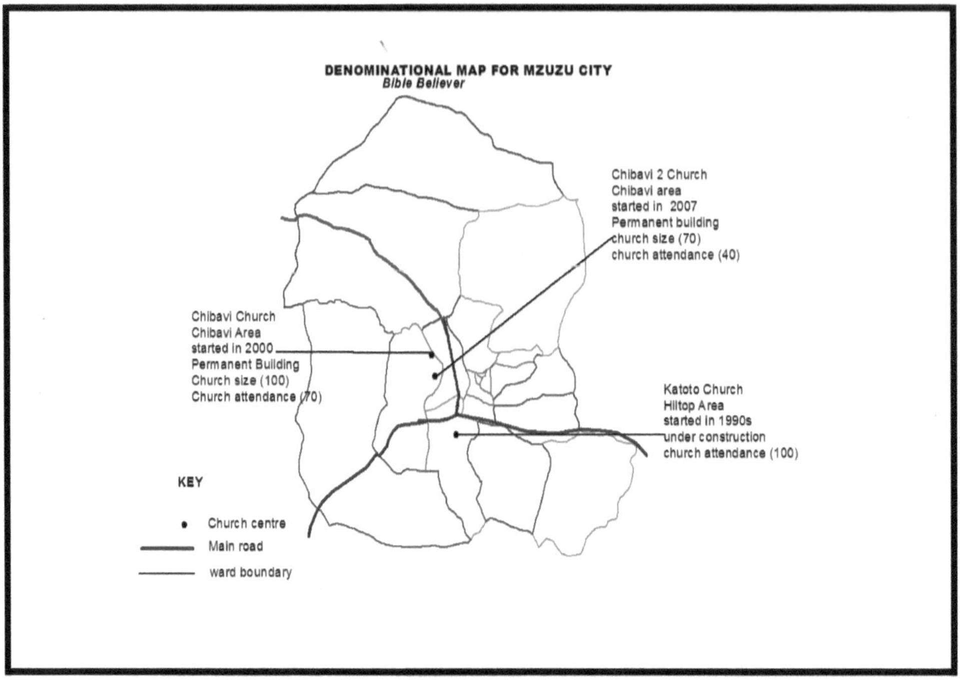

DENOMINATIONAL MAP FOR MZUZU CITY
Bible Believer

Chibavi 2 Church
Chibavi area
started in 2007
Permanent building
church size (70)
church attendance (40)

Chibavi Church
Chibavi Area
started in 2000
Permanent Building
Church size (100)
Church attendance (70)

Katoto Church
Hilltop Area
started in 1990s
under construction
church attendance (100)

KEY
• Church centre
— Main road
— ward boundary

A-46

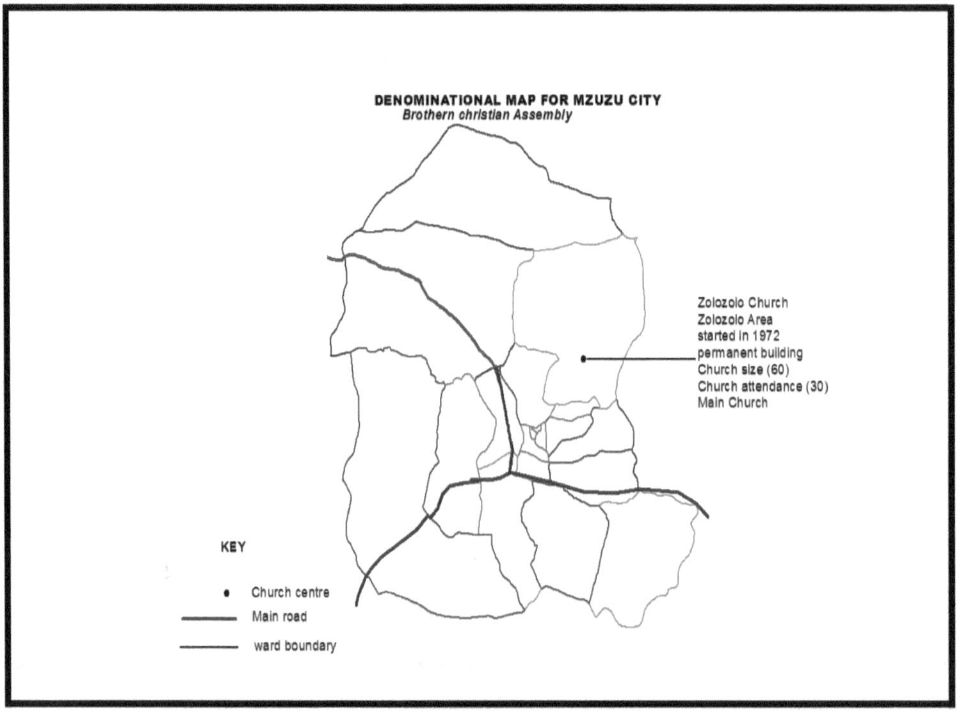

DENOMINATIONAL MAP FOR MZUZU CITY
Brothern christian Assembly

Zolozolo Church
Zolozolo Area
started in 1972
permanent building
Church size (60)
Church attendance (30)
Main Church

KEY
• Church centre
— Main road
— ward boundary

A-47

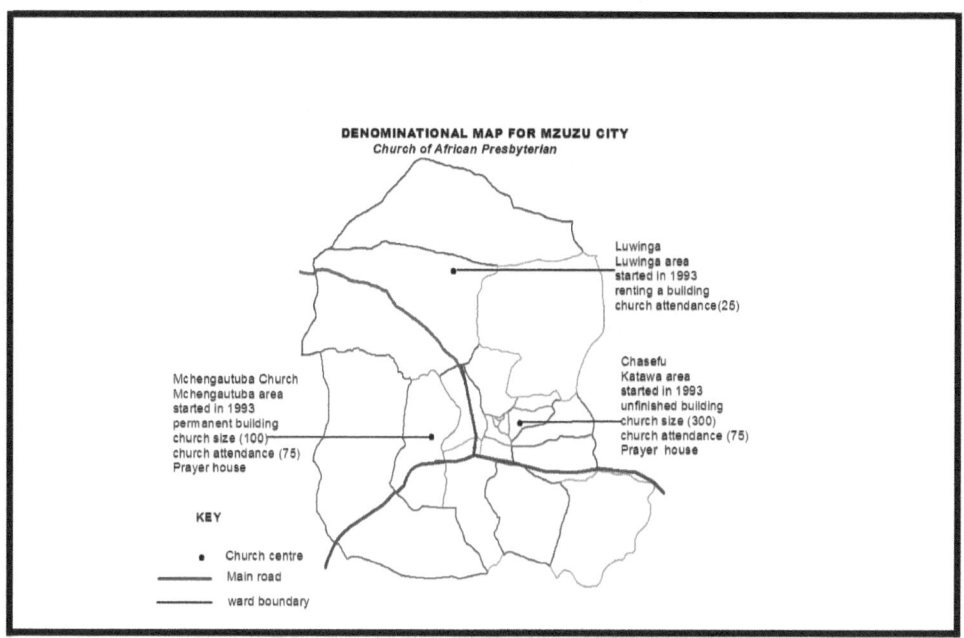

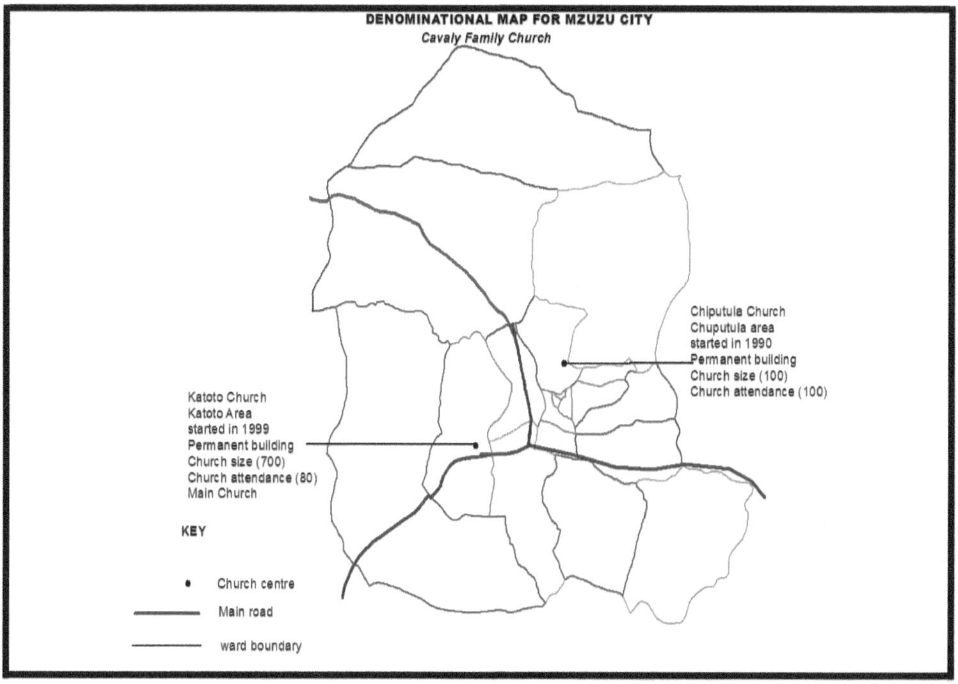

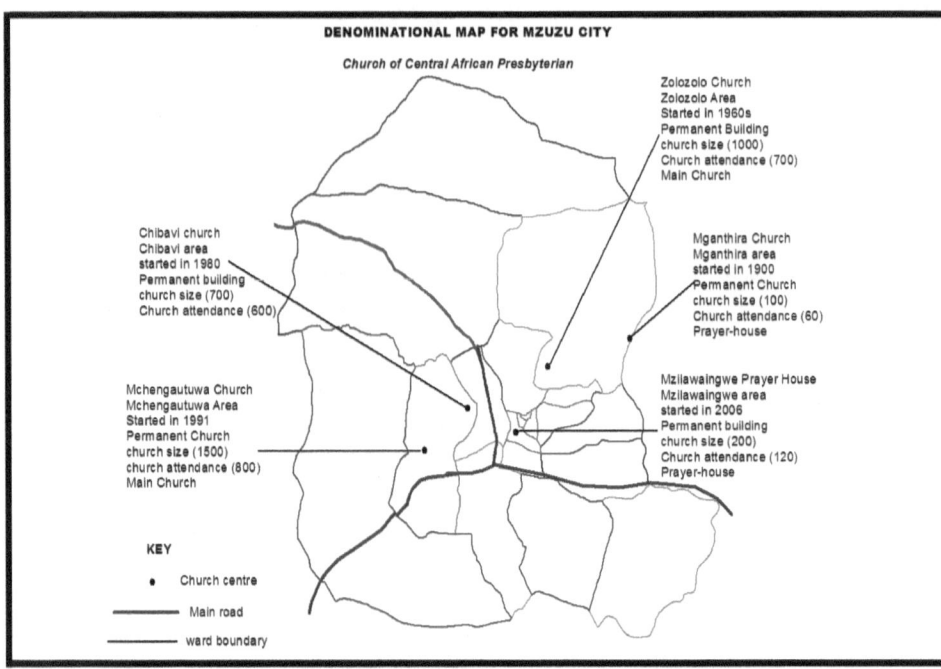

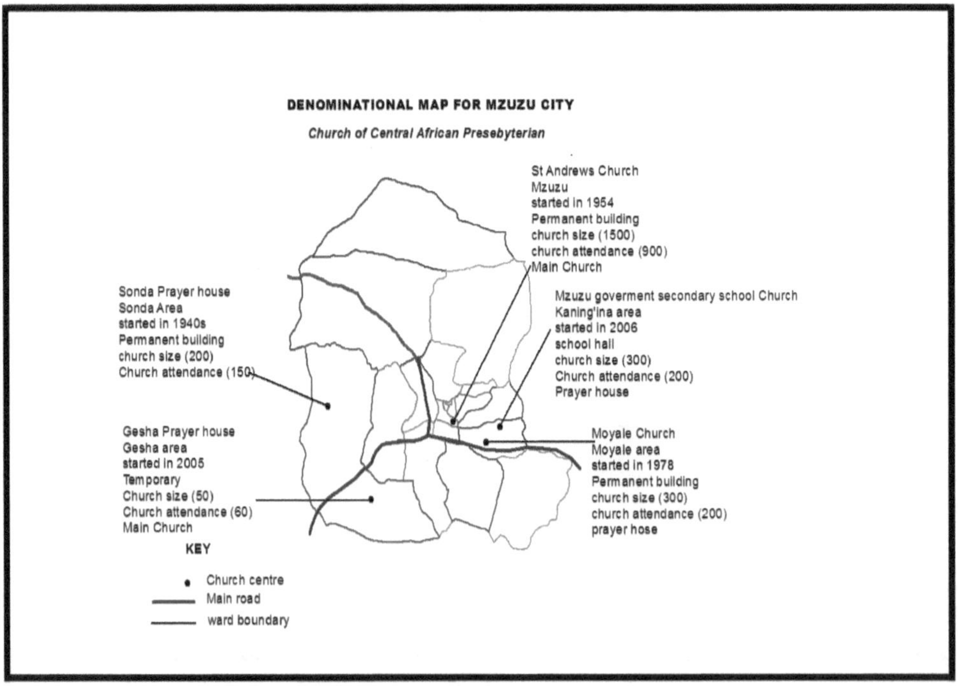

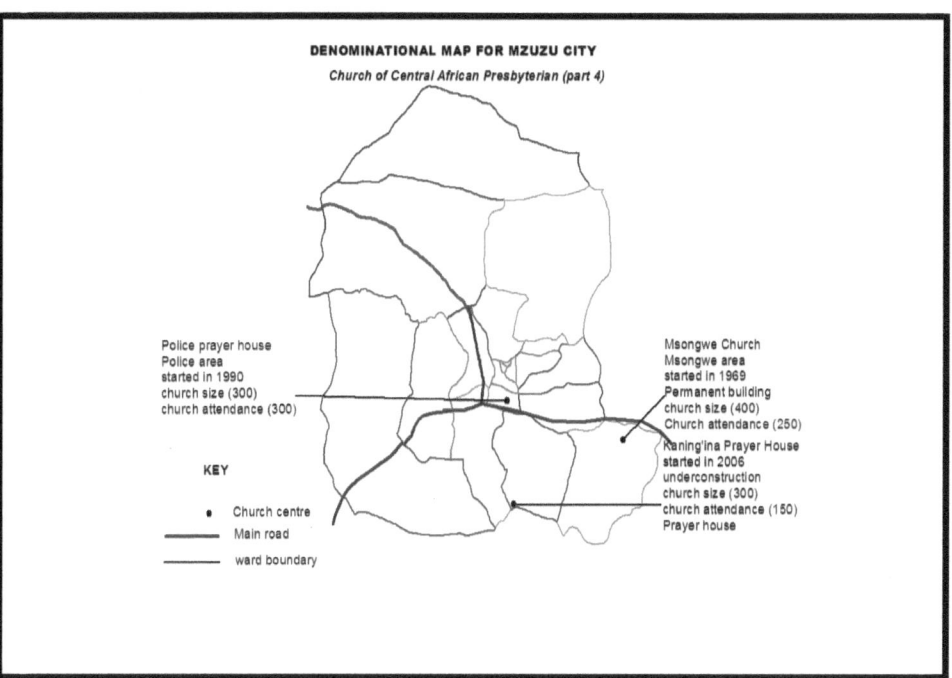

A-52

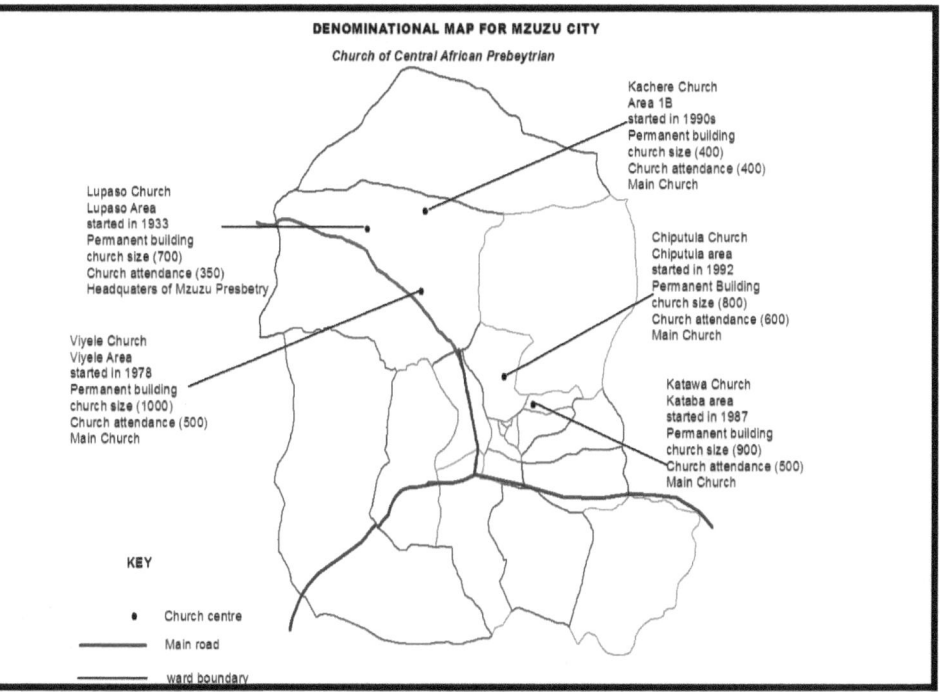

A-52

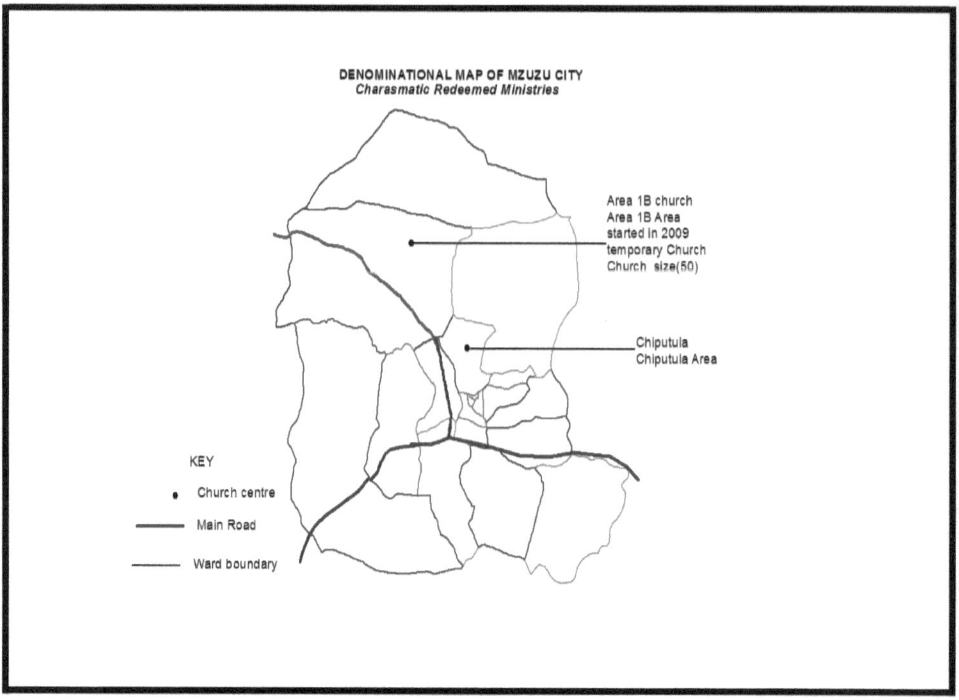

DENOMINATIONAL MAP OF MZUZU CITY
Charasmatic Redeemed Ministries

Area 1B church
Area 1B Area
started in 2009
temporary Church
Church size(50)

Chiputula
Chiputula Area

KEY
- Church centre
- Main Road
- Ward boundary

A-53

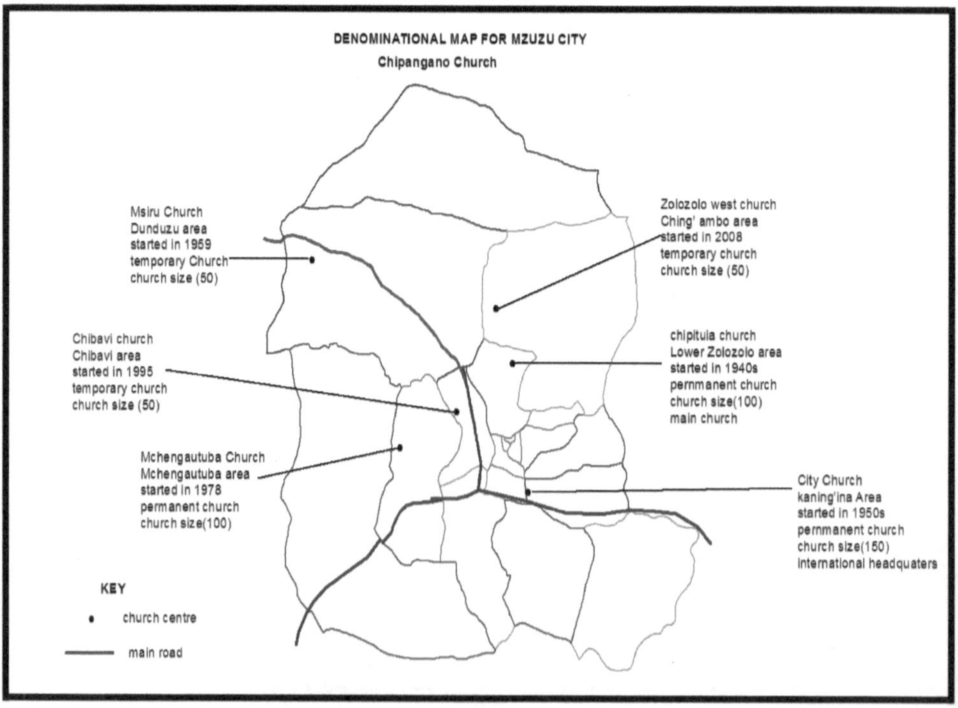

DENOMINATIONAL MAP FOR MZUZU CITY
Chipangano Church

Msiru Church
Dunduzu area
started in 1959
temporary Church
church size (50)

Zolozolo west church
Ching' ambo area
started in 2008
temporary church
church size (50)

Chibavi church
Chibavi area
started in 1995
temporary church
church size (50)

chiputula church
Lower Zolozolo area
started in 1940s
pernmanent church
church size(100)
main church

Mchengautuba Church
Mchengautuba area
started in 1978
permanent church
church size(100)

City Church
kaning'ina Area
started in 1950s
pernmanent church
church size(150)
international headquaters

KEY
- church centre
- main road

A-54

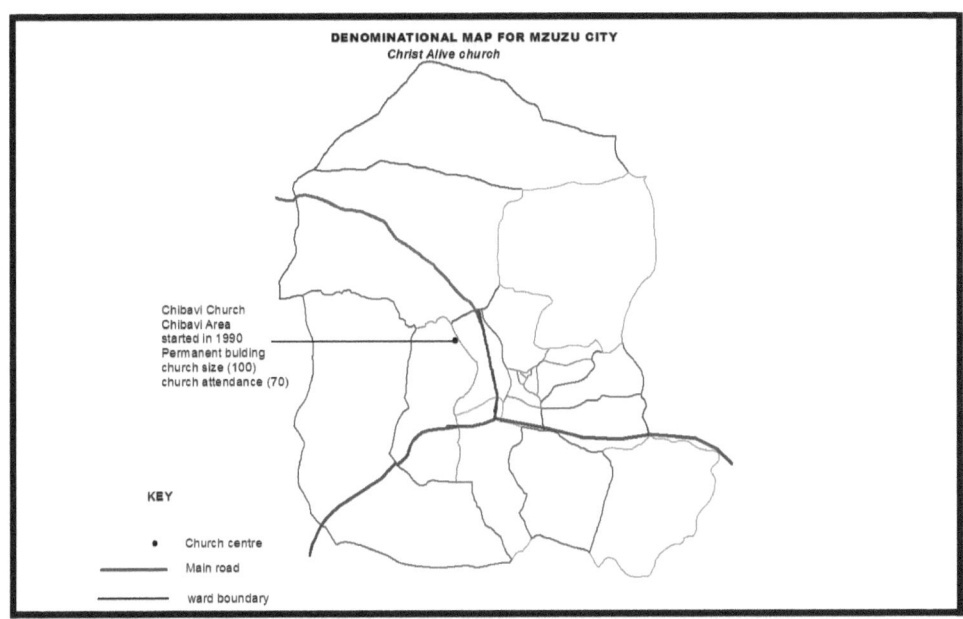

A-55

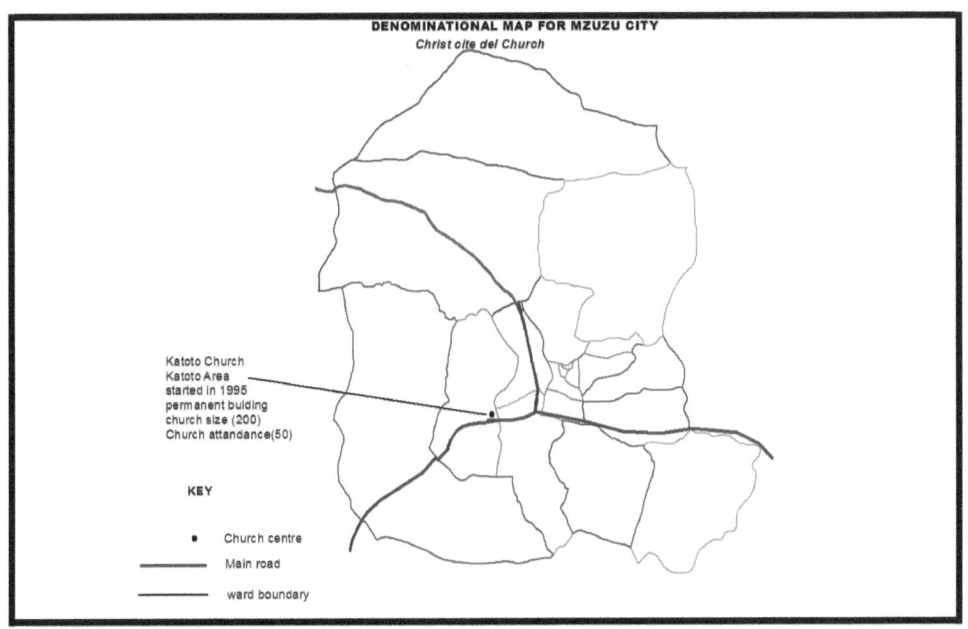

A-56

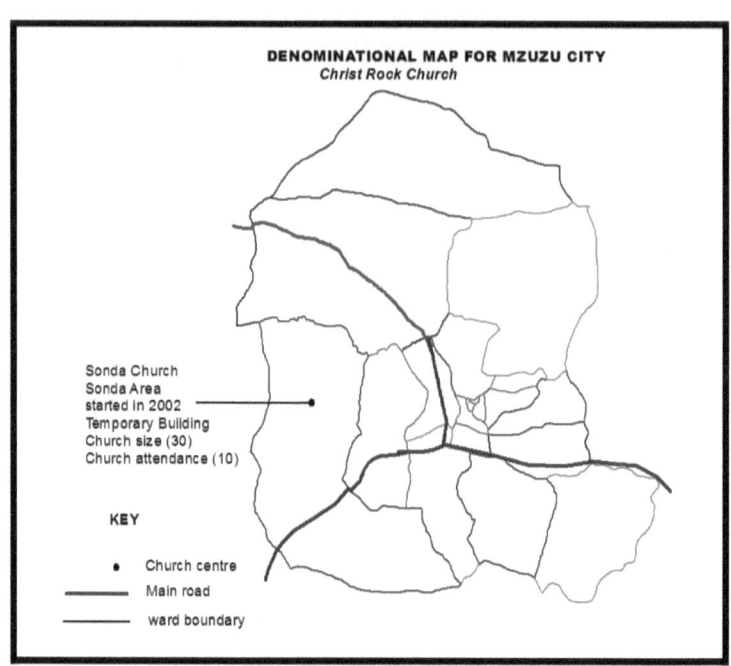

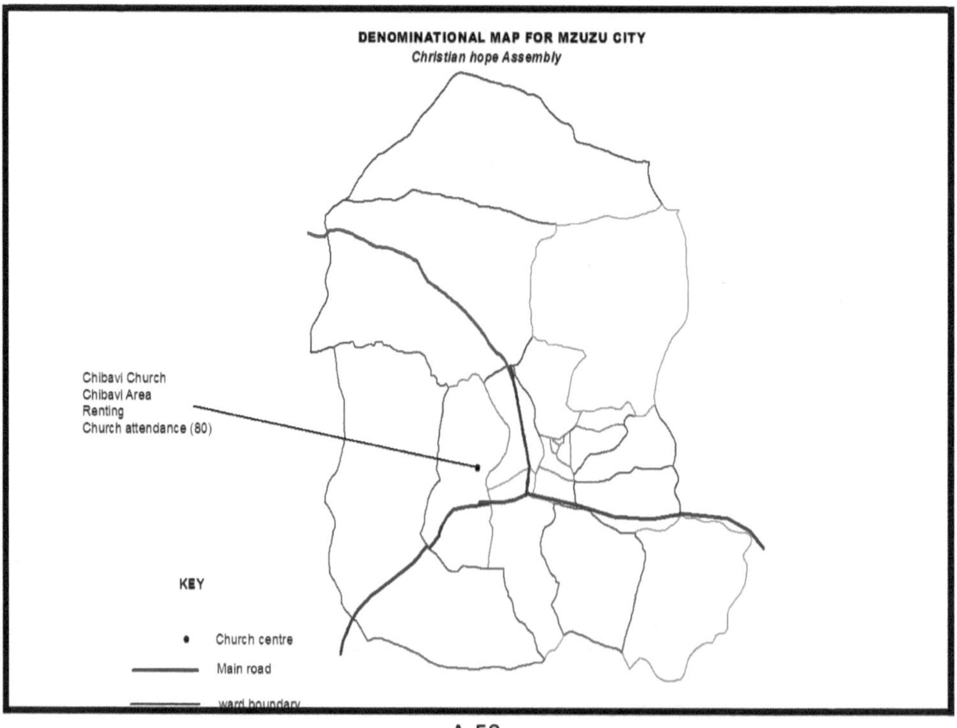

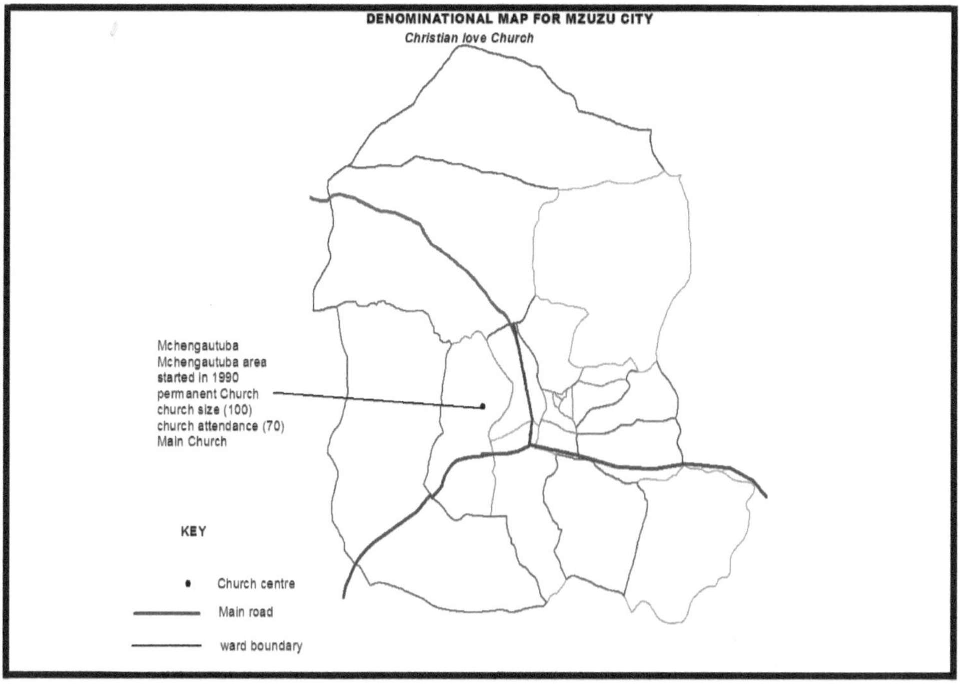
DENOMINATIONAL MAP FOR MZUZU CITY
Christian love Church
Mchengautuba
Mchengautuba area
started in 1990
permanent Church
church size (100)
church attendance (70)
Main Church
KEY
Church centre
Main road
ward boundary

A-60

Denominational Map of Mzuzu city
Church of Christ
Nkholongo church
Area 1B area
started in 1990
permanent church
church size(100)
Area 1B church
Area 1B area
started in 2008
permanent church
church size(60)
Zolozolo west Church
Lower zolozolo area
started in 1990s
permanent church
church size (150)
Mzuzu bible college
Luwinga area
started in 1992
permanent church
church size (300)
chiputula church
chiputula area
started in 2005
renting a building
Kaviwale Church
Sonda Area
started in 2004
temporary church
church size (70)
Jomo kenyatta Road
Kaning'ina Area
started in 1968
Permanent Church'
church size(500)
Regional central office

A-61

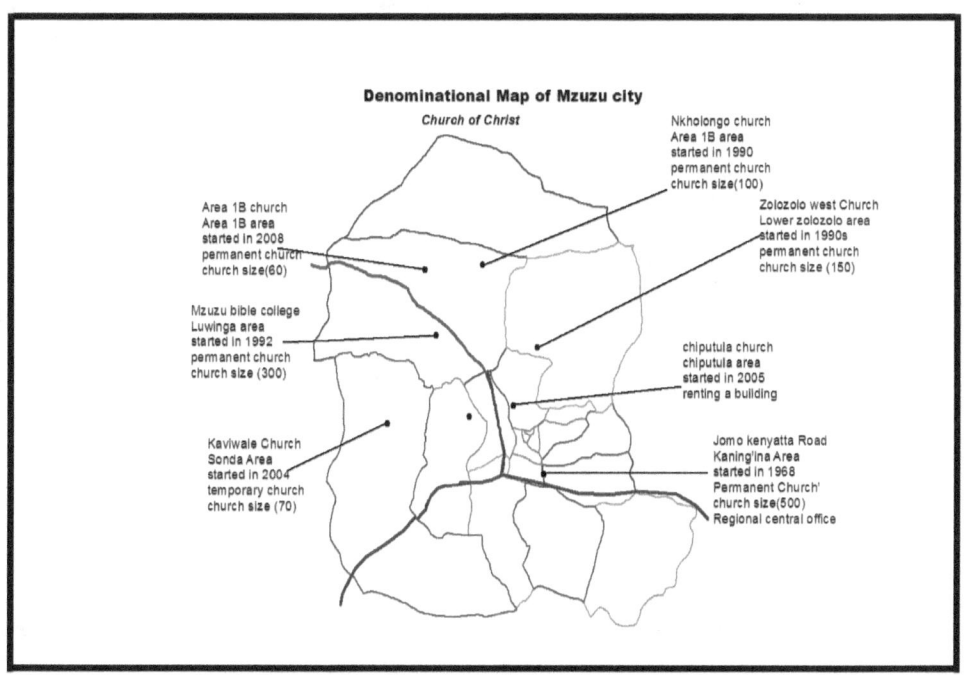

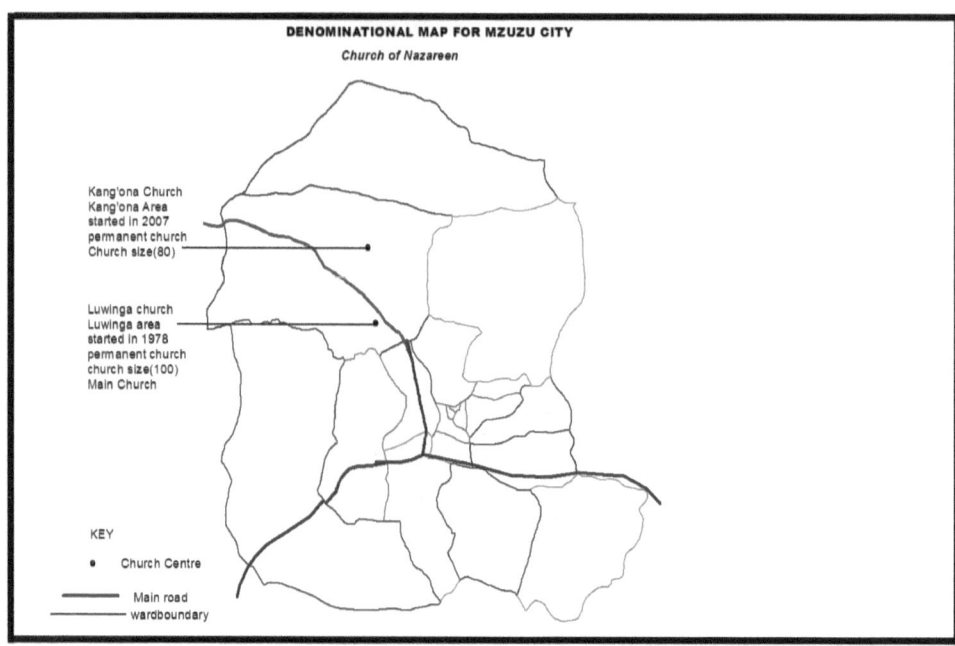

A-62

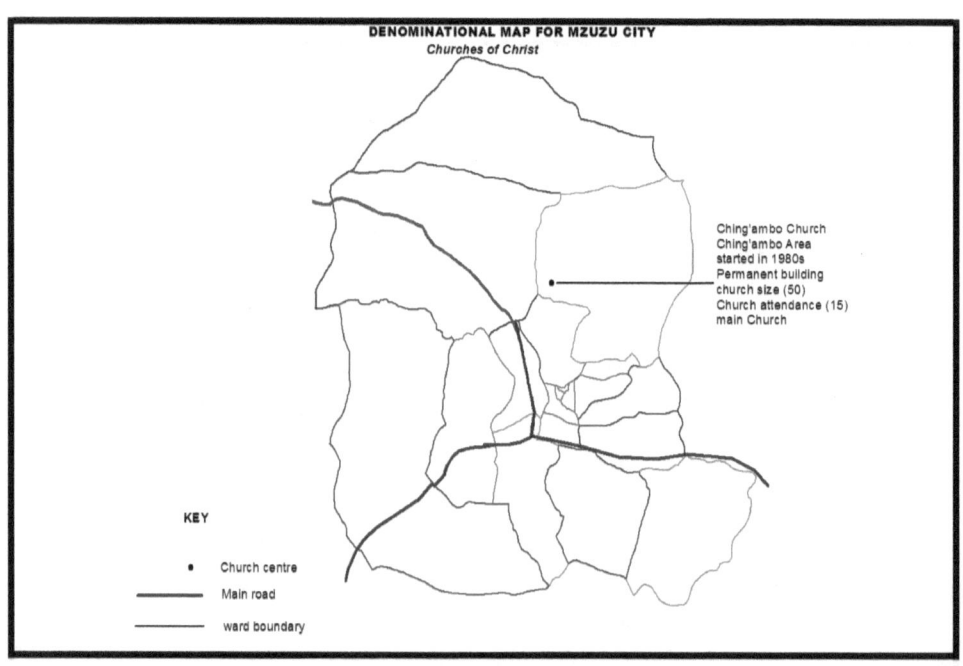

A-63

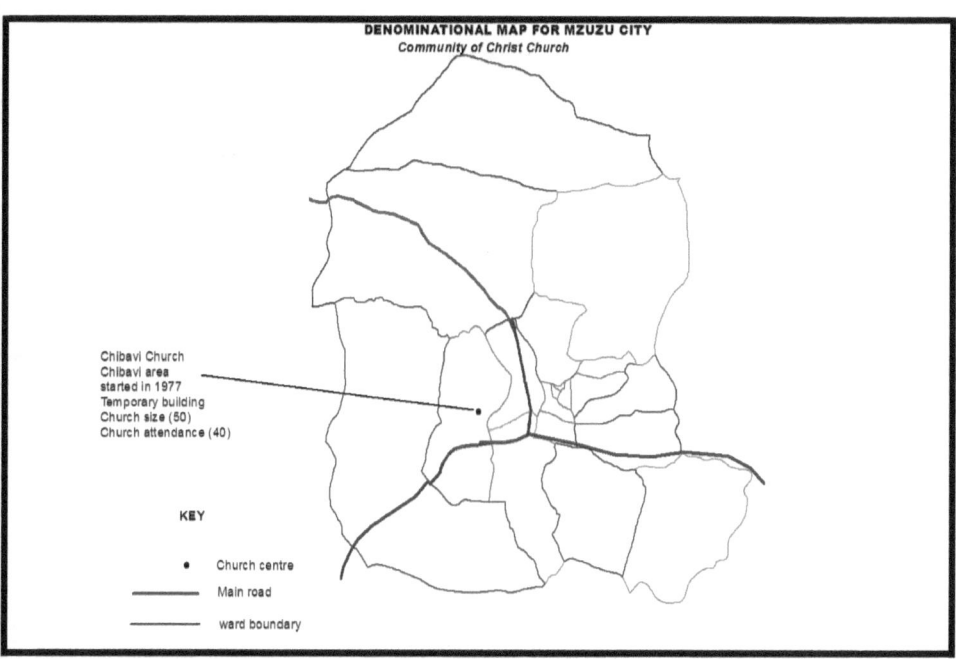

A-64

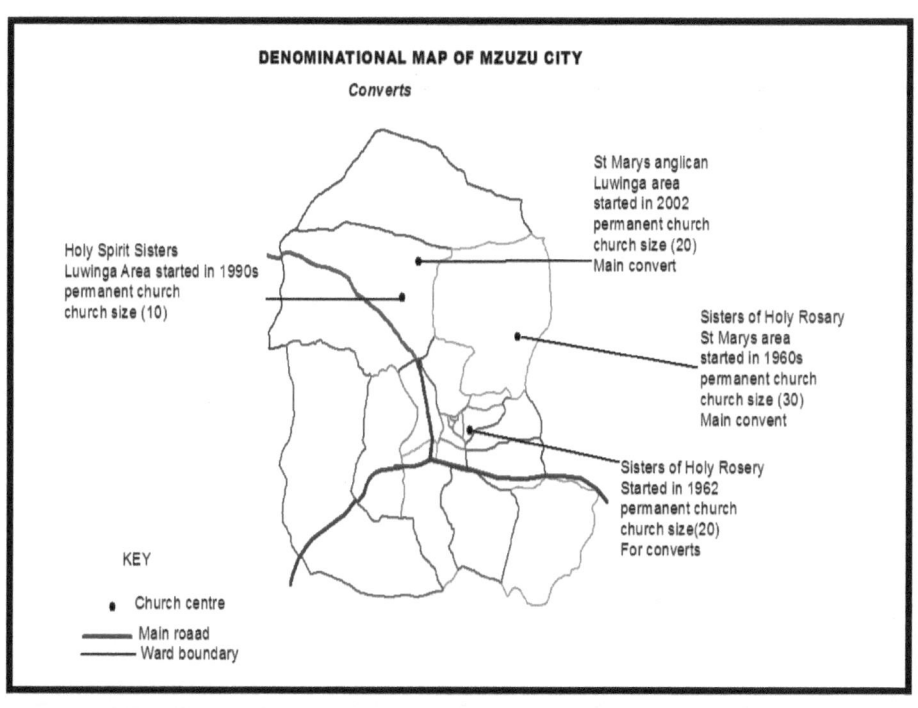

A-65

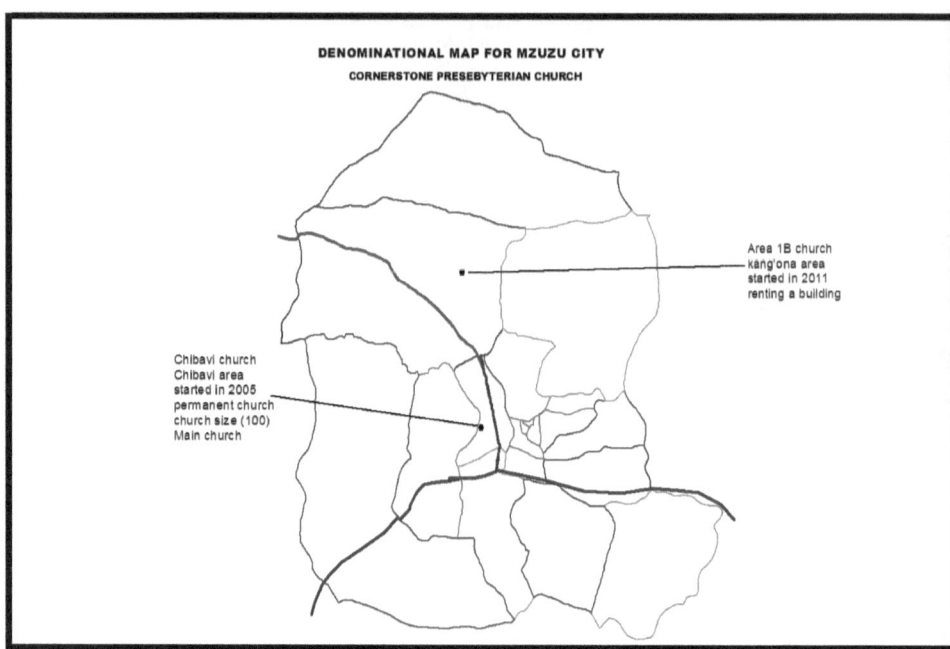

A-66

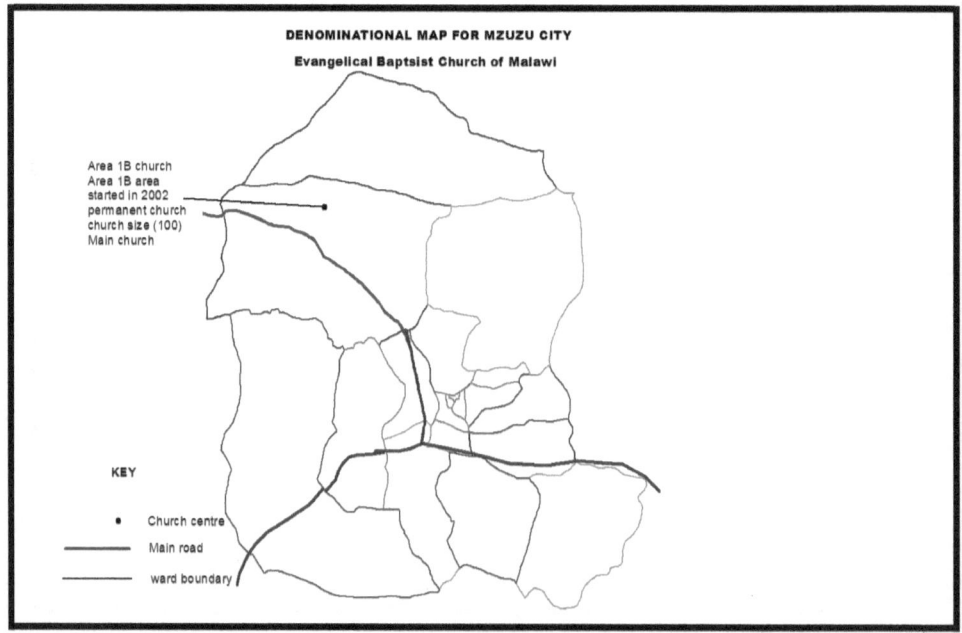

A-67

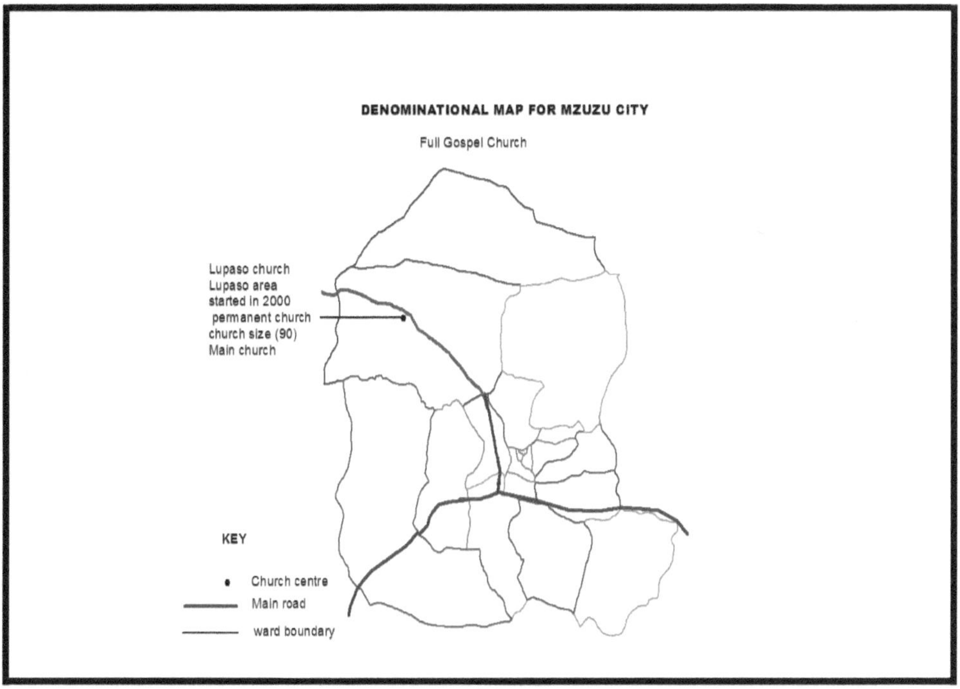
DENOMINATIONAL MAP FOR MZUZU CITY
Full Gospel Church
Lupaso church
Lupaso area
started in 2000
permanent church
church size (90)
Main church
KEY
Church centre
Main road
ward boundary

A-68

DENOMINATIONAL MAP FOR MZUZU CITY
Glorious Light Church
Kawuwa Church
started in 2003
renting a building
church size(50)
Church attandance (10)
KEY
Church centre
Main road
ward boundary

A-69

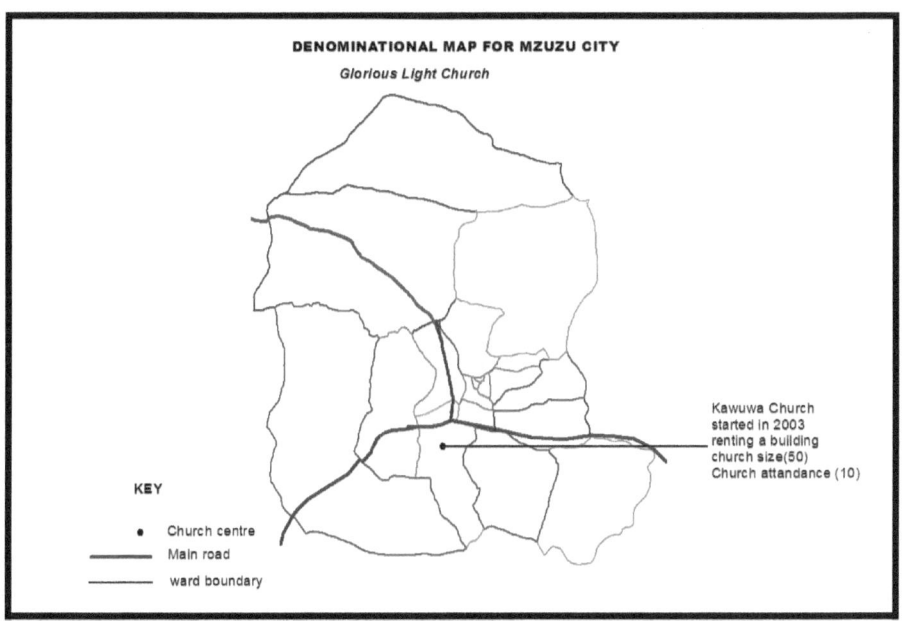

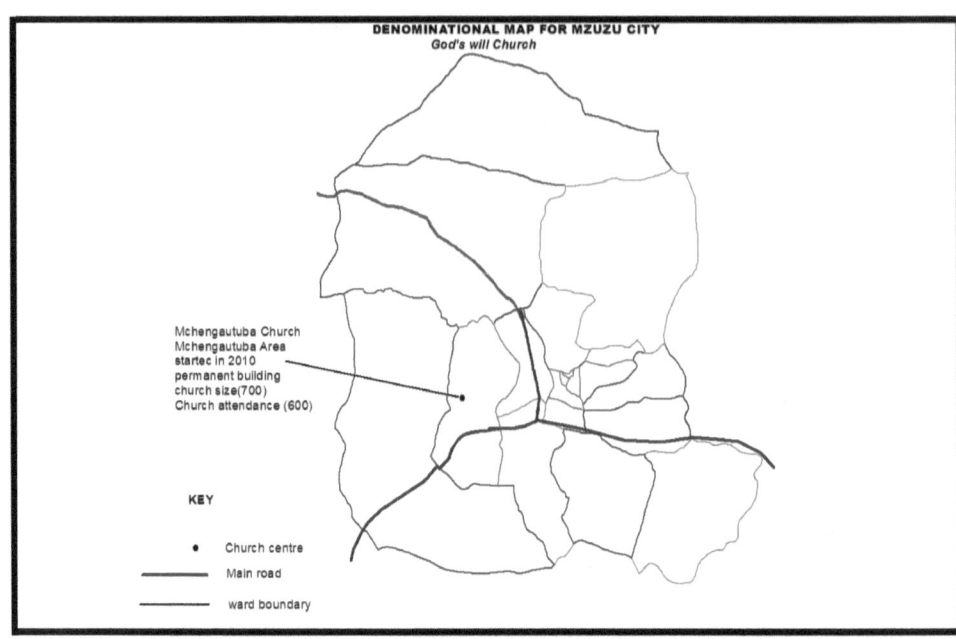

A-70

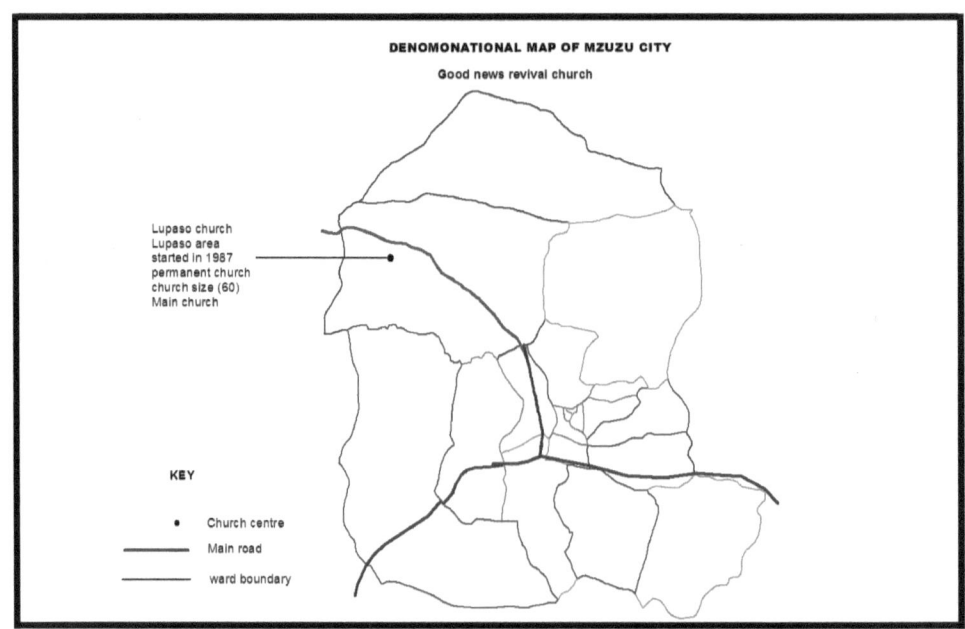

A-71

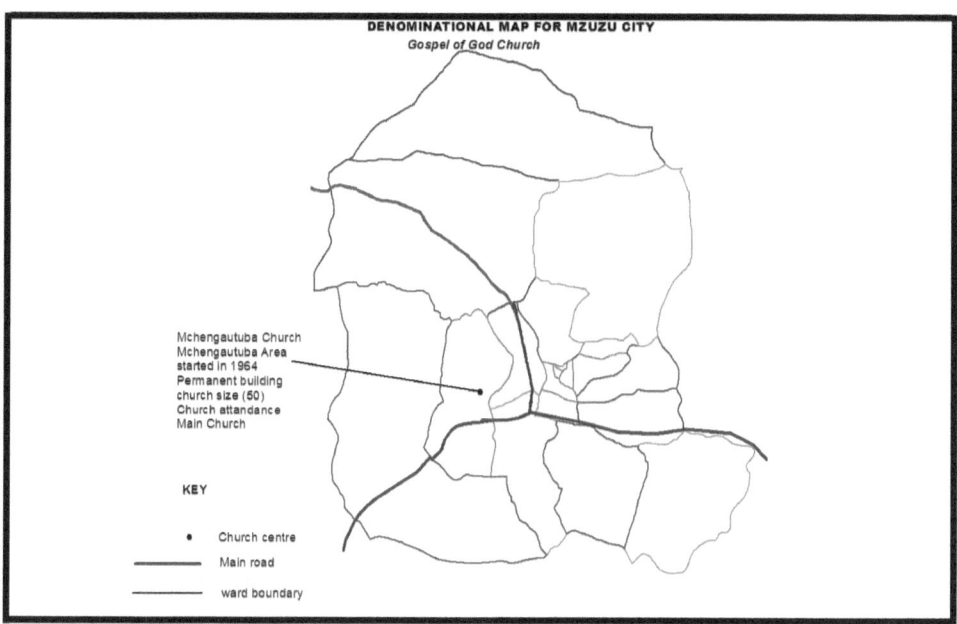

A-72

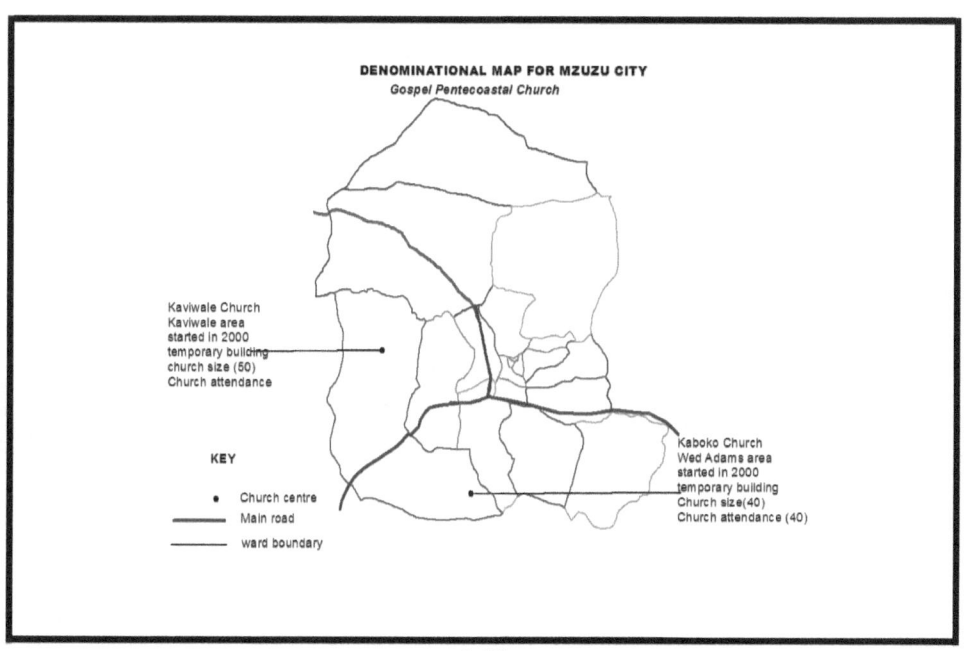

A-73

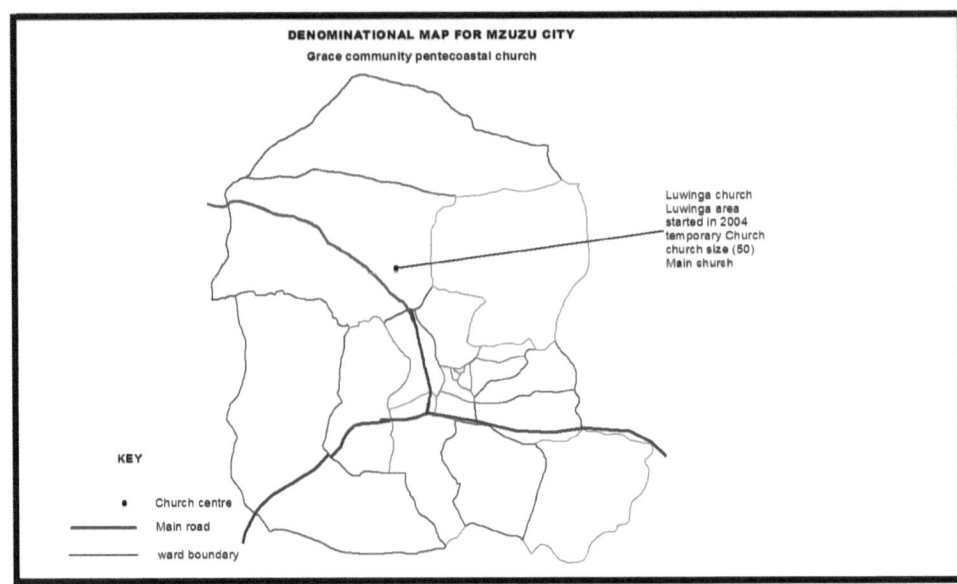

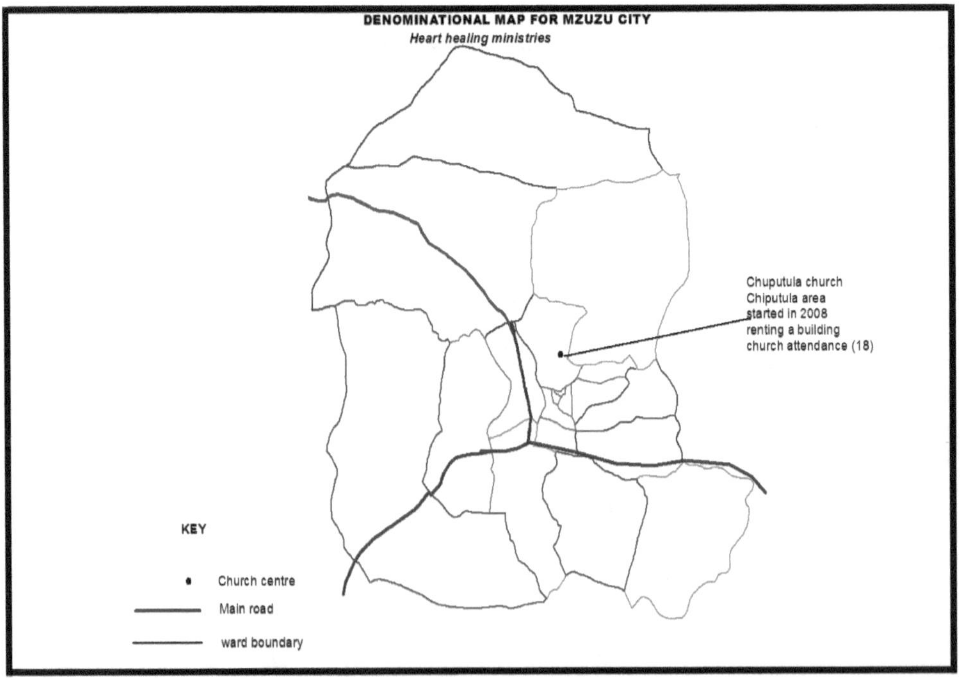

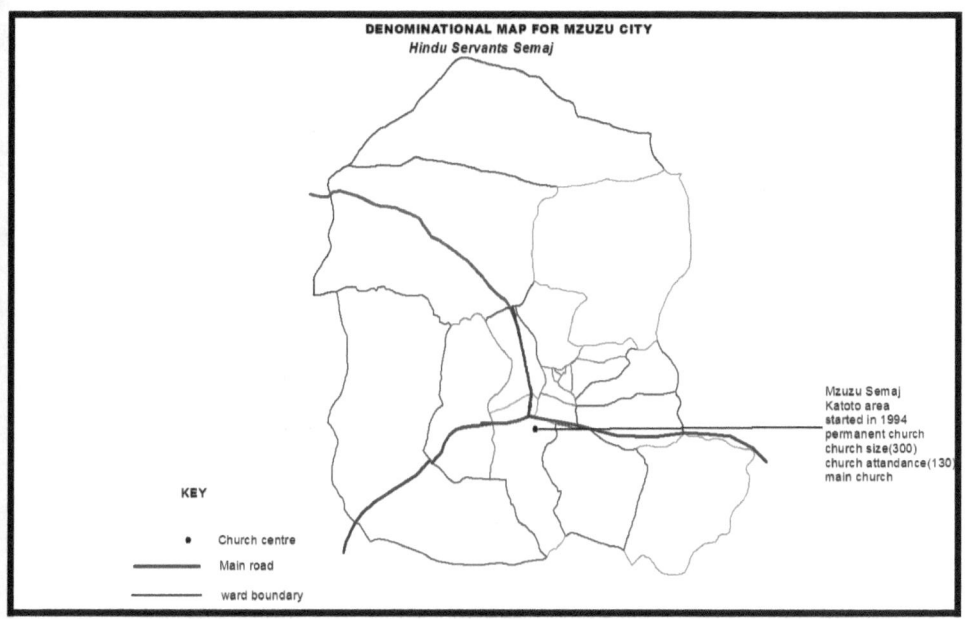

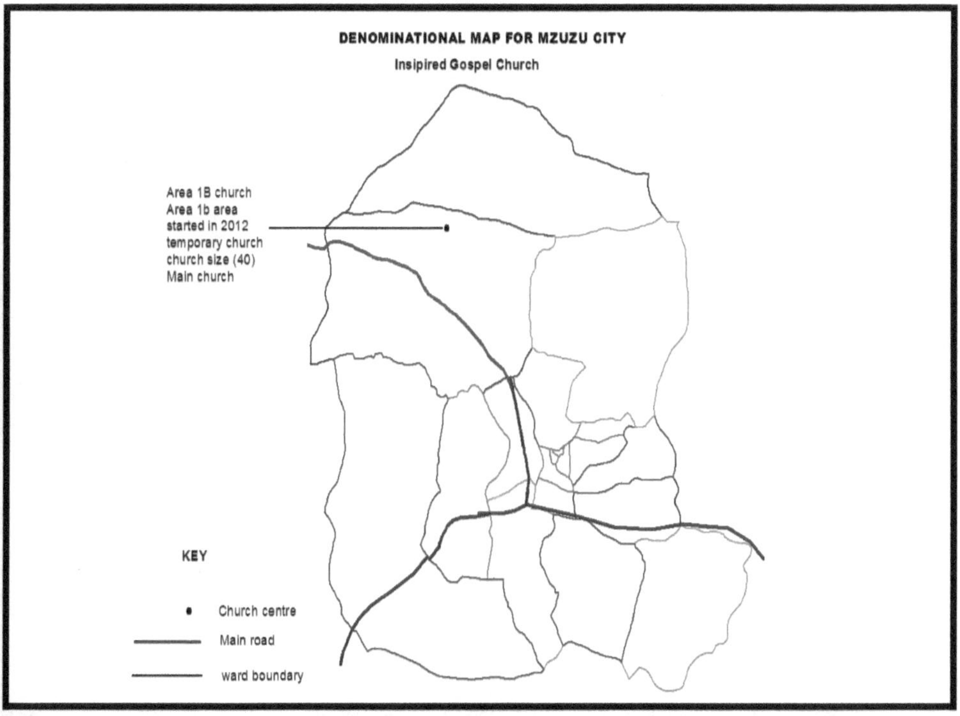

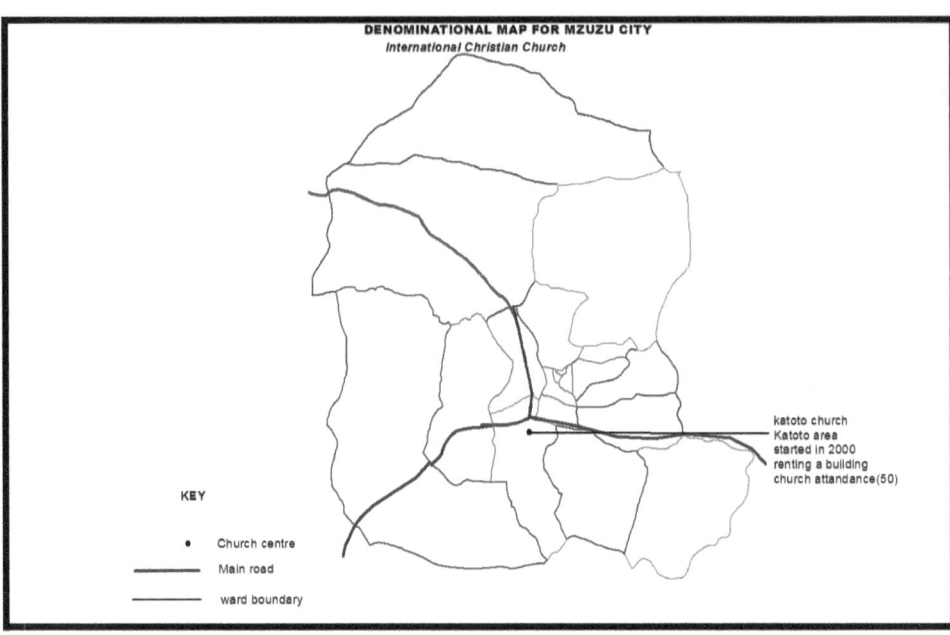

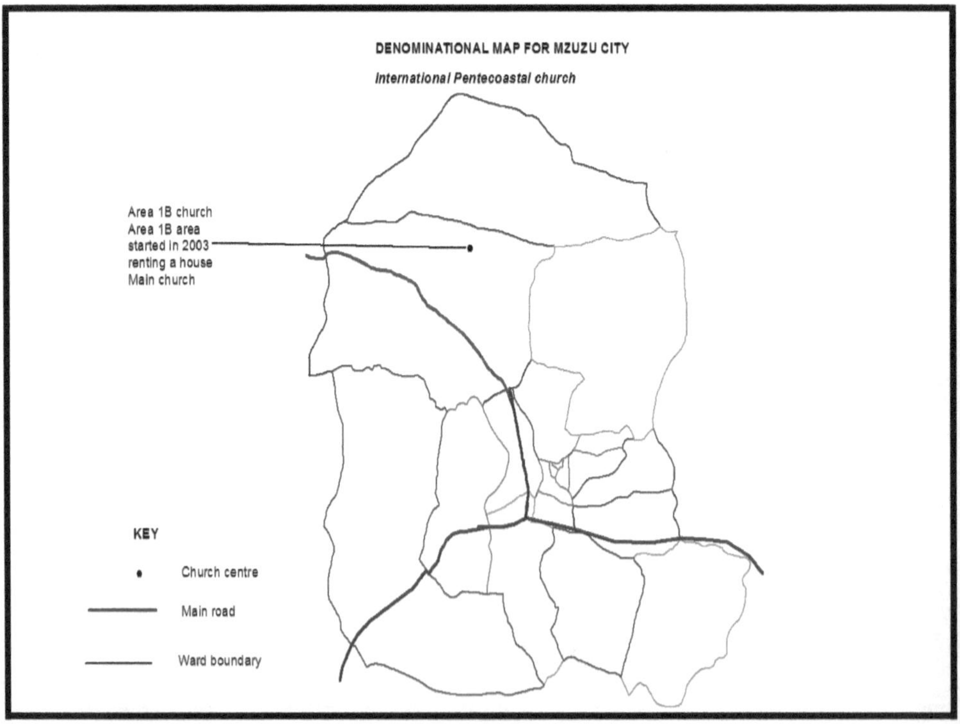

DENOMINATIONAL MAP
Jesus missionary Church
Dunduzu church
Dunduzu Area
started in 2003
Permanent Church
church size (70)
Main Church
KEY
Church centre
Ward boundary

A-80

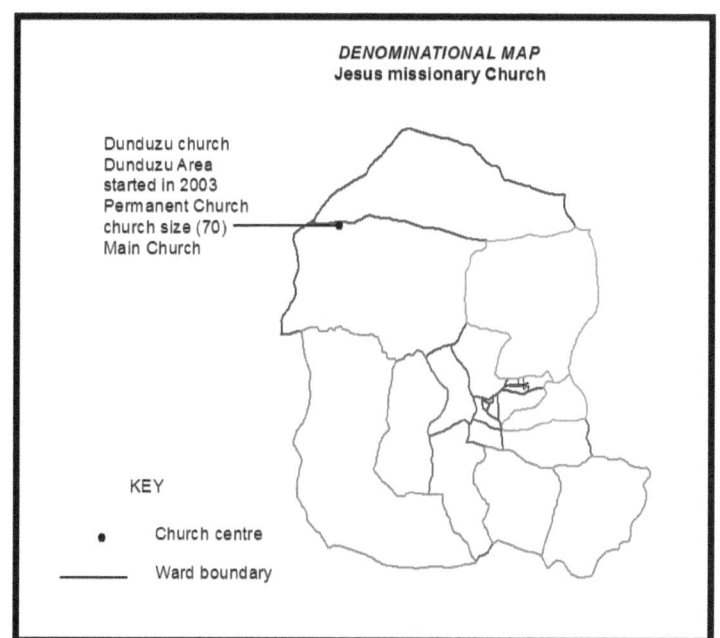

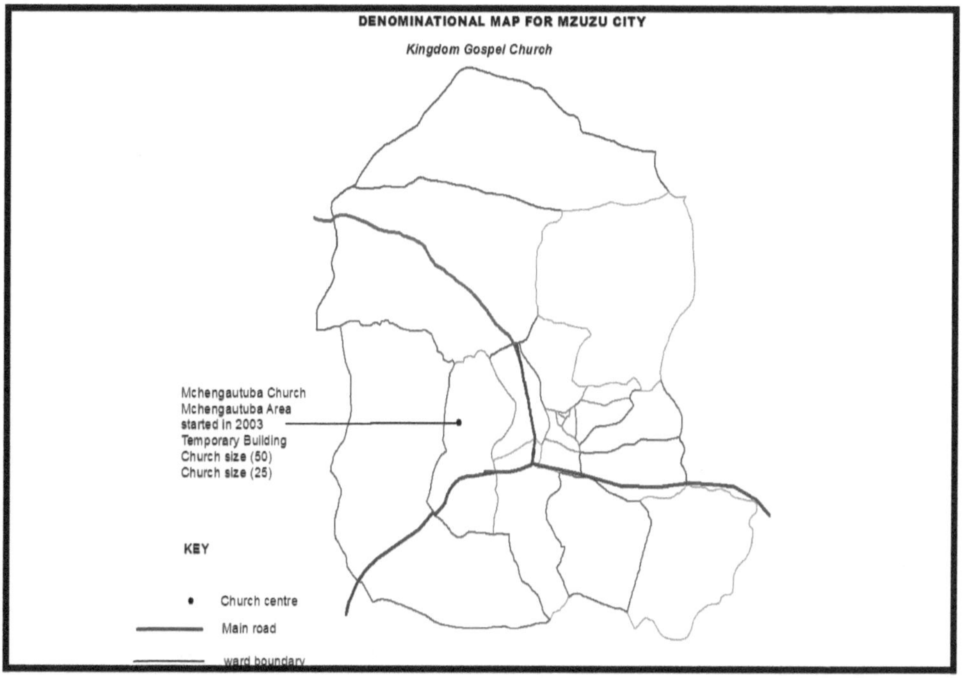
DENOMINATIONAL MAP FOR MZUZU CITY
Kingdom Gospel Church
Mchengautuba Church
Mchengautuba Area
started in 2003
Temporary Building
Church size (50)
Church size (25)
KEY
Church centre
Main road
ward boundary

A-81

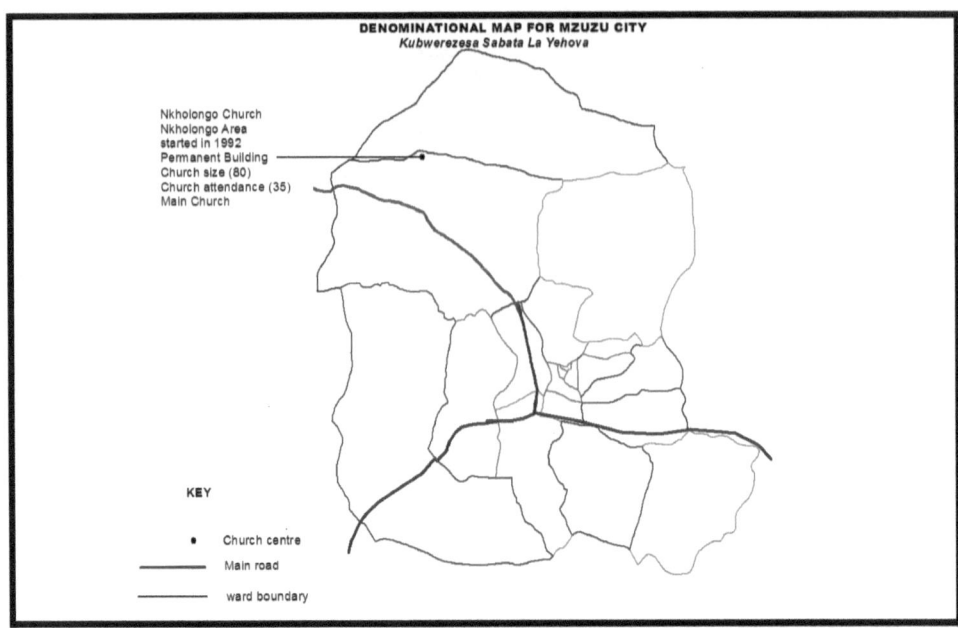

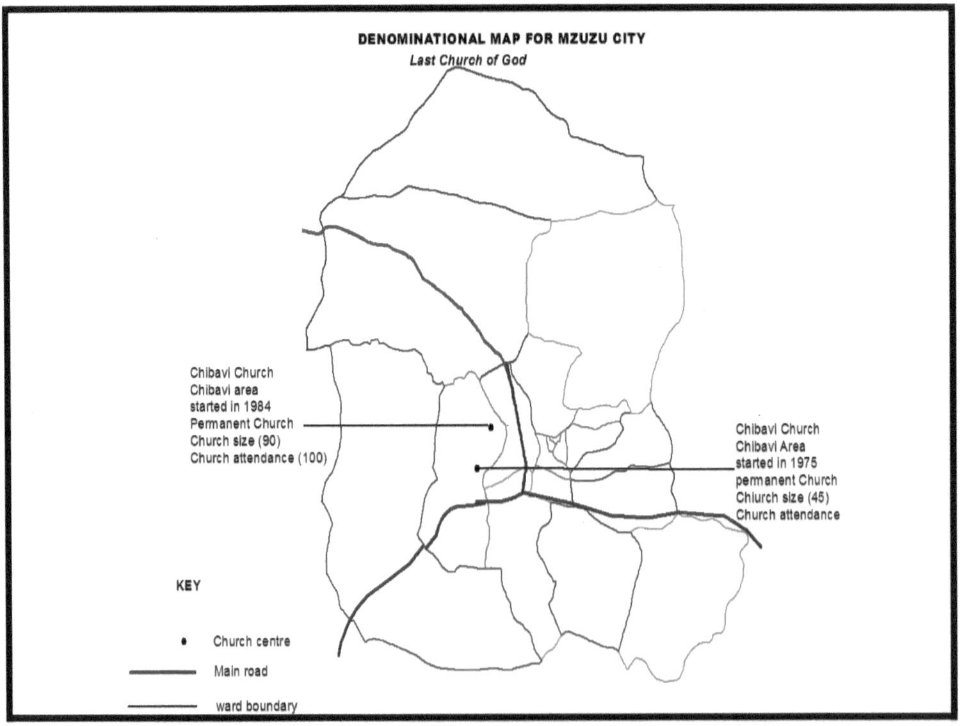

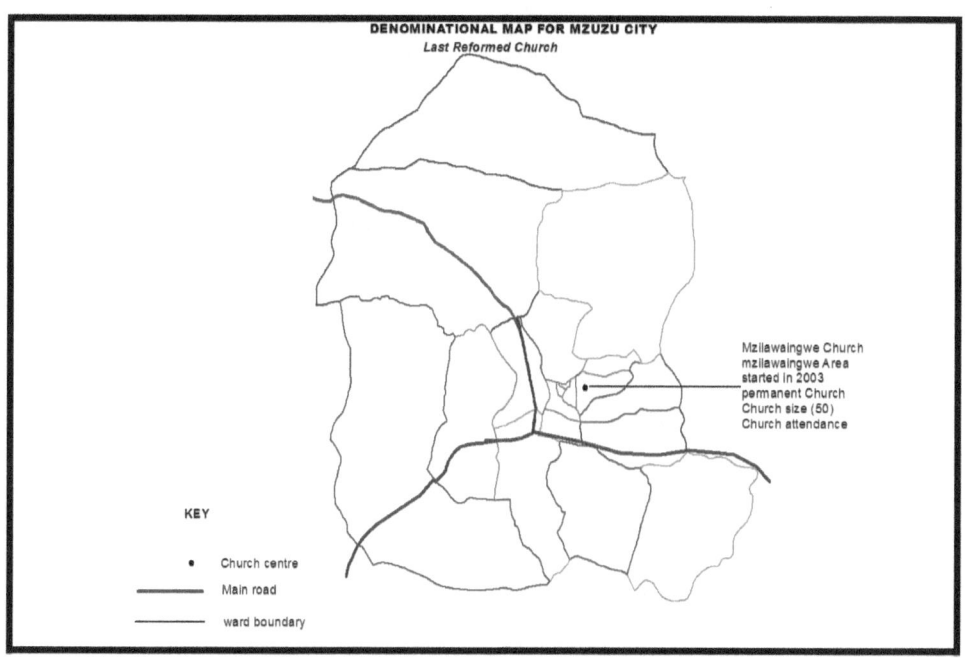

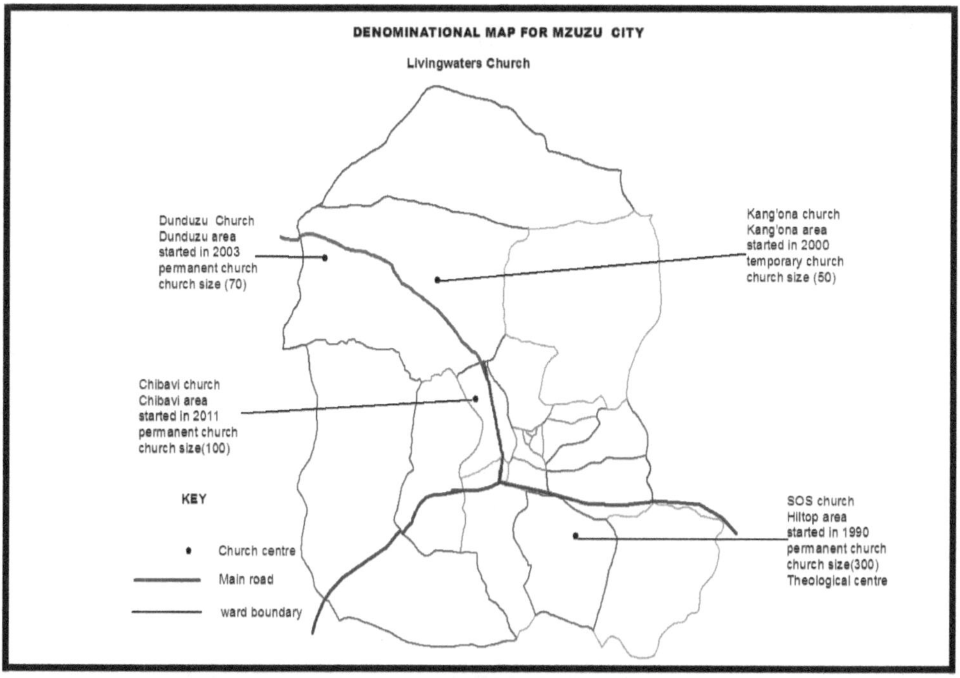

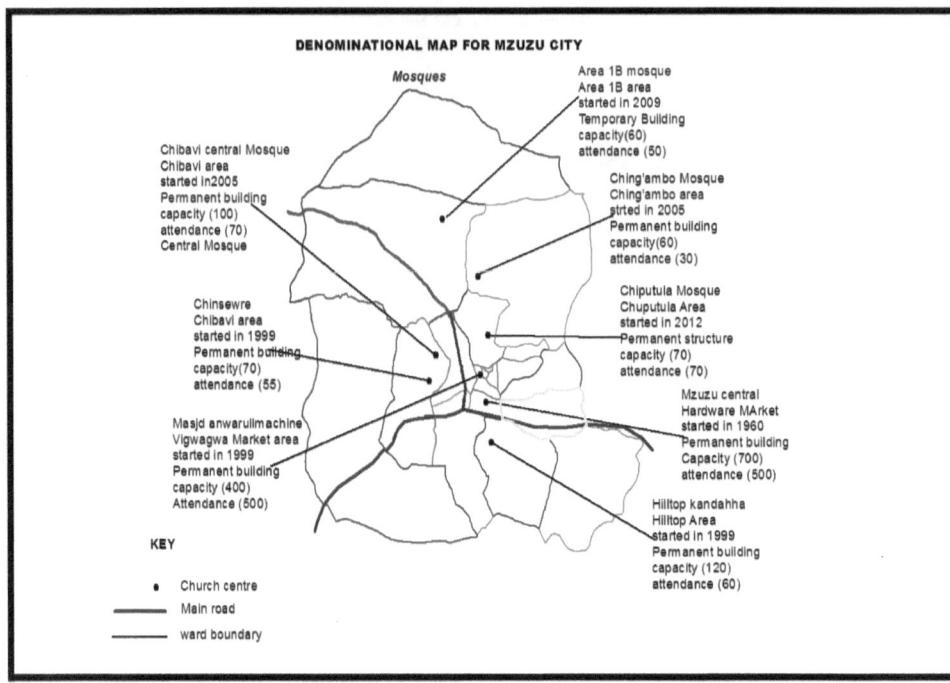

A-86

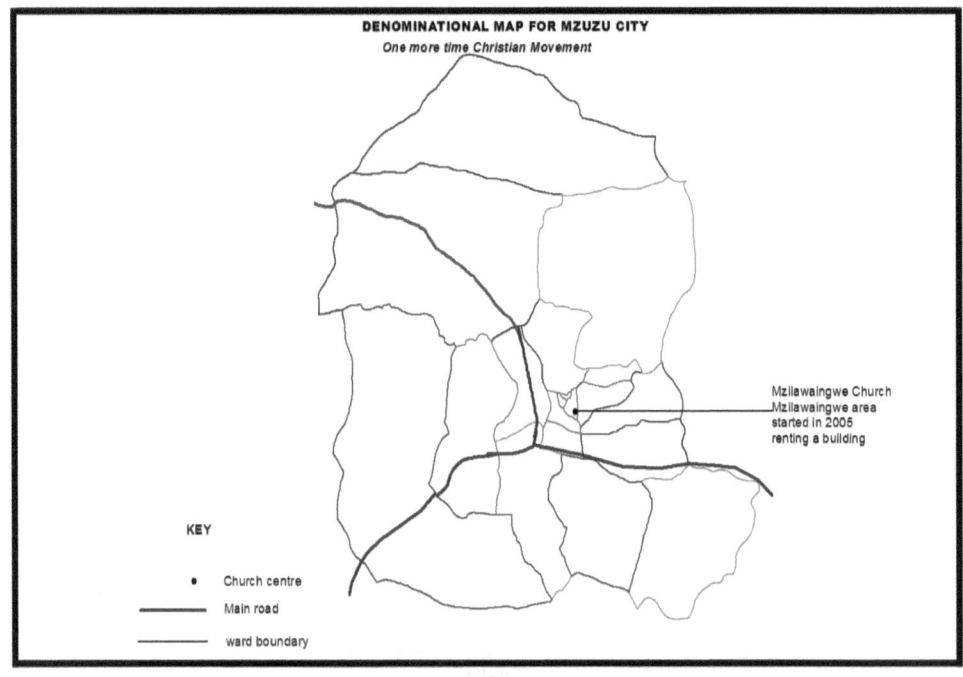

A-87

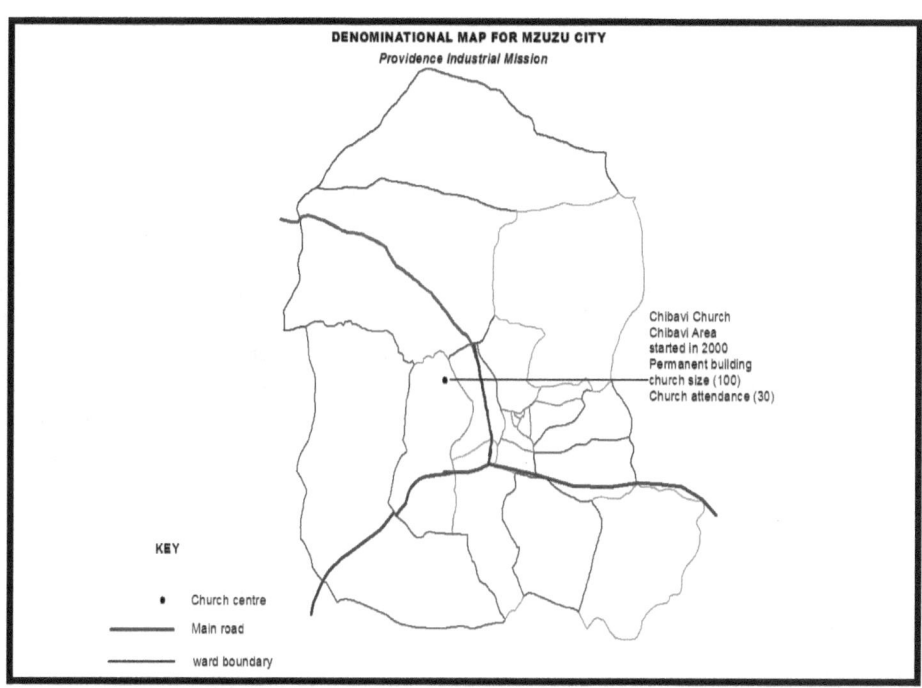

A-88

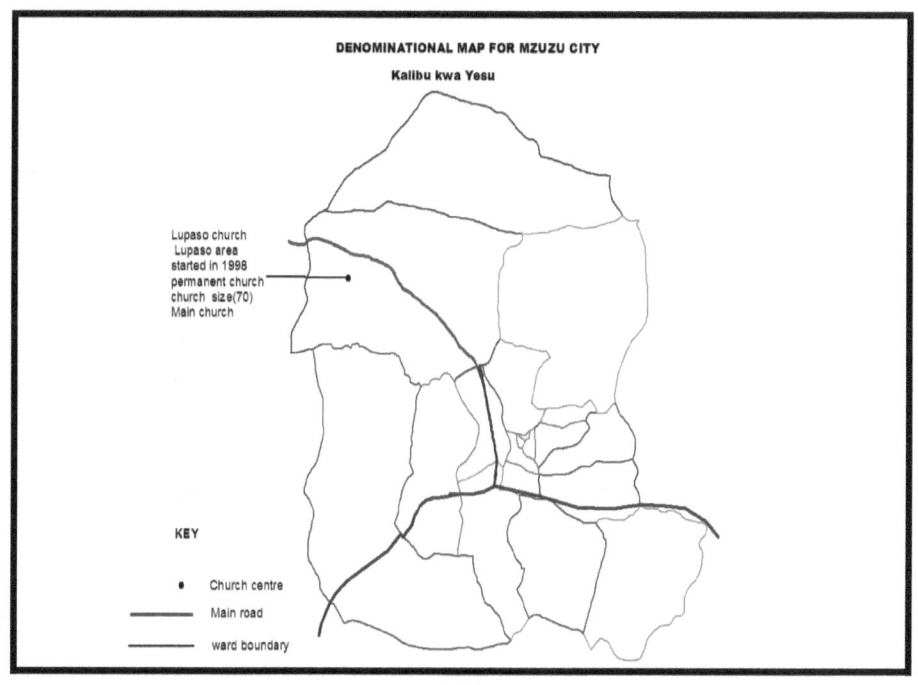

A-89

Index

African Evangelical Church 92f, 95, 258, 269, 358
African Instituted Churches 45, 231, 236, 238-240, 275, 287, 289, 291
African International Church 85f, 161f, 171, 178, 274, 288
African National Church 46, 87f, 116, 141, 247, 351
African Traditional Religion 28, 39, 42, 221-223, 225, 228, 230-234, 257, 274f, 283, 285, 288f, 291, 294, 338, 343, 360
Agape Life Church International 160
Anglican Church 45, 93-95, 184, 206f, 215, 222f, 225, 227f, 230, 237, 241, 255, 257, 274, 282, 285f, 288, 290, 325, 340, 357
Apostolic Church of Great Britain 95f
Baptist Church 59f, 78f, 82, 168, 200f, 222f, 225, 227f, 230, 260, 267, 274, 282, 285, 288, 357
Baptist Convention of Malawi 49, 56, 74, 78f, 147, 176, 205, 222f, 237, 256, 274, 285, 288, 361
Bethel Tabernacle Church 183
Bishop 47, 51, 63, 75f, 99f, 112, 130f, 133, 143, 172, 174, 185, 188-191, 193, 204, 207, 215, 237, 282, 286, 297f, 308f, 314, 325, 328f, 337, 339, 354, 357, 360
Brethren Christian Assembly 136
Brotherhood 266
Calvary Family Church 51, 119, 126f, 196, 198, 245f, 357
CCAP Church 25, 30, 39, 43, 58, 102-105, 108, 121-123, 125, 128f, 136-139, 141f, 145f, 154f, 157, 159, 172, 184, 190-192, 198, 209, 213f, 216f, 237, 244, 256f, 260, 262f, 267f, 270-274, 278, 281, 283f, 289, 291f, 299, 309, 337, 345, 347-350, 353f, 356f, 363
CCAP Nkhoma Synod 347f, 356, 359
CCAP Synod of Livingstonia 34, 42, 52, 56, 102, 123, 155, 157, 232, 243f, 277, 282, 289, 291f, 302f, 306, 313, 324, 332-334, 337f, 355, 358f, 362
Charismatic Redeemed Ministries and International Church 77f, 270
Chichewa language 92, 113, 127, 194, 290, 355
Chipangano church 45
Chipangano Church 46, 60, 63f, 141, 148f, 173, 179, 209f, 223, 254, 265f, 274, 285, 288, 357
Chitumbuka language 231, 287, 291
Christ Citadel International Church 198
Christ Rock Church 182, 295, 359
Christian Love Church 189f
Christian religion 31, 42f, 51f, 221, 232, 240, 243, 281, 287, 343
Christian Religion 42, 236, 281
Christian Sacred Structures 243
Church attendance 59-61, 117, 129
Church growth 345
Church leadership 57, 60, 62f, 67, 70, 72, 75f, 79f, 83f, 89f, 97, 100, 107f, 110f, 116, 118, 120, 122, 131f, 139f, 143-145, 148f, 151, 153, 156f, 161, 171, 176, 178f, 181f, 185f, 190, 192f, 200, 218
Church of Africa Presbyterian 107, 180f, 240
Church of Christ 47, 79f, 98f, 110f, 149-151, 178, 207f, 222f, 225, 227, 229f, 259, 274, 281f, 285, 288, 358
Churches of Christ 151f, 265, 277
Commonwealth Development Corporation 38, 314
Community of Christ Church 156
Convent 94, 127f, 207, 242, 255, 258, 314, 360
Cornerstone Presbyterian Church 83, 156f, 349
Cultural Religion 256

410

Culture 21, 23, 35-37, 39, 41, 43, 51, 232, 234, 271, 276f, 292, 299f, 360, 362
Diffusion of Religions 30, 38
Education System 305
Emmanuel Pentecostal Ministries 155
English language 231, 287, 355
Evangelical Baptist Church of Malawi 82f
Evangelism 182
Fellowship 145f, 177, 222f, 225, 227f, 230f, 236, 240, 274f, 285, 287f
Fellowships and Ministries 240
Free Methodist Church 151-153, 268
Glorious Light Church 204
Good News Revival Church 51, 67f
Gospel of God Church 147, 187f
Grace Community Pentecostal Church 73f, 261, 357
Grace Fellowship 176f
Healing and Deliverance 278, 292, 295
Heart Healing Ministries 146
Higher Learning Institutions 319
Hindu religion 55, 234f, 252, 281, 287, 291, 343f
Hindu Servants Semaj 211
Holy Spirit Filled Ministry 97f
Inspired Gospel Church 74f
International Christian Assemblies Church 195
International Pentecostal Church 75, 76, 273, 297
International Pentecostal Holiness Church 130, 206, 260f, 290, 359
Islam 24, 39, 52, 221-223, 226-228, 230, 232, 235f, 274, 285, 287f, 313, 317, 343f
Islamic Places of Worship 249
Jesus Missionary Church 76, 262, 357
Kingdom Gospel Church 185
Language 89, 215, 229f, 286, 288, 292, 354

Last Church of God 46, 107, 159, 164f, 240, 362
Last Reformed Church 131f
Locational Settlement 232
Madrassa 54, 120, 162f, 235, 317f, 356
Mainstream Denominations 236
Mboni za Yehova Church 89
Medicine Ministry Church 198
Membership Accession 225
Moravian Church 193f
Mosques 53, 100, 120, 162, 201, 236, 249-252, 280, 361
Mtambo Ministry 117f
Ngoni 23, 30, 34-38, 40-43, 51, 55, 287, 301, 304, 334, 358, 360, 362f
Njuyu 36f, 43, 257, 304
Open air rallies 51
Peace Ministries 197, 279, 346, 359
Pentecostal Assemblies 62, 298
Pentecostal Denomination 237
Pentecostal Holiness Association 112f
Power Ministry of the Living God Church 142, 248
Presbyterian Church of Malawi 84
Primary Education 305, 326, 359
Prophecy 91f, 294f
Providence Industrial Mission 165, 294, 357
Religion and Geography 21-23, 26, 38, 361, 363
Religions and denominations 23, 39, 55, 223, 293, 355
Religious adherents 25, 243, 292f
Religious centres 24, 42, 299
Religious geography 21f
Religious Human Rights 331
Religious Medical Care 327
Restorationist Revival 28, 47
Roman Catholic Church 46, 56, 64f, 81, 99f, 116, 149, 185f, 215, 241, 259, 270, 274, 318f, 326, 328, 332, 334, 337

Salvation Army Church 155, 157f
Scottish missionaries 34, 37
Secondary Education 313
Seventh- day Adventist Church 331, 358, 362
Seventh-day Baptist Church 137
Singini, Luwinga 305, 359
Social Services 258, 264
Social Status 257
Spiritual Gifts 258
Temple 66f, 183f, 203, 233, 253, 296, 301, 359
Theology 28, 39f, 124, 153, 157, 159, 233, 237, 266, 277, 324f, 331, 343, 353, 360, 362-364
Tonga 23, 30, 34-37, 40, 42, 55, 150f, 290, 304, 363
Tung Oil Estate 30, 38, 45, 138, 210, 213f, 217, 300, 305, 307
United Methodist Church 105, 261
Unity Pentecostal Church 219
Universalized religions 23
Victory Assemblies of God Pentecostal Church 175
Way of Life Church 86f
Women in Leadership 279, 282, 285
Word of Faith Temple International 142f, 357
Worship centres 24-26, 224, 228, 233, 235-237, 239, 255, 264, 266f, 269, 273, 279, 289
Worship Participation 269
Worship Structures 223
Zambezi Evangelical Church 121
Zion Christian Church 153, 239f, 357

www.ingramcontent.com/pod-product-compliance
Lightning Source LLC
Chambersburg PA
CBHW032145010526
44111CB00035B/1223